The Jesuits and Education

The Society's Teaching Principles and Practice, Especially in Secondary Education in the United States • • • *By*

WILLIAM J. McGUCKEN, S.J., Ph.D.
Professor of Education, St. Louis University

WIPF & STOCK · Eugene, Oregon

Wipf and Stock Publishers
199 W 8th Ave, Suite 3
Eugene, OR 97401

The Jesuits and Education
The Society's Teaching Principles and Practice,
Especially in Secondary Education in the United States
By McGucken, William J., S.J., Ph.D
ISBN 13: 978-1-60608-183-9
Publication date 11/03/2008
Previously published by Bruce Publishing Co., 1932

ST. IGNATIUS OF LOYOLA

PREFACE BY THE GENERAL EDITOR

FOR FOUR centuries the Jesuits have been engaged in the field of higher learning. During a considerable portion of that time they maintained a position of influence and prestige unique in the history of education. With the impetus given by them and under their fostering care, schools and universities arose in rapid succession throughout the length and breadth of Europe, all fully endowed, and thronged with eager students.

Since that period the growth of education has proceeded apace. The evolution of new systems has been rapid and often bewildering. Incalculable adaptation was necessitated by the economic, social, and scientific developments that now quickly followed upon the Industrial Revolution. Above all, there has been a steady expansion of opportunities in the field of learning during the past few decades. Fabulous sums have been expended and the clamor is for still greater resources to meet the rising demands made by increasing numbers of students and more exacting standards in educational administration.

It is obvious, then, that under existing circumstances, Jesuit schools must hold a relatively far less important place than at an earlier period. Yet, despite all these facts, it remains true that, in the United States at least, they are today easily and unquestionably the largest individual factor after public education itself, whether we consider the number of Jesuit high schools, of colleges, or of universities distributed throughout the land.

The importance, therefore, of an authoritative statement upon this subject, based upon thorough and reliable research, and written particularly from the American standpoint, must be clear to all. The author, in accomplishing his task, has rightly deemed it advisable to begin with the presentation of a historic background that should give the reader a sufficient knowledge of the origin, traditions, and development of Jesuit education itself. While his ultimate preoccupation has been with the secondary schools of the Society of Jesus in the United States, he does not fail to give an accurate view also of its higher educational institutions. His general discussion of the purpose and methods of Jesuit education necessarily embraces its entire range.

For a considerable time no authoritative volume in our own language, dealing with Jesuit education, has been obtainable. The only works on the subject, issued before the changes that came to the educational world since the turn of the century, have long ago disappeared from circulation. In consequence, the call for a book of this nature has been instant and imperative.

The author has for years been connected in an official position with the School of Education at St. Louis University. His first-hand contacts with original sources both in Europe and the United States have supplied him with much new information. Unpublished documents in Jesuit archives, catalogues of Jesuit schools, private and public pronouncements by members of the Order at various times have been placed at his disposal. In addition, the monumental literature, particularly on the history of the Society of Jesus, which within recent years, has made its appearance in Spain, France, England, and Germany, has greatly aided in this work.

For the part dealing specifically with the history of Jesuit educational institutions in the United States, the archives, not merely of the many Jesuit colleges, but of their respective Provinces as well, have been consulted no less than the published records and documents issued in England and America.

The book may be truly said to fill a threefold gap hitherto left in our educational literature. The first concerns the history of Jesuit education itself, the second regards its principles and practical methods, the third relates to the previous lack of any English rendition of the famous Jesuit *Ratio Studiorum.*

In the latter case we have here given in the Appendix a translation of that part of the 1832 *Ratio* which pertains to high-school instruction, besides an analysis of all the intervening sections, thus affording the reader a true concept of the entire document. The translation has been made with special attention to scientific accuracy. Serious misconceptions would necessarily result from a mere literal rendition. Words have vastly changed their meaning, and terms apparently familiar to us must be interpreted to convey the specific significance attached to them in the original document. This itself is certainly to be considered as one of the monumental works in the history of modern education. The attitude of the author, it need hardly be mentioned, is never partisan in discussion, but always purely scientific and critical in the best sense of the word.

The author at first traces the chain of circumstance that led the Society into the educational field, although not established for this work. He further finds that the original *Ratio* itself, drawn up in 1599, in reality deserves little credit for originality. The virtue of the teaching program of the Order consisted in this, that it embodied all the best traditions and practices of the sixteenth century. Latin naturally occupied the place of honor. From these beginnings to the developments we witness in the United States today, there is a far cry.

A complete evolution of Jesuit education may in fact be said to have taken place here. It began with the sporadic efforts made along traditional lines among the early Catholic colonists of Maryland during the seventeenth and eighteenth centuries, and was, for the time, abruptly terminated by the suppression of the Order, in 1773. The teachers in these schools were members of the English Province. The first permanent Catholic college in America was that opened at Georgetown in 1791 by Bishop John Carroll, who himself had been a member of the Society of Jesus. Finally, when with the restoration of the Order in 1814, the school at Georgetown was formally recognized as a Jesuit college, the work of education in the new Republic was vigorously promoted.

Since those days Jesuit education, like the Scriptural mustard seed, has grown into a mighty tree in whose branches and within whose shade North, East, South, and West of the great American nation have found intellectual nourishment, together with spiritual comfort and safe shelter. Its roots reach down deep into the very beginnings of American history. It is truly an indigenous and native growth as much as any education in the United States can claim to be, fostered under the best tradition which the Old World could give to the New. Even the Jesuit teachers themselves in the Maryland Mission, at that early period, were mostly Americans whose education had been completed at Liège and St. Omer's.

The next group, which now founded the Missouri Province in the Mid-West, was sprung from hardy Belgian stock, men with the brave heart and the strong arm of the typical Western pioneer, and with adventurous souls on fire for the glory of God and the extension of His Kingdom.

Then, from the chivalrous land of Jeanne d'Arc came the French blackrobes, who first chose their ground amid the blue grass of Kentucky, but thence journeyed eastward and joined their brethren of Maryland to form the Maryland-New York Province. Another group of the same nationality settled in Louisiana and established the New Orleans Province. They were followed, in turn, by the Italian Jesuits, who with native hardihood extended their missions and built their schools and colleges along the Pacific Coast and in Colorado. The last to arrive were the Germans, with sound educational standards along classic and scientific lines. Eager to bring to America the best learning of their Fatherland they began their earliest foundation at Buffalo in 1870. Their colleges and personnel were later apportioned between the Maryland-New York and the Missouri Provinces. Each of these has itself been recently divided into two new Provinces with the steady increase of members.

The different groups of Jesuit teachers, thus settled on our shores, definitely strove to acquire the American spirit and render themselves acceptable to the communities in which they lived. The infiltration of European members has long since ceased and the entire Jesuit personnel is recruited today from American stock.

The history of Jesuit education in the United States is therefore a replica of the growth of the country itself and of its assimilation, within a brief time, of many nationalities into one. This could be accomplished more speedily within the Jesuit houses themselves than throughout the land at large. So, too, the distinctive programs and methods brought from various cultural centers of Europe were in course of time merged into one essential unity. Yet the Jesuit teaching system in the Provinces was naturally affected in no slight degree by the educational differences in the various sections of the country. Definite measures are now being taken to bring about a more general uniformity, keeping constantly in mind whatever is best in the secular institutions, whether private or public.

Following out these developments, the author enters into the gradual internal transformation that took place in the Jesuit colleges. At first largely of the European gymnasium type, with a year or two of scholastic philosophy added, they gradually conformed themselves to the national system of distinct high school and college. The rapidity with which further adaptations, away from the letter of the *Ratio,* now followed within the Jesuit schools in different sections of the country, and the nature of these adaptations in each case was in no slight degree dependent upon the same forces that made the public high schools of the West develop along lines different from similar institutions in the East.

Yet despite all these external transformations, the same spirit which animated Jesuit education in the past can still be found, unchanged and uncontaminated, in the American Jesuit schools of today.

"Their traditions the Jesuits regard as a precious inheritance," the author elsewhere affirms. "There hangs about the stereotyped methods of their predecessors a glory which they are loath to lose. The American Jesuit high school of the present day has been adapted to modern requirements along conservative lines, but the American Jesuits have salvaged from the past a theory of education that is largely at variance with modern standards, a theory that mental discipline is a necessary factor in the training of the boy. This, partly at least, explains their emphasis on the classics as a splendid instrument for intellectual development."

A feature in which particularly he considers Jesuit education to be unique is the insistence placed by the Order on the preparation of its members for the work of teaching and the tremendous financial sacrifices made to insure efficiency in the schools. This held true even at a period when the standard for high-school teachers in the United States was lamentably low.

But over and above all else there stands out for him, as for his fellow members in the Society of Jesus, one supreme objective from which he finds the Jesuits have never wavered by a hair's breadth since the days of the Soldier-Saint Loyola. "That objective is the formation of the Christian citizen, obedient to the laws of God and the laws of the Church, obedient also to the laws of the State. God and man's duties to God are considered of sufficient importance to earn a prominent place in the Jesuit high school."

But for this the Jesuit educator does not rest content with the mere processes of learning and observation. The training of the will, the formation of Christian character, the grounding in true principles of conduct and right habits here become imperative, so that the pupil may ultimately attain to man's loftiest perfection, the motivating of the entire human being by the one great love of God. That alone can give to education its highest value.

JOSEPH HUSSLEIN, S.J., PH.D.,
General Editor, Science and Culture Series.

November 13, 1931,
St. Louis University.

AUTHOR'S PREFACE

THE PURPOSE of this study is to trace the history of Jesuit secondary education in America from its origins to the present day, to examine its characteristics, its objectives, its curricular development. An introductory chapter presents a brief account of the acceptance of educational work by the Society of Jesus in the sixteenth century. This chapter furnishes background for a proper understanding of the American Jesuit system of education which has its roots in the past.

The monograph is divided into three parts. Part One treats of the origins of Jesuit pedagogy in the sixteenth century and of those forces at work within and without the Order that resulted in the document known as the *Ratio Studiorum.* A brief study is given of the general characteristics of this plan of studies as it was applied in the Jesuit schools of the sixteenth and two succeeding centuries. Part Two treats of Jesuit educational foundations in the United States, recounts the educational activities of the various national groups that came to this country — English, Belgian, French, Italian, and German. The archives of the American houses and provinces of the Society, particularly the Georgetown and St. Louis archives, were consulted. Transcripts of documents, printed in the *Woodstock Letters,* a Jesuit publication, have also supplied material for this part.

Part Three deals specifically with the American Jesuit high school, tracing its development from the gymnasium type of school to the conventional American high school. In the study of the curriculum, data were taken from original sources, chiefly catalogues and courses of study, printed or in manuscript, reports of committees on studies in various provinces, circular letters of American provincials, and the like. In the chapters devoted to objectives, methodology, administration, and training of teachers, both unpublished and published material have been cited. The Appendix contains a translation of that part of the 1832 *Ratio* that deals with secondary education. As far as can be discovered, this is the only English translation of that document.

The author wishes to express his grateful appreciation to his superiors and to his brethren of the Society of Jesus in America who have given him loyal encouragement and needed assistance. He is especially thankful to Father Gilbert Garraghan of St. Louis University, who generously allowed him to use material he had gathered for his history of the Missouri Province; and to Fathers Bakewell Morrison and Alfred Brickel, of the same institution, who placed at his disposal their translation of the 1599 *Ratio*. Father Thomas Hughes, S.J., whose scholarly work, *The History of the Society of Jesus in North America*, has made all students of Jesuit history in America his debtors, graciously permitted the author to quote from his *Documents*.

Acknowledgments are also due to the following publishers who have permitted quotations from their works: Allyn and Bacon, The Bombay Press, B. Herder Company, Longmans, Green & Company, The Macmillan Company, and Charles Scribner's Sons.

WILLIAM J. McGUCKEN, S.J.

TABLE OF CONTENTS

CHAPTER PAGE

PART III. THE MODERN AMERICAN JESUIT HIGH SCHOOL

LIST OF TABLES

LIST OF MAPS

LIST OF FIGURES

INTRODUCTION

CHAPTER I

THE JESUITS AND EDUCATION

WHETHER or not one is prepared to admit that the Jesuits once occupied the front rank in education, it is undoubtedly true that for nearly a century and a half — roughly from 1600 to 1750 — they wielded a not inconsiderable influence on secondary education in Europe.[1] It is also equally true that this influence is no longer theirs; they never have regained, even in Catholic countries, the control of educational machinery which they lost at the time of the suppression of the Society in 1773. Yet their influence in Catholic educational circles, in the United States, for example, is still considerable.

Influence on Catholic Education in the United States

Of the 43 Catholic high schools for boys in the United States with an enrollment of 400 or over, the Jesuits control 18, including 11,073 of the 26,478 students. In all, they have 36 schools of secondary grade with 15,083 students.[2] Of the 56 liberal-arts colleges for men, conducted by Catholics in this country, 13 are under the direction of the Jesuits, with an enrollment of 13,545.[3] Of the 19 American Catholic universities offering professional courses, in addition to the arts and sciences, 14 are under Jesuit control.

At the present time, Jesuit influence on Catholic education is probably nowhere so great as in the United States. Although the American Jesuits constitute only 20 per cent of the personnel of the entire Order,[4] 36 of the 182 Jesuit secondary schools of the world are in the United States. Of the 72,582 students in Jesuit secondary schools throughout the world in 1921, 14,591 were in American Jesuit high schools. In addition, the American Jesuits conduct colleges and universities. In 1921, there were 5,091 students in American Jesuit colleges, and 12,723 in their universities, making a total of 32,405 students under the direction of the American branch of the Order. For the same year, there were only 95,966 students in Jesuit schools throughout the world, including students in theological seminaries.[5]

Naturally, with so much emphasis placed on teaching, the Society of Jesus is ordinarily spoken of as a teaching order.[6] Education is almost universally conceded, by Catholics, at least, to be the Jesuits' *forte*. With this in mind it is interesting to note that Ignatius of Loyola, the founder of the Order, who planned this vast organization, was himself not an educated man in the ordinary sense of the term, nor did he, at the outset, at least, intend to have his followers engage in teaching.

Loyola and the Foundation of the Order

It will be impossible here to give the story of Loyola's life, his abandonment of the profession of arms, his desire to serve Christ, a desire that saw its concrete realization in the formation of the Company of Jesus.[7] But it is important to see what intellectual equipment Ignatius had for the task in hand. Certainly his education up to the time of his conversion had been desultory in the extreme; a courtier-soldier, he had little need of a profound knowledge of either classics or philosophy, or of much else for that matter.

"His education," says Polanco, the chronicler of the pioneer Society, "as was the manner of the time, was carried out rather in accordance with the spirit of the world than in accordance with the spirit of God. For he had learned no more than to read and write when he was sent to the court of the King and was there engaged in those pursuits which are the ordinary occupations of the sons of noblemen and courtiers."[8]

Even after his conversion at the age of thirty, in 1521, he found polite letters but little to his taste. True, he went about a sort of vagrant student from Barcelona to Alcala, from Alcala to Salamanca. His change of schools seems to have been actuated not so much by a desire of better opportunities for learning as by the search for a wider field for winning souls.[9]

Finally his scholastic wanderings brought him to Paris in 1528,[10] where the truth came home to him, too late perhaps for his own good, but of inestimable benefit for his followers, that "the pen is mightier than the sword, intellect more powerful than muscle; and that if he wished to take part in the very best work being done in the world, he must find a place in the army of its scholars."[11]

At Paris, he went about the acquirement of an education in more methodical fashion, securing the master's degree from the University in 1534. Yet, despite his eleven years of study and his prized degree, Loyola was but indifferently educated; he never seemed to have acquired fluency in Latin, the common accomplishment of all educated men in his day. Both the book of the *Spiritual Exercises* and the *Constitutions of the Company* he wrote in Spanish; it was Polanco who translated them into Latin.

This is one of the curious anomalies in educational history: The renaissance of the study of antiquity and of *belles-lettres* in Catholic schools, the drawing up of a systematic course of humanities are intimately attached to the name of a man who was certainly not a scholar and who had little of the humanist about him.[12] What he did have was a "Roman strength of purpose . . . a rare genius for practical affairs of a kind that nature does not bestow on one in a hundred years."[13] It was this genius for organization that enabled him, when the time came, to use the instrument he had fashioned for God's service to control the educational machinery in Catholic Europe.

However, despite the earlier, uncritical biographies of Loyola, nothing is clearer in the light of impartial research by members of his own society than that St. Ignatius not only had no intention of founding a teaching order, but that he did not even have any idea of founding a religious order at all. In the course of the vicissitudes and tribulations he experienced from 1522 to 1539, there is no shred of evidence to show that he thought of founding one day a religious order to be called the Company of Jesus; no word or act of Ignatius indicates any such intention. True, at Paris, disciples gathered about him, men like himself, devoted to the "greater glory of God." Where that would lead was not clear either to St. Ignatius or to any of his companions; it was, at first, a soldier dream of reconquering the Holy Land. But his practical mind early saw the infeasibility of this; and he cast about for new fields of activity for his little band. Circumstances brought them to Rome. There, after mature deliberation, it was decided to form a religious order, bound by vows, to be known as the Company of Jesus. The new order was approved by Pope Paul III in 1540.[14]

Education of Youth not a Primary Objective

Even after the newly organized Company received its approval from the Holy See, there was still no thought of engaging in educational work. The Bull of Paul III[15] contains no word about teaching youth; the phrase, *"eruditio puerorum et rudium,"* means merely the catechetical instruction of poor and ignorant people in Christian doctrine, a duty to which the first companions had bound themselves. But this was obviously a work of the ministry, unconcerned with academic education. In fact, the idea of a vast order, devoted to education as one of its primary works,[16] did not come to St. Ignatius until many years after the foundation of the Company. His original concept of a very select body of men, limited in number—at first, the members of the Company were not to exceed sixty[17]—distinguished in every way, in practical judgment, in eloquence, in virtue was really incompatible with the development of the Order, even during the lifetime of the founder. Even Catholics speak of the Jesuits as the "shock troops of the Papacy." But Loyola had no intention of making his Company a troop at all. He had not visualized a vast organization, but rather a small group of men, gifted, trained, university men, of whom St. Francis Xavier was a perfect example; men of executive ability, bound by no petty parochial cares, much less by the daily routine of the classroom, ready to fly at a moment's notice to any part of the world at the Pope's command, there to sit in at the councils of kings, to argue with heresiarchs, or to captivate the university centers of Europe by their learning and eloquence.

The Acceptance of Colleges

The Society founded by Ignatius developed, however, along vastly different lines from the founder's intention, even in his lifetime.[18] Ignatius had looked for a select number of picked men, the most distinguished doctors in the universities. But great numbers clamored for admission to the new Company;[19] the ardor of undergraduate youth was stirred by Loyola's brilliant followers; they begged to be admitted to the Society. The admission of these younger men, the "scholastics," their university training not yet completed, presented a new problem to St. Ignatius, the problem of educating them. At first, they were dispatched in little groups to the universities; the first group of Jesuit "scholastics" came to Paris in 1540, where they were lodged in the Collège des Tresoriers.[20] Here they lived together under a superior and followed the ordinary exercises of community life — daily Mass, meditation, and the like. This is the first stage in the evolution of the Jesuit "college,"[21] in reality, merely a hostel or residence hall, a *collegium-seminarium,* for the scholastics of the Order at a university where they worked for a degree.

Naturally, these young men with their fixed hours for study and their regular manner of life were a striking contrast to the university youth of the sixteenth century.[22] Young seculars desirous of profiting by the favorable surroundings of the Jesuits asked to be taken into the Jesuit "college." Occasionally courses were given by Jesuit professors in these halls to counteract the none-too-orthodox university teaching, or to supplement a regular university treatise. To these, "externs"[23] were probably invited. Thus, about the year 1546, the *collegium-seminarium,* or house of studies, destined only for Jesuits, evolved into a college harboring both members of the Order and secular youth.[24]

The third stage in the evolution of the Jesuit college is the school for externs only, Jesuits acting as professors.[25] The college at Messina, founded in 1547,[26] the prototype of the seventeenth century — and later — Jesuit College, is regarded as the institution where the Society first exercised its new apostolate of teaching secular youth.[27] Finally, in 1550, the Bull of Julius III,[28] confirming the new order, mentions explicitly the work of teaching.

Educational Work Undertaken Reluctantly

It is obvious that the work of education, so intimately connected with the Order, was started almost in protest. In 1555, when Gonzales de Camarra asked Ignatius[29] who was the originator of the colleges, he was told that Lainez was the first to urge the matter and that he solved the scruples of the others relative to this new activity. To begin with, there was a current prejudice against a religious order devoting itself to secondary education, particularly to classical training; the medieval exaltation of philosophy and theology still held sway in certain circles. To teach these latter branches in the universities was to follow in the footsteps of the great schoolmen, Aquinas and Bonaventure, discerning dialecticians as well as model monks. But it was another matter when there was question of classical secondary schools, such as the Society had opened at Messina. Ridabeneira, who belongs to the first generation of Jesuits, and who was strongly attached to Ignatius and all his policies, naïvely attempts to prove that teaching the classics is not an unworthy type of work.[30] Lancicius is at pains to show that the teaching of humanities is one of the most precious services the new Order can render to the Catholic world.[31]

Echoes of this objection are to be found in the reproach of M. Etienne Pasquier, the clever lawyer of the University of Paris in its dispute with the Jesuits. In becoming humanists, he says, the Jesuits "violate an age-old tradition which forbids religious to become masters of arts. They should give themselves entirely to spiritual reading and to theology."[32] Of the attitude of Loyola himself, it can truly be said that "with all his advancement of education in the event, there can be no doubt that from first to last he looked upon it as a secondary matter; indeed, in some sense as a very dangerous serpent which, if he were not careful, might some day turn upon him and bite him."[33]

In the fourth part of an interesting document that preceded the actual Constitutions, there are nine chapters on education;[34] but not a word about the education of youth; all is concerned with the education of the Jesuit scholastics. This was written in 1541. In the actual Constitutions, however, St. Ignatius rewrote the fourth part, devoting seventeen chapters to secondary education and to the organization of universities.[35] And yet, even here, ten years after the rudimentary constitutions had appeared, there is no enthusiastic acceptance of the work of education. In the *Prooemium* to the *Pars Quarta* of the Constitutions, he writes:

> Since the purpose for which the Society is founded is to help the souls of its members and its neighbors to that end for which they were created; and since with this object in view, besides examples of life, doctrine and the power to express it are also necessary . . . we must now treat of the edifice of letters and the manner of making use of them. For this purpose the Society accepts colleges and sometimes even universities.[36]

In fact, one can almost accuse Loyola, the high idealist, of being purely utilitarian. First, he intended to conquer the Holy Land; then came the idea of a small group of highly trained men to stem the rising tide of heresy and save the nations of Europe to the Church. But, almost against his will, he and his followers came to see the power of education. This would be, not a cure for heresy, but a preventive of it. To save southern Germany for the Church, there was needed a genius like Peter Canisius; and even his heroic efforts were powerless to remedy all the ravages wrought by heresy and worldly prelates.[37] But once get control of the youth, train them in right principles, impart to them at the same time an education the equal or superior of any in Europe,[38] and the whole world is saved for the Church.

Aim of Jesuit Education

Some of these early Jesuits — and they were all distinguished, some exceptionally so — glimpsed the possibilities latent in a unified body of educators. Here was a sphere of influence greater than that exercised by any of the universities;

they would have professors from all the universities of the world; they would combine the best pedagogical principles of the different nations; their schools must and could be made so thoroughly systematized that they would be the envy of all the world.[39] Here was the concrete realization of Loyola's dream of conquering the land of the infidel.

Students of history have seen in the ambition the craft and wiles of Jesuitry. If it were merely a natural ambition, that would be true. But there is a spiritual significance to this work often missed or misinterpreted by the casual critic, that must be taken into account in order to have a full understanding of Jesuit educational activity. To the Jesuit, to every Catholic, for that matter, the Church was instituted by Christ, it constitutes the kingdom of God on earth. To spread that kingdom, to increase its influence, to keep Christians within its fold, to regain those who have strayed, from this point of view, is in no sense ignoble but highly commendable.

The aim of the Jesuits was not the control of the temporal powers of the world but of those inner forces that make up human life. They wanted to reform, to purify, to Catholicize, so to speak, the world; and to them this meant the Christian regeneration of the world. Regeneration must begin with reform in morals and thought. The vantage ground for this work was in the scholastic centers; from here the poison had spread; here must the polluted springs be purified. Under their guidance the universities and colleges would become disseminators of truth instead of agencies of error. Their hope was to elevate the morality of the age, to wrest back from heresy to the Church what was hers by every right; they hoped to give to the different countries of Europe men trained in their schools who would be upright citizens as well as loyal sons of the Church.[40]

Objection to such a system of education on the ground that it is unethical will, of course, be made by those who see in the Church an agency of evil. But to object to religious training in the schools, to regard nonsectarian teaching as the only possible ideal demands the rejection, not only of the Jesuit system, but of Sturm's also, who set piety and learning as his objective, and not a colorless, nonsectarian piety, but Lutheran piety.[41] Under the same condemnation must fall practically all educational systems up to the mid-nineteenth century. In the modern school, the training of citizens is generally regarded as a primary objective; the Jesuits aimed not merely at making good citizens, but good Christian citizens as well.[42]

The Jesuits and Primary Education

Compayré[43] objects to the Jesuits on the score that "a permanent and characteristic feature of the educational policy of the Jesuits is, that during the whole course of their history, they have deliberately neglected and disdained primary instruction." Laurie[44] echoes this, remarking that "while the Jesuit order does not forbid, they have never advanced the education of the masses. There is manifest danger to the Faith in so doing." It would be a simple matter to explode such sweeping universals by particulars. For instance, in the United States, there is not a Jesuit parish church that has not attached to it a flourishing parochial or elementary school, directed by one of the Jesuit fathers. Nevertheless, it remains true that the Society does not include primary instruction as one of the works to which its members are devoted. But it would be difficult to prove that this aim was excluded because the Jesuits placed no faith in primary education. Efficiency demanded that they should not spread their energies over too many fields; in education, they chose secondary and university instruction. Their personnel has never been large enough to attend even to this work as much as they would have liked. How, then, was it possible for them to spare men for the work of primary education? It is as unfair an objection as to say that because Harvard College did not take over the primary-school system of Massachusetts, therefore it has deliberately neglected and disdained primary education.

In conclusion, then, it may be said that the Society, after the reluctant acceptance of education, devoted itself wholeheartedly to the work. This field of activity was not so much their conscious choice as it was the result of circumstances of time and place over which they had no control. During the seventeenth and eighteenth centuries, "they were the real masters of education and they maintained this educational supremacy until the end of the eighteenth century."[45] That undisputed sway, lost by their suppression, they never have regained; yet their influence since the restoration in 1814, particularly in Catholic education, perhaps especially in the United States, has been in recent times not inconsiderable. The activity of this teaching order in this country, their contribution to educational theory and practice, whether one approves of Jesuit pedagogy or not, is hardly negligible; it constitutes a phenomenon well worth investigation by the student of the history of American education.

Footnotes

[1]It is not the purpose here to tell the story of Jesuit educational activity in Europe, but merely to give the necessary historical background for the proper understanding of the Order's educational work in America. For a complete treatment of Jesuit education in the period before the suppression, the monumental Jesuit histories of the Order may be consulted; Astrain, *Historia de la Compañia de Jesus en la Asistencia de España* in 7 vols., especially Vol. IV; Fouqueray, *Histoire de la Compagnie de Jésus en France*, 3 vols., especially Vol. II; Duhr, *Geschichte der Jesuiten in den Ländern Deutscher Zunge*, 3 vols., especially Vol. I, 163–357; and II, 494–703; Tacchi-Venturi, *Storia della Compagnia di Gesú in Italia*. For an excellent summary history of Jesuit educational work in this period, derived for the most part from these Jesuit histories, see Brucker, *La Compagnie de Jésus. Esquisse de son Institut et de son Histoire*. Boehmer, *Les Jésuites*, and Gothein, *Ignatius von Loyola und die Gegenreformation*, while not free from historical error, represent the non-Catholic viewpoint. Stoeckius, *Forschungen zur Lebensordnung der Gesellschaft Jesu im 16. Jahrhundert. Erstes Stück. Ordensangehörige und Externe* is more impartial. See also Paulsen, *Geschichte des Gelehrten Unterrichts*, I, 407 ff.

[2]See Table II, p. 122 and *N.C.W.C. Directory for 1928*.

[3]*N.C.W.C. Directory for 1928*. See also Table III, p. 122.

[4]*Catalogus Provinciae Missourianae, ineunte anno 1931*. In 1930, there were 16,956 priests and scholastics in the entire Society. Of these, 3,540 were in the American provinces.

[5]Data taken from official statistics for 1921 in *Woodstock Letters*, LI, 72 ff. With the exception of ecclesiastical seminaries, European Jesuits have few schools beyond the secondary level.

[6]Paulsen, *op. cit.*, I, 382. "Education so largely prevails in the activity of the Order that it can be called in a special sense a teaching order."

[7]See Astrain, *op. cit.*, I; Gothein, *op. cit.* An impartial biography of the saint by a non-Catholic is Boehmer's, *Studien zur Geschichte der Gesellschaft Jesu. I. Band: Loyola*. In accuracy, this far surpasses his earlier work, *Die Jesuiten*. For popular works, see Van Dyke, *Ignatius of Loyola;* Sedgwick, *Ignatius Loyola;* and especially Brucker, *La Compagnie de Jésus*.

[8]*Chronicon Soc. Jesu*, I, 10, in *Monumenta Historica*. ". . . cujus institutio prout illa tempora et mores ferebant, potius juxta mundi hujus quam Dei spiritum peracta est. Cum enim legere tantum et scribere didicisset, in curiam regis missus, in ejusmodi ministeriis, quibus pueri nobiles et aulici solebant, est versatus."

[9]See Fouqueray, *op. cit.*, I, 5–7; Astrain, *op. cit.*, IV, Chap. IV; *Chronicon Soc. Jesu*, I, 31–48.

[10]*Chronicon Soc. Jesu*, I, 41; Fouqueray, *op. cit.*, p. 8.

[11]Goodier, "The Society of Jesus and Education," *The Month*, CVIII, 461.

[12]See Astrain, *op. cit.*, I, Chap. I, "Estudios de San Ignacio." On page 61, he quotes Lainez' estimate of Ignatius's scholastic ability. "Cuanto al estudio, aunque tuviese más impedimentos que los otros, todavía tuvo tanta diligencia y tanto provecho ó mayor *ceteris paribus*, que los otros de su tiempo, viniendo á mediocres letras, como mostró en responder públicamente y platicando en el tiempo de su curso con sus condiscípulos." Astrain adds laconically: "Llegó, pues, San Ignacio a adquirir *una decente medianía en letras y nada más.*"

[13]Sedgwick, *op. cit.*, p. 321.

[14]Lainez wrote in 1547: "Mas porque nuestra intención primera, desde el tiempo que estáuamos en Paris hasta entonces, *no era de hazer congregación* mas viuir en pobreza, dedicámosnos al seruicio de nuestro Señor y provecho del próximo . . . y ir . . . á los pies del papa . . . y pedir licencia para ir á Hierusalem. . . ." *Scripta de S. Ignatio*, I, 114 f. (Italics inserted.) In 1553, Ignatius dictated a letter to his secretary, Polanco, for Francis Palmio, the rector of Bologna, correcting an error made by Palmio in his preliminary sketch of the origin of the Company. "Your Reverence may add," he writes, "come li primi, che congregò in Parigi N. P. Ignatio, et lui *non pasorno in Italia per far religione*, ma per passar in Hierusalem, et predicar, et morir fra infideli; ma dopoi, non potendo passare (il che mai si ha visto, se non quel anno, in nostri tempi, per la guerra de venetiani contra turchi), hebbeno a restare in Italia; et adoperandoli il papa in cose del diuino seruitio et della sede apostolica, *all ' hora trattorno di far un corpo;* et è stata confirmata per papa Paulo et Julio, etc., . . ." *S.P. Ignatii Epistolae et Instructiones*, V, 259–60. This formal declaration made by the founder of the Society toward the close of his life (1553) clearly shows that neither he nor his companions at the time of their quitting Paris in 1536–7 had any intention of founding a religious order. Even after the vows made at Montmartre, Loyola and his companions were merely a group of missionaries, destined to disappear as a corporate organization after the death of the last survivor. It was at Rome that they decided to form a company, that is, a new religious order, that would have a permanent existence. Lainez tells of the discussion held by the first companions on this point. "Primeramente, sin discrepar alguno, fué determinado que sería bien hazer una compañía, que durase y no se acabase en nosotros." *Scripta de S. Ignatio*, I, 121. See also Fouqueray, *op. cit.*, I, 33 ff.; and especially Van Ortroy, "Manrèse et les Origines de la Compagnie de Jésus," *Analecta Bollandiana*, XXVII (1908), 405–418.

[15]*Institutum Soc. Jesu.* I, "Bullarium et Compendium Privilegiorum," p. 4 (edit. Florence, 1892).

[16]Stoeckius, *Ordensangehörige und Externe*, supposes that the education of extern youth was intended from the first.

[17]Fouqueray, *op. cit.*, I, 147.

[18]Even in 1541, Ignatius hardly thought of his Order as engaged in teaching even of its own members, much less of externs. In the "Constitutiones de Paupertate" written in 1541, it was determined that the colleges (i.e., the *collegia seminaria*) should be located in the university cities. There were to be neither faculties nor lectures in the Company itself. "42. Hacer Colegios en Universidades. No estudios ni lecciones en la Compañía." *Constitutiones S.J., Latinae et Hispanicae cum earum Declarationibus*, p. 306. See also Fouqueray, *op. cit.*, I, 176.

[19]*Scripta de S. Ignatio*, I, 147: ". . . y muchos estudiantes se dedicaron á la Compañía que perseueran hasta oy. . . ." From a letter of Lainez, written in 1547.

[20]*Epistolae Mixtae*, I, 58.

[21]Jesuits are not monks like the Benedictines (despite Van Dyke, *Ignatius Loyola*, p. 7), nor friars like the Franciscans, but *regular clerks*, that is, clerics living in community, bound by vows and rules. Hence, it is quite incorrect to speak of a Jesuit monastery. If Jesuits live in an institution devoted to educational work, it is generally called a college; otherwise a house or residence.

[22]See Jourdain, *Histoire de l'Université de Paris*, I, Chap. I.

[23]"Extern" is a term that has been a stumblingblock to many writers on Jesuit education. Primarily, an extern is one following the Jesuit course of higher studies who is not a member of the Order. In later usage, however, an extern may be a lay professor in a Jesuit college; or, in a Jesuit boarding school, the students — none of whom are

Jesuits — are divided into *interns* or boarding students, and *externs*, or day students. Hence, the confusion.

[24]See Tournier, F., "Monseigneur Guillaume du Prat au Concile de Trent," *Études*, XCVIII (1904), 480 ff. It should be noted that this type of college has practically disappeared, except in a few European theological seminaries where Jesuits and extern students, preparing for the secular priesthood, pursue the same courses. Even here, they are not lodged in the same building.

[25]In the American provinces, Jesuits are never students in secondary schools. Before admission to the Society, the candidate must have finished his secondary studies. See *infra*, Chap. XIII, "Training of Jesuit Teachers." In the first century of Jesuit history, however, it is probable that Jesuit scholastics studied "rhetoric," the highest class in the *gymnasium*, with extern students.

[26]*Chronicon Soc. Jesu*, I, 242. The University of Gandia was not opened until 1549.

[27]Herman, *La Pédagogie des Jésuites*, p. 20; Gothein, *op. cit.*, pp. 350–1; Astrain, *op. cit.*, II, 553.

[28]*Institutum S.J.*, I, "*Bullarium*," p. 23. For the relations of the Popes to the new Society, Pastor, *Geschichte der Päpste*, Vol. VI, may be consulted.

[29]*Scripta de S. Ignatio*, I, 220 "Quién inuentó los colegios? Laynez fué el primero que tocó este punto. Nosotros halláuamos difficuldad por causa de la pobreza; y assí quién tocaua unos remedios, quién otros" (in the "Memoriale P. Consalvii de S. Ignatio"). The new Order was vowed to poverty; they did not see how they could accept foundations for educational work. Cf. Van Ortroy, "Manrèse et les Origines de la Compagnie," *Analecta Bollandiana*, XXVII, 416.

[30]*Acta Sanctorum, mense Julii*, t. VII, "Vita altera S. Ignatii," c. 23.

[31]Lancicii, N., *De Praestantia Instituti Societatis Jesu*, p. 175. Cited by Herman, *op. cit.*, p. 39.

[32]Cited by Herman, *op. cit.*, p. 40, from *Les Recherches de la France*, III, 43.

[33]Goodier, *The Month*, CVIII, 585.

[34]*Constitutiones Latinae et Hispanicae*, pp. 372–378.

[35]*Ibid.*, pp. 106–167. See also Pachtler, *Ratio*, I, 8–69.

[36]*Constitutiones Latinae et Hispanicae*, p. 106. Later on, in Cap. VII of the *Pars Quarta*, p. 134, there is more explicit treatment of the classes for *externs*. "Having due regard not only to the literary advancement of our own scholastics, but also to the progress in literature and character of the externs whom we have undertaken to train in our colleges, public classes should be instituted, wherever possible, at least in the humanities."

[37]Duhr, *op. cit.*, I, 66–91. See also Pastor, *Geschichte der Päpste*, VI.

[38]Gothein, *op. cit.*, p. 424 says: "Ignatius hatte erkannt, was den restaurierten Katholizismus Not hat: Theologen wollte er bilden, die das System des Mittelalters vom Boden des Humanismus aus verteidigten." But Ignatius — and his followers — desired to form more than theologians; they wanted to develop Catholic leaders throughout Europe.

[39]Laurie, *Studies in the History of Educational Opinion from the Renaissance*, p. 87, says: "How was it that the Jesuit schools so far excelled the humanistic secondary schools of the Reformation as wholly to eclipse them and to evoke the approval of Bacon and other Protestant men of eminence? The answer is contained in one word, *organization*." Macaulay, hardly a friendly critic, says in his *History of England*, II, Chap. 6: "The liberal education of youth passed almost entirely into their hands and was conducted by them with conspicuous ability. . . . Enmity itself was compelled to own that in the art of managing and forming the tender mind they had no equals." Adamson, *Pioneers of Modern Education*, p. 1, calls the Jesuits "without question the most efficient schoolmasters of their time." Von Ranke, a hostile critic, pays them tribute in the *History of the Popes*, I, Book V, sec. 418 (London edit., 1896): "It is found that young people gained more with them in six months than with other teachers in two years. Even Protestants removed their children from distant gymnasia to confide them to the care of the Jesuits."

[40]See Goodier, *The Month*, CX, 272 ff. See also Schimberg, *L'éducation morale dans les collèges de la Compagnie de Jésus*, Chap. 4.

[41]"Sapiens atque eloquens pietas." See Sohm, *Die Schule Johann Sturms*, pp. 100 ff.; Schiller, *Lehrbuch der Geschichte der Pädagogik*, p. 115.

[42]Naumann, a non-Catholic, in *Der Jesuitismus*, p. 77, says: "Ganz töricht aber ist der Tadel, der früher oft erhoben wurde, der 'unsittlichen' Methode der Erziehung der Jesuiten. Ich habe das Institutum auf das genaueste und sorgfältigste durchgelesen und ich erkläre, dass ich diesen Vorwurf für einen frivolen und völlig unbegründeten erachten muss. Wer das Institutum kennt, weiss dass ein Geist es beseelt, der nach einem hohen sittlichen Ideal strebt. Das Ideal ist nicht das meine; ich kann es nicht als solches akzeptieren, aber den Ernst und die Lauterkeit erkenne ich willig an, die den Männern innewohnen, welche ihm zustreben; ich erkenne sie an und mögen diese Männer zehnmal Jesuiten heissen."

[43]*History of Pedagogy* (Payne's translation), p. 142.

[44]*Op. cit.*, p. 90.

[45]Compayré, *op. cit.*, p. 141.

PART I

ORIGINS AND GENERAL CHARACTERISTICS OF JESUIT PEDAGOGY

CHAPTER II

ORIGINS OF JESUIT PEDAGOGY

TO UNDERSTAND the Jesuit system of education in any country at any period, there is need of studying its great educational document, the *Ratio Studiorum*.[1] Time and circumstances have undoubtedly brought about changes in Jesuit pedagogy both in America and Europe. The curriculum in Jesuit secondary schools in the United States, for example, would be quite unrecognizable by the framers of the *Ratio*. Nevertheless, it remains true that the kernel, the core, the soul of Jesuit pedagogy is found in that sixteenth-century document; the basic principles that underlie Jesuit teaching from that day to this are therein enunciated. It is this community of educational principles, however wide the divergence in practice in the modern American Jesuit high school and the Renaissance *collegium,* that gives to the Jesuit school of that day and this a common hallmark easily recognizable by the initiate.

Most historians focus attention on the *Ratio* of 1599.[2] But this was merely the culmination of many attempts at securing unity of instruction and administration in Jesuit colleges. In a body like the Jesuits, probably the most highly centralized organization in the world, with professors in the colleges subject to the local head, the rector; the rectors, in turn, subject to the regional head, the provincial; the provincials subject to the general; with their reports on the progress, number of students, new colleges accepted, and the like, there was bound to be some attempt at educational unity.

First Attempts

The first document, the ferment, so to say, of the entire Jesuit pedagogy,[3] is the fourth part of the Constitutions of the

Society, written by Ignatius himself. Even before these were finished in 1551, there was mention in Jesuit writing, of educational activity. Thus, one of the first companions of Ignatius drew up in 1541 a plan for the foundation of a college and traced the portrait of a scholastic of the Society.[4] But there is nothing here relating to the education of "extern" youth; nor is there anything in that rough draft of the Constitutions, written by Ignatius, called the Rudiments of the Constitutions.[5] The final edition of the Constitutions, however, makes mention of the education of secular youth. It is evident, as has been noted in the preceding chapter, that during the time that elapsed between these two editions of the Constitutions, St. Ignatius had definitely, though reluctantly, determined to devote the efforts of his Company to education. Still, at this early date, he had no desire to act arbitrarily; nor did he wish to impose a fixed course of study upon the colleges that the Company had taken over or founded. Each college was to draw up a tentative *ratio,* modeled as much as possible on the plan of the Roman College.

This recommendation was not without effect. In the *Monumenta Paedagogica*[6] are gathered together the extant pedagogical documents produced by Jesuits in the period that preceded the first *Ratio Studiorum* of 1586. In this collection[7] are to be found school programs, incompleted plans, often anonymous, without exact date; the thousand and one minutiæ in the scholastic life of colleges, as yet often but imperfectly organized; reports on the state of studies in a college or a province; words of praise or blame for individual masters, for the spirit of the students; embryo treatises on methodology. Here, too, are recorded the remarks of a provincial or of an official visitor on the state of a school, made on the occasion of his periodic visitation. This volume is invaluable for purposes of orientation to one who wishes to interpret the *Ratio;* it supplies the pedagogic atmosphere that preceded the definitive *Ratio*. Here and there in this volume are scattered rules for prefects of studies, for masters, for pupils, for classes — all of which leads one to believe that "about 1570 there was in all the provinces of the Society a *ratio studiorum* practically uniform, made up of documents sent to Rome at different times."[8]

The Ratio of 1586

In 1584, under the Father General, Claude Aquaviva, the General Congregation took up the question of the reform of studies. The proposal met with universal favor and Aquaviva set to work with characteristic energy to carry out this project.[9] Six fathers were commissioned to remain at Rome and draw up a plan of studies for the whole Society. After nine months of labor, their draft was submitted to the professors of the Roman College and to Aquaviva. This was meant to be a tentative draft, and was submitted as such by the General to all the provinces of the Society for their approval. Each province summoned its best scholars and ablest teachers to examine this plan of studies, to suggest amendments, to formulate in their turn a new *ratio*. The reports of each provincial or national committee were sent to Rome. Extraordinary candor was displayed by the critics, particularly those of the German provinces.[10] In fact, individual obstinacy and, perhaps, national jealousy seemed to combine to prevent the adoption of a uniform plan of studies for the whole Society. The two criticisms of vagueness and prolixity seem justified; the *Ratio* of 1586 gave the résumé of all the discussions of the first committee, the arguments pro and con; there was a succession of rather tedious treatises on the qualities of the Jesuit teacher, the formation he should receive, programs for the extern students, daily schedules, school exercises, together with hints on promoting discipline and study.

The Ratio of 1591

In 1591, Aquaviva issued an amended edition of the *Ratio.*[11] This differed from its predecessor in the omission of the pedagogical dissertation. An attempt is made at definiteness by the addition of regulations for the Provincial, the Rector, the Prefect of Studies, as well as rules for each of the five classes. However, this was received with hardly more enthusiasm than the preceding proposal. Again the German provinces broke forth in vigorous protest and candid criticism.[12]

The Ratio of 1599

Aquaviva, a forceful and decisive personality, determined to put an end to what he judged fruitless discussion. Accordingly on January 8, 1599, he sent to the provinces the final *Ratio Studiorum.*[13] This is much briefer, less prolix, to accede to the demands of the Germans.[14] The reasons for the various rules are omitted. The edition of 1591 had four hundred pages; this has two hundred. Yet even this did not give universal satisfaction. A German province protested again.[15] But Aquaviva was determined to have no more revisions for the time.[16] The *Ratio Studiorum* of 1599, in its general prescriptions at least, had the force of law for all Jesuit colleges until the suppression of the Society in 1773. While it no longer is binding on the colleges, even in the modified form given out by Roothaan in 1832,[17] yet it has had an enormous influence on Jesuit educators of all countries and all times; it has served to perpetuate the Jesuit tradition in their schools, to hand on to the modern Jesuit school the same spirit that animated the Jesuit college of the seventeenth century.

The Framers of the Ratio

Aquaviva's *Ratio* was the result of fifteen years[18] of collaboration (1584–1599), by a number of the most competent scholars and experienced teachers that could be found in the Society. In the *Monumenta Paedagogica* and other writings of this early period, some of the pioneers of Jesuit pedagogy stand out clearly. First of all, there is Loyola himself; he had devised a method of will training in the book of the Spiritual Exercises:[19] in a vague, indeterminate way, he had written a plan of organization for the colleges.[20] There is James Ledesma, the administrator, who developed this plan and attended to details of organization;[21] there is Jerome Nadal, who oriented the course of studies in Jesuit schools, directing them ever more and more toward unity;[22] finally, there is Perpiniani, the Jesuit humanist, friend of Marc Anthony Muretus, who gave to Jesuit teaching a final and effective impulse toward classicism.[23]

Borrowings from Other Sources

In a compilation such as this *Ratio,* it is impossible to determine the authorship or even to distinguish what is distinctively Jesuit and what are borrowings from other educators.[24] In the fifteen years of reports and correspondence from Jesuits of different nationalities, different antecedents, different teaching experience that went into the making of the *Ratio,* it would be exceedingly difficult to prove that there was no borrowing from other sources. On the other hand, it does not follow from chance resemblance between the Jesuit system and others that one must be necessarily derived from the other. The Jesuits of the period that produced the *Ratio* made no claim, as far as can be ascertained, to originality either in program or in method for this document.[25]

Sturm's Influence

Johann Sturm,[26] the Strassburg "gymnasial-magister," is most often cited as the source from which the Jesuits borrowed.[27] It may be that religious prejudice plays some part in the attempt to attribute the good points of the Jesuit system to the Lutheran schoolmaster. True, there are strong resemblances between Sturm's book, *De litterarum ludis recte aperiendis,* published in 1538, and the Jesuit *Ratio.* Von Raumer, who is bitterly anti-Jesuit, accuses the framers of the *Ratio* of immoral borrowings.

If one compares the Jesuit method with Sturm's, they have at first blush a great resemblance. The organization of the schools, the books, the courses, the ideal of their formation are the same. And yet in considering the matter more carefully, a Jesuit college is as different from Sturm's academy as a Jesuit is from a Protestant.[28]

Meyer, however, thinks it highly improbable that the Jesuit Nadal would borrow the regulations of a Protestant gymnasium for his foundation at Messina.[29] Yet Sturm himself thought the Jesuits had imitated his system. "I have seen the authors which the Jesuits explain, their exercises, their methods. So little different is this from our system and rules that it would seem to be borrowed from us."[30]

The Brethren of the Common Life

For want of more convincing evidence, it may be concluded that Sturm and the Jesuits both drew from a common source, the Brethren of the Common Life. That they influenced Sturm seems fairly well established; he spent three years, from 1521–1524, with the Brethren in their college at Liège.[31] The entire organization of this college made a profound impression on young Sturm; he adopted it, according to his biographers, as a model for the gymnasium at Strassburg.[32] Loyola, on the other hand, had lodged during his first months in Paris at the Collège Montaigú,[33] where the traditions of the Brethren were still strong. However, as Ignatius himself had little to do with the details of Jesuit education, it is not probable that the influence of the Brethren is due to this fact.[34] But at a later period, the educational system of the Brethren directly affected the Jesuits. In 1580, the college of the Brethren at Liège was handed over to the Society;[35] the school traditions and methods were, in all likelihood, appropriated by the newcomers. It may well be maintained that both Sturm and the Jesuits were influenced by the Hieronymites. Père J. B. Herman, a recent investigator in this field,[36] is of the opinion that the methods of the Brethren of the Common Life exercised an influence on the pedagogy of the Jesuits, at least indirectly. The schools of the Brethren in the Low Countries must have served as a stimulus and an example to the Netherland Jesuits, and through them to the whole Order.

Vives

Another educator whose theories are said to have been not without weight in drawing up the *Ratio* is Vives.[37] But this is based on very slight evidence, mainly on the fact that both Ignatius and Vives were Spaniards, and the *Chronicon Societatis Jesu*[38] tells of Loyola's visit to Vives at Bruges. The first reason would seem to have slight value, for as will be seen shortly, Jesuit pedagogy borrowed little or nothing from the Spanish Universities. Again, as in the case of Sturm, there are resemblances to the *Ratio* in Vives' writings. In both systems discipline is based on the dignity of the teacher; corporal punishment is to be rarely used; health education is imparted by means of sport and games; great emphasis is placed on Latin; *memoriter* work is given a prominent place. But resemblance does not imply community of origin. All the schools of the Renaissance period, as is probably true of every age, had many common elements.[39] In all likelihood, neither the Jesuits nor Sturm nor Vives deserve any particular credit as innovators of a new pedagogical system; their merit consists in the successful application of the current educational theories of their day. The Jesuits created a world-wide system, whose outstanding feature was a striving for uniformity.

Influence of the Universities

Two factors that played a large part in Jesuit pedagogy were the universities and the spirit of the age. This is almost a truism; for no teacher nor set of teachers can break away entirely from the *Zeitgeist*, nor can they completely sever their own pedagogical procedure from that which they saw imparted during their years of training.

The early Jesuits were, as has been seen, all products of the universities; they did not come from seminaries, not even from Jesuit institutions; practically all of that first generation entered the Society after graduation from the best universities of their day. Among the institutions that exerted a strong influence on Jesuit pedagogy, Paris stands out prominently. To begin with, Ignatius held his Alma Mater in the deepest veneration. He contrasted unfavorably the Italian university system and its lack of order with what he had known at Paris. He was insistent that his scholastics should follow the *modus Parisiensis*.[40] Messina, the first Jesuit college for externs, was modeled by his orders on the colleges of Paris.[41] He thought the method of Paris more thorough, more certain of assuring the intellectual advancement of his students. For this reason, he staffed the Roman College with Paris graduates to the great displeasure of some Roman authorities. Moreover, many of the scholastics were sent to study at Paris, although the university itself gave no enthusiastic welcome to the establishment of Jesuit houses there. Even in the matter of moral surroundings, Ignatius thought that Paris was superior to the other universities.[42] Undoubtedly, too, Loyola's esteem for obedience, his desire to see authority respected made him favor Paris,[43] where the professor was held in much higher esteem than at the democratic Italian universities where the professors were absolutely at the mercy of the students.

The Jesuit use of disputations and contests, the adoption of the scholastic ladder from rudiments, grammar, humanities, to rhetoric — all were in use at Paris.[44] However, the strongest confirmation of the theory that Paris was influential in shaping the Jesuit theory and practice comes from the early Jesuits themselves. Thus, Nadal, in his commentary on the Constitutions, says explicitly that the Society had appropriated the method of the University of Paris.[45] Later in the legal contest between the Jesuits and the University of Paris in 1612, when the Society was accused of cherishing the ambition of gaining control there, the Jesuits' advocate replied that the Company sought to teach there only because *"estant issue de cette université, elle l'honore singulièrement, souhaitant de lui dédier ses labeurs."*[46]

Influence of the Age

In the sixteenth century with its youthful impetuosity and its sometimes unreflecting ardor, three factors were at work distracting the minds of men. One was the exploration of the newly discovered lands beyond the seas; another, the rediscovery of antiquity; and the third, the revolt from the ancient Church. All three had their effects on the educational world and upon the new Society, but not in the same intensity. The discovery and exploration of the New World had little immediate effect upon school curricula; the pedagogue of that period thought the route of Julius Cæsar through Gaul of vastly more importance than Columbus' voyage of discovery.

Of the Reformation and its part in influencing education but little need be said here, as, with the possible exception of Sturm, Protestant schoolmasters in no wise influenced the framers of the *Ratio*. But the spirit of the Renaissance did color the thinking and the policy of the makers of the *Ratio;* the renaissance of pagan literature was accompanied by a pedagogic renaissance. This meant, on the part of many, a complete break with the Middle Ages, a contempt for all or nearly all that the medieval world held dear. Positively, it consisted in an almost idolatrous veneration, and a no less servile imitation, of pagan antiquity. Its pedagogic ideal was aristocratic; education was not for the many. The culture it aimed to impart was based on knowledge of the ancient classics. This cult of antiquity resulted not seldom in a new type of formalism; into the pit they had dug for what they held in supreme contempt — the dialect of the Middle Ages — the humanists themselves stumbled by their exaltation of form over thought. *Eloquentia,* the ability to write and speak Latin according to the Ciceronian form as interpreted by Quintilian, became the main objective of all secondary education.[47]

Attention was focused during this period on man and nature, not on God and the immortal life after death, as had been the case during the reign of scholasticism. But instead of the study of nature and man in themselves, the Renaissance pedagogue regarded him through the eyes of Cicero or Vergil. If one intends writing a description of a garden, the modern teacher would suggest a visit to a garden. Not so the sixteenth century pedagogue; he never dreamed of such a procedure. Had not Pliny the Younger described a garden in exquisite, cadenced prose? Nothing seemed more natural than to imitate in one's own writing the classical masterpiece. Even in education, a principle was sure of acceptance, if one could only quote Cicero or Horace or Quintilian in favor of it.[48]

Quintilian

Naturally this strong current of thought had its effect on the Jesuits and their pedagogy. They, like their contemporaries, succumbed to the influence of Quintilian[49] and joined in the chorus of praise of the Roman rhetorician.[50] The Jesuit objective, too, was *efformare ad eloquentiam,* and they took Quintilian's *Institutio Oratoria* as a treasure house from which they drew their pedagogical precepts. Not a page in the *Ratio* but bears the imprint of Quintilian's influence. The class exercises, memory lessons, literary composition, correction of exercises, declamation, all came from Quintilian.[51] Not that one should picture the framers of the *Ratio* as gathered about a table examining Quintilian's treatise and appropriating large excerpts for their work. But Quintilian and his *eloquentia* were in the air; *eloquentia* was the slogan of the intellectual world of that day much as evolution is of ours; there was no school or university where Quintilian was not in vogue; he was the interpreter of antiquity to the Renaissance as Aquinas in his day had been the interpreter of Aristotle in the schools. This influence lasted for long in Jesuit circles. Jouvancy, the one great pedagogical writer of the Society, intrusted by the fourteenth General Congregation with the task of writing a treatise on teaching, based on the *Ratio,* could find no better authority for his precepts than Quintilian.[52]

Scholasticism

Along with this veneration for Quintilian and *eloquentia,* another influence not yet dead had its effect on the framers of the *Ratio* — the medieval influence. For despite all the gibes of the humanists the sixteenth century was still the golden age of disputations. Loyola and his companions saw the disadvantages and the advantages of the disputations so characteristic of medieval Scholasticism. The Scholastics' contempt for style and their barbarous Latin provoked the sarcasm of the advocates of the New Learning. The Jesuits wished to save what was best in Scholasticism and unite it to humanism.[53] The result is evident in the *Ratio,* which provides for a thorough training in the classics, followed in the higher studies by courses in scholastic philosophy and theology. The *Ratio* is essentially a compromise between the old learning and the new.

Summary

The *Ratio Studiorum,* then, owes its origin first of all to the desire on the part of the Society for unity in its educational activity. It is the product of experience, the experience of Loyola and of Jesuit teachers and administrators generally. This experience was colored by factors at work in the intellectual world of the day; theories of other educators of which the members of the Order were cognizant; the practice of the universities where they had studied, notably the University of Paris; and most of all by the passion for antiquity, for *eloquentia,* whose exponent most held in honor during the Renaissance was Quintilian. How much of originality is in the document it is difficult to say; but this much is certain, that the application of these ideas to their schools produced a particular type of education, the Jesuit type. Its characteristics will be considered in the succeeding chapter.

Footnotes

[1]See Appendix.

[2]E.g., Compayré, *Histoire critique des doctrines de l'éducation.*

[3]Herman, *op. cit.,* p. 8.

[4]*Constitutiones Soc. Jesu latinae et hispanicae cum earum declarationibus* (Madrid, 1892), pp. 306–307.

[5]*Ibid.,* pp. 365–418. See especially "Cuarta Parte Principal," pp. 372–378.

[6]*Monumenta Paedagogica Societatis Jesu quae primam rationem studiorum anno 1586 praecessere* (Madrid, 1901).

[7]*Ibid.,* Introd., p. vii. The editors call it a "farrago."

[8]Herman, *op. cit.,* p. 18.

[9]The text of this 1586 *Ratio* is in Pachtler, II, 25–217. The legends that gathered about this document are examined pp. 18–24.

[10]*Judicia Provinciarum de ratione Studiorum de 1586.* See Herman, *op. cit.,* p. 25.

[11]*Ratio atq. Institutio Studiorum.* Romae: in Collegio Soc. Jesu, anno Dni. 1591. Pachtler, *op. cit.,* II, 218, does not seem to be aware of the existence of this edition. See Duhr, *Die Studienordnung der Gesellschaft Jesu,* pp. 19–22. All of this 1591 *Ratio* that pertains to the "lower" schools will be found in Dr. Corcoran's scholarly text, *Renatae Litterae* (Dublin, 1927), pp. 188 ff. This same work also contains excerpts from the *Monumenta Paedagogica,* the first *Ratio* (1586), and the definite *Ratio* (1599). An excellent source book for the study of Jesuit education.

[12]"Rückäusserung der vier deutschen Provinzen," Pachtler, *op. cit.*, II, 218–222. Pachtler supposes these are comments on the 1586 *Ratio;* but the numbering that puzzled him obviously refers to the 1591 edition.

[13]*Ratio atque Institutio Studiorum Societatis Jesu* (Neapoli, 1599).

[14]Pachtler, *op. cit.*, II, 218. "Librum judicant recipiendum et in breviorem formam praecisa omni sermonis asperitate redigendum."

[15]Pachtler, *op. cit.*, II, 483–507.

[16]For the history of these various *Ratios,* see Astrain, *op. cit.*, IV, lib. I, c. 1, 1–18.

[17]See Appendix. Roothaan's Revision of 1832 never secured the approval of a General Congregation. See *infra,* Chap. VIII, "The Evolution of the American Jesuit High School."

[18]It would be inexact to suppose that the long delay in presenting the final *Ratio* was due *merely* to a praiseworthy effort on the part of the Jesuits to secure an efficient program of secondary studies. First of all, the *Ratio* included philosophical and theological studies as well as humane letters. And in those feverish times, when accusations of heresy were in the air, a document that touched on theology was bound to be subjected to rigorous scrutiny. It was thought by the Dominicans that the new Order did not give to St. Thomas Aquinas and his teaching the place he deserved in the science of theology. For the part played by anti-Jesuit theologians, and particularly the Spanish Inquisition, in this dispute, see Astrain, *op. cit.*, IV, Chap. II, 18 ff. See also Broderick, James, S.J., *The Life and Works of Blessed Robert Francis Bellarmine* (New York, 1928), I, 374 ff.

[19]The *Exercitia Spiritualia.* For a translation, see Longridge, *Spiritual Exercises of St. Ignatius* (London, 1922). For an analysis and account of the genesis of the "Exercises," see Astrain, *op. cit.*, I, Chap. IX, 40–161; and Fouqueray, *op. cit.*, I, 82–100.

[20]See *Pars IV* of the Constitutions, *Constitutiones Latinae et Hispanicae,* etc., pp. 107–167.

[21]*Monumenta Paedagogica,* pp. 10–11; 141–149; 338–454 and *passim.*

[22]See *Chronicon Soc. Jesu,* III, 445, *Monumenta Paedagogica,* pp. 12, 14; 89–140 and *passim.*

[23]Herman, *op. cit.*, p. 17.

[24]Schwickerath, *Jesuit Education,* p. 136, admits that it is not easy to determine the sources from which the *Ratio* is derived. See also Fleischmann, in Rein, *Encyklopädisches Handbuch der Pädagogik,* IV, 671 ff.

[25]Astrain, *op. cit.*, IV, 15 f.: ". . . Todos saben no fué ninguna novedad en la enseñanza. Al hablar del *Ratio,* nadie piense que lo presentamos como un descubrimiento pedagógico. . . . El merito del P. Aquaviva fué metodizar sabiamente lo que pudiéremos llamar tradición escolar de los establecimientos docentes en el siglo XVI."

[26]Sohm, *Die Schule Johann Sturms und die Kirche Strassburgs in ihrem gegenseitigen Verhältnis, 1530–1581* (1912); Schmidt, *La vie et les oeuvres de Jean Sturm.*

[27]Sicard, *Les études classiques avant la révolution,* p. 12; Kämmel, *Geschichte des deutschen Schulwesens im Uebergange vom Mittelalter zur Neuzeit,* p. 227; Schiller, *Lehrbuch der Geschichte der Pädagogik,* p. 124.

[28]*Geschichte der Pädagogik,* 3 Auflage, I, 271.

[29]*Der Ursprung des Jesuitischen Schulwesens,* p. 54. Hyma, *The Christian Renaissance,* p. 298, thinks that Sturm's influence on the Jesuit school system cannot be proved. He is of the opinion that the Brethren of the Common Life influenced Lutherans, Calvinists, and Jesuits alike.

[30]Sturm, *Classicarum Epistolarum,* Liber III (Argentorati, 1565), f. A VI. Quoted by Duhr, *Die Studienordnung der Gesellschaft Jesu,* p. 7. "Vidi enim quos scriptores explicent et quas habeant exercitationes et quam rationem in docendo teneant quae a nostris praeceptis institutisque usque adeo proxime abest, ut a nostris fontibus derivata esse videatur."

[31]Sohm, *op. cit.*, p. 29. For the Brethren of the Common Life, see Hyma, *The Christian Renaissance,* especially pp. 268–275.

[32]Sohm, *loc. cit.;* Veil, *Sturms Unterrichtsziele und Schuleinrichtungen,* p. 23, Schmidt, *La vie et les Oeuvres de Jean Sturm,* pp. 5 and 36. Hyma, *op. cit.*, pp. 292 ff. enlarges on the influence of the Brethren on both Sturm's plan and the Jesuits'. The elements common to all three systems were the mild but effective discipline; fewer hours of class,

division into classes, one year for each class, advancement of the brighter pupils more frequently, etc.

[33]*Chronicon Soc. Jesu*, p. 41.

[34]Hyma, *op. cit.*, p. 272 seems to exaggerate the effect of Loyola's stay at Montaigú. "What he might have done," he writes, "if he had never seen the dormitory with its poor students at Montaigú, we do not know." And, on pp. 345 ff., he assumes that the entire organization of the Jesuits was borrowed from the Brethren. "They [the Jesuits] were the descendants of the Brethren of the Common Life."

[35]Daris, *Histoire du Diocèse et de la Principauté de Liège pendant le XVI siècle*, p. 433.

[36]*Op. cit.*, Chap. IV.

[37]Lange, *Encyklopädie des gesammten Erziehungs- und Unterrichtswesens*, IX, 776 ff.; Duhr, *op. cit.*, pp. 13 ff. See also Burger, *Erasmus von Rotterdam und der Spanier Vives* for an excellent outline and evaluation of Vives' pedagogical doctrine; and Sandys', *History of Classical Scholarship*, II, 214–215.

[38]I, p. 43.

[39]E.g., the purpose of education was, in general, the formation of Christian men. Thus Vives lays down the objective "ut sapientior fiat juvenis ac inde melior." Quoted by Burger, *op. cit.*, p. 22. And Erasmus: "Christus est totius eruditionis et eloquentiae scopus," *ibid.*, p. 20. According to Melanchton true eloquence is the "facultas res bonas sapienter et perspicue exponendi." *Ibid.*, p. 25. Cf. Sturm's *sapiens atque eloquens pietas.*

[40]*Chronicon Soc. Jesu*, III, 242. See also Astrain, *op. cit.*, II, 558 ff.; Herman, *op. cit.*, Chaps. 2 and 3.

[41]*Mon. Paed.*, pp. 615–616. Thus, p. 616, "conformando il tutto al modo Parisiense."

[42]See letter to his nephew, Bertrand, quoted by Herman, *op. cit.*, p. 63.

[43]Meyer, *Der Ursprung des Jesuitischen Schulwesens*, p. 20, says: "Es ist klar aus welchem Grunde Ignatius von Loyola den Modus Parisiensis vor dem Modus Italicus bevorzugte und zur Grundlage seines Ordensschulwesens machte. Es kam ihm ja nicht auf die Pflege der Wissenschaft und ihre Fortbildung an, sondern auf Erziehung. Nicht einen Orden von einzelnen Gelehrten im Dienste selbstloser Erforschung der Wahrheit wollte er gründen, sondern das war seine Absicht ein recht zahlreiches Heer von gehorsamen Kämpfern für die Zwecke seiner Kirche zu schulen." See also Renaudet, *Préréforme et Humanisme à Paris pendant les premières guerres d'Italie* (*1484–1517*), pp. 684–703, for an explanation of the *modus Parisiensis.*

[44]Herman, *op. cit.*, p. 68. Père Herman maintains that the system of classes was not invented by the Jesuits, but was in use at Paris. The program of studies for Messina (1548), prescribed three distinct Latin classes and adds: "Et nelle tre scuole dette oltra delle sue lettioni, si faranno per ordinario repetitioni, interrogationi, concertationi, compositioni, declamationi: et altri simili essercitij conuenuenti a ciascuno seguitando *il modo et ordine che s'usa in Parigi* essendo il meglio che tenere si possa per facilmente et perfectamente diuentare dotto nella lingua latina." *Mon. Paed.*, p. 615. But see Rochemonteix, *Un Collège de Jésuites aux XVII et XVIII siècles*, I, 5; and Goodier, *The Month*, CIX. 406.

[45]*Scholia in Constitutiones*, p. 350.

[46]*Plaidoyé de M. Jacques de Montholon, avocat en la cour* (Paris, 1613). Cited by Herman, *op. cit.*, p. 49.

[47]Dubois, *Le Problème Pédagogique*, "Le type humaniste," pp. 42 ff. For the development of this ideal by Sturm, see Sohm, *op. cit.*, pp. 100 ff.

[48]Jones, W., "Quintilian, Plutarch, and the Early Humanists," *The Classical Review*, 1907, pp. 41 ff.

[49]See Appel, *Das Bildungs- und Erziehungsideal Quintilians nach der Institutio Oratoria.*

[50]Thus Ribadeneira calls him, "Quintilianus noster exercitissimus et peritissimus pueros erudiendi magister." *Acta Sanctorum, Julii*, VII, 732.

[51]See Herman, *op. cit.*, Chap. 7, "Les Anciens."

[52]Juvencii, *Ratio discendi et docendi* (Parisiis, 1778), p. 240.

[53]Strowski, *Pascal et son temps*, "L'organe qui unit l'esprit religieux a l'esprit mondain ce fut la Compagnie de Jésus." Cited by Herman, *op. cit.* p. 196.

CHAPTER III

GENERAL CHARACTERISTICS OF JESUIT PEDAGOGY

To delineate the characteristics of Jesuit pedagogy as it was during the days of its supremacy is no easy task. The *Ratio Studiorum* alone will not suffice. First of all, this document[1] is not merely a *directorium,* so to speak, for the Jesuits in their conduct of secondary schools; it provides Jesuit students in their philosophical and theological studies with a plan of life. Obviously, the rules applicable to these "scholastics," bound by vows, have nothing to do with the boys of the lower or secondary schools, and very slight bearing on those *extern* students, usually candidates for the secular priesthood, who attended the same university lectures as the scholastics. At the risk of being tiresome, it must be repeated that members of the Order were rarely students in the secondary schools; before securing admission to the Society they were obliged to finish their gymnasial course. Yet these directions in the *Ratio,* sometimes for scholastics, sometimes for extern students in the university courses, sometimes for boys in the secondary schools, perfectly clear to the framers of the *Ratio,* as well as to one acquainted with the Jesuit system of education, have been a stumblingblock to many writers.

Misunderstanding of Jesuit System

Mertz,[2] for example, was so hopelessly confused that he gives an altogether ludicrous presentation of the matter. He seems convinced that the religious obedience and the disciplinary rules binding on the scholastics of the Society were regulations for boys in the lower schools as well. Nothing, of course, is farther from the truth. Students in Jesuit schools were expected to be obedient, respectful to authority, loyal to Church and

State. But in this, Jesuit schools differed but little from a Lutheran gymnasium. True, in the boarding schools, there was to the modern way of thinking too much supervision by the Jesuit master. The boy's waking hours, planned to give him a balanced routine of work and play, were left very little to individual taste or caprice. But the period we are considering was a stern one, and care must be taken not to apply the standards of the twentieth century to the customs of the seventeenth. The cult of individualism had only recently come into the world; its influence was very slight on school programs. A comparison of Jesuit secondary school régimes of the seventeenth and eighteenth centuries with others of the same period would not be altogether disadvantageous to the Jesuit system.

Discipline

The Jesuit schools were, for their day, not unpleasant places; this, in part, explains their success. They provided generously — under supervision, of course — for recreation. Variety was introduced into the school program by many devices. A time was assigned every day for play. That the Jesuit master took part in the boys' games must not be criticized too sharply. Even in our modern day, the masters in the great English public schools not only direct but participate in the games. To relieve the dull monotony of school life, plays were presented by the students, sometimes on a pretentious scale.[3]

All in all, the discipline in the seventeenth-century Jesuit college was mild.[4] There was, in sharp contrast to the prevailing practice of the day, very little corporal punishment. The Jesuits believed that prevention of disorder was better than post factum remedies and in general, they tried to win their students by love rather than fear. That the only ulterior purpose in their mind was the winning of souls for Christ and His Church many will not believe, and it would be quite useless here to argue the point.

Suffice it to say that the seventeenth-century Jesuit, and this holds for the modern Jesuit as well, did not engage in teaching merely for the love of teaching. Educational work was a means to an end, the furtherance of Christ's kingdom on earth.

Yet, it should be noted that their aim was not merely the making of good Catholics; that could be done by preaching, by missionary work, without schools; their objective was the formation of educated Catholic gentlemen able to take their proper places in the world. To this extent, the Society had what Dubois calls an extrapedagogical purpose.[5]

Ratio not a Pedagogical Treatise

Another point that must be kept in mind in the present discussion; one should not expect to find in a document that which its authors had no intention of placing there. The *Ratio Studiorum* is neither a pedagogical treatise nor a theory of education.[6] It merely mirrors, by way of rules, the methods and practices of Jesuit educational establishments of the sixteenth century. Nor is it altogether just to find fault with a document for not containing theories of life and education three centuries ahead of its time. A conservative institution like the school must be abreast of the times; but it is too much to hope that it will be ahead of its time.

Jesuit educators were in a sense utilitarians; they took existing educational practice as they found it, modified it to a certain extent, and by virtue of their splendid organization, imported to their system youthful vigor and abundant life. However one may quarrel with Jesuit principles or practice, it can hardly be denied that their system represents a distinct step forward in education, at least, from the administrative point of view. Their merit consists, not in the revolutionary rejection of existing educational theory and practice, but in a skillful retention of what was good in the old and in an adaptation of this to the needs of their day.

Secondary education had been aristocratic — the prerequisite of the well-born. The Jesuits kept it aristocratic, but theirs was an aristocracy not of wealth nor of birth, but of intellect. Instruction was by the law of their Institute absolutely gratuitous[7] and any youth, no matter how poor, could come to their schools provided he were able to satisfy the scholastic requirements. Secondary education had been largely in the hands of clerics. The Jesuits kept it there, but they saw to it that their scholastics received not only an ecclesiastical training, but a thorough grounding in classics and philosophy besides as a preparation for their teaching. Education aimed at developing all the powers of a man, imparting to him liberal culture. The Jesuits, and for that matter the whole educational world of the sixteenth and seventeenth centuries, were convinced that he was the educated man who was *eloquens;* in other words, eloquence in speech and writing was the aim of education. The portal to this culture was through *eloquentia latina.* The Jesuits accepted without question this theory of education.

Insistence on Latin

This explains the emphasis on the classics in the *Ratio.* It was not so much the cultural value of Latin that appealed to them — using "cultural" in the modern sense as an avenue of approach to an ancient civilization; Latin was accepted for its utility in fitting men for their place in the world.[8] In their acceptance of the rôle of champions or fosterers of classical studies, while they cannot be said to be in advance of their time, yet neither were they behind their times. The new humanism was suspected in certain orthodox quarters. The medieval tradition with its exaltation of dialectic, its contempt for the Quintilian canons of rhetoric, still had many advocates. In this struggle between humanists and dialecticians, the Jesuits were not found among the reactionaries.[9] They gave their own scholastics a thorough training in classics before allowing them to pass on to philosophy.[10] They were quite ready to be known as upholders of the classics. They tried to gain the front rank in the educational world, to capture the classical stronghold by a veritable flood of writings. Even by 1600, they had written Greek and Latin grammars, textbooks of rhetoric, Latin conversation books; they edited Vergil, Martial, Catullus, Cicero, the Greek and Latin Fathers.[11]

Unity a Primary Objective

Latin was the core of the curriculum; indeed the sum and substance of the curriculum of the secondary school. It occupied nine tenths of the time. This made for unity of content. There was, as Herman remarks,[12] unity of professor, of method, of matter in the Jesuit school. Unity was further solidified by a corps of teachers, animated by the same principles, formed in the same school, tending to the same objective through the same means.[13] It is a question whether this unity may not have been purchased at too dear a cost; the inbreeding of the Jesuit personnel prevented direct contact during the formative years with the educated world outside. It is interesting that St. Ignatius himself sent the scholastics to non-Jesuit universities, but this practice was largely discontinued early in the seventeenth century, probably for economic reasons.

Unity had to be secured at all costs. *Non nisi unum uno tempore*. Even a casual glance at the *Ratio* makes manifest the evident striving for this harmony. The objective of each year of the course is clearly defined; exercises are prescribed to attain that end. But in Jesuit administration particularly, unity is apparent; here an almost military uniformity is secured. The masters were responsible to the prefect of studies; he was responsible to the rector; the rector to the provincial; and the provincial to the general.

Jesuit Educational Devices

In viewing the methods of the Jesuit school, we find certain devices in honor. Foremost among these, was emulation. Theoretically, at least, modern educators regard emulation as highly unethical, but in practice there has hardly been a school where it has not been employed to some extent. The Jesuits frankly accepted it; they believed that competition in school was a good preparation for competition in later life. Classes were divided into camps; the "Romans" were pitted against the "Carthaginians"; each boy had his competitor or *aemulus*; he was ever on the alert to catch his opponent.[14] Classwork became an absorbing game; the Jesuits saw no reason why competition, altogether correct on the playing field, should be immoral in the classroom. Premiums were awarded to the best students in each branch. Perhaps the Jesuit system carried emulation to extremes;[15] but it must be remembered that what seems puerile to the modern, was quite acceptable to the seventeenth-century boy who was at once younger and less sophisticated than, let us say, our present-day American high-school youth.

Another device much in honor in the Jesuit system was repetition. Every day there was a repetition of the matter seen; Saturday there was repetition of the work of the week; there were monthly repetitions and there were repetitions of the work of the entire year.[16] Truly, the Jesuits made a pedagogical cult of repetition; for them it was indeed *mater studiorum*. Yet it is doubtful if there is a surer way to mastery, as modern educators are beginning to realize.

The Prelection

The prelection was a teaching device made much of by the Jesuits. Père Bainvel believes that this is the soul of Jesuit pedagogy. "To summarize the pedagogy of the early Jesuits," he says, "in a short and simple formula, one may propose the following: A study and imitation of a model under the direction of the master."[17] There were two parts to the prelection; the first was largely the work of the master — reading the text, the argument, explanation of difficult passages, translation, erudition, that is, remarks that tended to throw light on the text; the second part was the work of the pupil and consisted of exercises based on the passage, retranslation, and repetition of what had been said by the master.[18]

Pupil Activity

An obvious criticism of the prelection is that too much work was demanded of the master, too little of the boy. Yet, the Jesuit system provided for pupil activity under the initial impulse of the master. *Ut excitetur ingenium,* occurring so often in the *Ratio,*[19] indicates that the method of teaching is essentially active. True, the master is the pivot of the system;[20] the master's fund of information was at the disposal of his students in a day when reference books, available for youth, were rare. But it would be quite inexact to say that no personal initiative was encouraged, although no doubt the Jesuit schools, like other schools of their day, insisted on the pupils following the program laid down, and that program was from first to last a Latin program.

Compayré[21] is not correct when he says that he could find no trace in the *Ratio* of a desire to awaken personal reflection in the pupil; on the other hand, it would be absurd to deny that the primary pedagogical objective — though not the only one, as Compayré contends — of the Jesuits was to make the pupils good Latinists. Even in modern times there are educators of note who believe that this objective does not necessarily exclude mental activity on the part of the pupil. Latin, then, occupied in Jesuit school programs of that day, as in practically all others, a predominant place. But the Jesuits never claimed that their schools were other than Latin schools; *eloquentia* was not only the formal element of their teaching but the material element as well.

Vernacular in Jesuit Schools

They even went to extreme lengths in their glorification of Latinity. The vernacular tried to gain a place on their program, but was vigorously, though not entirely, repulsed.[22] Even out of class, the use of Latin was recommended.[23] But the reason for this was not devotion to Latin because of its place in the liturgy of the Church, nor any fear of the newer national tongues. Indifference toward the vernacular was merely an outcropping of the spirit of the age; the mother tongue was not regarded as a vehicle for culture — the very term, *lingua vulgaris*, crystallizes the sentiment of the period.

Nor were the Jesuits alone in their, to us, unreasoned stand against the vernacular. Trotzendorf and Sturm strove to have their pupils unlearn German;[24] Melanchton banished German from the school programs of Saxony;[25] the Wurtemburg plan of studies, the most important program in Protestant lands in the sixteenth century, forced pupils to talk Latin in class as well as outside of class.[26]

The Other Subjects in the Curriculum

It was the same with other branches. If an historical or geographical allusion came in the Latin text, it was explained; and that was all.[27]

Latin remained almost absolutely supreme in the school program, says Père Herman. We say, almost; for after long and painful discussion, Greek was finally given a very small place. The school program is well named; it is the program of the sixteenth-century Latin school. In this program, perfect in its simplicity, one word predominates throughout — *eloquentia*.[28]

Still it must not be supposed that the Jesuits remained insensible to the growing demands for change in the curriculum. Geography and history did eventually find place in the program;[29] the vernacular, too, managed to secure a foothold, particularly in the French schools, due, at least partially, to the influence of the Little Schools of Port Royal.[30] An apologist for the Society must regret that they did not adapt themselves more readily to the needs of the time. Still, an educational system like the Jesuits, designed by its fashioners to do service in many lands, must of its very nature be conservative. That is the penalty an organization must pay for efficiency; a machine that has cost much time and effort in the making is not readily scrapped by its creators at every suggestion of novelty seekers.

Rigidity and Unity

If an educational system is to be effective, standards must be set; and standards are of their very nature not elastic. Rigidity and unity characterized the *Ratio* during these days of Jesuit educational success. And thereby efficiency was gained.

It aimed at efficiency in masters and in boys. It made a master strive to be in himself what his place expected of him; it made a boy not only learn but also produce the fruit of his learning. It maintained a carefully graduated system, assuming that time is one of the essentials required for the making of a scholar. And these two qualities [efficiency and method] . . . may be said to be the bequest which the Society has made to the world of education. Before its time, it is true, there were efficient men teaching in schools and universities; henceforth, there were not only efficient men, but also efficient teachers as such. In a true sense, the Society instituted tests for teachers.[31]

Another contribution made by the Jesuits of that early day was this: education and instruction were united. They avoided what Père Daniel calls the *"dualisme funeste"*[32] of intrusting the instruction to one agency and the character formation to another.[33]

An objective perfectly defined, namely, the formation of cultured Christian men; a method demanding activity on the part of the pupil by means of exercises carefully graded and adapted to the purpose in hand; a Latin curriculum, sound for its day, however it may appear to moderns; and through it all the master as the soul, the vivifying force of the entire system — these seem to be the outstanding features of the *Ratio Studiorum* as it was applied in the schools of Europe during the seventeenth and eighteenth centuries.[34]

Footnotes

[1]See Appendix.

[2]*Die Pädagogik der Jesuiten,* Chaps. III and IV.

[3]Duhr, *Die Studienordnung der Jesuiten,* pp. 136–148; Boysse, E., *Le théâtre des Jésuites* (Paris, 1880); Reinhardstöttner, "Zur Geschichte des Jesuitendramas in München" in *Jahrbuch für Münchener Geschichte* (Bamberg, 1889), III, 53 ff.

[4]See Schimberg, *L'Éducation Morale dans les Collèges de la Compagnie de Jésus en France sous l'Ancien Régime,* especially Chap. IV.

[5]A fuller treatment of the purpose of Jesuit teaching is reserved for a later chapter.

[6]Compayré, *History of Education* (Payne's Translation), p. 168.

[7]Compayré in his *History of Pedagogy* (Payne's translation), p. 258, says: "What the Jesuits did in the matter of secondary instruction, with immense resources and for pupils who paid them for their efforts, LaSalle attempted in primary instruction through a thousand obstacles and for pupils who did not pay." Until the nineteenth century the Jesuits were absolutely forbidden to accept tuition money from their students. Of course, in a boarding school, students paid for their meals and lodging. But no charge was ever made — until the nineteenth century — for tuition. Day schools were, of course, absolutely free. See Paulsen, *Geschichte des gelehrten Unterrichts,* I, 383.

[8]Chossat, *Les Jésuites et leurs oeuvres à Avignon,* p. 256: "Je dirai simplement que les Jésuites furent autrefois des utilitaires. Le Latin était indispensable à nos aïeux bien pour la physique et la médicine que pour le droit canon et la théologie; et les Jésuites commirent, comme ils font encore, le crime abominable de préparer l'enfant qui fréquentait leurs classes à faire bonne figure dans le monde, à s'y créer une carrière et à devenir, comme on disait, 'un honnête homme." And Rochemonteix, *Un Collège de Jésuites* III,

42: "Le latin était en honneur [in the seventeenth century]. Alors on ne cherchait à former ni des mathematiciens ni des physiciens, ni des artistes, ni des agronomes, ni des spécialistes; on étudiait le latin, parce qu'on se faisait gloire de le savoir, de l'écrire et de le parler; parce qui'l était indispensable pour la philosophie, couronnement des études classiques; parce que c'était l'idiome de l'Église et de la science; parce que c'était la langue de tout le passé religieux, littéraire, philosophique et théologique; parce que personne ne se figurait une éducation liberale sans le latin."

[9]See Herman, *op. cit.*, p. 19; *Historia Societatis*, Pars V, lib. xv, No. 13; *Epistolae S.P. Ignatii*, I, 519–526.

[10]*Ratio Stud.*, "Reg. rectoris," 12; *Const.* Pars IV, c. vi.

[11]Herman, *op. cit.*, p. 195

[12]*Ibid.*, p. 174

[13]Willmann, *Didaktik*, II, 233–235, cites Herbart: Er lobt darum die Schulen der Jesuiten wo immer ein Gegenstand zur Hauptsache gemacht wurde und bemerkt, dass dies "zwar nicht durchweg, aber in manchen Punkten der einzige mögliche Schlüssel zu einer richtigen Zeiteinteilung des Jugendunterrichts ist."

[14]*Rat. Stud.* "Reg. Praef. Class. Inf.," 3, 13, 32, 35, 36; "Reg. Comm. Prof. Class. Inf.," 31, 34, 35. See also *Constitutiones S.J.*, Pars IV, cap. vi, 2. For an interesting picture of a seventeenth-century Jesuit school at work, see Corcoran, *Studies in the History of Classical Teaching*, Chap. 15, pp. 229–247, "A Description of a Transmarine Schoole," a transcript of a seventeenth-century document.

[15]There were certainly abuses. See Herman, *op. cit.*, p. 121, note 6. There is a significant remark in the *Monumenta Paedagogica*, dated 1553. "Quod redegit aliquos ad insaniam nimium studium vincendi aut non succumbendi." *Mon. Paed.*, p. 619. See also p. 306.

[16]Pachtler, *op. cit.*, II, 167; *Mon. Paed.*, pp. 260, 269, 298, 110, 111, 236, 257, and *passim;* see also the *Ratio, passim.*

[17]*Causeries pédagogiques*, p. 17; "À qui voudrait résumer la pédagogie des anciens Jésuites dans une formule courte et simple, on pourrait, ce me semble, proposer celle-ci: Étude et imitation d'un modèle sous la direction du maître."

[18]Schwickerath, *Jesuit Education*, pp. 484 ff.

[19]*Rat. Stud.*, Reg. 6, prof. class. hum.; Reg. 32, reg. comm. class, inf.

[20]Chossat, *op. cit.*, p. 283: "La plupart des régles du Ratio ne sont, nous l'avouons, que des régles de détail; il est néanmoins, facile de deviner, derrière ces applications particulières, que le pivot du système est l'instruction de l'élève par le maître."

[21]*Histoire critique des doctrines de l'Éducation*, I, 254: "Dans le Ratio Studiorum nous n'avons pas trouvé un mot qui annonça le desir d'éveiller la reflexion personelle et d'accroître l'intelligence. Dans les *Regulae* de la Société de Jésus tout semble converger vers un objet unique, la connaissance des tournures et des élégances de la langue latine. Peu importe que le jeune homme soît une intelligence, active et vivante, ou plutôt ce serait un danger qu'il le fût; l'essentiel, c'est qu'il devienne un bon latiniste."

[22]See Rochemonteix, *op. cit.*, Tome III, Chap. II, p. 131, for the place granted French at La Flèche in the eighteenth century; and Duhr, *op. cit.*, pp. 51 ff. Nevertheless, as Astrain remarks, many of the official recommendations given to Jesuits to cultivate the vernacular had a practical purpose, not a literary one, that is, to fit Jesuits to carry on apostolic work more efficiently in the country in which they were living. Astrain's words, *op. cit.*, IV, 15, are worth quoting: "Se encargaba aprender la lengua vulgar, como se recommendaba á los misioneros aprender la lengua de los indios: para satisfacer una necesidad, no para la cultura y formación literaria de los sujetos. Esta educación artistica y literaria se buscaba sólo en las lenguas y literaturas de la clásica antigüedad."

[23]*Mon. Paed.*, pp. 721, 746.

[24]Von Raumer, *Geschichte der Pädagokik*, I, 335.

[25]Herman, *op. cit.*, p. 213, citing Schmidt.

[26]*Ibid.*

[27]But see Schwickerath, *op. cit.*, pp. 125–129.

[28]*Op. cit.*, p. 225. Chossat, *op. cit.*, p. 254, quotes a document found in the Museum Calvet, 565, fol. 175. It is a conference addressed to the Jesuit Juniors of Avignon who

are preparing to teach. "Il leur apprendra (i.e., the master will teach the pupils) donc parfaitement les langues savantes et les beaux-arts. Savoir une langue, cela signifie l'entendre, l'expliquer, et la parler élégamment dans la composition ou le discours familier. Pour arriver à ce resultat, poursuit le conférencier, il faut l'instruction et les exercises; l'instruction ou l'enseignement du maître se donne par les preceptes et par l'explication des auteurs; les exercises consistent à apprendre par coeur à tourner du français en latin, en grec, etc., et à composer." C'est en quelques lignes, says Chossat, tout le programme et même en dépit du paradoxe, presque tout le système d'enseignement du Ratio studiorum.

[29]See Daniel, *Les Jésuites Instituteurs de la Jeunesse française au XVIIe siècle et au XVIIIe siècle.*

[30]Rochemonteix, *op. cit.*, Tome III, Chap. II.

[31]Goodier, "The Society of Jesus and Education," *The Month*, CIX, 406–7.

[32]*Des études classiques dans la société chrétienne*, p. 292.

[33]Körner, Friedrich, *Geschichte der Pädagogik*, p. 120. "Erst die Jesuiten gründeten ein Schulwesen, welches das bestorganisierte ihrer Zeit war und daher sehr bald einen sehr wohlverdienten Ruf in der ganzen Welt erhielt. . . . Die Ankläger wissen nicht, dass die Jesuiten im Grunde gar kein neues System aufgestellt haben, sondern nur die Erziehungsmethode Trotzendorfs mit der Unterrichtsmethode Sturms verbunden zu einem Ganzen organisierten. *Im Schulwesen bezeichnen sie einen neuen Wendepunkt, indem sie Erziehung und Unterricht zu einem Ganzen vereinigten, also das antike Element mit dem christlichen verbinden.* Darin stehen sie auf der Höhe ihrer Zeit, darum haben sie so Grosses geleistet, welches auch der Protestant neidlos anerkennen muss, dass sie das Studium der Alten auch von der praktischen Seite fassten und die Erziehung in ihre Lehranstalten als gleich wichtigen Teil aufnahmen."

[34]See also Herman, *op. cit.*, p. 314.

PART II

JESUIT EDUCATIONAL ACTIVITY IN THE UNITED STATES

CHAPTER IV

JESUIT SCHOOLS IN THE AMERICAN COLONIES

THE Society founded by Ignatius, bound by a special vow to serve the foreign missions, naturally turned with enthusiasm to the New World across the sea. The Spanish Jesuits worked among the aborigines and the white colonists in Chile, Peru, and Columbia, and established the Paraguay Reductions, early in the seventeenth century. Colleges were founded at Arauco, at Valdivia, at Lima, at Bogota, and elsewhere in South America.[1] To the north, Jesuits of the same nationality preached the Gospel in Mexico and founded in 1573 the "Royal and Most Ancient College of San Pedro, San Pablo, and San Ildefonso" in Mexico City; elsewhere, too, they established their schools.[2] From this center, members of the order carried on missionary work in Lower California, but conditions did not warrant the undertaking of educational work.

The Jesuits of France arrived in Canada in 1603, but their regular mission work did not commence until 1625. The story of their heroic labors among the Indians is told in the *Jesuit Relations*.[3] Père Lejeune opened the College of Quebeck in 1635.[4] Missionaries from Canada visited what is now the United States in an effort to convert the Indians to Christianity, but no attempt was made to establish schools in this region. This was left to the Jesuits of the English Province of the Society.

The Newtown School

The story of the English Province is an interesting one. The main work of the English Jesuits was to strengthen the adherents of the old religion in England, to win back those who had fallen away, and to convert what heretics they could. The penal laws of those days of bitter controversy, so stringent against all Catholics, were especially so against the Jesuits. In order to carry on their work, they had to resort to all sorts of subterfuges, disguise themselves as merchants, peddlers, sailors, or lords. It is this, no doubt, that gave rise in both England and America to the legend that persisted well into the nineteenth century that every prominent Catholic, lay or clerical, was a "Jesuit in disguise." Schools and seminaries were essential to save the faith of the younger generation of England and to supply the island with priests. But Catholic schools, and most of all Jesuit schools, were out of the question in England.[4a] So the English Jesuits founded establishments in Flanders and elsewhere during the seventeenth century whither resorted English youth many of whom, fired with enthusiasm by Campion's example or Parson's pleading, promised to devote themselves to the spiritual care of the English mission. Thither also, despite fines and imprisonment, the Catholic gentry sent their sons to be schooled in the old Faith as well as to receive a training in arts and letters.

Although the Jesuits of the English missions were few in number — in 1636 there were in all only 374 members[5] — yet in 1634 they sent Father Andrew White and four other Jesuits with the expedition of Cecil Calvert to the territory now comprising the State of Maryland.[6] This marks the foundation of the first Jesuit mission within the limits of the United States, a mission that has continued with hardly a break until our time, and constitutes the present Maryland-New York Province of the Society.

The account of the trials of this Jesuit mission among the Indians, the ascendancy of the Protestant party in Maryland which shattered their hopes of having a free field for missionary and educational work, will not be treated here.[7] It is worthy of note that, despite difficulties, Maryland Jesuits never entirely abandoned the project of establishing a school in the colony and actually made several attempts to provide the sons of the Catholic gentry with Jesuit schoolmasters. But owing to the religious persecution of the Protestant colonists, none of these attained to any degree of permanency. However, it is beyond dispute that schools of a sort were established and directed by the Jesuits of Maryland in colonial days.

In a letter of General Vitelleschi to John Brooke (*alias* Ferdinand Poulton) under date of Sept. 15, 1640, preserved in the General Archives of the Society at Rome, occurs this significant phrase, "The hope of establishing a college which you hold forth I embrace with pleasure; and shall not delay my sanction to the plan when it shall have reached maturity."[8] This is evidently an answer to Brooke's report on the condition of the Maryland Mission of which he was superior; he, at least, was sanguine in the expectation of founding a school.

However, this hope was apparently not realized, for on August 20, 1650, the new General of the Society, Piccolomini, writing to the Provincial of England, Francis Foster, calls attention to the fact that something is lacking in the organization of the Maryland mission; it is without a college. He urges that the mission be joined to some college as soon as possible, if this has not already been done.[9] It must be observed here that the General uses the term *collegium* in a technical sense; it does not necessarily imply that there was no educational activity in the mission. Indeed, in a letter of the same date (1650) addressed to Philip Fisher,[10] the Maryland Superior, he says: "I haven't any doubt that the school started by the Father, your companion, will be a success."[11]

Where was this school? And was it a school of secondary grade or merely a primary school? The probability is that the General would not have gone out of his way to congratulate the superior on the opening of a primary school. Shea, in his *History of Georgetown College,*[12] is of the opinion that the chaplains residing at the manors in Maryland in the seventeenth century often were tutors to the sons of the proprietors. Might it be that one of these chaplains gathered together the sons of the neighboring gentry at one of these manor houses?

Ralph Crouch, the ex-Jesuit

It is fairly certain that some sort of school was conducted under Jesuit auspices as early as 1650. It is probably to this school, conducted by Mr. Ralph Crouch or Crouche, that the

General refers in the letter mentioned above. Crouch was a layman, born at Oxford in 1620. He was a man of some education and had made his collegiate studies,[13] probably at St. Omer's. He entered the English novitiate at Watten in Flanders in 1639, but quitted it in the same year and went to Maryland where "for nearly twenty years he was the right hand and solace of the English Fathers in that laborious and extensive mission. Being a man of some education, he opened schools[14] for teaching humanities, gave catechetical instructions to the poorer class, and was assiduous in visiting the sick. He was a man full of zeal and charity, and ready for every good and pious work. Being at length readmitted to the Society in 1659, he returned to Europe, completed his noviceship at Watten, and was admitted to his vows in 1669.[15] He died November 18, 1679.[16]

Crouch's school was probably conducted at Newtown Manor where the Jesuits had a residence at this time which served as a combination church and school.[17] Burns[18] is of the opinion that the "three R's" doubtless constituted the main curriculum of studies in the Newtown School, but admits as highly probable that Latin was taught and Greek also. It is more than likely that the school was conducted along approved Jesuit lines as a Latin grammar school, with a preparatory class of *abcedarii*. That the school was under the control of the Jesuits, despite the fact that Crouch was not at the time a member of the Society, would seem to be the logical inference.[19] Father Sankey or Starkey, "the other Father," may have directed the school; occasionally he may have even taught the older boys, although there is no documentary evidence for this.

Edward Cotton, a rich and influential planter near Newtown, a member of the assembly in 1648, who died in 1653, made Ralph Crouch one of his two executors, and left the bulk of his estate, consisting of 450 acres of land and many cattle, for the endowment of the Catholic school. This is the first educational bequest in Maryland, certainly the first in the colonies in behalf of Catholic education.[20] Part of the will is subjoined:

The Last Will and Testament of Edward Cotton, made the 4th of April, 1653, he having perfect sense and memory as followeth. First,

I bequeath my soul to God my Maker and Redeemer to the fellowship of the Holy Angells and Saints and my body to the earth from whence it came to be decently buried with all Christian Rites and Ceremonies according to my quality. . . . I do appoint my Loving friends Thomas Mathews and Ralph Crouch my Executors. . . . I doe give all my female Cattle and their Increase for Ever to be disposed of by my aforesaid Executors as they shall think Fitt unto charitable uses which may be most to God's honor, the Stock to be preserved and the profit to be made use of to the use of a schooll, if they shall think convenient . . . my desire is if they shall think convenient that the Schooll be kept at Newtowne, and that the Cattle may be in the care of John Warren upon such agreement as my Executors shall make Provided that this my desire do not hinder them from doing a greater good to the honour of God otherwise which I do leave absolute in their power and to their discretion.[21]

To imagine the Newtown school as a fully equipped and fully staffed grammar school during this period would, of course, be absurd. Treacy, in an investigation of the records of Jesuit activity at Newtown,[22] makes no mention of Crouch's school. He believes that the first Catholic school for classical scholars in Maryland was opened at Newtown in the last year of Father Warren's superiorship (1675). Father Hughes, the historian of the American Assistancy of the Society, says that there was a school of some sort in Maryland under Father Sankey in 1650, but adds that it did not last long.[23] With the fragmentary evidence at hand, it can be asserted that Ralph Crouch, the ex-Jesuit brother, under the direction of the Fathers, taught the Maryland youth sometime during his stay in the colony from 1640 to 1659; that this is probably the school referred to in 1650 by the General of the Society as opened by the "Father, your companion"; that the rudiments of Latin and Greek in all likelihood were taught by Crouch;[24] that Newtown, in St. Mary's County, was the place where Crouch held his classes, as this was the center of Jesuit activity during this period, and here dwelt the most influential Catholics of the colony. Whether the Jesuits actually engaged in teaching or merely exercised a supervision over the school cannot be determined. But as we examine the number of Jesuit missionaries in Maryland during this time,[25] never more than five, and some years only one, it seems more probable that whatever teaching was done was entirely in Crouch's hands and the supervision by the Jesuits was merely nominal.

What happened to Crouch's school after his reëntry into the Society in 1659, and his return to Europe must be left to conjecture. It would be an interesting hypothesis to suppose that the lay brother[26] that came over to Maryland this year of Crouch's departure carried on his work. However, it is more likely that the Jesuits waited for a more favorable time to continue their educational activity, as these years from 1657 to 1676 were lean years in the Maryland Mission; very few Fathers came over from England during this period.

In 1673, a Mr. Robert Dowglas (or Douglas) had come over from England and was employed in the education of Governor Calvert's children.[27] Charles Calvert wrote to his father under date of June 2, 1673:

TABLE I. JESUITS ON THE MARYLAND MISSION FROM 1634 TO 1773 (*a*)

Year	*Number of Jesuits on the Maryland Mission*			*Superiors of the Mission*
	Priests	*Scholastics (b)*	*Temporal Coadjutors (c)*	
1634	4		1	Andrew White
1636	2		1	
1639–41	4			John Brooke, or Brock
1642	3			Andrew White
1643	5			Philip Fisher
1644–45	5			Bernard Harkwell
1646	3			
1646–51	2			Philip Fisher
1652	1			
1653	2			
1654	3			
1655–56	2		1	
1657	1			
1658	2			
1659	2		1	Francis Fitzherbert
1660	1		1	
1661	2		1	
1663	3		1	
1664	3		1	Henry Warren
1667	3		2	
1672	2		2	
1673–74	2		1	
1676	3		2	Michael Forster
1678–80	4		2	
1681	4	1	3	
1682	5	1	3	
1683	4	1	3	
1684	6 (*d*)	1	2	Francis Pennington
1685	6 (*d*)	1	3	
1686	5 (*d*)	1	3	
1687	6 (*e*)	1	3	

Year	*Priests*	*Scholastics (b)*	*Temporal Coadjutors (c)*	*Superiors of the Mission*
1689	5 (*f*)	1	3	
1690	3 (*g*)	1	3	
1691	4 (*g*)	1	3	
1692	5 (*g*)	1	3	
1693–95	6 (*g*)	1	3	
1696	5	1	3	William Hunter
1697	4	1	4	
1699	3		2	
1700	6		4	
1701	5		4	
1703	8		4	
1704	8		3	
1705	9		5	
1706	7		6	
1709	5		4	Robert Brooke
1710	5		5	
1711	6		6	
1712	9		6	
1714	9		7	Thomas Mansell
1715	9		5	
1716–20	9		4	
1723–25 (*h*)	12		4	George Thorold
1733	13		2	
1734	13		3	Peter Atwood
1735	14			Richard Molyneux
1736	13			
1737	10		2	
1738–40	11		2	
1741	14		2	
1743	17		2	Thos. Poulton
1744–45	17		1	
1746	16		1	
1747–48	17		1	
1749	16		1	Richard Molyneux
1750	13		1	Thos. Diggs
1752	17		1	
1753	15		1	
1754	16		1	
1755–58	14		1	
1763	14		1	Geo. Hunter
1764	18			
1768	23			
1769	26			
1771	23			

(*a*) Material supplied from Foley, *op. cit.*, Vol. VII, Part I, pp. lxxviii ff.

(*b*) "Scholastic," a Jesuit who is preparing for the priesthood. His studies are interrupted for a few years in order to engage in teaching. The scholastic on this list was Mr. Thos. Hothersall, who, because of ill health or religious scruples, remained a scholastic all his life. This is quite contrary to the usual practice in the Society.

(*c*) "A temporal coadjutor," a Jesuit lay brother, destined for domestic service, farming, household duties, and the like. Ordinarily they did not engage in teaching; occasionally, however, they taught catechism or even conducted classes in an elementary school in a missionary country.

(*d*) This includes two priests in New York.

(*e*) Includes three priests in New York.

(*f*) Includes two priests in New York.

(*g*) Includes one priest in New York.

(*h*) The catalogues of the English Province for the years 1726 to 1730 give only names; they do not indicate the men on the Maryland Mission.

Your lordship's of the 21st of November on the behalf of Mr. Robt. Douglas I received by his own hand, whom at present I entertain at my own house and employ him to teach my children. . . . Shall endeavor the promoting of a school here and make him the master.[28]

It is possible that since the Jesuits were unable to supply men for a school they induced Calvert to bring over a schoolmaster. There is, however, no evidence to show that they exercised any control or supervision over this school.

A Second School at Newtown?

There seems to have been a preparatory school in the colony about this time, for in the will of Luke Gardner, a Catholic, made in 1673, provision is made for the education of his sons until they reach the age of eighteen.

My will is that my three sons, John, Luke and Thomas Gardner, be kept at school and have such education as this country and their estates will afford them until they successively attain unto the age of eighteen years.[29]

In the Annual Letters of the English Province, preserved in the General Archives of the Society at Rome, there appears, under date of 1681, in the autograph of John Warner, the Provincial of England, the following:

The mission in Maryland is in a flourishing condition. . . . Four years ago, a school for humanities was opened by our Society in the center of the country, directed by two of the Fathers; and the native youth, applying themselves assiduously to study, made good progress. Maryland and the recently established school sent two boys to St. Omer who yielded in abilities to few Europeans, when competing for the honor of being first in their class. So that not gold, nor silver, nor the other products of the earth alone, but men also are gathered from thence to bring those regions, which foreigners have unjustly called ferocious, to a higher state of virtue and cultivation.[30]

There can be no doubt that this school for humanities, established in 1677, was located at Newtown, as this was still the center of Jesuit activity in the colony. The fact that the youths were sent to St. Omer's in Flanders to finish their collegiate studies would indicate that Newtown did not have a complete collegiate curriculum. Probably it never did possess the entire five to six classes of the typical Jesuit *collegium,* but was content with the grammar classes, sending abroad the more promising youth for the two higher classes of humanities and rhetoric. Still, in the *Annual Letters,* quoted previously, the Provincial, Father Warner, adds: "Two of the Society were sent out to Maryland this year to assist the labourers in that most ample vineyard of the Lord."[31] The context would indicate that these men were sent out for the work in the Newtown School, possibly to conduct the higher classes. Burns thinks it has a right to the name of college and can claim to be "the second institution of the kind, in point of time, established within the present limits of the United States, being preceded only by Harvard."[32]

In 1677, Father Thomas Gavan (or Gawen)[33] arrived in Maryland. Brother Turberville, who had come over earlier, had made his collegiate studies in Europe, but not wishing to become a priest, had entered the Society as a temporal coadjutor.[34] These two were probably masters in the revived Newtown School. The two men sent out by the English Provincial in 1681, were the scholastic, Mr. Thomas Hothersall, and a lay brother.[35]

Hothersall, The Scholastic Master

Mr. Hothersall, who had studied both at St. Omer's and at the English College in Rome, entered the Society in 1665 at the age of 26.[36] Before going to Maryland in 1681, he had made some of his higher studies, but had not been promoted to the priesthood because of headaches so acute that further study seemed out of the question. The fear of insanity seemed to hang over him during the years in Maryland, as he never was ordained a priest. His status for thirty years was that of a scholastic, a most unusual procedure in the Society. In 1698, General Gonzales wrote to Henry Humberston, the English Provincial, ordering him to settle Hothersall's case, promoting him to the priesthood if there is no imminent danger of insanity. If his condition is such that he is not fitted for any exercise of the sacred ministry, he is to be asked to become a lay brother.[37] Before these orders could be forwarded by the English Provincial to the Maryland superior, Mr. Hothersall died in the colony, aged 56.[38] It is reasonably certain that all during Hothersall's stay in the colony a school of secondary grade was conducted in Maryland, since the only work he could engage in was schoolwork. As a scholastic, he could not exercise any of the functions of the sacred ministry. In the triennial catalogues of this period sent to the General, among the members of the Society working in the Maryland Mission, there is listed *"unus magister,"* one master.[39]

It is certain that young Marylanders were trained in this school in the humanities; some were sent abroad to St. Omer's to finish their studies. Of these, some returned to America; others entered the Society of Jesus, later laboring in the mission field either in England or Maryland.[40] Thus, Robert Brooke (or Brooks), a member of a Catholic family in Maryland, born in 1663, who entered the Society at Watten in Flanders in 1684, and very likely the first American-born member of the Society, in all probability received his preparatory training here.[41]

The last mention of the school at Newtown is in the will of Thomas Rasin, made April 18, 1687, wherein it is stated: "My desire is that if Mr. Pennington desires to have the educating of my youngest son that my executors do put him to him."[42] This Mr. Pennington was the Jesuit Superior in Maryland, who died in Newtown in 1699.[43]

Proscriptive legislative enactment by the Maryland Colony in the early eighteenth century sought to make it impossible for a Catholic parent to secure a Catholic education for his children. In 1704, a law was passed prohibiting "persons professing to be of the Church of Rome" from taking upon themselves "the education, government, or boarding of youth at any place in the province"; offenders were to be "transported to England to undergo the penalties provided there by Statutes 11 and 13, of William III, 'for the further preventing the growth of Popery.'" Another section of the same law provided that any person sending his child abroad to be educated in the Catholic faith should forfeit one hundred pounds.[44] Consequently, if the Jesuits continued their school, great precautions must have been taken to prevent discovery. It is highly probable that for some years after Hothersall's death, no formal school was conducted; but some of the fathers may have prepared the sons of Catholics for St. Omer's at private manor houses. There is, however, no documentary evidence for this.

The Jesuit School in New York

Before this time a favorable opportunity offered itself to the English Jesuits to enter New York. The Duke of York, a Catholic, lord of the colony, had appointed an Irish Catholic Governor, Thomas Dongan. The latter objected to the missionary activities of the French Jesuits among the Indians and wished to have English Jesuits in their place in order to make the Indians friendly to the English cause.[45] In a letter of the English Provincial, Father Warner, to the General of the Society, he says:

> Father Thomas Hervey (or Harvey), the missioner, passes to New York by consent of the Governor of the Colony. In that Colony is a respectable city, fit for the foundation of a College, if faculties are given, to which College those who are now scattered throughout Maryland may betake themselves and make excursions from thence into Maryland. The Duke of York, the lord of that Colony, greatly encourages the undertaking of a new mission. He did not consent to Father Thomas Hervey's sailing until he had advised with the Provincial, the Consultors, and other grave Fathers.[46]

Later followed Henry Harrison[47] and Charles Gage,[48] both priests. Mention is made of them and the New York mission in the triennial catalogues and annual letters from 1685 to 1696.[49] In the appendix to the triennial catalogue for 1696, it is said that in New York "one of Ours spent seven years, but three years ago he was forced to leave, owing to the fury of the wife of the new governor (Fletcher), that had been appointed by the Prince of Orange."[50]

Clear evidence exists that a Jesuit school was founded in New York, and that classes were conducted there during Dongan's administration. It must have opened about 1685 and was certainly closed before 1690. It was held apparently on the King's Farm, subsequently leased to Trinity Church.[51] Among the pupils were the sons of Judges Palmer and Graham, Captain Tudor, and others.[52] The bell of the Dutch Reformed

Church in the fort was rung to summon the students.[53] There is extant a letter of Leisler, a merchant in the New York colony, to the governor of Massachusetts, under date of August 13, 1689, that says:

> I have formerly urged to inform your Honor that Coll: Dongan in his time did erect a Jesuite College upon cullour to learne latine to the Judges West ———— Mr. Graham Judge Palmer and John Tudor did contribute their sones for some time, but no boddy imitating them the collidge vanished. . . .[54]

Again, there is a fragment of a letter supposed to be from Leisler written apparently about June, 1690:

> . . . then I told him [one of the men he is accusing of being too well affected to the Papists] that he did contribute not with silver, gold or precious stones to erect a Jesuit Collidge in this Citty, but he with Judge Palmer & Graham offered their sones to it who went daily twyce to be instructed by that hellish brude of Jesuits.[55]

When the news of the downfall of James II, and of the landing in England of William of Orange reached the colony, the fanatical Leisler seized the government and Dongan was obliged to flee. The Jesuits, Harrison and Harvey, just managed to escape Leisler's hands.[56] Father Harvey made his way to Maryland, but later returned to New York. All hope of educational activity, however, in that colony had to be abandoned for over a century.

The School at Bohemia Manor

During the eighteenth century due to the penal laws the number of Catholics in the Maryland colony had dwindled to one twelfth or less of the population.[57] To save the faith of the younger generation, the Jesuits made another brave effort to establish a secondary school, "the first successful attempt to establish secondary Catholic education in the United States."[58] Only fragmentary records remain of this school. "Its origin is wrapped in obscurity; it was begun by stealth; its existence was precarious; and it appears to have been closed several times owing to fresh outbursts of persecution."[59] The Jesuits had a residence, Bohemia Manor, on the eastern shore of Maryland, near the Pennsylvania border. The mission had been established about 1704 by Thomas Mansell.[60] Father Thomas Poulton, who came to America in 1738, was in charge at Bohemia from about 1742 to 1749.[61] It was while he was there that a school was started, probably in 1745 or 1746. Certainly there is no documentary evidence for assigning an earlier date. It was apparently discontinued after the death of Father Poulton in 1749. It is safe to assume that its span of life did not exceed a decade. McLaughlin[62] and others are wont to refer to this academy of Bohemia as the predecessor of Georgetown, and they seem to suppose that it had a continued existence until the American Revolution or even later. But they are probably in error;[63] certainly there is no shred of evidence for it. The only connection between Georgetown and Bohemia is that both were conducted by Jesuits and that John Carroll, the founder of Georgetown, was once a student at Bohemia Manor.

A fragment of an old account book[64] furnishes nearly all that is known directly concerning the Bohemia Manor school:

> 1745–6 Peter Lopez to your son's board. Feb. 17.
> " May 20. Daniel Carroll to your son's board.
> " June 24. Edward Neale, to board of your two sons; £43 - 16 - 3.
> 1748. April 22. Daniel Carroll, 2nd Time, son John came here.
> Jackey Carroll to Marlborough, July 8.
> August 5. Robert Brent.
> August 20. Bennett Neale, Archibald Richard.
> June 24. Ben Neale, Ed. Neale, John Carroll, James Heath went first to school.
> N. B. All those that learn Latin at 40 currency pound. The rest at £30 as by agreement this day.[65]

The Jackey Carroll mentioned became the first Bishop of Baltimore. In 1748 or early in 1749, he left Bohemia to go to St. Omer's where he remained six years completing the classical course. Charles Carroll of Carrollton, future signer of the Declaration of Independence, was probably a pupil at Bohemia at the same time;[66] but there is no certain evidence of this.

Studies at the Bohemia Manor School

The school comprised at most, it may be legitimately inferred, two courses, an elementary course for *abcedarii,* and a preparatory course consisting in all probability of the two

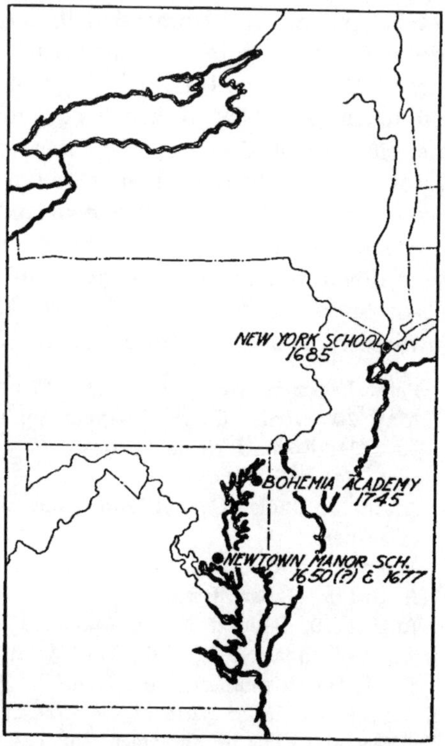

MAP I. JESUIT SCHOOLS IN COLONIAL DAYS

divisions of the *infima grammatica* of the *Ratio,* designed to impart the rudiments of Latin grammar. This saved the Maryland Catholics the expense of sending their sons abroad at too tender an age. If the case of Jackey Carroll, who spent one or at most two years at the Bohemia school, is typical, this is a reasonably safe assumption. It is said that there were as many as twenty students boarding at the school at one time.[67] This is probably a fairly accurate estimate. To assume that algebra, history, and perhaps Greek,[68] as well as Latin, were taught is quite unwarranted.

A later document seems to indicate that the school was still in existence in 1760. In that year, the Rev. Mr. Reading, an Episcopal minister at Apoquiniminck, Delaware, reported that there was "a very considerable Popish Seminary in the neighboring province of Maryland, under the direction of the Jesuits."[69] A liberal discount must be made for the "considerable" in this report, if the temper of the times and the tendency to exaggeration when fanatical bigotry is aroused are taken into consideration.

It is possible that some sort of preparation for St. Omer's was imparted at various times even after the closing of the Bohemia Academy, but again no documentary evidence is forthcoming. The death blow to Jesuit educational activity in the colony came when news reached America of the suppression of the Society by Clement XIV in 1773. In order to safeguard the possessions of the Society for happier days, the ex-Jesuits in Maryland formed an association which was later incorporated, December 23, 1792, as "The Corporation of the Roman Catholic Clergymen." Bishop Carroll secured verbal approval for the revival of the Society in America in 1805 and united it with the branch in Russia under Father Gruber that had not been suppressed.[70]

Footnotes

[1]Campbell, *The Jesuits*, pp. 296 ff.

[2]Crivelli, "Mexico," *Catholic Encyclopedia*, X, 259 ff. See also Decorme, "Catholic Education in Mexico," *The Catholic Historical Review*, II, 168 ff.

[3]Edited by Reuben Gold Thwaites.

[4]Fournet, "Canada," *Catholic Encyclopedia*, III, 232.

[4a]However, there were two Jesuit schools in London in the time of James II. See Lingard, *History of England*, X, 220 ff.

[5]Pollen, J. H., "The Society of Jesus," *Catholic Encyclopedia*, XIV, 92.

[6]*Ibid.*, p. 95.

[7]See Hughes, Thomas, *History of the Society of Jesus in North America: Colonial and Federal.*

[8]"Spem ostentatam collegii laetus amplector et cum maturuerit non cunctabor admittere." The entire text of this letter is printed in Hughes, *op. cit.*, "Documents," I, Part I, 25. McLaughlin, *College Days at Georgetown*, p. 16, wrongly attributes this letter to Edward Knott, the Provincial of the English Province.

[9]Hughes, *op. cit.*, "Documents," I, Part I, 38. There is need of care in interpreting

collegium when the word occurs in correspondence relating to the English Province and its missions at this time. The Institute of the Society forbids missions or residences to possess landed properties and revenues. As there were no colleges in England itself during these years, and as, on the other hand, it was essential that some moral person be constituted who could receive bequests and donations necessary for the support of the missionary activity of the Fathers, the English Province resorted to the unusual expedient of constituting "missionary colleges," corresponding in a certain sense to a diocese among the secular clergy. The head of this college was a Rector. This was done to meet a practical difficulty. It was probably the intention to have these administrative districts merge into *real* colleges after the days of persecution passed. Thus, in England there were five such "colleges" in 1651. (See Foley, *Records of the English Province of the Society of Jesus*, VII, Part I, lxxxiii.) Now, it is highly probable that when the General in 1650 gave orders to the English Provincial, Francis Foster, to attach the Mission of Maryland to some college he had in mind a "college" such as existed in England at the time, that is, a corporation that might legally possess landed property and revenues without contravening the laws of the Society. (See Hughes, Thomas, "Properties of Jesuits in Pennsylvania," *Records of the American Catholic Historical Society*, XI, 180–181.) This was the more necessary as the expenses of the mission were heavy, and the inheritances of the members of the Society working in Maryland, most of whom were of good family, were needed to meet living expenses. If a college did not exist, these inheritances and other bequests could not be accepted; the individual members could possess nothing by reason of their vow of poverty according to ecclesiastical law and the regulations of their institute. By 1713 the whole mission of Maryland had the status of a missionary (or *ideal*) college (Hughes, *ibid.*, p. 181).

[10]*Alias*, Thomas Copley. See Hughes, *op. cit.*, "Text," II, 679.

[11]Hughes, "Documents," I, Part I, 39. "Nec dubito scholas a socio patre apertas operae pretium laturas."

[12]P. 2.

[13]Foley, *op. cit.*, V. 943, and VII, 184.

[14]"Schools" is used here in the sense, common in England, of classes. It does not mean that Crouch founded several schools.

[15]Burns, James, "Early Jesuit Schools in Maryland," *Catholic University Bulletin*, XIII, 363, is in error when he says that Crouch died a Jesuit priest. He was a temporal coadjutor or lay brother.

[16]Foley, *op. cit.*, V. 953.

[17]*Woodstock Letters*, XIII, 269.

[18]*Op. cit.*, p. 368.

[19]Dexter, *History of Education in the United States*, p. 65, although he says that Crouch was "the first schoolmaster to make his way across the Potomac," seems to be unaware of his connection with the Maryland Jesuits. It is highly probable that Crouch, unable for some reason or other to persevere in his religious vocation in the Society, yet wishing to help the Fathers on the Maryland Mission, came over for the express purpose of starting a school. See also Treacy, Wm. P., "Some Early Catholic Grammar Schools," *United States Catholic Historical Magazine*, I, 71; Shea, *Catholic Church in Colonial Days*, p. 404; McLaughlin, *College Days at Georgetown*, p. 21; Steiner, *History of Education in Maryland*, p. 16; Treacy, Wm. P., *Old Catholic Maryland*, p. 72.

[20]Burns, *op. cit.*, p. 366.

[21]*Will-Books* in the Office of the Register of Wills, Annapolis Lib. I, 46. Burns (*op. cit.*, p. 367) calls attention to the fact that Steiner in his *History of Education in Maryland*, does not seem to be aware of the existence of this will. Steiner cites the will of Herman, who died in 1684, as containing the first educational bequest made by a citizen of Maryland.

[22]*Woodstock Letters*, XIII, 269.

[23]Hughes, *op. cit.*, "Text," II, 46.

[24]See Foley, *supra*. Foley's account of Crouch's life is taken from a contemporary *Historia domus*. This account says "he opened a school for humanities."

[25]See Table I, p. 50.

[26]See Table I, p. 50. Hughes, *op. cit.*, "Text," II, 680, says of the Brother in question,

Gregory Turberville, that he, like Crouch, "had studied the lower humanities." He was competent, therefore, to carry on Crouch's work.

[27]Hughes, *op. cit.*, "Text," II, 136.

[28]Steiner, *History of Education in Maryland*, p. 15.

[29]*Maryland Will-books*, Annapolis, Lib. I, 634. See also Burns, *op. cit.*, p. 369.

[30]The original text is given in full by Hughes, *op. cit.*, "Documents," I, Part I, 136: "Marilandica missio floret. . . . Ante quadriennium aperta illic a nostris, in media barbarie, humaniorum litterarum schola, quam duo regunt, et juventus illic nata, supra modum litteris dedita, proficit. Duos illa missio, illa recens nata schola Audomarum transmisit, qui paucis Europaeis ingenio cedant, cum suae classis primis de palma contendant. Unde collegimus non auri tantum et argenti aut aliarum terrae frugum, sed et hominum ad virtutem et altiores disciplinas factorum regiones illas. quas immerito barbarae audiunt, esse feracissimas." Dexter, *op. cit.*, p. 65, supposes from the phrase "native youth," that this was an Indian school. In this he follows Steiner, *op. cit.*, p. 16. But this is obviously an error. "Juventus illic nata" evidently means the sons of the white colonists born in Maryland. Further, in the *Annual Letters*, etc., there is no reference to Indians receiving a training in humane letters. See Foley, *op. cit.*, III, 394, and *passim*. Nor is there any mention in Vol. VII of the same work, containing the history of St. Omer's, of any Indian coming to that college from America. On the contrary, mention is made of the native Marylanders, sons of the colonists, who came there to finish their studies during the seventeenth and eighteenth centuries. See also Hughes, *op. cit.*, "Documents," I, Part I, 252, 253, 257.

[31]Hughes, *op. cit.*, "Documents," I, Part I, 137. "Submissi eo hoc anno duo qui laborantes in illa amplissima Domini vinea sublevent." See also Foley, *op. cit.*, III, 394.

[32]Burns, *op. cit.*, p. 370. In support of the view that a complete college course, that is, up to "rhetoric," was supplied at the school, the following may be offered. In September, 1683, the authorities in Maryland petitioned the General to allow them to receive into the Society a young man of the colony, Robert Brooks. They wished to have him receive his religious training in America (privately, no doubt) as they found the expense of sending a subject to Europe too onerous. The General disapproved, as there was neither novitiate nor novice-master in Maryland. In the following year, young Brooks was received into the novitiate at Watten in Flanders. Presumably Brooks had finished his classical studies as required before entry into the Society; presumably he had not been abroad; if that had been the case, he would have applied to the Society there. The inference, then, is that he received all his classical training in Maryland. Of course, this might merely indicate that Hothersall or one of the Fathers supervised the private study of Brooks. He was a mature youth, 20 years of age, when he entered the Society.

[33]Foley, *op. cit.*, VII, Part I, 29.

[34]*Ibid.*, VII, Part II, 785. Hughes, *op. cit.*, "Text," II, 136, is of the opinion that Robert Douglas assisted in the teaching.

[35]*Ibid.*

[36]Foley, *Records*, VII, Part I, 374; VI, 410. See also Hughes, *op. cit.*, "Text," II, 137; Shea, *History of Georgetown College*, p. 4.

[37]The letter of Father General Gonzales to the English Provincial is in the General Archives of the Society at Rome. Text is given in Hughes, *op. cit.*, "Documents," I, Part I, 61: "Quod attinet magistrum, qui degit in Marilandia, jamque annum prope trigesimum agit in Societate, sacris ordinibus insigniendus et ad gradum coadjutoris spiritualis promovendus erit, si quidem propinquum absit periculum incidendi in maniam; eamque habeat, vel sibi comparari [*comparare?*] possit doctrinam, quae requiritur ad sacerdotium, etsi non sufficeret pro sacro tribunali, a quo poterit abstinere. Quod, si ea sit illius conditio, ut incapax censeatur sacerdotii, inquirat R. Va., velitne formari in coadjutorem temporalem, mittatque informationes consuetas, si contentus sit hoc gradu" (April 12, 1698). In the appendix to the Triennial Catalogue of 1696, under the heading "De Missione Americana," occurs the following mention of Hothersall: "Jam numeramus in Marilandia 4 sacerdotes, *unum magistrum, qui puerorum educationi praeest, ob capitis debilitatem ad sacerdotium non promotus. . . .*" Hughes, *op. cit.*, "Documents," I, Part I, 374. And Hughes, *op. cit.*, "Text," II, 682, quotes the following estimate of Hothersall sent to the General in the Triennial Catalogue of 1685: "Ingenio optimo, sed laeso; judicio

similiter; prudentia pariter; scientia insigni in philosophia et theologia; complexione temperata nisi ob morbum; talento ad multa si sanaretur, nunc ad pauca."

[38]Foley, *op. cit.*, VII, Part I, 374.

[39]Hughes, *op. cit.*, "Documents," I, Part I, 138 ff.

[40]Shea, *Catholic Church in Colonial Days*, p. 83; Foley, *op. cit.*, VII, Part I, 275; *Ibid.*, p. 90; *Woodstock Letters*, XIII, 269.

[41]Foley, *op. cit.*, VII, Part I, 90–91; Shea, *op. cit.*, p. 84. In the *Annual Letters* for 1674, there is mention of twelve youths sent from Maryland to pursue their studies at St. Omer's. ". . . ac duodecim adolescentes ad Seminarium Audomarense studiorum causa transmissi." Hughes, *op. cit.*, "Documents," I, Part I, 135.

[42]*Maryland Will-books*, lib. IV, fol. 302; Burns, *Catholic University Bulletin*, XIII, 373.

[43]*Woodstock Letters*, XIII, 271. Foley, *op. cit.*, VII, Part I, 583, says he died on his way back to England, but Treacy (*Woodstock Letters*, *loc. cit.*) claims to have found documentary evidence of his death at Newtown.

[44]*A Compleat Collection of the Laws of Maryland*, Annapolis, 1727, p. 201. Acts of 1704, Chap. 59. See also Shea, *op. cit.*, pp. 358–9; Burns, *op. cit.*, pp. 373–4.

[45]*Ecclesiastical Records of the State of New York*, II, 877 ff.

[46]Foley, *op. cit.*, VII, Part I, 343.

[47]*Ibid.*, p. 335.

[48]*Ibid.*, p. 282.

[49]Hughes, *op. cit.*, "Documents," I, Part I, 138–140.

[50]*Ibid.*, p. 140. "Hic septennium exegit unus e nostris, sed ante triennium coactus exire, ut furori cederet uxoris novi gubernatoris, a principe Auriaco submissi."

[51]*Documents Relative to the Colonial History of New York*, IV., 490.

[52]*Documentary History of the State of New York*, II, 14.

[53]Shea, *The Catholic Church in Colonial Days*, p. 91, citing Broadhead.

[54]*Documentary History*, II, 14.

[55]*Ibid.*, p. 262.

[56]Shea, *op. cit.*, 97–98. And Hughes, *op. cit.*, "Documents," I, Part I, 138.

[57]*Life and Select Letters of Rev. Thomas Bray*, p. 160.

[58]*Catholic Historical Review*, II (old series), 231.

[59]Burns, *Catholic University Bulletin*, XIII, 376.

[60]Devitt, "Bohemia," *Records of the American Catholic Historical Society*, XXIII, 102.

[61]*Ibid.*, p. 105.

[62]*College Days at Georgetown*, p. 17.

[63]Devitt, *op. cit.*, p. 107.

[64]In the Archives of the Maryland-New York Province.

[65]This school was, of course, a boarding school. It is not clear why more was charged for the board of the Latin students than for the non-Latins. This may possibly be a slip for 40 shillings and 30 shillings respectively, or it may be the Jesuit bookkeeper's original way of indicating shillings. Apparently the sum of 40 sh. was paid to Mr. Wayt, a lay teacher for each Latin student. Thus, the entry for 1745, 1746: "Mr. Wayt, the Schoolmaster . . . Cr. By schooling for the 2 Neales and John Carroll, in all for 32 months, at 40 sh. per year: each £5. 7." Hughes, *op. cit.*, "Text," II, 520, note 7, says that the terms for boarding were £20 for one boy; £35 for two brothers.

[66]Burns, *Catholic University Bulletin*, XIII, 378; Boyle, *Biographical Sketches of Distinguished Marylanders*, p. 104; *ibid.*, p. 81.

[67]Devitt, *Records of the Catholic Historical Society*, XIII, 107.

[68]Burns, *op. cit.*, p. 377.

[69]Shea, *op. cit.*, p. 404, quoting Perry. It is difficult to see how Shea (p. 405) can find in the complaint of the Rev. Hugh Jones to the S.P.G. about the activities of the Jesuits at Bohemia any reference to the academy. In the first place, Jones wrote in 1739, certainly before the school was started; secondly, there is no mention of a school, but only of the Jesuits' "propagation of schism, popery and apostacy."

[70]Shea, *Life and Times of Archbishop Carroll*, pp. 525–6; Campbell, *The Jesuits*, p. 684; Hughes, *op. cit.*, "Documents," I, Part II, 816 ff.

CHAPTER V

THE MARYLAND-NEW YORK PROVINCE

THE ex-Jesuits in Maryland, who later constituted "The Corporation of Roman Catholic Clergymen," remained strongly attached to the Society that had been suppressed and entertained lively hopes of its restoration, especially when news came of the Jesuits living in community in White Russia. Indeed their attachment to the Society and their fear of undertaking any educational work as ex-Jesuits, lest the funds needed for this purpose might cripple the usefulness of the Society in America when restored, threw difficulties in the way of establishing Georgetown College[1] and interfered with its usefulness and prosperity during the pioneer days.[2]

Bishop Carroll and the Jesuits

All the ex-Jesuits in Maryland had hopes of founding a school for the education of youth on the Jesuit plan. To none, however, was the need so pressing as to John Carroll, the Prefect-Apostolic in the new republic. His was the responsibility of providing priests for the Church intrusted to his care. For this purpose a classical school was needed that would supply him with suitable candidates for the priesthood. The problem puzzled him. In 1785, he seemed to think that the lately founded secular institution in Philadelphia[3] and the two colleges Maryland proposed to build might solve the difficulty. His plan was, therefore, to build a seminary where young men who had finished their classical studies at one of the secular schools might study theology.[4] For this seminary he had in mind the Sulpician Fathers, a congregation whose primary object is the training of the secular clergy. They arrived in Baltimore shortly after the opening of the Georgetown School in 1789. But he soon realized the futility of expecting candidates for the priesthood from secular schools and the old dream of a Jesuit college revived; for in 1787, Cardinal Antonelli, the Secretary of Propaganda at Rome, wrote to Carroll congratulating him both on the seminary project, and the proposed school for youth.[5]

Father Ashton, a member of the Corporation in Maryland, wrote to Father Strickland, an ex-Jesuit in England, under date of September 13, 1786:

> I will give every encouragement in my power to disposed people to send their children to the Liège Academy [the successor to the old St. Omer's, conducted by ex-Jesuits of the English Province] on the terms you propose; but as we are about to institute a school in this state, for the education of youth and perpetuity of the body of clergy here, it may suit parents better to have their children brought up nearer to them, though their education may not at first be so perfect as what they would get abroad.[6]

At length, at a meeting of the clergy, all of whom were ex-Jesuits, held at White Marsh in November, 1786, the following resolutions were passed:

Resolves Concerning the Institution of a School

1o. That a school be erected for the education of youth and the perpetuity of the body of clergy in this country.

2o. That the following plan be adopted for the carrying of same into execution.

Plan of the School

1o. In order to raise the money necessary for erecting the aforesaid school, a general subscription shall be opened immediately.

2o. Proper persons shall be appointed in different parts of the continent, West India Islands and Europe, to solicit subscriptions and collect the same.

3o. Five directors of the school and the business relative thereto shall be appointed by the General Chapter.

4o. The monies collected by subscription shall be lodged in the hands of the five aforesaid directors.

5o. Masters and tutors to be procured and paid by the directors quarterly and subject to their directions.

6o. The students are to be received by the managers on the following terms:

Terms of the School

1o. The students shall be boarded at the parents' expense.

2o. The pension for tuition shall be £10 currency per annum, and is to be paid quarterly and always in advance.

3o. With this pension the students shall be provided with masters, books, paper, pens, ink and firewood in the school.

4o. The directors shall have power to make further regulations, as circumstances may point out necessary.

Other Resolves Concerning the School

1o. The General Chapter, in order to forward the above institution, grants £100 sterling towards building the school. . . .

4o. The General Chapter orders the school to be erected in Georgetown in the State of Maryland.

5o. A Clergyman shall be appointed by the directors to superintend the masters and tuition of the students, and shall be removable by them.

6o. The said clergyman shall be allowed a decent living.

7o. The General Chapter has appointed the Rev. Messrs. John Carroll, James Pellentz, Rob Molyneux, John Ashton, and Leonard Neale, directors of the school.[7]

The project apparently hung fire for several years due to the opposition of some of the members of the Chapter who wished to save all the property of the "Select Body"[8] intact for the Society which, they hoped, would soon be restored. Carroll complains of this in a letter to Father Charles Plowden, an English ex-Jesuit. He had written to Plowden on January 22, 1787, asking Plowden to help him in securing a suitable president for the new Academy. He also asked him to recommend textbooks and to secure pecuniary aid from friends in England. In the same letter, but dated February 28, he adds, "I am sorry to inform you that since writing the above an opposition has broken out of some of our good gentlemen [the ex-Jesuits] against the establishment of a school."[9]

Carroll, however, urged the point with the "Select Body." Writing to one of the opposing clergymen in 1787, he tried to make his correspondent see that the extinct Society was not being wronged by having its property used for this new academy; it was, indeed, only fitting to apply these funds to such a work; "it could not be applied to a fund more conducive to the end of the Society" if it were in existence at the present moment; the Society in the old days "rendered no service more extensively useful than that of the education of youth."[10] Carroll and four colleagues addressed a circular letter in similar vein to the "Reverend Gentlemen of the Southern District," who were opposing his plan. "A school," he urges, "will certainly be a nursery from whence postulants [i.e., for the Society, if it be restored] can alone be expected." He presents further reasons for the school, taking his arguments from the antecedents of the Society.[11]

Beginnings of Georgetown College

Carroll finally prevailed. On May 15, 1789, the Chapter voted an appropriation for the new school.

May 15th. Business of the Academy

Resolved, 1o. That a subscription be proposed to the general Offices [Officers?] and members of clergy to relieve the public exigencies to which it is likely the general fund will not be adequate.

2o. That the present members of Chapter do circulate and encourage the aforesaid subscription among their fellow clergymen in their respective Districts, and the monies collected be paid into the hands of their Directors of the Academy.

3o. That the sum arising therefrom be applied to the finishing of the Academy at Georgetown, and that the Procurator General be authorized to apply all savings out of the Office, which may be made till next sitting of Chapter, to the same purpose.

4o. That the Superior be requested by the senior member of Chapter to nominate a clergyman to superintend the Academy at Georgetown as soon as the schools[12] shall be opened for the education of youth, and that the said clergymen be presented to the Directors thereof, and if approved by them, be constituted Principal.

5o. That the income from a certain tract of land subject to the care of the Procurator General be by him annually paid to the Principal for his support, as far as the amount of £100 current money, and that all deficiency be made up to him out of the general fund.

6o. That the said Principal be *ex officio* one of the Directors of the Academy and have a vote in all matters belonging to the government thereof, except wherein he is personally concerned.

7o. That the Principal shall be removeable by a majority of votes of the other Directors.[13]

The year 1789 is usually regarded as the date of the foundation of the college, but the building was not finished at this date. Carroll wrote to Plowden, March 13, 1788:

> We shall begin the building of our Academy this summer. In the beginning we shall confine our plan to a house of 63 or 64 feet by 50, on one of the most lovely situations that imagination can frame. . . . Do not forget to give and procure assistance. On this Academy is built all my hope of permanency and success to our Holy Religion in the United States.[14]

The college was ready for occupancy in 1791. In that year under date of October 12, Carroll wrote again to Plowden:

> The academy will be opened in a few days; but not so advantageously as I hoped. No president *pro dignitate loci.* I can hardly forgive my friends at Liège [for not sending him a capable president]. Here was an opportunity for infinite service to the cause of God and His Church. Mr. Molyneux [an ex-Jesuit in Maryland, who, while a scholastic, had been a master at the English college of the Society at Bruges in 1764; at this date he was fifty-three years old[15]] cannot be prevailed on; and indeed he has not the activity of body nor the *vivida vis animi* for such employment. I have recurred to Mr. Plunkett, but cannot get his answer yet. . . .[16]

According to Father Grassi, a European Jesuit who came to the United States in 1810, the first president of Georgetown was Robert Plunkett, an Englishman. Grassi's letter of October 8, 1811, is addressed to Plowden at Stonyhurst.[17] Plunkett had come from England about 1791.[18] He was succeeded by Molyneux; then came Dubourg, a Sulpician.[19] The latter was elected September 30, 1796. Evidently he was not altogether acceptable to the faculty, made up mostly of ex-Jesuits. He resigned in January, 1799.[20] Later, in August, 1799, the Sulpicians started an Academy of their own in Baltimore. At first, out of deference to "Messieurs du collège de Georgetown," native Americans were not admitted. But in 1803 they threw open their doors to Americans, much to the consternation of the authorities at Georgetown.[21] Carroll himself was in sympathy with the undertaking[22] which threatened to close Georgetown permanently. The strange thing was that the ex-Jesuits' institution, intended primarily for the instruction of secular youth, was "governed on the principles and in the system of a convent,"[23] while Dubourg's academy in Baltimore, though directed by Sulpicians whose work is the training of candidates for the priesthood, was conducted along very liberal lines.[24]

Early Difficulties at Georgetown

The early days of Georgetown were crowded with difficulties. In the first place, while the men that made up its faculty in the first decade of its existence had received as Jesuits excellent training for their profession of teaching, yet it is doubtful if many of them had ever actually engaged in teaching before the Georgetown experience. Molyneux had been a master at Bruges, but that was thirty years before. All of them had been employed in missionary work in Maryland, an employment hardly calculated to produce classical scholars, much less able teachers. Carroll realized this and was appealing continually to his former associates of the old Society in England to send some of their masters from Liège. In the meantime, the school founded by Dubourg, the French Sulpician, "a man of very pleasing manners and towering genius,"[25] was in striking contrast to Georgetown. Even in 1808 Carroll wrote that the College of Georgetown "has sunk lamentably in character; and no wonder it should; . . . Mr. Leonard Neale was its president for many years, and his brother Francis his right-hand man. You know that the latter is piety and virtue itself, but too illiterate to have any share in the direction of a literary institution."[26] Elsewhere he says of Francis Neale: "he had no ability for his station [he was the seventh president], and was nominated by a strange combination."[27]

In addition to the lack of a suitable faculty in the first decade, Georgetown also suffered from the fact mentioned in the foregoing, that many of the ex-Jesuits did not enter heartily into the college plan, because they wished to guard intact the properties of the old Society over against its restoration. The Society was not canonically restored until 1814, but Pius VII legalized the existence of the Russian branch of the Order in 1801, and in 1802, by a *viva voce* pronouncement, permitted them to receive foreign ex-Jesuits. Carroll was empowered by the General, Father Gruber, in 1806 to reëstablish the Society in the United States.[28] From this date, 1806, Georgetown became a Jesuit college with a Jesuit rector, the Reverend Robert Molyneux.[29]

English Tradition at Georgetown

Henceforth the Maryland Mission was, unlike its status before the suppression, independent of England. Yet it continued to owe a great deal to England and the English tradition. Georgetown's founders and first professors and presidents — with the solitary exception of the Frenchman Dubourg — had all studied, and some of them had taught at the English college at St. Omer and at Liège. In these early years, there was frequent communication with Stonyhurst, whither the Liège college had been moved in 1794, for counsel as to methods, textbooks, and the like. So much influence had the English that when the Reverend Edward I. Purbrick, president of Stonyhurst College, visited Georgetown in 1878, he expressed delight at "the prosperity indicated. He could feel that all the work of the Society which he witnessed in Maryland was an outgrowth of the old English Province to which he belonged."[30]

Grassi's Arrival

The growth of the school was slow. In 1792 there were 66 students enrolled, but it did not reach the century mark until 1818 with 101.[31] In 1810 a remarkable European Jesuit came to Georgetown, John Anthony Grassi. Originally destined by his superiors to revive the missions in China, he set out with a companion from St. Petersburg in February, 1805, beginning a "strange Odyssey that was to last five years and was to end not in Pekin but in Baltimore." Through Russia and Finland they crossed over to Stockholm, then to Copenhagen. But everywhere there were difficulties in the way of their voyage to China. They went to London, then to Lisbon for another trial. Here, while awaiting orders, they studied astronomy. Once more Grassi went to England where he spent considerable time at Stonyhurst, familiarizing himself with the system of education and discipline of that college, with the collection of physical instruments and books on mathematics. Finally he arrived in Baltimore in October, 1810. He was made superior of the mission in 1811, and president of Georgetown in 1812.[32] He remained in Maryland only until 1817, but he left his impress on the educational work there.

To him, says Shea, Georgetown College owes its first great impulse and thorough organization. He came directly from countries where colleges of the Society were in successful operation, he had been formed to the strict discipline which characterized the revived Society, and was admirably fitted by his learning, his administrative ability, and by every refinement to direct a college, introduce discipline, and win the approbation of parents by the manifest progress of their sons.[33]

Archbishop Carroll wrote to Father Plowden in 1813: "Mr. Grassi has revived the College of Georgetown, which has received great improvements in the number of students, and course of studies."[34] He not only gave a new impetus to the study of mathematics and science,[35] but he definitely took the college out of the experimental stage and placed it on a secure footing. From this time, although the College had its vicissitudes, its periods of stress and storm, yet in general it advanced steadily, developing from a rather primitive Latin academy into a great Catholic University.[36]

The Georgetown Curriculum

In the first decades, Georgetown was largely a typical Jesuit Latin School. No catalogue was issued until 1851; before this time an annual prospectus was printed. In the Georgetown Archives there is one dated January 1, 1798, during the presidency of Dubourg. It states:

> The study of the dead languages, that foundation of universal knowledge, which in every Academy calculated for the purposes of extensive utility, ought to engage a large proportion of the attention of the professors, must have been indeed cultivated in *this* with uncommon application, of which the extraordinary proficiency of many of its pupils, in so short a period is unequivocal proof. . . .

In the prospectus of 1814, issued by Grassi, there are many interesting items. The annual charge for board and tuition is $125; for day scholars $34. The Sunday and "holyday dress" is prescribed, "a plain coat and pantaloons of blue cloth with yellow buttons and red cloth waistcoat." The object of the institution is "principally for the education of those who profess the Catholic religion." Grassi's influence is evident in the enlarged curriculum. Besides English, French, Latin, Greek, and all the other branches of classical education, the students are taught "Sacred and Profane History, Geography, Use of the Globes, Arithmetic, Book Keeping, Algebra, Geometry, Trigonometry, Mensuration, Navigation, Surveying, Astronomy, Fluxions and the other parts of Mathematics, in general comprising a complete and regular course."[37]

The age of admission was from eight to fourteen. "When children are not sufficiently advanced to begin a regular course of classical education, they are placed in an elementary class, attended by a particular teacher, from whom they may learn to spell, read, and write."[38] But in the first annual catalogue (1850–51), it is stated: "No student is admitted who cannot read and write." In 1820, the classes were named: Rudiments, first year; Third Class of Grammar, second year, in which Latin was begun; Second Class of Grammar; First Class of Grammar, in which Greek was begun. Two other classes were added, Humanities and Rhetoric, after which the degree of bachelor of arts was conferred.[39] Later, especially after the appearance of Roothaan's Revised *Ratio* in 1832, the curriculum was changed, largely in the direction of giving more emphasis to Latin.[40]

New York Literary Institution

The first offshoot of Georgetown was the New York Literary Institution. Anthony Kohlmann, one of the Jesuits who had come to America in the first decade of the nineteenth century, opened a school in a house on Mulberry Street in 1808. When Kohlmann wrote to Carroll toward the end of 1808 he already had seventeen pupils.[41] Four scholastics were sent from Georgetown in 1809; Adam Marshall, James Redmond, James Wallace, and William White.[42] In July, 1809, Kohlmann wrote to Carroll; "It now consists of about thirty-five of the most respectable children of the city, Catholic as well as Protestant."[43] In September, 1809, the school was moved to Broadway and in March, 1810, a new site was secured "far out in the country" just opposite the old Elgin Botanical Gardens, the present location of St. Patrick's Cathedral.[44] Kohlmann was enthusiastic about its future. He wrote in August, 1810: "Everyone thinks that if the reputation of the house is kept up, it will in a short time rivalize any college in the country. . . . We have the finest set of globes in America."[45] In November, 1810, he wrote to Father Strickland in England: "Our College . . . is in a very prosperous way. In the space of about eight months we received thirty-six pupils, that is as many as the house can possibly admit, among whom are the son of the late Governor Livingston and the son of the present Governor Tompkins."[46]

During its short existence the number of pupils reached seventy-five;[47] probably more than half were day scholars. Mr. Wallace, the Jesuit scholastic, one of its first professors, published in 1812, the first Jesuit contribution to exact science in the United States:

> *A New Treatise on the Use of the Globes and Practical Astronomy*, the whole serving as an introduction to the *Higher Astronomy and Natural Philosophy*. Designed for the instruction of youth and particularly suited to the United States. Published by Smith and Forman at the Franklin Juvenile Bookstore, 195 and 213 Greenwich Street, New York.[48]

Despite Kohlmann's enthusiasm and the seeming success of the new school, it was destined to a brief existence. The Jesuits could not supply both the New York school and Georgetown with masters. Kohlmann was in favor of closing Georgetown and transferring the faculty to New York. New York is "of greater importance to the Society than all the other states together," he wrote to Grassi in 1815. He speaks contemptuously of the Superior's policy of recalling all the Jesuits "to a state [Maryland] the worst and poorest in the Union . . . in which the Society will be eternally buried in a tomb."[49]

But the American group in the Order, most of whom were native Marylanders, with strong attachments to their own state, prevailed; the New York school was closed in 1813;[50] Kohlmann himself was recalled to Maryland in 1815.[51] The next, and permanent foundation in New York, was made, not from Maryland but by the French Fathers from St. Mary's, Kentucky.[52]

The Washington Seminary

This institution in the city of Washington was originally intended as early as 1815[53] by Father Grassi as a novitiate for members of the Order, but it was never used for that purpose.[54] It was opened as a "*scholasticate,*" or house of studies, for members of the Society in 1820.[55] Three classes of grammar for extern students were started in 1822;[56] the Jesuit scholastics taught Latin and studied divinity at the same time.[57] In 1824, the Jesuit students were withdrawn, but the school for boys taught by the Jesuits continued for a few more years.[58] In 1827, Washington Seminary had to be closed for lack of funds, the superiors in Rome having ordered that the rule of the Society about not accepting tuition money was to be strictly enforced.[59]

An interesting figure among the faculty members was Father Adam Marshall, the former professor at the New York Literary Institution. For a time, he was employed by the government as an instructor of the midshipmen on board the *North Carolina.*[60]

Washington Seminary was reopened in 1848; the name was changed to Gonzaga College in 1858,[61] and under this name it has continued to the present day, although now it conducts only a high-school department.[62]

St. John's Literary Institution, Frederick, Maryland

This school was opened by the Jesuits in November, 1829, with an enrollment of forty boys.[63] This soon increased to one hundred, "which has been the average number since," wrote Father McElroy in 1844 to Father James Ryder, the President of Georgetown.[64] It apparently enjoyed fair prosperity for some years, although it never got beyond the stage of a *collegium inchoatum*[65] in the official records of the Society. It went out of existence gradually, the Jesuit personnel and number of classes decreasing during the last decade of its existence. In 1853, a great number of students was expelled for some breach of discipline, and St. John's never recovered.[66]

By the end of 1859, the *collegium inchoatum* ceased appearing in the province catalogue, although a day school of a sort was conducted there until the beginning of the twentieth century with a Jesuit or two teaching, assisted by a few seculars.[67] It is now a parish high school for boys and girls, taught by the Sisters of Notre Dame.[68]

Holy Cross College, Worcester, Massachusetts

The first permanent foundation by the Fathers of the Province of Maryland,[69] after Georgetown, was made at Worcester, Massachusetts, in 1843. The Reverend James Fitton, a parish priest of that city, had established a school, the Seminary of Mt. St. James, which he intrusted to a layman, a Mr. Brigden, whom Bishop Fenwick of the Maryland Mission, in his diary, calls "a worthy and excellent master." Bishop Fenwick, an ex-Jesuit of the Maryland Mission, took over this school and property in 1843. In November of that year, the Jesuits accepted the charge of the school, changing the name to Holy Cross College. It opened with twelve students; at the end of December that number had increased to seventeen. The order of exercises, distribution of classes, system of administration and discipline were similar to those that existed at Georgetown from which institution nearly all of the officials and professors were drawn.[70] Indeed, its first graduates received their degrees from the sister institution in the District of Columbia.[71]

Holy Cross never developed into a university, but concentrated on the classical courses in its preparatory and college department. After 1914, the high-school department was discontinued because of a great increase in college students. In 1930–31, there were 1,039 college students of whom 771 were boarders, the largest Catholic boarding college in the United States.

St. John's College, Fordham

This school had been founded June 24, 1842, and classes were begun the same year under the charge of the secular clergy.[72] In 1844, Bishop Hughes made overtures to the French Jesuits of St. Mary's College, Kentucky,[73] offering them his college in the suburbs of New York. He did not call upon the Maryland Jesuits because he feared that they would make Fordham secondary to Georgetown, whereas he ambitioned for Fordham a brilliant future as the foremost Catholic college in the country.[74] St. John's College was sold to the fathers of St. Mary's in 1846 and in April of the same year Fathers Thebaud and Murphy arrived at Fordham. The entire faculty of St. Mary's, consisting of sixteen priests, eighteen scholastics, and thirteen lay brothers, arrived at Fordham in July, 1846.[75] The Jesuit system was introduced in 1847 and from that date the Jesuits were in complete control. The old method of subject professors, in use while the secular clergy was in charge, was abolished and the plan laid down by the *Ratio Studiorum* was introduced.[76] For a time, Fordham was a boarding college, a seminary, a novitiate, and a house of studies for the divinity students of the Society.[77] It was incorporated as a college in 1846; as a university in 1907, under the name Fordham University. It still continues its preparatory department at St. John's College High School.

The Jesuits at Fordham were, for the most part, Frenchmen; they constituted with the Canadian colleges and missions the New York and Canada Mission, and until 1879 they were quite distinct in local administration from the American Jesuits of the Maryland Province. However, as their school was based on the *Ratio*, and since they modeled their courses at Fordham on the Georgetown plan,[78] it is not probable that

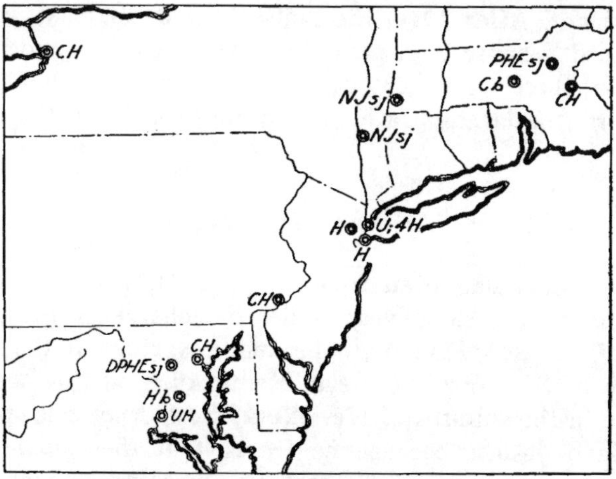

MAP II. MARYLAND-NEW YORK PROVINCE OF THE SOCIETY OF JESUS, 1928*

U — University. C — College. H — High School. b — Boarding school. NJsj — Novitiate and Juniorate for Jesuits, undergraduates. D — Divinity. PHEsj — School of Philosophy and Education for Jesuits, graduate students.

there was a great deal of difference between the two institutions with the exception of that which came from varying national traits. In 1879, Maryland and New York were united into one province.

St. Francis Xavier College, New York City

A year after Fordham had been intrusted to the Jesuits, the same group of Jesuits opened a school in the city of New York, the "College of the Holy Name of Jesus."[79] In 1850 it was

*The New England institutions were detached from the Maryland-New York Province in 1926 to form the independent Province of New England.

moved to the present location on Sixteenth Street where two courses were offered, the commercial and classical. The college department was discontinued in 1908. Since that date, a large classical high school has been conducted under the name of "The Xavier High School of St. Francis Xavier College."[80]

Other Schools of the Maryland-New York Province

A classical school, St. Joseph's College, was opened by the Fathers of the Maryland Province in September, 1851, at Philadelphia.[81] Loyola College, Baltimore began classes two years later.[82] Boston College, Boston, opened its doors for secular students, September 5, 1864. It had commenced in 1850 as a house of studies for the divinity students of the Society in the United States.[83] In 1913, the college department was moved to University Heights in the suburbs of Boston; the high school remained in the old location. For many years it had the distinction of being the largest Jesuit high school in the United States. There were 1,275 students in 1925–26, all of them in the classical course.[84] However, in 1930–31, Xavier High School, New York City, outdistanced the Boston Institution.[85]

St. Peter's College, Jersey City, was the last American foundation of the New York-Canadian Mission; it was opened with an enrollment of 123 on September 2, 1878.[86] The New York and New Jersey Jesuits were united with the Maryland Fathers in 1879. There have been three schools opened since the union: Brooklyn College in 1908 at Brooklyn,[87] at present only a high school; Loyola School in New York City in 1900, a select school, comprising junior- and senior-high-school classes;[88] and Regis High School, also New York City, in 1914,[89] an endowed school, open to Catholic students only. The course is strictly classical; students are selected from the parochial schools by competitive examinations. Regis High School is the only free high school in the Maryland-New York Province; there are at present only two Jesuit free schools in the United States. Canisius College, Buffalo, started by the Fathers of the German Province in 1870, was incorporated into the Maryland-New York Province in 1907.[90]

Footnotes

[1]The word *college* has an interesting history. In Jesuit usage, it originally meant a school designed to cover the whole field of secondary education, practically the equivalent of the German *gymnasium,* or the French *lycée.* In fact, this usage still persists, for example, in France and Belgium. In England, certain public schools still retain the word *college;* thus, Eton College, as well as the Jesuit institutions, Stonyhurst College, Beaumont College. In the United States, in the beginning a Jesuit college ordinarily did not go beyond the level of European secondary schools. But soon classes in philosophy were added to the top class, and finally the division made into high school and college on the American plan. See *Oxford Dictionary,* s.v. "college."

[2]See Hughes, *op. cit.,* "Documents," I, Part II, 668 ff.

[3]This was the Academy and Charitable School of Philadelphia, founded in 1749. See Davis, *Public Secondary Education,* p. 37.

[4]Hughes, *ibid.,* p. 634. "Ad procurandos in Religionis ministerio successores, quid faciendum sit non sane intelligimus. Est jam Philadelphiae collegium, agiturque de duobus in Marilandia extruendis, ad quae admitti poterunt Catholici aeque ac alii. . . . Fore speramus ut hos inter aliqui vitam ecclesiasticam velint amplecti. Cogitamus igitur de seminario instituendo, in quo valeant deinceps ad mores et doctrinam statui illi convenientes formari." (Copy in the "Shea Transcripts," *Georgetown Archives.*)

[5]In "Shea Transcripts," *Georgetown Archives.*

[6]Hughes, *ibid.,* p. 658.

[7]*Georgetown Archives,* "Proceedings of the General Chapter." 1786; see also Hughes, *op. cit.,* "Documents," I, Part II, 665–7; and Shea, *History of the Catholic Church in the United States,* II, 301–4.

[8]Later (1793) incorporated as "The Corporation of Roman Catholic Clergymen." See Hughes, *ibid.,* pp. 743–4.

[9]*Maryland-New York Province Archives,* 1787; see also Hughes, *ibid.,* p. 673.

[10]"Shea Transcripts," *Georgetown Archives;* see Hughes, *ibid.,* pp. 673–5.

[11]*Georgetown Archives,* MSS. Excerpts given in Hughes, *ibid.,* pp. 676–679.

[12]In the sense of "classes."

[13]*Maryland-New York Province Archives,* 1789. See Hughes, *ibid.,* p. 695.

[14]*Maryland-New York Province Archives,* 1788; Hughes, *ibid.,* p. 695.

[15]Foley, *op. cit.,* VII, Part I, 514.

[16]*Maryland-New York Province Archives,* 1791; Hughes, *ibid.,* p. 746.

[17]Hughes, *ibid.,* p. 837.

[18]Shea, *History of Georgetown University,* p. 15.

[19]Hughes, *ibid.,* p. 833, citing Grassi's letter of 1811 to Plowden.

[20]*Georgetown Archives,* "Shea Transcripts," "Époques du Seminaire de Baltimore par Mons. Tessier"; and Hughes, *ibid.,* p. 767.

[21]"Shea Transcripts," "Jusqu'à ce jour on n'avait admis à l'académie [of the Sulpicians] aucun sujet du pays par déférence pour les Messieurs du Collège de Georgetown. Mais enfin on pensa que la necessité de soutenir un établissement, lequel seul pouvait nous mettre en état d'élever des jeunes gens pour l'église, devait suffire pour nous excuser aux yeux de ces Messieurs; et on annonça publiquement qu'on recevrait les Américains dans l'académie de quelque religion qu'ils fussent." See also Hughes, *ibid.,* p. 797

[22]See Hughes, *ibid.,* pp. 757–799.

[23]*Ibid.* Carroll's remark to Strickland.

[24]*Ibid.,* p. 797, note 47.

[25]Carroll to Plowden, Jan. 10, 1808. *Ibid.,* p. 799.

[26]Carroll to Strickland, April 2, 1808. *Ibid.*

[27]Carroll to Plowden, Dec. 12, 1813. *Ibid.,* p. 801. Father Charles Sewall, of Maryland, wrote to his brother Nicholas in England, also an ex-Jesuit, under date of July 29, 1803: "I am sorry to inform you that the College of Georgetown does not flourish, but has for some time past been declining in numbers, character and reputation; so that there

are only about 40 boys at present; and I am told by one who is better acquainted with the College than I am that its bad success is owing to the want of proper masters, and better administration in sundry points. Though the gentleman, who presides at present [Leonard Neale] is certainly a very virtuous and zealous bishop, yet it appears that something is wanting to give satisfaction to parents, many of whom have withdrawn their children and sent them to Protestant schools and academies. We [the ex-Jesuits] are so few in number, and are now so far advanced in years, that unless Mr. Stone [the first Provincial of the restored Society in England] will be pleased to send us a proper superior and president for the College, to say nothing of some masters, it will, I fear, come to nothing, to the great detriment of religion and our great disgrace. . . ." *Ibid.*, p. 799.

[28]"Shea Transcripts," *Georgetown Archives;* Hughes, *ibid.*, p. 820.

[29]Devitt, "Notes on Georgetown College," MS. in *Georgetown Archives,* 136. No. 11.

[30]Shea, *History of Georgetown University*, p. 267.

[31]Devitt, *loc. cit.*

[32]Parsons, J. Wilfrid, "The Catholic Church in America in 1819," *The Catholic Historical Review,* V, 301.

[33]Shea, *History of Georgetown University*, p. 41.

[34]Carroll to Plowden, Dec. 12, 1813. Quoted in Hughes, *op. cit.*, "Documents," I, Part II, 801.

[35]Devitt, "Notes on Georgetown," *Georgetown Archives.*

[36]An Act of Congress, dated March 1, 1815, granted the power of conferring degrees, and on March 30, 1833, the Holy See empowered Georgetown to confer degrees in Philosophy and Theology. The formal incorporation of the institution was effected by Congress in 1844. The School of Medicine was opened in 1851, the School of Law in 1870, the first session of the Dental School was held in 1901, and in February, 1919, the School of Foreign Service was opened. The secondary department was removed from Washington to Garrett Park, Maryland, in 1918, but it is still known as the Georgetown Preparatory School.

[37]A MS. copy of the prospectus of 1814, signed, "John Grassi, President," in *Georgetown Archives,* VII, 8.

[38]*Ibid.*

[39]"Prospectus of 1820," *Georgetown Archives.*

[40]See *infra,* Chap. VIII, "The Evolution of the American Jesuit High School" and Chap. X, "The High School Curriculum."

[41]Parson, J. Wilfrid, in *The Catholic Historical Review,* IV (old series), 38.

[42]Father McElroy's Diary, *Maryland-New York Province Archives.*

[43]Quoted by Parsons, *loc. cit.*

[44]*Ibid.;* McGuire, Edward J., "The Elgin Botanical Garden and the New York Literary Institution," *Historical Records and Studies,* IV, Parts I and II, 332.

[45]Meehan, Thomas F., "Catholic Literary New York," *The Catholic Historical Review,* IV, 405.

[46]McGuire, *loc. cit.;* McElroy's *Diary.*

[47]McElroy's *Diary.*

[48]Meehan, *loc. cit.*

[49]Hughes, *op. cit.*, "Documents," I, Part II, 945, 946, and note 14.

[50]McElroy's *Diary;* Shea, *History of Georgetown University,* p. 36.

[51]Hughes, *ibid.*, note 12.

[52]See *infra,* Chap. VI, "The Jesuits in Kentucky."

[53]Grassi to Kohlmann, March 4, 1815. *Maryland-New York Province Archives.*

[54]Devitt, E. I., "History of Maryland-New York Province." MS. in *Georgetown Archives.*

[55]*Woodstock Letters,* XVIII, 280.

[56]Devitt, *op. cit.*

[57]*Sketch of Gonzaga College,* p. 13; MS. "Catalogus Missionis Americae Foederatae," *Maryland-New York Province Archives.*

[58]*Sketch of Gonzaga College,* p. 13.

[59]Devitt, *op. cit.* In 1825, at the annual exhibition, held at the close of the school

year, Washington Seminary had as an honored guest, the President of the United States, John Quincy Adams. The following account is taken from the *Truth Teller* of New York, August 6, 1825.

"The following is extracted from the *National Journal* of August 2:

'Mr. Editor:

'On Tuesday last I had the gratification of being present at the annual exhibition of the Catholic Seminary of this city and cannot help expressing, though late, owing to various avocations, the pleasure I there received. The young gentlemen performed their parts in such a manner as showed, evidently, not the particular pains that had been taken for the occasion, but the regular and steady habits in which they had been trained during the preceding year. Were I to particularize, I might justly be esteemed interested, which I really am not, inasmuch as I have children who have never been to that Seminary. This, however, shall not long be the case.

'A part of the young gentlemen were examined in Greek and Latin by the President of the United States (who thereby showed, not only his usual urbanity, but his really paternal affection for the rising generation), and by other literary gentlemen, among whom I could distinguish the Chargé d'Affaires from Brazil, Judge José Silvestre Ribello, with the Secretary of the Legation, and several of the clergymen of the city. The specimens of the acquirements of the scholars showed very plainly the assiduity and industry of the gentlemen under whose tuition they had been placed, and also the spirit which they had infused into those under their charge.

'Everything was conducted with the utmost order and regularity; and although the room was small, a great number was accommodated. At regular intervals too the mellifluous tones of the excellent Marine Band added zest and satisfaction to the mental and moral entertainment. After the exercises were finished, the President of the United States, with a readiness and satisfaction which really added to the dignity of his character, at the request of the President of the Seminary, consented to distribute the premiums to those to whom they had been adjudged; and if we can augur from the unsophisticated countenance of innocent youth, the favor and kind feeling which his benevolent countenance expressed will never be eradicated from their minds.

. . . .

Very respectfully, etc.,
PHILOTECNOS.' "

(Communicated to *Woodstock Letters*, XXVII, 47–48.)

[60]Devitt, *op. cit.*

[61]*Ibid.*

[62]*Gonzaga College and High School Catalogue for 1925–26.*

[63]Letter of McElroy to Ryder, *Maryland-New York Province Archives;* see also *Woodstock Letters,* V, 108; XXX, 232.

[64]McElroy to Ryder, *loc. cit.*

[65]A college not yet on a firm financial basis.

[66]*Woodstock Letters, ibid.*

[67]*Catalogus Provinciae Marylandiae,* 1860; *Woodstock Letters,* XXX, 245.

[68]A word should be said about the educational work at Conewago, Pennsylvania, one of the old mission stations of the old Maryland Mission, situated in the southern corner of Pennsylvania, about ten miles from the historic field of Gettysburg. About 1800, before the restoration of the Society, a secular priest, F. X. Brosius, was in charge of the parish, and conducted a school for boys where at least the rudiments of Latin were taught. It is impossible even to conjecture how long it lasted. From 1835–38. Father Virgil H. Barber, S.J., a convert who had taught school before his entry into the Society, taught five boys at this place "among other branches, Latin and Chemistry." Six years later, the Brothers of the Society had charge of the Conewago School; during this period from 1844–48 it was probably little more than an elementary school for boys, with instruction in commercial branches possibly for a few. The school was opened again from 1856–61, taught in the main by the lay brothers; a Father F. X. DeNeckere had charge of the school, probably from 1856–68; he was stationed there again from 1864–1879, and during part of this time conducted a Latin school. From 1881–84, and from 1887–89, and from 1890–92, the Latin school at Conewago was revived, the sole teaching during

these later periods being carried on by a layman, under the direction of the Jesuit pastors (See MS. *History of Maryland-New York Province* in *Georgetown Archives* and *Woodstock Letters,* LXIII, 56–66).

[69]Before the suppression, the Jesuit foundations were known as the Maryland Mission. After the reëstablishment in 1805, it was called *Missio Americae Foederatae,* the Mission of the United States. It was raised to the rank of a province in 1833 with the name Province of Maryland. In 1879, it was united to the New York Mission of the Canadian Province as the Province of New York. In 1880, the name was changed to the present title Maryland-New York Province. In 1926, New England was cut off from Maryland-New York and raised to the rank of a Province, the Province of New England.

[70]Devitt, *History of Maryland-New York Province,* MS. in *Georgetown Archives.*

[71]*Ibid.;* and *Historical Sketch of the College of the Holy Cross.*

[72]De Courcy, *Catholic Church in the United States,* p. 240.

[73]Taafe, *History of St. John's College, Fordham,* p. 58; Devitt, *op. cit.*

[74]Taafe, *loc. cit.*

[75]Devitt, *op. cit.,* Taafe, *op. cit.,* p. 68.

[76]Taafe, *op. cit.,* p. 73.

[77]Devitt, *op. cit.*

[78]Taafe, *op. cit.,* p. 73

[79]Devitt, *op. cit.*

[80]*Catalogue of the Xavier High School, 1925–26.*

[81]Devitt, *op. cit.;* Shea, *History of the Catholic Church in the U. S.,* IV, 400.

[82]*Historical Sketch of Loyola College,* p. 11; Devitt, *op. cit.*

[83]Devitt, *op. cit.;* Shea, *op. cit.,* p. 515; *Woodstock Letters,* LI, 81.

[84]*Woodstock Letters,* LXIII, 352.

[85]*Ibid.,* LX (February, 1931), supplement.

[86]Devitt, *op. cit.*

[87]*Woodstock Letters,* LI, 80.

[88]*Ibid.,* XXX, 99.

[89]*Ibid.,* LI, 80.

[90]See *infra,* Chap. VII, "The Buffalo Mission."

CHAPTER VI

THE MIDDLE WEST. THE MISSOURI PROVINCE

THE Missouri Province of the Society, the second Jesuit Province to be established in the United States, furnishes in its origin, and to a certain extent, in its later development a distinct contrast to the Maryland Jesuits. The latter inherited the English Jesuit tradition, modified by the national consciousness which the Maryland members of the Society, along with their fellow citizens, imbibed during the first decades of the new republic; this was further modified by superiors like Grassi and subjects like Kohlmann who brought the European influence to bear on the growing province. The Missouri Province, on the other hand, was from its inception subject to the continental influence.

Founding of the Missouri Mission

Father Anthony Kohlmann, on his arrival in Maryland, felt the need of more subjects for the work of the Society. America and England seemed unable to supply sufficient candidates; so he wrote to Belgium begging the assistance of young seminarists.[1] In 1820, several young Belgians came to America and entered the Maryland novitiate at White Marsh, where they were put under the care of their countryman, Father Van Quickenborne, who had come from Ghent in 1817.[2]

It would seem that there was friction between the foreign and American Jesuits. Archbishop Marechal, in a letter dated January 15, 1826, to Cardinal Della Somaglia, speaks of it as a "*Magnum quidem et publicum dissidium*"; but Marechal's evidence must be discounted because of his well-known *animus* to the Maryland Jesuits.[3] Still it was probably felt by the

American Jesuits that the Flemish subjects, because of their unfamiliarity with English, were quite unsuited to the work in Maryland, whereas in the West they might find a field of usefulness where their knowledge of French would stand them in good stead in their ministrations to their coreligionists of French descent in St. Louis and vicinity. In this strain, Father B. Fenwick, of Maryland, wrote in 1823 to the General.[4]

However, it is clear from correspondence supplied by Hughes[5] that as early as 1814 Bishop Dubourg had asked the Jesuits both in Maryland and abroad to send him helpers for his vast diocese. The tense situation that existed between the Maryland Jesuits and Marechal, as well as the belief that the Belgians were unsuited to work in Maryland, undoubtedly induced Charles Neale, the Superior of the Maryland Mission, to grant Dubourg in 1823, Charles Van Quickenborne and eleven others for work among the Indians in Missouri.[6] Two priests, seven scholastics, and three lay brothers made up the party. Among them was Peter De Smet, later famous for his work among the Indians of the Far West.

The principal object of Dubourg in bringing the Jesuits to Missouri was to have them care for the Indians; the concordat entered into between Neale and the Bishop makes only incidental mention of colleges.[7] The little band of Jesuits arrived at St. Louis on May 31, 1823, whence they proceeded to Florissant, Missouri. Here they established a house of studies for the younger Jesuits and a school for Indians.[8]

This was the beginning of the Missouri Mission of the Society, later to become the Missouri Province,[9] numerically the second largest of all the American provinces. The Jesuits arrived in May; in November, Bishop Dubourg wrote to Father Neale offering the Society "two beautiful squares of ground in the city of St. Louis" and promising "to help in the erection of a house for an academy, as a preparation for a college, if you thought you could spare a couple or three of your Maryland brethren, even scholastics, to commence that establishment; in which case I will shut up the one that is now kept by some of my priests."[10] This school had been opened in 1819 under the name of St. Louis Academy with the secular priests of the St. Louis Cathedral in charge.[11]

St. Louis University

The Missouri Jesuits were unable at first to accede to the bishop's request. The young Jesuits were busy with their divinity studies and their attempts to master the English language; in addition they were employed as teachers of the Indians at the Florissant Seminary.[12] In December, 1825, Father Van Quickenborne wrote to the Maryland Superior, Father Dzierozynski, that four white boys were in residence at the seminary.[13] This may be regarded as the beginning of the St. Louis institution as a Jesuit school.[14]

The "St. Louis College" conducted by secular priests closed its doors in 1826; and the need of a school for the Catholic youth of the city of St. Louis became imperative. Accordingly, in 1828, the Jesuits accepted the bishop's offer. While their building was being erected in St. Louis during the session of 1828–29, there were about fifteen white boys from St. Louis and the vicinity registered at the "Indian Seminary" at Florissant.[15] In the *Catalogus Missionis Americae Foederatae* for 1829, there occurs this entry: *"Domus seu Collegium Inchoans Apud S. Louis in Missouri,"* with the information that two of the Fathers made trips from Florissant to St. Louis while the college was being built.[16] The register of the St. Louis Institution contains the names of all the white boys at the Indian Seminary after 1828.[17] Classes were opened in the new building in St. Louis on November 2, 1829, with the Reverend Peter J. Verhaegen as its first president.[18] The St. Louis College in its first year of existence had a faculty of five Jesuit teachers[19] and a total registration of 150, of whom 30 were boarders.[20]

Despite the rather flamboyant prospectus, it is probable that in the first years of its existence, the college was hardly much better than a grammar school. In the first year, Father De Theux taught French,[21] but this was undoubtedly a necessity, as the register shows a preponderance of French names. In 1830–31, De Theux is listed as teaching Latin, Greek, and French. But in 1831, De Theux wrote to his mother, the Countess De Theux, at Liège, Belgium. "I thank you for the

Greek books. They will begin to teach this branch in St. Louis College at Easter or the following October, 1832. Father Van Quickenborne replaces me at St. Louis in Latin. . . . He has a good class of almost fifteen. Last year I sometimes had only two or three pupils."[22]

The superior of the mission, Father Van Quickenborne, was less optimistic than the others. Apparently he was in favor of devoting their efforts to a grammar school, believing it more suited to the pioneer conditions of St. Louis. But his advisers were insistent that the institution should come before the public as a Jesuit college, offering the traditional classical course.[23] During this first year only two classes were conducted, Higher and Lower English.[24] Lower English was for those who, as a contemporary expresses it, "have never studied English Grammar, and are learning their A, B, C and reading." Among the textbooks used during the first session were Webster's Spelling Book, Murray's English Reader, Murray's Small Grammar, Murray's Large Grammar, Pike's Arithmetic, Hutton's Mathematics, Smiler's Geography, Reeve's History of the Bible, Goldsmith's Greece and Rome, and Levizac's French Grammar.[25] Latin was first taught in the session of 1830–31, and Greek probably at the end of the 1831–32 session.[26] The rate for boarders was $120 yearly, while the day scholars paid only $5 a year for "fuel and servants"; no charge being made any of the students for tuition according to the Jesuit rule of gratuitous instruction then in force.[27]

Whatever the character of instruction imparted at the St. Louis College, there is no doubt that the discipline conformed to continental standards. In the *Maryland-New York Province Archives* there is a set of regulations which Van Quickenborne forwarded to Father Dzierozynski, the superior of the Maryland Mission, for his approval. They are in Van Quickenborne's handwriting and were probably composed by him. The following extracts picture the seminary atmosphere that pervaded the institution:

1. Studies are held in the Common Hall. One of the professors presides and one or more tribunes according to the number of students.

2. The tribunes are charged with what regards good order and discipline in the study hall and the same obedience is to be paid them in

whatever has reference to their office and to the professor. This post is filled by the most exact and diligent. [Presumably he speaks of the tribune's office.]

3. The first studies of the day are commenced by morning prayers, the other by *Veni Sancte Spiritus* and *Ave Maria* and close with *Sub tuum,* etc.

4. After prayer each student takes from his desk whatsoever he may want during studies. At the expiration of three minutes the first tribune will give the signal to shut them [i.e., the desks]. During the time of school [i.e., class] it will be permitted to open them once or twice at a given signal, but independently of those occasions it will not be allowed and every infringement will be noted by the tribune, unless permission for doing so has been granted.

5. Profound silence must reign during the time of studies. The first tribune has an elevated and a distinguished place, having a sheet of paper divided into several columns before him. In one are inserted the names of those who talk or are noisy; the second will contain the names of such as are idle; the third of those who move from their place or open their desks; the fourth of such as having been three times marked as idlers, or talkers or noisy continue to merit the same reproach. In the last place the tribune shall go to the place of the delinquent and place thereon these words, *Signum pigritiae,* to which he affixes the delinquent's name. The culprit is to present this note to the rector at the end of evening studies.

6. They must attend the lectures [i.e., reading during meals] which are performed in turns by the best readers and they are to be prepared to give an account of it when the presiding person shall require it.

The students walk three by three and talk in a moderate tone of voice until they arrive in the country. Then they are allowed to confound their ranks when the prefect gives the sign. They resume their ranks when they draw near the city and no one shall take or admit of any other companions than those appointed. At the head of the band is a conductor, ordinarily one of those who have the crosses of diligence. No one can precede him nor must they have a great interval between the ranks.

To go to grog shops is forbidden under pain of dismission.[28]

The Curriculum at the St. Louis School

In the catalogue of St. Louis University for 1832–33 the course of studies is announced:

It embraces both a mercantile and classical education, but so conducted that the student may apply himself to either or both of these, according to his destination or the desire of his parents. The mercantile department embraces reading, writing, the English and French languages, poetry, rhetoric, history, geography, mythology, bookkeeping, arithmetic, algebra, geometry, the use of the globes, trigonometry, mensuration, and surveying.

The classical department besides the above-specified subjects comprises the Latin and Greek languages, logic, metaphysics, moral and natural philosophy, and the higher branches of the mathematics. The Spanish, if required, is taught to the students of both departments without any additional charge. The English is the ordinary language of communication in all the classes, the French and Spanish excepted; but the students speak French and English indiscriminately during the hours of recreation.[29]

In the same catalogue it is announced that "no student is admitted under the age of eight years nor above that of sixteen, unless for special reasons, and in all cases it is required that he bear a good moral character and know how to write and read his vernacular language." The St. Louis Jesuits borrowed the Georgetown regulation, for it solemnly declared that "with regard to pocket money, it is the wish of the faculty that no more than 12½ or 25 cents a week be allowed to the students." Violations "of the established discipline of the university are repressed in a kind, paternal manner; corporal punishment is inflicted only for grievous offences and by none but the president, or in his absence by the vice-president."

Father Kenney's Comments on the New School

About this time a remarkable man arrived on the scene, the Reverend Patrick Kenney, an Irish Jesuit, appointed by the General of the Society as Visitor of the American houses of the Society. He gave a realistic account of the educational situation at the St. Louis school. In a letter to Father John McElroy, the head of the classical school at Frederick, Maryland, dated February 9, 1832, he says:

We are all well here. The college at St. Louis has an increase of pupils. . . . Of the whole number of 152, which through the whole of this severe winter attended school (with few exceptions) every day, only 51 are not Catholics. . . . They do not indeed oblige the non-

Catholics to learn catechism; but they make the Catholics recite their lessons in it in the class in the presence of the others. The lesson, too, is explained to all alike and they have no difficulty in questioning the one as well as the other with regard to the meaning of what has been explained. Besides, the Protestants join in all the prayers, hear all the instructions, have books and beads as well as the Catholics. Thus the most important object of our schools is fully realized with regard to the greater number, nay to double the number of pupils, and this majority is like to increase every day and the same object is forwarded even by the non-Catholics by learning the true principles of Catholic faith and morals. But I am sorry to say that the object next in importance, which is that of a classical education, is very far from being realized; nor is there any immediate prospect of this department being more flourishing. Poor as your classical school was this time last year, it was then double the number of those who study Latin now in St. Louis College. There is great flourishing in the Prospectus about rhetoric, philosophy, classics, etc. But *details* such as I am giving you, because I know that you wished to know how all was arranged here, *tell the truth* and more truth than the fine descriptions, glowing hopes, and brilliant course of studies found in the pages of a Prospectus or in the reports of an Exhibition, but for which we seek in vain *a parte rei!* It is said that high sounds and a little boasting does much in this country. If it do, it will not last long. Such mists disappear as the sun rises. There are five classes. The two lowest teach the alphabet, spelling, and reading. These are taught by Br. Yates and Mr. Taylor who has himself been a scholar in the house, and they are the most numerous. The next two are divided more on account of numbers than of matter. They were only one school [class] until Mr. Van de Velde arrived. Here to reading are added geography, some action of elocution, a little history, some elementary composition. These are taught by FF. Walsh and Elet. Next comes rhetoric (God bless us), the pupils when all together may be twelve. They learn by heart Jameson's Elements of Rhetoric. They study and give an account of an abridgement of Blair. They write English letters and alternately compose in some subject or write an amplification theme. To teach some twelve boys is Mr. Van de Velde's sole occupation! With the exception of a class of mathematics three times in the week; which, however, is included in his five hours per day, the limit now fixed to the Master's labors. Here, then, is Mr. V. d. V., fifteen years in the Society, the most of which time he has been employed teaching, without being allowed to finish his theology; again condemned to teach another year (tho' I specially warned Mr. De Theux, before I sent him, that his undoubted right and the interests of the Society required that he should finish his theology). Could the school [class] in any way contribute to his improvement — had he the English language yet to study or could the elementary exercises improve him in English composition, some fruit would be derived from his labors, like that which the Society wishes her masters to gather for themselves that thus they may be prepared for higher duties; has anything like this to be gained! patience. But so it is. There is a class of French taught by Mr. Verhaegen, the rector, three times a week and good F. V. Quickenborne spends his (?) hours every day with *eight Latin scholars,* who being also half-rhetoricians and therefore give only one hour to Latin threaten to revive the Augustan age with their proficiency in Cornelius Nepos. Mr. Van Sweevelt [scholastic S.J.] has hitherto been clothes keeper and sacristan — when I just discovered these appointments in which good F. De Theux did not even consult me. I very quietly remonstrated . . . ; he told me they were both to study their theology at the same time! Every one but himself saw the impossibility of such a combination. I let the experimentum be made and now he finds that theology was lost in all the clothes, bed and table linen of the house, to say nothing of the duties of the sacristan and infirmarian; all of which Van Sweevelt had to do whilst without any professor he was to prepare for his examen ad gradum in order that on the vote of four men he might become a professed father of four vows. . . .[30]

Unsatisfactory Condition of the St. Louis School

Kenney wrote to the General, Father John Roothaan, more formally but not less pessimistically, of the condition at the St. Louis College. He asked whether it were worth while for the members of the Order to conduct institutions of this type. There would be no cause for complaint if circumstances of time and place permitted the faculty to impart a more serious type of education. But "the young men go forth superficially educated in every way. They speak proudly of eloquence, rhetoric, and of its figures, but of the Greek and Latin authors there is ignorance profound. . . ." The greatest difficulty to his mind was that American parents did not desire any better training for their children. He deprecates the fact that some fatality has driven the Jesuits to avoid the better-known cities and take in charge the cultivation of the stubborn soil of small and unimportant places. "Is it in the interest of the common good," he asks, "that our priests wear out their strength in the management of colleges such as this?"[31]

In the same letter, the visitor urges the general to command the St. Louis authorities to promote Latin and Greek studies. Accordingly, Roothaan wrote in October 23, 1832, pleading strongly for a classical education even in the uncongenial environment of the American West.

> I should wish, however, he says, that the education and instruction imparted be brought into closer alignment with the standards of the Society and that the Latin and Greek languages be better cultivated. For to give the majority of the students only those subjects which are everywhere given equally well by junior clergymen and even laymen is not an affair of such great moment that so many of our priests should spend their time and strength in occupation of this sort. . . . You ought to see whether persons [i.e., laymen] cannot be found among you willing and able to teach schools of this kind under our direction.[32]

At the same time, Roothaan wrote to Kenney deploring the state of affairs at St. Louis. "The College of St. Louis! What is to be done? It certainly cannot now be abolished and so must be tolerated. Meantime the Fathers there are to be urged to come nearer by degrees to our system of studies and especially to give more attention to Latin."[33]

Verhaegen, the Rector of the new institution, had written August 25, 1832, to the General explaining the educational situation in St. Louis.

> We are placing, he says, just that degree of emphasis which the state of our infant country allows. Things here, Reverend Father, are all new and must be molded into shape. The study of languages, if you except English and French, has no great attraction for the young. This defect will be remedied only in the course of time, namely when the family affairs of the inhabitants become more settled and an end be put to all these changes and shiftings of residence.[34]

Verhaegen realized that a classical school on the European plan was out of the question for the present in St. Louis; the Latin classes were falling off, the Greek class had been discontinued by July, 1834; it was resumed, however, in the following year.[35] Three years was the average stay of a boy at college and so Verhaegen observes "since they scarcely know anything when they come to college, few are permitted to finish the classical course as it is called."[36]

Yet Verhaegen was hopeful for the future. He was a man "whose learning, administrative capacity, and social gifts eminently fitted him for the position of president."[37] It was long, however, before St. Louis reached the status of a University. Eventually, Verhaegen's hopes were realized and his dream came true. St. Louis University, besides its undergraduate departments, possesses at the present time flourishing schools of philosophy, theology, medicine, law, dentistry, and education. In addition, St. Stanislaus Seminary at Florissant, where candidates for the Society have their novitiate and receive their normal and classical training, is affiliated with the university. The graduate school in St. Louis, which all the younger members of the province attend after their course at Florissant, is an integral part of the university and supplies the various high schools of the Missouri Province with their Jesuit personnel.

Courage of the St. Louis Jesuits

One cannot but be impressed by the courage of the little band of Belgian priests who began this educational venture amid such adverse surroundings. Catholic education in the Middle West owes an immense debt to their heroic effort. "With the history of this institution begins the history of secondary education in the Trans-Mississippi West. Not only is the St. Louis school the oldest school of its type west of the Father of Waters; but to many of its alumni and one-time instructors belongs the distinction of setting up other pioneer high schools in the Western States."[38] What Georgetown was to Catholic education on the Atlantic seaboard, that St. Louis was to the Middle West. The faculty was eminently competent for the work in hand, the direction of a classical school, and could compare favorably with their contemporaries in Eastern classical schools. During the first decades of its existence, practically all the professors were men who had received thorough classical training in European schools. Verhaegen and Van de Velde had taught in Europe. Nor were they unduly hampered by their unfamiliarity with English. Of Van de Velde, for example, it was said by one who knew him, "Few scholars even among those whose vernacular tongue was English ever acquired more thorough mastery of the language or could speak and write it with more purity and propriety than he could when he was raised to the priesthood."[39] Van de Velde deserves more than a passing notice. He had come to America in 1817, joined the Society in Maryland, and taught for a time at Georgetown. In 1831, he came to St. Louis; in 1840, he was appointed president, "and gave a new impulse to the studies and the classes in the college, elevating them to a higher grade. He accomplished this improvement especially by the pains he took to train up and form his young teachers. He insisted that in order for them to be successful as professors, it was necessary that they should acquire proficiency in the English language, and in its best literature. . . . [He convinced them] that no degree of superior learning could be made by them any means of important good for the people of this country, unless they became well trained in the idioms of the language, the words and phrases that reach the heart of the people and unless they learned their national history, their allusions, their models of literature, their ideal of style and taste."[40]

Other influences besides the Flemish were felt in the province. Maryland sent a few men, experienced in their schools, to the new province. In 1847, revolutionary troubles in Europe brought to the Missouri Province a great many Germans. Since the Civil War, however, the majority of the candidates entering this province have been native Americans.

The St. Louis school gave up its original location at Ninth and Washington Avenues in 1888, moving to the present location of the Administration Building on Grand Avenue. The high-school department was transferred from Grand Avenue to the west end of the city in 1925.

The Jesuits in Kentucky

An interesting episode in the history of the Catholic Church in the United States is the trek of the Maryland Catholics of

English stock to Kentucky, in the post-revolutionary period. Monseigneur Flaget, Bishop of Bardstown, began, in 1819, a small day school at Bardstown which boasted the imposing title of St. Joseph's College. The teachers were secular priests and lay professors.[41] So many calls were made on the priests in charge for parochial work that they found the school an impossible burden; accordingly in 1828, Flaget applied to the Provincial of France for members of the Society to man his college. The Provincial was unable to accede to the request at the time, but in 1830 a revolutionary storm swept over France closing the Jesuit colleges. The Provincial, believing that circumstances were still unchanged in Kentucky, sent four of his subjects to America. They arrived in 1831; and from New Orleans enthusiastically sent word of their arrival to the bishop.[42]

The bishop was in a quandary. Not receiving Jesuit aid when he asked for it, he had intrusted the Bardstown school to some of his own priests who naturally resented the coming of the Jesuits. Fortunately for the latter, another school, St. Mary's College, opened in the spring of 1821 by the Rev. Wm. Byrne as a sort of preparatory seminary[43] and located near Lebanon, in Marion County about twenty-five miles from Bardstown, needed teachers. This was offered to the French Jesuits on condition that the Rev. Wm. Byrne be permitted to remain as president. On the 7th of July, 1832, word came from the General, Father Roothaan, approving this arrangement.[44] Father Byrne retained the presidency until his death in June, 1833.[45] From this date the Jesuits were in complete control and gradually introduced their system of education. It offered a "classical course of four years and a commercial course of three years."[46]

In many respects this was a remarkable college; the contrast must have been striking between the primitive manners of the natives and the old-world courtesy of the teachers, most of whom had been educated and had taught in the best Catholic schools of France. Charles Herbermann, who knew many of them personally after their transfer to New York, says of them:

They were all good instances of that almost extinct species, the gentlemen of the old school. Among them . . . Father William Stark Murphy, a man of great executive power and an English scholar of very high attainments; Father Larkin, whose scholarship ranged from Latin and Greek grammar (he wrote a very original work on Greek grammar) to the highest flights of theology; Father Charles Hippolyte de Luynes, a courtly man, of comely and impressive appearance, a correct and powerful orator, a learned exegete and a deep and original thinker. . . . ; Father Simon Fouché, the most amiable and gentle of teachers and scholars; lastly Father Thebaud, a man enthusiastic for all that was charitable . . . a convinced American . . . a warm admirer of the great work of Washington . . . [these men] worked with zeal, energy, and intelligence in bringing up the boys of Kentucky and the Southwest from 1831 to 1846. . . . The tuition fee was only six dollars per session. And the boys, future judges, governors, and attorney-generals readily gave one day weekly to farming, hewing of wood, etc. . . . Place in this frame as a setting the picture of one hundred and fifty or two hundred sturdy Kentuckian youths struggling away morning, noon and night to master the difficulties of the classics, mathematics, and English, spurred on by their teachers, most of whom would have been ornaments to the best faculty at that time in the United States, and we enjoy a sight that the United States will probably never see again.[47]

Plays composed by the Fathers, after the best Jesuit tradition, formed a conspicuous feature of the commencement-day exercises at this backwoods college, says the diary manuscript preserved at Fordham. The exercises took place on a rustic stage erected under the shady trees that surrounded the house. Père Chazelle, the Rector, convinced that to promote the glory of God in America and in Kentucky, he must first become a real American and a Kentuckian, wrote a tragedy called "Redhawk" for the commencement of 1834, designed to illustrate the ancient customs of the Indians, and the labors of the early American settlers, all turning to praise of Christianity. The bright costumes of the natives, in which the actors were arrayed, contributed not a little to the success of the drama.[48]

In 1844, the Fathers from St. Mary's announced the opening of a new school in the growing town of Louisville, the "St. Ignatius Literary Institution," where the "system of studies embraces all the branches of a classical education." John Larkin is listed as its president, assisted by one priest and two scholastics.[49] It was probably opened in the fall of 1845[50] and was closed at the end of the scholastic year. For in 1846, the entire faculty of St. Mary's College was transferred to St. John's College, Fordham, New York, the French Jesuits having accepted Bishop Hughes' invitation to take over his institution.[51] Henceforth, the history of the French Jesuits' educational establishments in Kentucky becomes merged in the history of Fordham. The real reason for closing the Kentucky schools seems to have been, not only difficulties with Chabrat, Flaget's coadjutor,[52] but also the little apparent opportunity offered for educational expansion in this section of the country.[53]

The Missouri Jesuits at Bardstown

Bishop Flaget, a warm friend of the Society, was determined that his diocese should not be without a Jesuit school. In 1848, shortly after the departure of the French Jesuits, he offered the Missouri Provincial St. Joseph's College at Bardstown, the institution that had been opened in 1819 and conducted ever since with varying success by the secular priests of the diocese. Father Verhaegen, the first president of the St. Louis College, with a faculty of Missouri Jesuits, went to Bardstown in the summer of 1848 to take charge.[54] The Missouri Province was able to do this the more easily as a great increase in their numbers took place in 1848 due to the expulsion of the Jesuits from Italy and Switzerland by the anticlerical revolutions in Europe. About forty of these exiles, mostly Germans and Swiss, received a hospitable welcome at St. Louis University.[55]

The college at Bardstown was prosperous enough under Jesuit régime. Its clientele was largely drawn from the South. When the Civil War broke out, classes were "temporarily suspended, the college having been used for more than a year as a military hospital."[56] The number registered for the last year of classes at Bardstown 1860–61, was 280; of the number 118 were from Kentucky, 82 from Louisiana, and 22 from Mississippi. After the war, it is probable the Jesuits would have reopened the school but for a financial disagreement with Dr.

McCloskey, the bishop of the diocese.[57] Their announcements ceased appearing in the *Catholic Almanac* after 1864.

The Missouri Jesuits also attempted a school in Louisville, St. Aloysius College, but it was of short duration. It was opened on the "second Monday of September, 1849."[58] and it had a prosperous beginning. In 1849–50, "about two hundred boys attend and it bids fair to do much good."[59] But some fatality seemed to attach to all Jesuit educational ventures in the State of Kentucky. The last session of the Louisville school was 1851–52.[60]

Other Colleges of the Missouri Jesuits

Even before the Jesuits took charge of the Bardstown College, the vice-province of Missouri had made a second educational venture. Bishop Edward Fenwick, of Cincinnati, founded a school for boys in October, 1831, called "The Athenaeum."[61] The Athenaeum began auspiciously but soon its directors, secular priests of the diocese, found it difficult to carry on and engage in heavy ministerial work at the same time. It could hardly have been a very successful school when Archbishop Purcell asked the Jesuits of Missouri to take charge in 1840. They changed the name to St. Xavier College, and Father Elet, one of the original band that came from Maryland with Van Quickenborne, was the first president under the new régime.[62] It was conducted as a combination boarding and day college until 1854, much on the lines of the St. Louis school. The tuition was $130 for boarders and $40 for day scholars.[63] College courses as well as preparatory classes were conducted from the beginning, St. Xavier's having been granted a temporary charter to grant degrees by the state legislature in 1842, and a perpetual charter in 1869.

In 1847, the preparatory department of the college was moved to the Purcell Mansion on Walnut Hills. It was brought back to the old location in the city in 1849 where the present St. Xavier High School is located. In 1920, the college department was transferred to Avondale, a suburb of Cincinnati, where from 1912 to 1919 a branch high school had been conducted.[64] In 1930, St. Xavier College became Xavier University.

From 1838 to 1847 the Missouri Jesuits had charge of Louisiana and of St. Charles College, Grand Coteau.[65] Toward the end of 1847,[66] however, the French Jesuits from the province of Lyons took over its direction.

In 1848, the Missouri Jesuits founded an Indian school at St. Mary's, Kansas. In 1869 the provincial decided to establish a boarding college at St. Mary's; a charter was obtained on December 24th of the same year. The college building was not begun until 1870. Evidently they taught the classics on a modest scale; one scholastic is listed in the catalogue of the province as teaching there in the year 1870–71.[67] In fact, several years after its inception as a college the *catalogus* of the Missouri Province lists St. Mary's as a residence, with a certain number of *magistri.* Not until 1878 does the school appear as "*Collegium et Convictus Stae Mariae.*" It was a decade before they had a complete college and high-school course, as the first graduates were given diplomas in 1882.[68] Due to financial difficulties, St. Mary's in June, 1931, ended a long and glorious career. At present, the divinity school for the Missouri Province is housed there.

The Jesuits opened St. Ignatius College, Twelfth Street, Chicago, on September 5, 1870,[69] although the picturesque and zealous Jesuit, Arnold Damen, had long been engaged in missionary and parochial activity in this city with some of his companions.[70] This first year there were four classes; twenty-six were enrolled in the classical, nine in the commercial, and two in the preparatory course. By the end of the year the enrollment was 99.[71] A branch school, "the North Side Collegiate School," was opened on LaSalle Street near North Avenue in 1887, only to be abandoned for lack of patronage in 1888.[72]

Twenty-two years later, Loyola Academy was opened, Sept. 20, 1909, on Sheridan Road. In the same year, St. Ignatius College obtained a university charter as "Loyola University"; it has two affiliated high schools, Loyola Academy, on the North Side campus and St. Ignatius High School, on the original foundation on the west side. The latter institution was for many years the largest high school in the Missouri Province. The college was transferred to the north-side campus in 1923.

In June, 1877, the Jesuits arrived in Detroit. Classes were held for the first time in Detroit College, September, 1877.[73] This institution too, secured a university charter in 1911. It is now known as the University of Detroit, and its preparatory school as the University of Detroit High School.

On Sept. 2, 1878, Creighton College, Omaha, Nebraska, opened with 120 students in attendance.[74] This new venture of the Missouri Jesuits was due to the generosity of the Creightons, a Catholic pioneer family.[75] It was the first Catholic endowed college in the United States. Tuition was free for many years, but recently, the endowment proving insufficient for the upkeep, a tuition fee has been charged.[76]

Omaha in the early 80's was a frontier town, hardly a happy location for a classical school. One of the early professors, Father Patrick A. Murphy, speaking of those times, says: "Though the College was free, the number of students was small, which, however, is no valid proof that they all belonged to the select aristocracy. They could neither understand the beauty of Greek nor the utility of Latin."[77] The low standard of studies can be judged by this; the English branches of the Third Humanities, which was the highest class in 1878–79, were on a par with those of the sixth-reader class. The only requirement for admission to the "college" was ability to read in the second reader.[78] Until 1887, Creighton offered only four years of instruction "to fit the student for a practical business life, for literary or scientific pursuits."[79] However, in the 90's more prosperous times and a better class of students came to Creighton. Continued benefactions of the Creighton family enabled the Jesuits to develop the unpromising Creighton College into Creighton University.

Marquette College, Milwaukee, though not opened until 1881, was planned much earlier. In fact, the Jesuits were engaged in educational work in Wisconsin as early as the 50's. Some of the German and Swiss Jesuits who, driven out of Europe by the revolution of 1848, had taken refuge in the

Missouri Province, evidently had high hopes of an educational venture in this state. In the *catalogus* of the vice-province for 1850, under Green Bay, Wisconsin, there is the entry *"Collegium Marquettense brevi inchoandum."*[80] Two priests and a lay brother were assigned to this "college." One of them, Anthony Anderledy, was later General of the Society. But classes were never conducted in this "college."

The Missouri Jesuits came to Milwaukee in September, 1857, and opened a preparatory school, "St. Aloysius Academy." The total number of pupils was fifty, the faculty two, consisting of one priest, the Reverend Stanislaus Lalumière, and a scho-

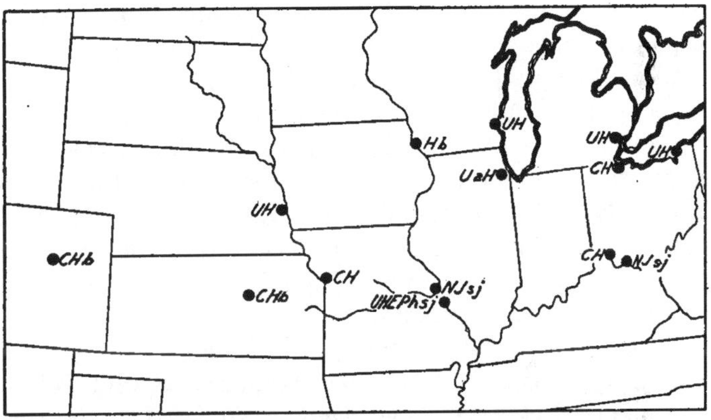

MAP III. MISSOURI PROVINCE OF THE SOCIETY OF JESUS, 1928*

U — University. C — College. H — High School. b — Boarding School. NJsj — Novitiate and Juniorate for Jesuits, undergraduates. PHEsj — School of Philosophy and Education for Jesuits, graduate students.

lastic, Mr. Cornelius O'Brien. Latin and bookkeeping, as well as more elementary subjects, were taught.[81] The school was not a success and in 1859, the Jesuits withdrew. They returned, however, in 1861. A new building was erected in 1864 and the name of the school was changed to "St. Gall's Academy." Un-

*Since 1928, Chicago, Northern Illinois, and the four states, Michigan, Ohio, Indiana, and Kentucky have been separated from the Missouri Province to form the Chicago Province.

til the close of the institution in 1872, the academy gave some of its students at least a smattering of the classics and the elements of rhetoric.[82]

In 1881, Marquette College, Milwaukee, was opened with a registration of only 35; this number increased to 77 before the close of the year. The first year, besides a preparatory class, only two commercial classes and the lowest class of the classical course were conducted.[83] The growth of the college was slow during the first two decades of its existence; but in 1907 the college affiliated with several existing professional schools to form the Marquette University. It has made remarkable progress since that date and today is one of the foremost Catholic universities in the Middle West. A modern high school, the Marquette University High School, with accommodations for fifteen hundred students, was opened in 1925.[84]

In September, 1907, the General of the Society assigned three colleges, founded by the German Jesuits of the Buffalo Mission, to the Missouri Province, together with their personnel, namely, St. Ignatius College, Cleveland, Ohio, Sacred Heart College, Prairie du Chien, Wisconsin, and St. John's College, Toledo, Ohio,[85] thus bringing a total of ten colleges under the control of the Missouri Province Jesuits.

In 1914, a high school and junior college was opened at Kansas City, Missouri, Rockhurst High School and College.[86] In 1920, Sacred Heart College, Denver, founded by the Italian Jesuits, was assigned to the Missouri Province.[87]

Since the Chicago Province was established in 1928, the Missouri Province administers the following secondary schools: Campion Preparatory at Prairie du Chien, Wisconsin, Regis High School at Denver, Marquette University High School at Milwaukee, Creighton High School at Omaha, St. Louis University High School, St. Mary's College High School at St. Mary's, Kansas (closed in June, 1931), Rockhurst High School, at Kansas City, Missouri. The total number of high-school students in this province, in 1930–31, not including the mission college in Belize, British Honduras, was 2,346.

The Chicago Province controls the following secondary schools: Xavier High School at Cincinnati, St. Ignatius High School at Chicago, Loyola Academy at Chicago, St. Ignatius

High School at Cleveland, Detroit University High School, St. John's High School at Toledo. The number of students in this group of schools in 1930–31 was 2,257, a total for these two provinces of 4,603.[88]

Besides this, they control five colleges and six universities.[89]

Footnotes

[1]Marechal to Della Somaglia. See *infra.*

[2]Hill, *Sketch of St. Louis University,* p. 7.

[3]Marechal's letter to Della Somaglia, Pro-Prefect of the Congregation of the Propaganda, is in the "Shea Transcripts," *Georgetown Archives.* Hughes, *op. cit.,* "Documents," I, Part I, 548–9 ff., quotes it *in extenso.* The letter is dated January 15, 1826. "Ex quo Jesuitae Russiaci et Belgae adhuc advenerunt, magnum et quidem publicum extitit dissidium inter eos et Americanos Jesuitas. Istos extraneos fratres Americani ab initio judicarunt tanquam nostris missionibus minime idoneos, tum propter rusticos eorum mores, tum propter barbarum eorum loquendi modum. . . . Unus ex istis Jesuitis, nomine Ant. Kohlmann, et qui nunc in collegio Romano residet, scripsit circularem epistolam quae in Belgio fuit impressa, in qua invitabat suae provinciae juniores clericos ut in Americam venirent. . . . Novem seminaristae, hac epistola inflammati, a seminario Mecklinensi secreto aufugerunt et Baltimori appulerunt anno 1821. [This date is evidently wrong; Marechal is writing in 1826.] Septem eorum collegium Geeorgiopolitanum adiere. . . . Americani Jesuitae irati sunt valde. . . . P. Kohlmann eos misit White Marsh et ipsorum religiosam educationem duobus Belgis sacerdotibus qui hic morabantur commisit. . . . DD. Dubourg [the Bishop of New Orleans; as a Sulpician, he had been rector of Georgetown] certior factus malevolentiae qua Americani Jesuitae istos extraneos prosequebantur, P. Carolum Neale Americanum et tunc Superiorem Societatis clam adiit, eum induxit ut mandaret illis Belgis ut in statu Missouriensi migrarent." Marechal felt that he had a grievance because the Jesuits in his diocese were not entirely under his control; he resented the departure of any of them without his permission. Copious reference to the Jesuit-Marechal controversy may be found in Hughes, *passim.* From an obituary notice of Father Van Assche, a member of this band, written in all probability by one of the older members of the Missouri Province and published in the *St. Louis Times,* June 27, 1877, it would seem that it was not Kohlmann's appeal that induced the Belgians to come to America, but Father Charles Nerinckx, a famous pioneer missionary of Kentucky, not a member of the Society, who visited Belgium in 1816 and in 1820. This, too, is the tradition in the Missouri Province.

[4]Hughes, *op. cit.,* "Documents," I, Part II, 1025. The original is in the General Archives of the Society at Rome.

[5]*Ibid.,* 1008–1015.

[6]*Ibid.,* pp. 1021–24.

[7]See Concordat in Hughes, *ibid.,* p. 1023.

[8]Hill, *Sketch of St. Louis University,* pp. 20 ff.

[9]Missouri began as a mission dependent on the *Missio Americae Foederatae* in 1823; in 1831 it was an independent mission; in 1839 it was raised to the rank of a vice-province, and in 1863 it became a province. In 1925, the four states, Michigan, Ohio, Kentucky, and Indiana, were separated from it and made into the vice-province of Ohio. In 1928, all of the State of Illinois except the southern section was added to this territory to constitute the new Chicago Province. From 1837–1840, the Missouri catalogue was printed as an appendix to the Belgian province. Actually it was never administratively under the control of the Belgian or any European province, although its founders and many of its first subjects were Belgians. See *Woodstock Letters,* XX, 58–9.

[10]*Maryland-New York Province Archives,* Dubourg to Neale.

[11]Hill, *Sketch of St. Louis University,* p. 5.

[12]In the *Maryland-New York Province Archives* are preserved in lithograph the catalogues of the *Missio Americae Foederatae* (Maryland Mission) for the years 1824–1832. Here the Missouri houses and subjects are listed. For 1824, Florissant has two priests listed as *operarii*, i.e., missionaries; all the scholastics are "auditores theologiae." In 1827, after each scholastic's name is this entry, "*Stud. theol. et doc. schol,*" that is, "is studying theology and teaching class."

[13]*Maryland-New York Province Archives,* Van Quickenborne to Dzierozynski, Dec. 19, 1825.

[14]Garraghan, *St. Louis Catholic Historical Review,* I, 85.

[15]Hill, *op. cit.*, p. 39.

[16]"P. Van Quickenborne et P. Jos. Verhaegen se excurrunt donec aedificium perficiatur, et stabilem ibi habitationem figant."

[17]Hill, *ibid.*

[18]"*Catalogus Missionis Americae Foederatae, 1830.*" Lithograph in *Maryland-New York Province Archives.*

[19]*Ibid.*

[20]Hill, *op. cit.*, p. 41.

[21]*Catalogus* . . . 1831. P. Theodorus M. De Theux . . . *Prof. ling. latin. graec. et gall.*

[22]Quoted by Garraghan, in *St. Louis Catholic Historical Review,* I, No. 2.

[23]Garraghan, in *The Dauphin,* II, 105.

[24]*Catalogus Missionis Americae Foederatae, 1830, Maryland-New York Archives.*

[25]Van Quickenborne to Dzierozynski, Nov. 13, 1829, in the *Maryland-New York Province Archives.*

[26]*Catalogus Missionis Amer. Foed., 1831,* and De Theux's letter, *supra.*

[27]Garraghan, *The Dauphin,* II, 105.

[28]*Maryland-New York Province Archives.* See Garraghan, *The Jesuits in the Middle United States* (not yet published, 1931).

[29]*St. Louis University Archives.*

[30]Kenney to McElroy, February 9, 1832. In *Maryland-New York Province Archives.* Quoted from Garraghan, *op. cit.*

[31]Kenney to Roothaan, April 25, 1832, in the *General Archives of the Society.* Quoted by Garraghan, *op. cit.*

[32]Roothaan to Verhaegen, Oct. 23, 1832. In Garraghan, *op. cit.*

[33]Roothaan to Kenney, Oct. 23, 1832. In Garraghan, *op. cit.*

[34]Verhaegen to Roothaan, Aug. 25, 1832. In Garraghan, *op. cit.*

[35]A premium in Greek was given in 1836. *Catalogue of St. Louis University,* 1835–6 in *St. Louis University Archives.*

[36]Verhaegen to Roothaan. In Garraghan, *op. cit.*

[37]*St. Louis Catholic Historical Review,* I, No. 2, 100.

[38]Garraghan, in *The Dauphin,* II, 105.

[39]"A Short Biographical Sketch of James Van de Velde, S.J." *Woodstock Letters,* VIII, 65 ff.

[40]*Ibid.*

[41]W. H. Hill, in *Woodstock Letters,* XXVI, 90 ff.

[42]*Woodstock Letters,* II, 109 ff. Transcript of the Latin MS. diary of St. Mary's College

[43]Shea, *History of The Catholic Church in the U. S.*, III, 294.

[44]*Woodstock Letters,* II, 111–13.

[45]Taafe, *A History of St. John's College, Fordham,* p. 60.

[46]*U. S. Catholic Almanac or Laity's Directory,* 1837, p. 143.

[47]"Forty Years in the U. S. of America," by the late Rev. Augustus J. Thebaud, S.J. Edited by Charles George Herbermann. *U. S. Catholic Historical Society Monograph Series,* p. 330.

[48]*Woodstock Letters,* II, 109 ff. Transcript of the Latin diary.

[49]*U. S. Catholic Almanac,* 1844.

[50]Shea, *op. cit.*, III, 190.

[51]MS. *History of the Maryland-New York Province;* Shea, *loc. cit.*

[52]Taafe, *op. cit.*, p. 68.

[53]*Woodstock Letters*, III, 27.

[54]Hill, *Historical Sketch of St. Louis University*, pp. 70–1; *Catalogus Vice-Provinciae Missourianae ineunte anno MCMXLIX.*

[55]Hill, *loc. cit.*

[56]*Catholic Almanac*, 1864, p. 143.

[57]Hill, "Some Facts and Incidents Relating to St. Joseph's College, Bardstown, Kentucky," *Woodstock Letters*, XXVI, 90.

[58]*Catholic Almanac*, 1851, p. 76.

[59]*Catholic Almanac*, 1849, p. 201; *Catalogus Vice-Provinciae Missourianae ineunte anno MCMXLIX.*

[60]Hill, *op. cit.*, p. 95. In the Catalogue for the Vice-Province for 1852 (that is, recording the actual state of the school for 1851–2) a faculty of nine Jesuits is attached to this school. In the same records for the years following (1853–8) one or two Jesuits are stationed at Louisville, mostly engaged in parochial work. But apparently some sort of school was continued, as after two names during this period appears this entry "doc. in gymn.," i.e., "docent in gymnasio." In the *gymnasium* probably little more than the rudiments was taught.

[61]Shea, *op. cit.*, III, 351. An early prospectus announces, "The College course will embrace the Greek and Latin authors — both historians and poets — which are usually read; the Hebrew, Spanish, French, and English languages; the various branches of the mathematics; reading, writing, geography and the use of globes." *St. Xavier College Archives.*

[62]"The Jesuits in Cincinnati," *Woodstock Letters*, V, 115; Shea, *op. cit.*, p. 628, Hill, *Historical Sketch*, pp. 60–61; *Catalogus Vice-Provinciae Missourianae*, 1841.

[63]*Woodstock Letters, loc. cit.*

[64]*St. Xavier College Catalogue* (1925–26), pp. 18–19.

[65]*Catalogus Vice Provinciae Missourianae* (1840–47). It was actually founded by Nicholas Point of the Lyons Province. In the 1840 *Catalogus*, Nicholas Point is listed as "Rector a die 31 Julii, 1837." The Fathers of the Missouri Province helped him to man the college and it was attached to the Missouri Province during these years.

[66]*Woodstock Letters*, V, 17 ff. In the *Index Domorum et Sociorum Universae Societatis Jesu* lithographed at Rome in 1847, St. Charles College is listed as belonging to the Province of Lyons, France.

[67]*Catalogus Provinciae Missourianae ineunte anno 1870.* Sadlier's *Catholic Directory* lists St. Mary's College for the first time in 1872.

[68]*Historical Sketch of St. Mary's College.*

[69]Garraghan, *Catholic Church in Chicago*, p. 217.

[70]*Ibid.*

[71]"The Jesuits in Chicago," *St. Ignatius Collegian*, V, 4.

[72]Mulkerins, *History of Holy Family Parish*, p. 164.

[73]*Woodstock Letters*, I, pp. 303 ff; *Catalogus Provinciae Missourianae*, 1878.

[74]Dowling, *Creighton University: Reminiscences of Twenty-Five Years*, p. 58. Listed in the *Catalogus Provinciae Missourianae ineunte anno 1879*, which contains the report for the scholastic year 1878–79, as "Collegium Omahense inchoatum." A faculty of five Jesuits was stationed here this year.

[75]*Ibid.*

[76]*The Creighton University High School Catalogue for 1925–6.*

[77]Quoted in Dowling, *op. cit.*, p. 60.

[78]Dowling, *op. cit.*, pp. 58–9.

[79]*Creighton Catalogue*, 1884–5.

[80]*Catalogus Vice-Provinciae Missourianae ineunte anno MCML*, p. 15: "Missiones Provinciae Germaniae Superioris sub regimine praepositi V. Provinciae Missourianae.

COLLEGIUM MARQUETTENSE BREVI INCHOANDUM

Missio in Green Bay, Wisconsin."

[81]In the *Catalogus* for 1858, giving the status for the year 1857–58, appears the entry under *Residentia ad S. Galli Milwaukee:* "Stanislaus Lalumière, Praes. gymn.," i.e., Praeses gymnasii. Gymnasium seems to have been the term used for a school where the rudiments of the classics were taught. (See St. Aloysius, Louisville, Kentucky *supra.*) See also

Marquette College: A Quarter Century, Stray Leaves from the College History, p. 5.

[82]*Marquette College: A Quarter Century,* p. 6.

[83]*Ibid.*, p. 13.

[84]*Marquette University Catalogue,* 1925–6.

[85]See *infra* Chap. VII, "The Buffalo Mission."

[86]*Woodstock Letters,* V, 81.

[87]See *infra* Chap. VII, "The Italian Jesuits in the Western States."

[88]Supplement to *Woodstock Letters,* February, 1931.

[89]*Woodstock Letters,* LIV, 352–353.

CHAPTER VII

LOUISIANA. CALIFORNIA. THE BUFFALO MISSION

Jesuits in Louisiana

THE French Jesuits of the old Society had engaged in missionary work in Louisiana as early as 1700.[1] There they labored until the suppression, without, however, engaging in educational activity. In 1835, Monseigneur Blanc, the second Bishop of New Orleans, invited the Jesuits to take charge of a college at Iberville, Louisiana. He went to Europe in 1836 and obtained from Père Guidée, the Provincial of France, eight members of that province for his new school.[2] Iberville was abandoned for financial reasons, and Donaldsonville chosen as a more suitable place, because of its situation at the junction of Bayou La Fourche and the Mississippi, only eighty miles from New Orleans by river route. All arrangements were made for the establishment of a Jesuit school at this place, when unexpected opposition from the inhabitants put an end to the project.[3] Accordingly, Grand Coteau was selected as the site for the first Jesuit college in the South.

St. Charles College, Grand Coteau, Louisiana

Here, on January 5, 1838, the Jesuits opened a boarding college with Father Point as president and Father Abbadie as vice-president. But this date being Friday, superstition seized hold of the prospective students and not one boy appeared.[4] Before the end of the month, however, there were 24 students while the scholastic term ended with 56. Even at Grand Coteau much opposition was encountered; anonymous letters, threats of "tar-and-feather treatment" for the priests were received,

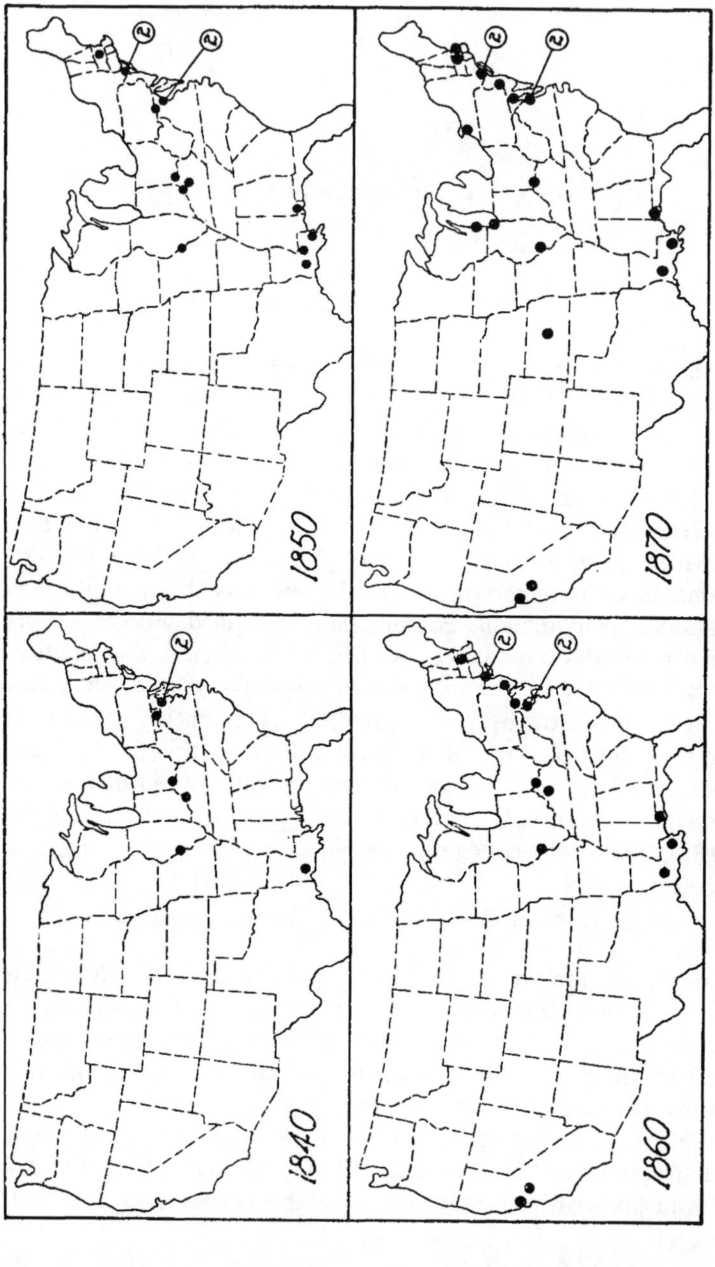

MAP IV. JESUIT EDUCATIONAL FOUNDATIONS IN THE UNITED STATES, 1840–1870

and an organization was formed for the avowed purpose of driving out the Jesuits so that the first superior could say with perfect truth, *"Ah! le voilà enfin, le collège St. Charles, enfanté dans la douleur!"*[5]

From 1840 to 1847, the little college went through various vicissitudes. Sometimes the attendance was so low that the question of closing it was proposed. In 1847, the college, which had been under the supervision of the St. Louis Jesuits up to the present, was transferred to the French Province of Lyons.[6] A few years later, October 28, 1853, the college was closed because of lack of patronage, but it was reopened in 1856 to house the students of Spring Hill College who were forced to leave Mobile on account of the yellow fever.[7] All during the Civil War the college managed to keep going after a fashion, but an order from the General closed the institution in 1868. In the following year, the burning of Spring Hill College again brought the students and faculty of the Mobile institution to Grand Coteau. They remained only a year. Since that date Grand Coteau has been a novitiate for the Jesuits of the New Orleans Province, serving at intervals as a college as well. Its last year as a college was 1921–2.[8]

Spring Hill College, Mobile

This college, the best known and oldest Catholic college in the South, was opened as a boarding school in May, 1830, with 30 students.[9] Monseigneur Portier, the first bishop of Mobile, intended it not only as a college, but also as an ecclesiastical seminary. In 1840, it received from Pope Gregory XVI the title and privilege of a papal university with the right to confer degrees in canon law and theology.[10] The real founder of Spring Hill is Cardinal Joseph Fesch, the uncle of the first Napoleon; he contributed 30,000 francs to Bishop Portier for this college.[11] The first staff of the college was composed of secular priests of the diocese. In 1839 the school was handed over to the Fathers of Mercy, a French congregation, and from 1841 to 1846 it was directed by the Eudist Fathers. But for some reason or other the college did not prosper; the number of students never reached one hundred, and there were few, if any, graduates.[12] The college was closed during the scholastic year 1846–47, and the bishop sent his vicar-general to Europe to find a body of religious to take charge of the school.

Although it would seem that the bishop was not very eager to get Jesuits for this work, yet he could find no others. The French Fathers had just disbanded their houses because of the revolution and the Provincial of Lyons was willing to send a colony of his subjects to America. On September 1, 1847, Spring Hill College opened under the presidency of Father Gautrelet, with 86 students.[13] The French Fathers found the American youths very unsatisfactory material to work with. The Annual Letters of 1848 reports: "Their dispositions are worse than I can say. . . . [They believe] that they can succeed in life and get rich without work." The chronicler speaks further of the "weakness of parents who tolerate and encourage everything; of the ungodly connections formed from earliest years," etc.[14]

Among the Jesuit professors at Spring Hill must be mentioned Dominic Yenni, the author of a Latin and a Greek grammar; both works were used in all Jesuit schools in America for many years. Spring Hill still continues as a select boarding college; in 1930–31 there were 156 high-school students and 143 college students.[15]

Other Jesuit Schools in the South

In 1847, the Jesuits secured a charter for a school in New Orleans, called Jesus School until 1853, when the name was changed to the College of the Immaculate Conception.[16] For over three quarters of a century, this college has been the center of Catholic intellectual life in New Orleans. Despite the ravages of yellow fever in the early days, the dark days of the Civil War, and the darker days of reconstruction, the College of the Immaculate Conception maintained a high scholastic standard and supplied the Catholic youth of the southern city with an excellent education. In 1904 another Jesuit college, Loyola College, was opened in New Orleans. The first years were hardly prosperous, but with the completion of its splendid group of buildings and the removal of all college classes from Immaculate Conception to Loyola in 1911, the new school advanced rapidly. In 1912, it was incorporated as a university by the state legislature.[17] The College of the Immaculate Conception, popularly known as "Jesuit High School," is now located in a new building on Carrollton Avenue.

The College of SS. Peter and Paul at Baton Rouge, Louisiana, destined to have but a brief existence, was opened in September, 1849, with 25 boys. It was closed at the end of the scholastic year 1854–55.[18] For a long time the Jesuits of

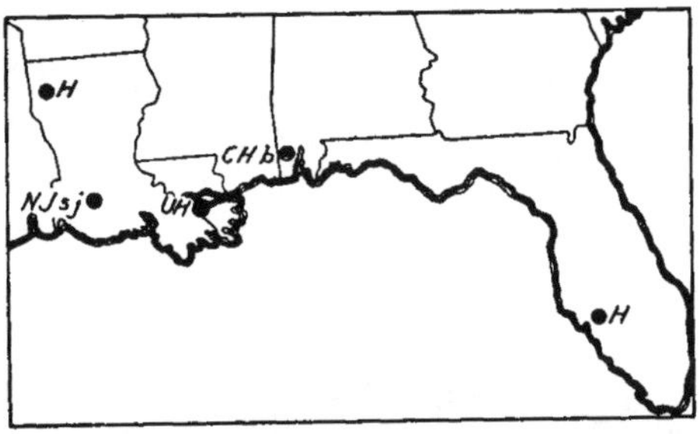

MAP V. NEW ORLEANS PROVINCE OF THE SOCIETY OF JESUS, 1928

U — University. C — College. H — High School. b — Boarding School. NJsj — Novitiate and Juniorate for Jesuits, undergraduate students.

the South attempted no other schools but concentrated their efforts on Spring Hill and New Orleans, with sporadic attempts to revive Grand Coteau. But in 1884, the ecclesiastical authorities at Galveston intrusted to the Jesuits of the New Orleans Mission the University of St. Mary's at Galveston, an institution founded in 1852, which in its brief history before the coming of the Jesuits had struggled along under eight different changes of directors.[19] At the end of June, 1922, the college was discontinued.[20]

Sacred Heart College, Augusta, Georgia, was opened in 1900,[21] but it was never largely patronized, and in 1917 it was closed. Two other schools have been opened in recent years by the southern Jesuits, St. John's College High School, at Shreveport, Louisiana, in 1908, a free high school, and Sacred Heart High School, at Tampa, Florida, in 1913.

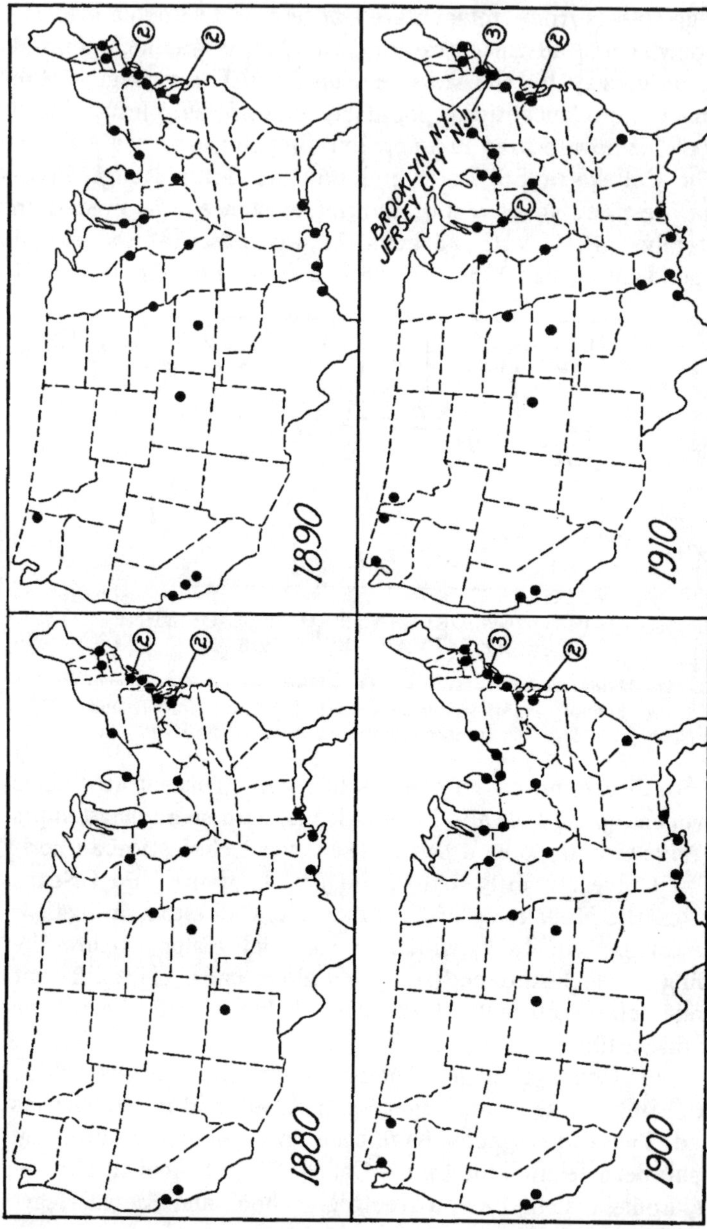

MAP VI. JESUIT EDUCATIONAL FOUNDATIONS IN THE UNITED STATES, 1880–1910

At present (1931) the New Orleans Province conducts four high schools at New Orleans, Shreveport, Spring Hill, and Tampa. In addition there is a university in New Orleans, and a college department at Spring Hill. This province is the smallest numerically of the American Jesuit Provinces; the relatively few Catholics in the South and the economic condition of this region after the Civil War have interfered with the development of Jesuit educational activity. In recent years there has been a considerable increase of students; this is particularly noticeable at New Orleans.

The Jesuits in the Far West

The first Jesuit of the restored Society to penetrate the Far West was the picturesque Belgian, Pierre De Smet, one of the Missouri pioneers, who in 1840 on the urgent appeal for Black Robes by a delegation of Flatheads,[22] was sent to preach the Gospel to the tribes beyond the Rockies. Other men from America and Europe joined him in Oregon. Thus, Nicholas Point, the founder and first rector of Grand Coteau, abandoned the classroom for the life of a missionary with De Smet in 1841. Two of his other assistants, Giovanni Nobili and Michael Accolti, Italians, left the missionary field in the Northwest in 1849 to engage in work in California at the invitation of the diocesan administrator, Fra Gonzalez.[23]

The gold rush to California in 1848 had brought lawlessness in its train; consequently the administrator welcomed the help of the two Jesuits in this difficult situation. In a letter, dated March 5, 1850, he writes to them:[24]

> I give infinite thanks to God for the favor He has conferred in the so opportune arrival of your Reverence and worthy colleague to aid me by your holy ministrations in correcting the morals of my flock, the education of youth and the preservation of Catholic worship through this vast diocese. . . .
>
> I have already expressed my earnest desire that two colleges of the Society of Jesus should be established here, one in the North where you are [San José] and another in the South. . . . As soon as you assure me you have collected from the people of the diocese enough funds for founding the first college and that you have permission from

your Superiors to found it, I am ready to send the corresponding permission of the diocesan authority in the prescribed form. . . .

I should take it as a great favor if your Reverences would ask of your Father General two good priests to come to Los Angeles, where the foundation of a college is of great importance. . . .

Fathers Accolti and Nobili were overjoyed at the friendly disposition of the administrator. In a letter dated April 9, 1850,[25] they expressed their gratitude, telling him his desire to establish a college coincided with their own views.

Nothing remains for us now, they wrote, but the approbation of our Father General, which we have little doubt in promising ourselves.

Your Reverence urges also the foundation of a second college in Los Angeles. We would venture to observe that once our Society shall have taken root in California, it will be easy for it to spread branches. When we shall have one college it will be easy to start another. Thus everything will be more solid than if we keep many projects at once before our eyes. . . .

In the meantime a new bishop had been appointed, a Dominican Friar, Joseph S. Alemany. In 1851, he wrote to Father Nobili urging him to apply to the Society for the Propagation of the Faith for funds to establish a college.[26] At the same time, the bishop wrote to the Jesuit Superior at Jamaica, asking him to send some Fathers. No priests could be sent from Jamaica, however; equally unsuccessful were the applications made to the superiors of the Missouri Vice-Province and those of Chile and Ecuador.[27] About this time the General of the Society wrote to Father Accolti, then in Oregon, giving the needed permission to establish a college in California, but adding that at present he saw no way of supplying the teachers unless the Provincial of Spain could come to their assistance with some of the dispersed members of his Province; while awaiting such aid, they might open a small school with the help of pious seculars, and a couple of Fathers might be sent down from Oregon. Three of the Indian missionaries were sent to Nobili from Oregon in 1851, the Belgians, Fathers De Vos and Goetz, and the Frenchman, Father Veyret.[28] This aid enabled Father Nobili to start the school at Santa Clara, the first Jesuit College in the West.

Santa Clara College

Accordingly, a very primitive sort of college was started by Father Nobili at Santa Clara, March 19, 1851. Nobili with two lay teachers constituted the first staff. Sixteen pupils enrolled as boarders, most of them children of the ranchers around Santa Clara.[29] That Father Nobili himself regarded the school with a critical eye is evident from a letter of his in the *Daily Evening Picayune,* of February 18, 1852:

> As yet we have issued no regular prospectus nor did we intend doing so until we should be able to enlarge and fit out the establishment so as to put it on an equal footing with the other colleges of our Order. We do not now claim for it even the name of a college, but have looked upon it merely as a select boarding and day school — the germ only of such an institution as we should wish to make it, and as the wants of the community will require. . . . It is, of course, a Catholic school, yet those of a different faith are admitted, and their religious opinions are not interfered with. . . .
>
> The rule of prepayment was not rigidly enforced during the past year, in which time, it is well known, the current expenses far exceeded the income from pupils. Had pecuniary profit been our object in the establishment it would have run its course and ceased to exist many months ago. You need have no fear of the college's permanence.[30]

And Father Accolti, the Superior of the Mission, writing of the little college at Santa Clara in 1852, says: "Although to the eyes of one who has seen better things, such an establishment must seem a mass of irregularities, it was the only one and the best that there was or could have been in California."[31]

One of the lay teachers in the college, Mr. Bernard J. Reid, afterwards a lawyer in Pennsylvania, writing to the *Pittsburgh Catholic* under the name of "Gerald" on August 21, 1852, said: "The Jesuits' College at Santa Clara is doing well, so much so as to provoke the envy and ire of some of the parsons, who storm furiously at the idea of Protestants sending their children there. One half of the boarders are Protestants, their parents preferring that school to any of the Protestant schools in the country."[32]

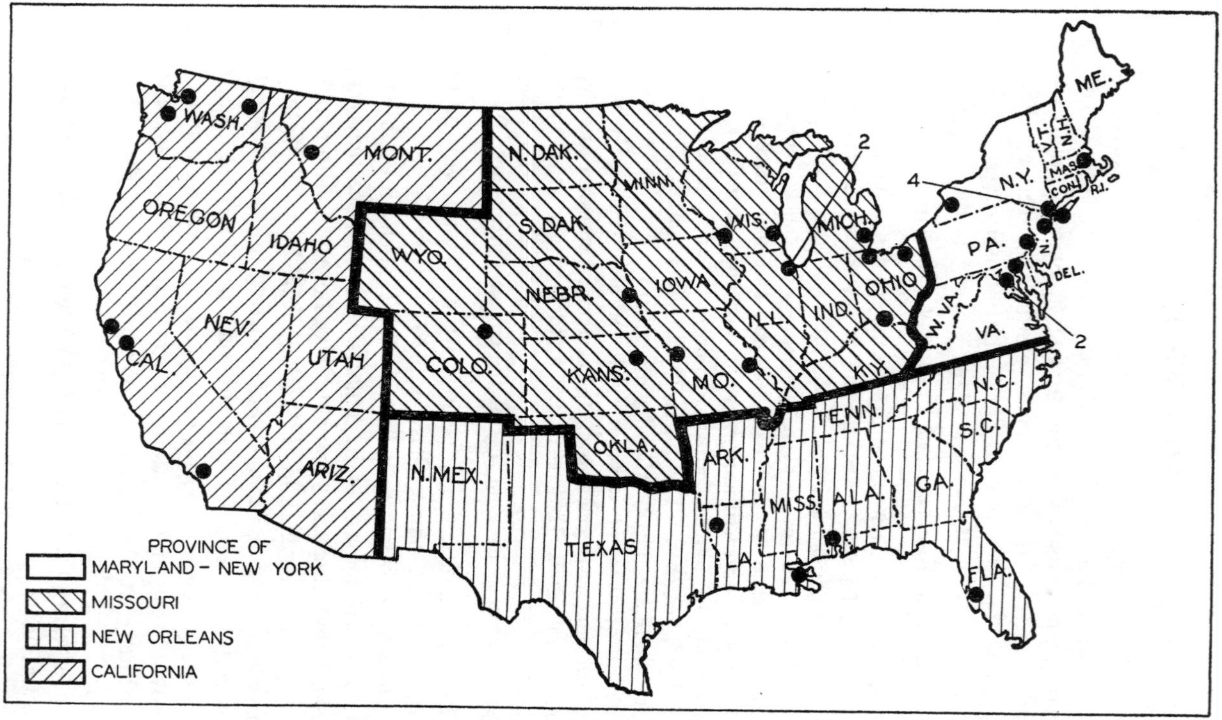

MAP VII. JESUIT HIGH SCHOOLS IN THE UNITED STATES, 1928

(Note: New England was formed into a separate province distinct from Maryland-New York in 1926; Chicago, northern Illinois, and the four states of Michigan, Ohio, Indiana, and Kentucky, were separated from the Missouri Province to form the new Province of Chicago in 1928.)

In 1853, the missions of California and Oregon were affiliated to the Province of Turin, in Italy, instead of to Missouri, in order to obtain a readier supply of teachers. The Jesuits had been banished from the kingdom of Sardinia in 1848, and the members of the Province of Turin were scattered in various countries. Five of the Turin Jesuits, already in the United States, reached California before the end of 1854, and four more came with Father Accolti from Europe the next year.[33] All of them had taught in the best schools of the Italian Jesuits in Europe; the first five had also been professors in American Jesuit institutions. Father Maraschi had been at Cincinnati, Messea at Louisville, Masnato at Georgetown, and Careddo and Congiato at Bardstown.[34] The last named had been rector of the college at Bardstown and, before his ordination, had been vice-rector of the Turin College of Nobles and the Swiss Jesuit College at Freiburg in Switzerland.[35] The next year, besides the four Italians, two Americans, Fathers Kenney and Howard, came from Maryland.[36]

The augmented staff at Santa Clara was undoubtedly unequaled in California at the time for scholarship, both literary and scientific. The number of pupils in 1855 was 114. There were fifteen professors, twelve priests, and three laymen.[37] The college continued to prosper; it was incorporated by the state in 1855.[38] In 1912, it became a university; in 1926, the University of Santa Clara High School, which up till the present had been on the university campus, was transferred to a new site halfway between Santa Clara and San José, formerly occupied by the Methodist College of the Pacific.[39]

St. Ignatius College, San Francisco

A nondescript school had been opened at Mission Dolores in San Francisco by Father Flavien, a Picpus Father, some time before 1852; there were some students there in 1852.[40] Later, Father Fontaine, a French Marist, had tried to carry on the school but with no success.[41] Father Veyret, whom Accolti had sent to Nobili's assistance in 1851, took over the school probably in 1854.[42] This attempt, however, was not successful.[43]

In 1854, Father Congiato arranged for the purchase of a site for a church and school in the city itself. The school was opened in October, 1855, with Mr. Haley, a layman, as its first teacher, although Father Maraschi was in general charge.

MAP VIII. CALIFORNIA PROVINCE OF THE SOCIETY OF JESUS, 1928*

U — University. C — College. H — High School. b — Boarding School. NJsj — Novitiate and Juniorate for Jesuits, undergraduate students. PHEsj — School of Philosophy and Education for Jesuits, graduate students.

This was the school of St. Ignatius, the predecessor of the present St. Ignatius College.[44] In 1859, the General of the Society recognized the school officially as a *collegium inchoatum;* the same year it was incorporated under the laws of the state, and empowered to give the usual academic degrees.[45] In 1861, the first catalogue appeared; its course of studies as outlined was much the same as in the Jesuit institutions in the

*Brophy College at Phoenix, Arizona, was opened in 1929.

East. This lists 144 pupils, of whom only 10 were above the grammar grades. Yet there were classes in Latin and Greek for these few.[46] Not until 1864 does St. Ignatius appear in the official catalogues of the Society as a complete college. In 1930, the official registration for St. Ignatius College was 780 for the high school, and 527 for the college department. Since 1930, St. Ignatius College assumed the title of the University of San Francisco.

Other Jesuit Schools in the West

A *collegium inchoatum* was opened at San José in 1886;[47] it was closed, however, at the end of the scholastic year 1895–96. In 1887, the Fathers of the Rocky Mountain Mission, also dependent like the California Mission on the Turin Province, opened a boarding school, Gonzaga College, at Spokane, Washington. Since 1912, it has been Gonzaga University.[48] Loyola College, Los Angeles, founded by the Vincentian Fathers in 1865, as St. Vincent's College, was taken over by the California Jesuits in 1911 under the new name. This year high-school classes were conducted and in 1914, the collegiate department was begun.[49] Seattle College High School, Seattle, Washington, was founded in 1892.

In September, 1929, Brophy College at Phoenix, Arizona, was opened with an enrollment of 72 high-school students. In the same year, Bellarmine College, Tacoma, was dedicated. There are moreover, two small high schools at Missoula, Montana, and Yakima, Washington, conducted by the Jesuits, assisted by teaching Sisters. At the present date (1930) the California Province of the Society controls seven high schools, besides the two just mentioned. Five of them are affiliated with colleges at the same location, also conducted by the Jesuits, namely, Los Angeles, Santa Clara, San Francisco, Spokane, and Seattle.[50]

The Colorado Mission and the College at Denver

Other Italian Jesuits came to America later to work in Colorado and New Mexico; these Fathers were members of

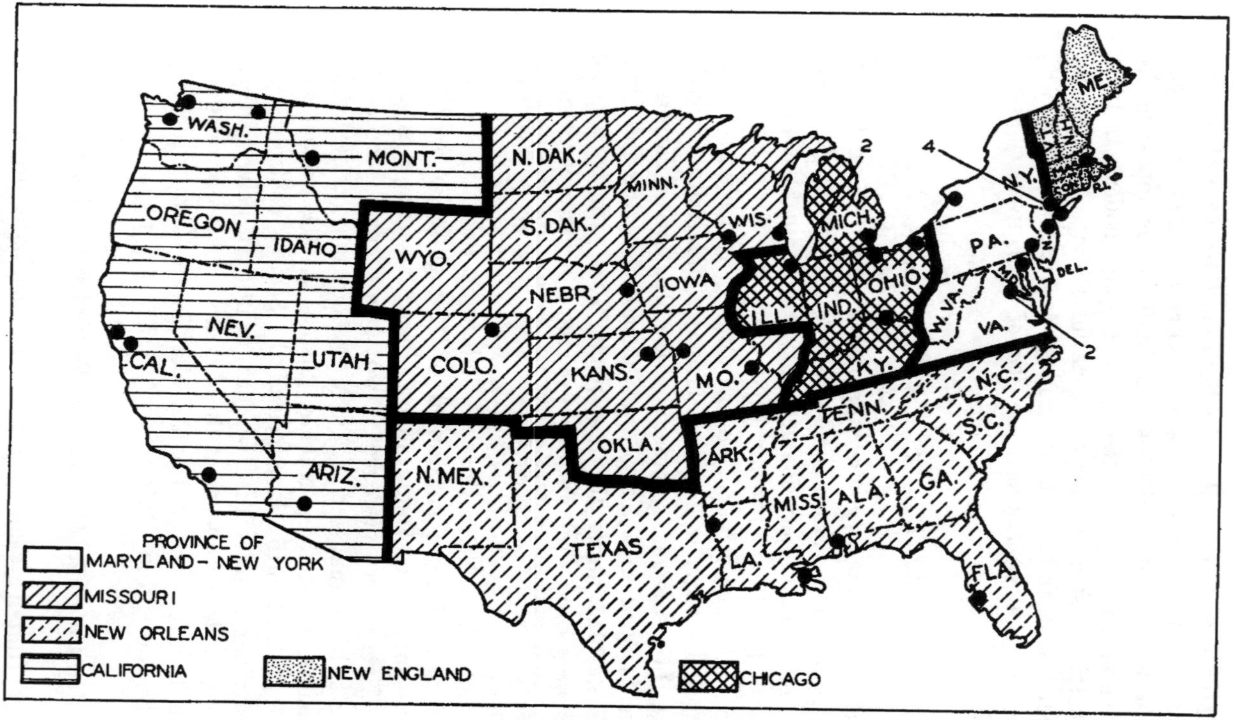

MAP IX. JESUIT HIGH SCHOOLS IN THE UNITED STATES, 1930

(Note.—In 1931, the states of Oregon, Washington, Idaho, and Montana were separated from the California Province to constitute the new Province of Oregon.)

the Province of Naples. A combination day and boarding college was opened, November 7, 1877, in Las Vegas, New Mexico, called at first St. Mary's College, but later changed to Las Vegas College.

"Only such matters will be taught as are deemed to meet the special requirements of our Territory," says the first prospectus, "and will be adapted to the capacity and gradual proficiency of pupils. Consequently, reading and writing, and elementary lessons in English and Spanish grammar, in history, geography, arithmetic, and bookkeeping will be part of the regular scholastic course. A few applications for the study of Latin having been already received, that language, together with French, Italian and music of piano or organ, will be left to the option of parents. . . ."[51]

In 1884, this same mission founded Sacred Heart College at Morrison, Colorado; in June, 1888, both Las Vegas College and the Morrison institution were merged in a new school at Denver, Colorado, called Sacred Heart College, a combination day and boarding college.[52] This remained under the control of the Province of Naples until 1919, when it was transferred to the Missouri Province and the name changed to Regis College. Its enrollment in 1930–31 was 160 high-school students and 220 college students, the majority of whom were day students.[53]

The German Jesuits and the Buffalo Mission

Jesuits of the German Province came to America in 1868 and the Buffalo Mission was founded in 1869, *Missio Germanica Americae Septentrionalis*.[54] Previous to their arrival, the New York Fathers had attempted a Latin school at Buffalo in 1856; but the enterprise was short-lived, only eight students attending and it was soon abandoned.[55] In September, 1870, the German Jesuits began a school with two classes, a Latin and a commercial class. The school was conducted in a private house; about 15 boys enrolled the first day, but this soon increased.[56] The school prospered; in 1872 the corner stone of the present Canisius High School was laid. In 1895–96 the Board of Regents of New York recognized both the high-school and college course of Canisius College. In 1907, the personnel and colleges of the Buffalo Mission were divided between the Maryland-New York and the Missouri Provinces. Canisius College came under the control of the Maryland-New York Province.[57] It ceased to be a boarding school, and in 1911 the college department was transferred to a new building at the corner of Main and Jefferson Streets, the high school continuing in the old site on Washington Street.[58]

The next venture of the German Jesuits was in Wisconsin. On September 5, 1880, they opened Sacred Heart College, Prairie du Chien, Wisconsin, in a building that had originally been a railway hotel, then a Methodist College, during the Civil War a hospital for wounded soldiers, and for a time (1871–1880) a Christian Brothers' College.[59] The Jesuits began with 50 boarders; three years later they had a six-year Latin course and four commercial classes.[60] In 1888, the college was discontinued and the buildings became a novitiate and juniorate for the German Jesuits in America. Lay students were readmitted in 1898.[61] During the first years that the Missouri Jesuits took charge of the school (1907), the Wisconsin college had its period of greatest prosperity. At this time the name was changed to Campion College. In 1925, the college department was discontinued and the institution became known as Campion Preparatory School.

Two other schools were founded by the German Jesuits: St. Ignatius College, Cleveland, Ohio, in 1886, now known as John Carroll University, with its preparatory school St. Ignatius High School; and in 1898, St. John's College, Toledo, Ohio.[62] Both of these schools, as well as Campion College, were transferred to the Missouri Province by the General of the Society in September, 1907.[63]

Summary

This ends the story of Jesuit educational activity in the United States;[64] it often had humble, and in colonial times, even furtive beginnings.

With the growth of the Catholic population in the United States, Jesuit schools have increased in numbers and attendance.[65] From 6 schools in 1840, the Jesuit secondary system has grown until now it includes 36 high schools.[66] Besides they control 13 universities, 13 colleges of liberal arts, and 6 juniorates where the undergraduate members of the Society receive their classical and normal training.[67] The high-school population in Jesuit schools has increased from a little over 3,000 in 1880 to 14,233 in 1930.[68] There has been a distinct trend in the past five years in the two larger provinces, Missouri and Maryland-New York, to limit the high-school attendance in favor of the college. The college population in the Maryland-New York institutions has trebled since 1910; in Missouri it has increased almost six times during the same period.[69]

That Jesuit high schools exert a potent influence in the Catholic educational system in the United States is evident from the fact that the boys in Jesuit high schools constitute nearly 20 per cent of all the boys in Catholic high schools in the United States. If the number of boys in Jesuit high schools is contrasted with the number of boys in Catholic schools of the same type, that is, private schools exclusively for boys, they make up nearly 30 per cent of the total.[70] As there are 230 schools of this type in the United States according to the census taken by the Bureau of Education of the National Catholic Welfare Conference, and as there are 36 Jesuit high schools, approximately 16 per cent of the total, the fact is not without interest. Of Catholic high schools and academies for boys with an enrollment of over 400, there are 18 Jesuit high schools out of a total of 43, approximately 41.9 per cent.[71]

The prestige of Jesuit schools among Catholics, the number of their students, the uniformity of curriculum and unity of government, the emphasis placed on the classics in their schools give the Jesuit educational system a unique place in Catholic education in America; and it is a phenomenon not without interest to the student of the history of education.

TABLE II. INCREASE IN STUDENTS IN JESUIT COLLEGES IN THE UNITED STATES FROM 1880 TO 1930 (*a*)

Year	College Students	High-School Students	Total
	Number of Students Attending American Jesuit Schools		
1880–81 (*b*)	866	3,118	3,984
1885–86 (*c*)	1,166	4,199	5,365
1890–91 (*d*)	1,196	4,309	5,506
1895–96 (*e*)	1,946	3,547	5,493
1900–01	1,920	3,550	5,487
1905–06	1,859	5,263	7,122
1910–11	2,298	7,440	9,738
1915–16	3,206	9,675	12,881
1920–21	5,091	13,041	18,132
1925–26	8,454	15,083	23,537
1930–31	13,545	14,233	27,778

(*a*) Data supplied by *Woodstock Letters* of the respective years. The first year that complete figures are given is 1878–79; the total is 4,104. On the estimate that 20 per cent are college students and 10 per cent of the remainder are preparatory students below high school, there would be 820 college students and 2,956 high-school students for that year, a total of 3,776.

(*b*) Total given in *Woodstock Letters* is 4,330. Twenty per cent of these are estimated to be college students; 10 per cent of the remainder preparatory students, that is, pre-high school.

(*c*) Estimated. The total is 5,831, no distinction being made between preparatory, high-school, and college students.

(*d*) Estimated. The total is 5,983.

(*e*) From this year, the *Woodstock Letters* separates college and high-school students. Preparatory students are listed separately and are not included in these totals.

TABLE III. ENROLLMENT IN JESUIT HIGH SCHOOLS IN THE FOUR AMERICAN PROVINCES FROM 1910 TO 1930

Year	Maryland-New York Province (*a*)	Missouri Province (*b*)	New Orleans Province	California Province (*c*)	Total
	Number of Students Attending American Jesuit High Schools				
1910–11	3,175	3,207	420	638	7,440
1911–12	3,184	3,160	462	771	7,577
1912–13	3,380	3,549	478	931	8,338
1913–14	3,567	3,715	462	982	8,726
1914–15	3,964	3,801	482	816	9,063
1915–16	4,364	3,973	500	838	9,675
1916–17	4,592	3,997	509	857	9,955
1917–18	4,746	4,162	502	919	10,329
1918–19	4,825	4,403	589	998	10,815
1919–20	4,986	5,150	622	1,234	11,992
1920–21	5,541	5,261	724	1,515	13,041
1921–22	6,525	5,599	822	1,645	14,591
1922–23	7,195	5,668	665	1,794	15,322
1923–24	6,908	5,538	718	1,916	15,080
1924–25	6,995	5,476	734	1,924	15,129
1925–26	6,891	5,387	814	1,991	15,083
1926–27	7,088	5,324	823	2,174	15,409
1927–28 (*d*)	6,034	4,699	911	1,972	13,616
1928–29	6,707	5,003	1,003	2,149	14,862
1929–30	6,699	4,929	993	2,231	14,852
1930–31	6,515	4,603	1,005	2,110	14,233

(*a*) Boston College High School is included here, although since 1927 it has been administered by the New England Province.

(*b*) Including Regis High School, Denver. After 1928, the following schools were administered by the new Chicago Province; namely, Loyola Academy, Chicago; St. Ignatius, Chicago; University of Detroit High School; St. John's, Toledo; St. Ignatius, Cleveland; and St. Xavier, Cincinnati. For comparative study, they are included here with the Missouri Province schools to which they belonged until 1928.

(*c*) Since 1930, Seattle High School, Gonzaga at Spokane, and Bellarmine High School at Tacoma have been under the jurisdiction of the new Vice-Province of the Rocky Mountain Region. Figures for these schools are included here, however, for the sake of comparative study.

(*d*) Figures for this year in the *Woodstock Letters* are incomplete. Consequently, an estimate from the preceding and subsequent years has been made.

TABLE IV. ENROLLMENT OF COLLEGE STUDENTS IN JESUIT INSTITUTIONS FOR THE FOUR AMERICAN PROVINCES FROM 1910 TO 1930

Number of Students Attending American Jesuit Colleges

Year	*Md.-N. Y. Province*	*Missouri Province* (*a*)	*New Orleans Province*	*California Province*	*Total in Colleges*	*Total in Colleges and High Schools*
1910–11	1,189	694	149	266	2,298	9,738
1911–12	1,358	689	209	261	2,517	10,094
1912–13	1,455	658	141	278	2,532	10,870
1913–14	1,662	687	130	318	2,797	11,523
1914–15	1,868	796	110	226	3,000	12,063
1915–16	1,998	853	136	219	3,206	12,881
1916–17	2,305	910	137	241	3,593	13,548
1917–18	2,248	964	154	185	3,551	13,880
1918–19	Figures not available; S.A.T.C. in some colleges					
1919–20	2,568	1,962	142	208	4,880	16,872
1920–21	2,851	1,822	210	208	5,091	18,132
1921–22	3,226	2,027	194	320	5,767	20,358
1922–23	3,498	1,998	165	405	6,066	21,388
1923–24	3,770	3,068	180	545	7,563	22,643
1924–25	4,885	3,226	179	568	8,858	23,987
1925–26	3,333	4,069	251	801	8,454	23,537
1926–27	5,341	4,436	346	822	10,945	26,354
1927–28 (*b*)	5,633	3,706	278	744	10,361	23,977
1928–29	7,764	4,204	241	912	13,121	27,983
1929–30	5,712	5,373	342	1,266	12,693	27,545
1930–31	5,852	6,201	334	1,158	13,545	27,778

(*a*) Including Regis College, Denver. As in the preceding table, in order to make a comparative study, no account has been made here of the administrative changes brought about by the establishment of the New England Province in 1927, the Chicago Province in 1928, or the Vice-Province of the Rocky Mountain Region in 1930.

(*b*) The statistics for this year are incomplete in the *Woodstock Letters*. Consequently, an estimate has been made. In fact, some of these statistics need careful interpretation as the editorial policy of this publication has not been consistent in presenting statistics. Some years, for example, extension students are obviously included in the list of college students by some of the colleges.

TABLE V. ENROLLMENT IN JESUIT HIGH SCHOOLS COMPARED WITH ENROLLMENT IN OTHER CATHOLIC HIGH SCHOOLS

Number of Boys in Catholic High Schools in the United States for the Year 1926

Total Enrollment All Schools (*a*)	*Enrollment in Jesuit Schools* (*b*)	*Percentage in Jesuit Schools*	*Enrollment in all Schools of Same Type as Jesuit* (*c*)	*Percentage in Jesuit Schools*
86,490	15,409	17.8	52,369	29.4

(*a*) Data taken from *N.C.W.C. Directory of Catholic Colleges and Schools for 1928.*

(*b*) See Table III.

(*c*) *N.C.W.C. Directory.* Figures include enrollment in all Catholic private schools, exclusively for boys.

TABLE VI. LIST OF JESUIT HIGH SCHOOLS IN THE UNITED STATES, 1930–31

Location	*Name of School*	*Year of Foundation*	*Year Jesuits in Charge*	*Province*
Baltimore	Loyola H. S.	1853	1853	Md.-N. Y.
Boston	Boston College H. S.	1864	1864	Md.-N. Y.
Brooklyn, N. Y.	Brooklyn Academy	1908	1908	Md.-N. Y.
Buffalo	Canisius H. S.	1870	1870	Md.-N. Y.
Chicago	Loyola Academy	1909	1909	Missouri
Chicago	St. Ignatius H. S.	1870	1870	Missouri
Cincinnati	St. Xavier H. S.	1831	1840	Missouri
Cleveland	St. Ignatius H. S.	1886	1886	Missouri
Denver	Regis High School (B)*	1888	1888	Missouri
Detroit	U. of Detroit H. S.	1877	1877	Missouri
Garrett Park, Md.	Georgetown Prep. (B)	1789	1805	Md.-N. Y.
Jersey City, N. J.	St. Peter's H. S.	1878	1878	Md.-N. Y.
Kansas City, Mo.	Rockhurst H. S.	1914	1914	Missouri
Los Angeles	Loyola H. S.	1865	1911	California
Milwaukee	Marquette U. H. S.	1881	1881	Missouri
New Orleans	Immaculate Conception H. S.	1847	1847	New Orleans
New York	Loyola School	1900	1900	Md.-N. Y.
New York	Regis High School	1914	1914	Md.-N. Y.
New York	St. John's College H. S.	1841	1846	Md.-N. Y.
New York	The Xavier H. S.	1847	1847	Md.-N. Y.
Omaha, Nebr.	Creighton H. S.	1878	1878	Missouri
Philadelphia	St. Joseph College H. S.	1851	1851	Md.-N. Y.
Phoenix, Ariz.	Brophy High School	1928	1928	California
Prairie du Chien, Wis.	Campion Preparatory (B)	1871	1880	Missouri
St. Louis, Mo.	St. Louis U. H. S.	1819	1828	Missouri
St. Mary's, Kansas	St. Mary's College H. S. (B)(*a*)	1869	1869	Missouri
San Francisco	St. Ignatius H. S.	1855	1855	California
Santa Clara, Cal.	Santa Clara U. H. S. (B)	1851	1851	California
Seattle, Wash.	Seattle College H. S.	1892	1892	California
Shreveport, La.	St. John's College H. S.	1908	1908	New Orleans
Spokane, Wash.	Gonzaga H. S. (B)	1887	1887	California
Spring Hill, Ala.	Spring Hill H. S. (B)	1830	1847	New Orleans
Tacoma, Wash.	Bellarmine H. S.	1912	1912	California
Tampa, Fla.	Sacred Heart College H. S.	1913	1913	New Orleans
Toledo, O.	St. John's H. S.	1898	1898	Missouri
Washington, D. C.	Gonzaga H. S.	1822	1822	Md.-N. Y.

(*a*) St. Mary's was closed in June, 1931.
*(B) Indicates a boarding school.

TABLE VII. AMERICAN JESUIT HIGH SCHOOLS NO LONGER IN EXISTENCE

Location	*Name*	*Founded*	*Discontinued*	*Province*
Newtown, Md.(?)	Newtown Manor School (?) I	1650(?)	?	Md.-Mission
Newtown, Md.(?)	Newtown Manor School (?)II	1677	1698(?)	Md.-Mission
New York	Jesuit School (?)	1685(?)	1690(?)	Md.-Mission
Bohemia, Md.	Bohemia Academy (?)	1745(?)	1760(?)	Md.-Mission
New York	N. Y. Literary Institution	1808	1813	Md.-Mission
Bardstown, Ky.	St. Joseph's College	1819(*a*)	1861	Missouri
Lebanon, Ky.	St. Mary's College	1821(*b*)	1846	French Jesuits
Frederick, Md.	St. John's Literary Institute	1829	1859	Md.-Mission
Conewago, Pa.	Conewago Latin School	1835(?)	1892(*c*)	Maryland
Grand Coteau, La.	St. Charles College	1838	1922	New Orleans
Worcester, Mass.	Holy Cross H. S.	1843	1914(*d*)	Md.-N. Y.
Louisville, Ky.	St. Ignatius Literary Inst.	1845	1846	French Jesuits
Louisville, Ky.	St. Aloysius Academy	1857	1859	Missouri
Baton Rouge, La.	College of SS. Peter and Paul	1849	1852	New Orleans
Galveston, Tex.	St. Mary's	1852(*e*)	1922	New Orleans
Milwaukee, Wis.	St. Aloysius Academy	1857	1859	Missouri
Milwaukee, Wis.	St. Gall's Academy	1864	1872	Missouri
Las Vegas, N. M.	Las Vegas College	1877	1888(*f*)	Italian Jesuits

Location	*Name*	*Founded*	*Discontinued*	*Province*
Morrison, Col.	Sacred Heart College	1884	1888(*f*)	Italian Jesuits
San Jose, Cal.	San Jose College	1886	1896	California
Augusta, Ga.	Sacred Heart College	1900	1917	New Orleans

(*a*) Jesuits in charge in 1848.
(*b*) Jesuits in charge in 1832.
(*c*) This was never a typical Jesuit school; Jesuits taught here at different times.
(*d*) The high-school department of Holy Cross was closed to make room for their increased college enrollment.
(*e*) Jesuits in charge in 1884.
(*f*) Both schools were merged with Sacred Heart (later Regis) College, Denver.

Footnotes

[1]*Jesuit Relations*, LXV, 103, 265, 271. See also, Biever, *The Jesuits in New Orleans and the Mississippi Valley*, pp. 17 ff.

[2]Shea, *History of the Catholic Church*, III, 675; Biever, *op. cit.*, pp. 73 ff. See also Kenney, *Catholic Culture in Alabama*, pp. 125 ff.

[3]*Woodstock Letters*, V, 17 ff.; XXIV, 24 ff.

[4]Shea, *op. cit.*, p. 675; *Woodstock Letters*, XXIV, 21.

[5]*Woodstock Letters*, V, 21.

[6]See *supra*, Chap. VI.

[7]*Woodstock Letters*, XXIV, 26.

[8]*Ibid.*, L, 468.

[9]*Spring Hill College*, p. 11; *Woodstock Letters*, XXVIII, 269; Shea, *op. cit.*, III, 697.

[10]*Woodstock Letters*, XXVIII, 270.

[11]*Spring Hill College*, p. 5; *Woodstock Letters*, XXVIII, 268–9.

[12]*Woodstock Letters*, *loc. cit.*

[13]*Spring Hill College*, p. 43; *Woodstock Letters*, XXVIII, 271.

[14]See *Woodstock Letters*, XXVII, 271–2.

[15]*Ibid.*, LX (Feb., 1931), supplement.

[16]*Catholic Almanac*, 1848–53; *Catalogus Provinciae Lugdunensis;* see also Biever, *The Jesuits in New Orleans and the Mississippi Valley*, p. 130.

[17]*Woodstock Letters*, VI, 90; Biever, *op. cit.*, pp. 170 ff.

[18]*Catholic Almanac;* Shea, *op. cit.*, IV, 272, Shea says the college did not open until January, 1850, but the Reverend Hippolyte Gache, the first superior at Baton Rouge, in an account of the college given in the *Woodstock Letters*, XXVII, 5, says that it opened in September, 1849.

[19]*Woodstock Letters*, XVI, 283.

[20]*Ibid.*, VI, 451.

[21]*Ibid.*, XXXIV, 381.

[22]Clinch, Bryan J., "The Jesuits in American California," *Records of the American Catholic Historical Society*, XVII, 64 ff.

[23]*Ibid.*, p. 65; *Woodstock Letters*, XX, 343 ff.; *Notizie Storiche et Descrittive delle Missioni della Provincia Torinese della Compagnia di Gesú nell'America del Nord*, p. 9. See also *Golden Jubilee of Santa Clara College and University of Santa Clara. A History from the Founding of Santa Clara Mission to the beginning of the University, 1912.*

[24]Original in *St. Ignatius College Archives*, San Francisco. See Clinch, *op. cit.*, pp. 126 ff.

[25]Original in Latin, preserved in *Santa Clara Mission Archives;* Clinch, *op. cit.*, p. 128.

[26]Alemany to Nobili, August 8, 1851, in *Santa Clara Archives;* Clinch, *op. cit.*, p. 138; *Woodstock Letters*, XX, 349.

[27]Clinch, *op. cit.*, pp. 132–3; *Woodstock Letters*, XX, 350.

[28]Clinch, *op. cit.*, p. 133; *Woodstock Letters*, XX, 352.

[29]Clinch, *op. cit.*, p. 136.

[30]See Clinch, *op. cit.*, p. 137; *Woodstock Letters*, XX, 352.

[31]*Golden Jubilee Santa Clara College*, p. 35.

[32]*Woodstock Letters*, XX, 352.

[33]*Notizie Storiche*, etc., p. 15.

[34]*Catalogus Maryland-New York and Missouri Province;* Clinch, *op. cit.*, p. 138; *Woodstock Letters*, XX, 353.

[35]*Notizie Storiche, loc. cit.*

[36]Clinch, *op. cit.*, p. 138.

[37]*Ibid.*, p. 139.

[38]*Ibid.; Woodstock Letters*, XX, p. 355.

[39]*University of Santa Clara Diamond Jubilee Volume*, p. 100.

[40]Riordan, Joseph W., *First Half Century of St. Ignatius Church and College*, p. 50.

[41]Clinch, *op. cit.*, p. 140.

[42]Riordan, *loc. cit.; Woodstock Letters*, XX, 252.

[43]Veyret to Nobili, Oct. 22, 1854, *Santa Clara Archives;* see Riordan, *loc. cit.*, and Clinch, *loc. cit.*

[44]*Woodstock Letters*, XX, 355; Clinch, *op. cit.*, p. 141; Riordan, *op. cit.*, p. 50.

[45]Riordan, *op. cit.*, p. 93; Clinch, *op. cit.*, p. 142; *Woodstock Letters, loc. cit.*

[46]Clinch, *loc. cit.*

[47]*Woodstock Letters*, XX, 362; Clinch, *op. cit.*, p. 321.

[48]*Gonzaga's Silver Jubilee: A Memoir*, pp. 77 ff.

[49]*Woodstock Letters*, XLI, 298; LI, 87.

[50]Since 1930, the Rocky Mountain Region has been cut off administratively from the California Province and is now constituted a Vice-Province. In 1931 it was definitely constituted a province, the Province of Oregon. Under its charge are the following secondary schools: Seattle High School; Bellarmine High School, Tacoma; Gonzaga University High School, Spokane. Jesuits of this Vice-Province also have administrative relations with the schools at Missoula and Yakima.

[51]*Prospectus of Las Vegas College*, 1877; *Woodstock Letters*, VII, 41 ff.

[52]*Catalogue of Sacred Heart College*, 1888; *Woodstock Letters*, XVII, 399.

[53]*Woodstock Letters*, LX (February, 1931), supplement.

[54]*Mittheilungen aus der Deutschen Provinz*, II Band, Nr. 16, 34.

[55]Devitt, *History of Maryland-New York Province*, MS. in *Georgetown Archives;* "Leaves from an Old Diary," *The Canisius Monthly*, Vol. III, No. 2. *Historia Domus*, MS. in Canisius College: "Collegium Canisianum . . . nunc inchoaturi sumus. September, 1870"; *Mittheilungen, loc. cit.*

[56]Devitt, *op. cit.*

[57]*Ibid.; Woodstock Letters*, XXXVII, 39.

[58]*Woodstock Letters*, LIV, 352.

[59]*Mittheilungen aus der Deutschen Provinz*, Nr. 30 (Ostern, 1907); *Woodstock Letters*, XIV, 192.

[60]*Woodstock Letters*, XIII, 13 ff.

[61]*Prospectus of Sacred Heart College, Prairie du Chien, Wis.* (1898).

[62]*Mittheilungen*, etc., Band III, Nr. 18; *Woodstock Letters*, XXXI, 254.

[63]*Woodstock Letters*, XXXVII, 39.

[64]The Mexican Jesuits had a college for Mexicans at Seguin, Texas, for a time (1878–79); but this has no place in a history of American Jesuit education (See *Woodstock Letters, VIII, supplement*). Neither has it been thought necessary to mention the two preparatory departments of St. Louis University, Gonzaga Hall and Loyola Hall, that were conducted separately for a time in St. Louis. These, together with the St. Louis University High School, constituted the preparatory department of the University. They represented a temporary expediency, resorted to because of lack of space. In Cleveland, too, a separate high school, Loyola Academy, was maintained for over a decade. Its doors were closed and the students transferred to St. Ignatius High School in 1922.

[65]See Maps IV, p. 106, and VI, p. 110 and Tables II, p. 122, III, p. 122, IV, p. 123, VI, p. 124.

[66]See Map VII, p. 114.

[67]See Maps II, p. 76, III, p. 99, V, p. 109, VIII, p. 116.

[68]See Table II, p. 122.

[69]See Tables III and V, p. 123.

[70]See Table IV, p. 123.

[71]*N.C.W.C., Directory of Catholic Colleges and Schools*, 1928.

PART III

THE MODERN AMERICAN JESUIT HIGH SCHOOL

CHAPTER VIII

THE EVOLUTION OF THE AMERICAN JESUIT HIGH SCHOOL

A THOROUGHLY interesting phenomenon is the change brought about in a social institution like the school through the influence of environment. The springing up of Jesuit schools on American soil during the nineteenth century is an instance in point. Here was an institution, definitely continental in origin, tradition, and spirit; the founders, with the exception of the Marylanders, were all European. The French in New Orleans and New York, the Belgians in Missouri, the Italians in the Far West, the Germans in Buffalo brought with them the gymnasium type of education. Even Georgetown, with its English tradition from St. Omer's, Liège, and Stonyhurst, conformed to the general pattern. All had common factors, namely, the definite Jesuit spirit, the Jesuit system of pedagogy, and, most of all, the Jesuit organization. Moreover, there were close relations among these different provinces of the Society in America, independent though they were in administration; they borrowed freely from one another ideals, theories, and practical procedures adapted to American needs. Not infrequently men were loaned from one well-established college to a newly founded institution. As a consequence, despite the divergence of nationality in the various provinces, there was uniformity to a high degree. This was, of course, further secured by the relations of the different colleges with the General of the Order.

Two currents were at work during the nineteenth century shaping American Jesuit secondary education; now one predominated, now the other. These two forces were, first, the influence of the American *milieu* — social, educational, economic; secondly, the directive force that came from the head of the Order in Europe, a force constantly striving for the casting of the Jesuit type of education everywhere into a common mold, a force, too, that kept alive the common traditions of the Society in all the provinces. It is this latter factor that will be considered first in the present chapter.

The Influence of Jesuit Theory and Practice

In the period that elapsed between the suppression of the Society in 1773 and its restoration in 1814, momentous changes had taken place in the world. Various factors of tremendous import were at work; it would be too much to expect that even so conservative a body as the Jesuit Order could remain uninfluenced by these movements. True, the members of the Order were loyal to the traditions and spirit of the Old Society; they still regarded the *Ratio* as an educational Magna Charta. It had been successful in the past; they saw no reason why it should not prove equally successful in the future.

This much must be granted to the Order: they wanted efficient schools. It would be incorrect to imagine that they clung tenaciously to the *Ratio Studiorum* merely out of reverence for the past or because of an obscurantist theory of education. In all sincerity, they thought that the *Ratio,* or an adaptation of the *Ratio* suited to modern needs, was the best instrument at hand to revive their seventeenth-century educational triumphs.

Roothaan's Revision of the Ratio in 1832

Shortly after the restored Society resumed its educational activity the question of a revision of the *Ratio* to meet modern requirements was proposed in the 20th General Congregation in 1820.[1] The General, Father Aloysius Fortis, was instructed to choose competent men for this revision. The work begun in 1821 was not finished until Roothaan's time. In 1832, the revised *Ratio* was published.[2]

Before this revision appeared, tentative *schemata* had been drawn up by provincial committees, their findings collated and submitted again to the provinces for their approval. Pachtler has gathered together the comments of the German Provinces.[3]

Entire liberty of criticism was permitted and throughout all, while there is an earnest desire manifested to retain the good points of the old *Ratio,* there is no less earnest insistence on allotting a larger place to the vernacular, to mathematics, and to history.[4]

In presenting this revised *Ratio* to the Society, Father Roothaan desired that it be adopted by all the colleges; yet it was by no means his intention to close the door to further revision. In the circular letter that accompanied the *Ratio,* he said:

> It remains, then, to put to the test zealously and diligently the plan which I am offering you. For although some provisions are only temporary, until, tested by experience, it is discovered what must be changed, what added, what dropped completely; nevertheless, if it be only half-heartedly put into practice because it is not yet entirely defined and established, we will never be able to form a sure judgment of its success.[5]

The *Ratio* of 1832 never had the force of law in the Society as it was never approved by a General Congregation.[6]

The criticism of Roothaan's *Ratio* is that it attempted too much and too little; too much, insofar as it was quite impossible in the changing conditions of modern society to devise a pedagogical program equally suited to German, French, Italian, Spanish, English, and American schools; too little, in that it did not take into sufficient account modern demands for change in the curriculum. True, there is provision made for the vernacular, for history, mathematics, and geography in the lower schools; but they are entirely subsidiary to Latin.

All in all, this *Ratio* of 1832 was not an unqualified success.[7] The growing demand for *realien,* and the contempt into which Latin and Greek studies had fallen were probably responsible for this. Yet, it did attach the Jesuits of the restored Society rather definitely to the classical tradition. It emphasized anew the Jesuit system of administration with its centralization of authority. But beyond that it never went; it is doubtful if Roothaan's *Ratio* was introduced anywhere in its entirety;[8] certainly, the strenuous Latin curriculum — four hours daily[9] — was never attempted in America, at least.

Attempts at Further Revision

Enrico Vasco, an Italian Jesuit, made the most notable attempt in the nineteenth century at a further adaptation or modernization of the *Ratio*. Vasco was a man of wide experience both as master and administrator in various Italian colleges.[10] In 1848, he drew up a plan for reorganization of the curriculum in Jesuit secondary schools. The General, Father Roothaan, heartily approved this plan and submitted it to experienced professors in the different colleges. Vasco was asked to draw up his proposals more in detail. Before a distinguished Jesuit gathering in Rome, he delivered an address "*De ephebis recte instituendis*"[11] in which he outlined his plan of reorganization. Almost all his hearers approved emendations of the *Ratio*. Some, however, feared that the introduction of so many branches would interfere with solidity of training; but others were convinced that the adoption of this plan was the only way to remove modern complaints against the Jesuit method of teaching.[12]

In 1851, Vasco's reorganization of the *Ratio* was printed for private circulation in four volumes under the formidable title: *Il Ratio Studiorum adattato ai tempi presenti, ossia esposizione ragionata di alcune modificazioni che salva la sostanza del Ratio Studiorum potrebbero introdursi etc., dal P. Enrico Vasco, S.J.*, (Roma, 1851), 4 vols.

The work is in many respects astonishingly modern in method and content. He seems to have anticipated the need of dividing education along the modern American line of junior high school, senior high school, and junior college, although, of course, his terminology is quite dissimilar. Step by step he builds up his curriculum and the reasons therefor; evidently he expected opposition and left no stone unturned to make his position unassailable.

His proposed course consisted of four stages. He began with a preliminary course, *anno preliminare*. Here two hours daily are given to the vernacular; *Squarci d'autore facili ed ameni.* This class is to serve as a preparation to the study of the classics, ancient and modern. Besides the class in Italian, instruction was to be given in history, religion, and what the author calls *Erudizione Infantile,* comprising arithmetic, zoölogy, botany, mineralogy, physical, and political geography. The purpose is to give "*un idea generale del mundo.*" The resemblance to the objective set forth in many modern programs is obvious.

The next stage Vasco called *Primo Stadio ossia quadriennio di letteratura inferiore.* This was to last two, three, or four years according to the individual's capacity. Two hours each morning were to be given to languages — Italian, Latin, and Greek. One hour was assigned for an outline course in history, including considerable geographic detail. In the afternoon, another hour and a half was spent on languages; one hour was set aside for *Erudizione Civile,* that is, arithmetic, geography, fundamental notions of botany, zoölogy, cosmography, and the like. Once a week there was to be a class in oral and written expression.

The third stage is the *triennio di letteratura superiore.* Two hours daily were devoted to the study of classical eloquence, including composition in those languages. One hour was spent on *eloquenza nazzionale,* comprising a course in the art of oratorical composition. The national classics were used as models. Along with this there was to be a course in the history of Italian literature. Instruction was also given in history, mathematics, elementary physics, and religion. The fourth stage is a two-year course in philosophy and science. This need not concern us as it belongs above the secondary level.[13]

While Vasco's ideal *ginnasio* remained strongly classical, yet enormous concessions were made to the modern side. Nevertheless, despite the revolutionary character of this curriculum, Vasco's work was highly praised by the General.[14] Indeed, Father Roothaan was very eager to have Vasco try out his plan in its entirety in some college and advised him to select some school in the Province of Venice as an experimental station. But the local head of this province was timorous; he felt that the responsibility was too great for "*tam gravem ac multiplicem innovationem.*" Therefore, he urged the postponement of the project to a more favorable time. All Vasco's efforts were unable to move the Provincial from this position. Accordingly Vasco abandoned the whole undertaking, apparently in disgust.[15]

It is difficult to say whether Vasco's book influenced Jesuit educational procedure in succeeding years. Certainly it was read by Jesuits everywhere with interest. A ferment was surely at work; whether it was due to *Il Ratio Adattato* or whether this itself is a resultant of the same forces, it is quite impossible to say. It seems certain that Roothaan's *Ratio* was being modified in practice in European Jesuit schools. Thus, Creti-neau-Joly[16] cites the example of the College of Brugelette in Belgium where curricular innovations had been made even before Vasco's time. There was a *cours préparatoire*, comprising the elements of French, history, geography, and arithmetic, together with the rudiments of Latin. The second course, a *cours des lettres,* corresponds more closely to the modern high-school course, with Latin, Greek, and French grammar, arithmetic, elements of algebra and geometry, history, and geography.

Ebner[17] gives the *programme scolaire* for the Collège de St. Michel at Freiburg in Switzerland. Here a set course in French was prescribed for all the gymnasium classes, consisting of grammar, composition, reading, and explanation of authors. There were also courses in history, geography, and mathematics. Algebra was begun in the fourth class and continued in the fifth and sixth, together with the elements of geometry.

Stonyhurst College in England affiliated as early as 1838 with the University of London and candidates were presented for matriculation. "From the first there was a zealous movement in the direction of science . . . for of the first matriculators, three took honors in zoölogy and one in chemistry."[18] Later, in 1895, Stonyhurst abandoned the affiliation and adopted in its place the Oxford and Cambridge higher certificate. In this "Stonyhurst is returning to her ideals," say the writers cited above. "The fifty-five years of her affiliation with London were productive, no doubt, of great good but it was obtained by the sacrifice of much that was characteristic of the traditional Jesuit training."[19]

American Deviation from Literal Interpretation of Ratio

In the chapter on "The High-School Curriculum," it will be seen that in America, too, from the very beginning there was considerable deviation from the letter of Roothaan's *Ratio*. Indeed, it may be safely said, though it would be difficult to prove from existing documents, that two distinct schools of educational thought have been at work in the restored Society; one striving for a literal interpretation of the *Ratio* and an acceptation of all its prescriptions; another, more liberal, that would disregard the letter and keep the spirit. This was true both in America and in Europe.

Father R. Bakewell Morrison of the Missouri Province presents the latter point of view in the *Province News Letter*.[20]

> The *Ratio* has always exercised a more or less elastic control of the matter used in Jesuit schools. It is a principle laid down by St. Ignatius himself in Const. IV, c. vii, No. 2: "In particularibus multum varietatis esse oportebit pro varietate locorum et personarum. . . ." And so the *Ratio* was understood up to the time of the suppression. It was a guide but not an absolute dictator. . . . The practice of the restored Society is then quite in keeping with the traditions of the past when it yields to time and widens its curriculum.

Official Approval for Adaptation of Ratio

That this is the official teaching of the Society today is evident from an address made by the General of the Society, Father Louis Martin, in 1893, to the scholastics at Exaaten in Holland. On that occasion he called attention to the fact that those who find fault with the *Ratio* do not really understand the document; they look only at the content, not at the spirit that animates it. "As to content," he says, "we are not free at the present day. That is prescribed for us [by government programs, etc.], and if we should try to retain the same content as before, we could close the doors of our colleges. Nevertheless, we are still free in the spirit and method of teaching."[21]

In the Twenty-fifth General Congregation, held in 1906, the

question of a new revision of the *Ratio* came up for discussion. Some provinces were in favor of this, but the Congregation decided that this was not opportune in the present age with so much diversity of school legislation and practice. The Congregation, however, strongly recommended the study of Jesuit pedagogy, as outlined in the fourth part of the Constitutions, in the *Ratio*, and in the writings of members of the Order. The different provinces were told to draw up their own courses of studies, care being taken to provide a thorough training, not only in knowledge, but in piety.[22] Here was definite and official recognition by the highest authority in the Society that Roothaan's *Ratio* as a program of studies, at least, was impracticable in the modern age.

Influences Shaping Jesuit Educational Policy in America

The changes that took place in Jesuit educational procedure in Europe during the nineteenth century were not without their reverberations in America. For long, there was no essential difference between the Jesuit secondary school in Europe and that in America, save the accidental divergence that followed upon a change of *milieu*. Naturally, a rigorous classical program, such as the Jesuit system demanded, could hardly be introduced in its entirety in a frontier community, like St. Louis in the early 30's, or among the pioneer Kentucky farmers.

The American Jesuit college was, at the beginning, as has been said, purely a secondary school. What the Jesuit pioneers had done was to transfer the continental *gymnasium* or *lycée* to the American scene. But they discovered that there were no institutions quite corresponding to the gymnasium in the United States. Already education was tripartite here — elementary, secondary, and collegiate. There was emerging from the Latin grammar schools and the academies a new type of school[23] complete in itself, of four years' duration, "a unique feature of our American educational system, having for the most part no counterpart in the educational system of countries other than our own"[24] — the modern American high school.

Where did the Jesuit six-year course belong? They felt, and probably with considerable justice, that this six-year course was much superior to the ordinary four-year high school; yet the Jesuit course did not include enough work of collegiate grade to warrant their assuming the title of college. Consequently, a course in scholastic philosophy was added to the classical curriculum, and thus the American Jesuit college came into being. This was the universal practice of Jesuit schools throughout the country; in some places, the upper classes were lopped off, and the Jesuit school remained only an academy.

The development of one Jesuit high school is told by the Rev. Gilbert J. Garraghan in *The Dauphin*:[25]

> From 1829 to 1887, the undergraduate instruction (at St. Louis) was of six years' duration, with no hard-and-fast line drawn between secondary and collegiate instruction. Beginning with 1858, the classes in the classical course bore the names Philosophy, Rhetoric, Poetry, First Humanities, Second Humanities, Third Humanities. At a later period, the three last were designated, First Academic, Second Academic, Third Academic. High-school education was the business of the classes named Humanities or Academic. St. Louis University High School was, consequently, during all these years (1829–1887), functioning as a school of secondary education, though not standing apart in administration and certain other respects from the department of Arts and Sciences. In 1887–88, the Academics (the first three classes of the classical course) are grouped together in the college catalogue as the Academic Department.
>
> Gradually the St. Louis University High School adjusted itself in every detail to the now fully established conception of the high school in the United States as an educational unit, standing on its own feet, imparting a type of education complete within its own limits, and equipped with its own administrative officers, teaching-staff, and buildings. In 1901, the Academic Department changed its name to the St. Louis Academy and was given a special section in the general catalogue of the University, which section a few years later began to be issued separately from the other catalogues of the institution. Beginning with the session 1903–4, instruction in the Academy was lengthened to a four-year period by the addition of a class called Humanities; and with the season 1908–9, it was still further standardized by the adoption of the eighth-grade entrance requirement.

This was typical of what took place in Jesuit institutions throughout the United States, although the western schools generally, under the leadership of St. Louis, have perhaps been more ready to conform to the general pattern of the American public high school and have been less tenacious of the letter of the *Ratio* than the Maryland-New York group.

At the end of the scale, then, there is a European gymnasium turned into an American college by the addition of a year of scholastic philosophy together with courses in physics and chemistry. There was little or no distinction in either administration or teaching technique between the secondary and collegiate classes. Today, everywhere in America, the Jesuit high school is distinct in administration and teaching personnel from the Jesuit college,[26] conforming in nearly all particulars to the conventional American high school, and yet retaining at the same time the distinctive *ethos,* common to Jesuit schools the world over.

What has brought about this change? First of all, there was a period when the American Jesuit school went its own way, quite undisturbed by the educational world outside. Social conditions in part explain this. The Catholic population, particularly in the West, were for the most part immigrants or children of immigrants. Comparatively few went into the professions. Very seldom did they pursue their education in secular institutions. Students of Jesuit schools rarely transferred to other colleges. As a consequence, standards and methods of American secular schools had little direct influence in Jesuit circles. Jesuit and secular education flowed in parallel grooves; the Jesuit institution was an institution complete in itself, providing the Catholic boy from ten to eighteen with his entire educational equipment.

The Parochial School

The first factor that brought about change came from the Catholic body itself. In the beginning, the American Jesuits had been forced, much against their will, to conduct preparatory classes, below the high-school level. In many places there were no Catholic elementary schools, and where they did exist they rarely went beyond the sixth grade. Consequently, the Jesuits had to admit rather small boys, nine and ten years of age, into their academies, and give them a year or more of preparation before commencing the high-school or academic course.

But with the development of the parochial-school system, especially after the 90's,[27] the pastors were resentful when the Jesuits took the best boys from their seventh and eighth grades, believing that this practice tended to weaken their parish schools. Eventually, the Jesuits demanded the completion of the eighth grade as a requisite for entering their schools. This, of course, made the preparatory classes unnecessary, although in schools of the type of Loyola School, New York City, and Georgetown Preparatory School a junior division is still maintained. By 1910, the Jesuit high school had become, throughout the United States, an institution distinct from the Jesuit college, comprising a four-year course, and requiring completion of eighth grade for entrance.

Contact with Secular Colleges

With the raising of the social status of the Catholic population through increasing prosperity, more and more Catholics began entering the professions. Many of them matriculated in secular institutions. Difficulties arose when students from Jesuit schools presented their credits. The Jesuit institution did not show a clear demarcation between secondary and collegiate instruction; there seemed a preponderance of classics in their courses; the technical terminology employed was quite different from that of outside institutions.

At first, the Jesuits felt that an injustice was being done to their schools. They believed that the Jesuit instructors, by reason of their long and severe training, were better equipped for their work than the average public high-school teacher, whose preparation was, at this period, admittedly inadequate. They were willing to have their students meet any tests that students in other institutions had to undergo.

Relations with Educational Associations

Accordingly, the Jesuits determined to find out just what outside institutions wanted. The first recorded mention of Jesuit contact with outside educational associations occurred in the West in 1878. The Reverend F. H. Votel tells in the *Woodstock Letters*[28] of the participation of several members of the St. Xavier College faculty of Cincinnati in the meetings of the Ohio College Association in December, 1877. Five Jesuits attended the meeting; one of them read a paper on the "Jesuit System of Teaching the Classics." An excellent impression, it would seem, was made on both sides by this *rapprochement.*

> It was a great pleasure, writes Fr. Votel, to those of Ours who took part in these proceedings to meet so many teachers who are at one with us in the importance to be attached to classical training. It is an encouragement to us all to aim still higher in our collegiate labors, to know that our work is appreciated by those who are most capable of understanding it.

At the meeting of the College Association of the Middle States and Maryland, held at Princeton, in 1890, Jesuit schools were represented. Father Thomas Hughes, the author of *Loyola and the Educational System of the Jesuits,* read a paper. His comments on this meeting are not without interest.

> The impression left on the mind seems to be that such occasions as this offer a compendious means for understanding the modern mind . . . for knowing and being known. To hear these experienced men explain themselves *viva voce* is a very different thing from reading their lucubrations in reviews and books.[29]

A significant controversy arose in 1896 between the authorities at Georgetown and the New York Board of Regents.[30] Columbia refused to accept a Georgetown student who had finished his academic course; the Columbia authorities insisted on two years of college as well. The Reverend J. Havens Richards, the president of Georgetown, protested, maintaining that "the far more thorough and careful methods of our institution, and the amount of time devoted to each branch taught by us"[31] more than compensates for the smaller number of branches taught in the Jesuit school. The Regents sent inspectors to Fordham and to St. Francis Xavier, New York, to visit classes and evaluate the course of studies with a view of coming to a satisfactory basis for registration of Jesuit schools. The inspectors were very much impressed by what they saw. Mr. Parsons wrote as follows to Father Richards, November 4, 1895:

> The verbal statement made to me up to date [by the inspectors relative to the work at the two New York schools] is certainly creditable to the highest degree.[32]

On November 7, the final report came from Mr. Parsons, granting freshman college standing to all students who completed four years in the preparatory department of Georgetown or affiliated schools.[33]

President Richards, in his account of the affair, has some interesting comments.[34]

> The importance of the controversy is probably much greater than may at first sight appear. It points to the rapid growth of conditions altogether different from those under which our colleges have thus far existed. Hitherto, education has been entirely free, and the value of a diploma has been measured only by the public appreciation, or want of appreciation, of the merits of the institution conferring it.
>
> But this state of affairs is apparently about to change. . . . A government control of education, stringent and effective, even if indirect, is probably the program of the near future throughout the greater part of our country. . . . From all this the practical inference is plain that we must be on the alert to adjust our colleges to the altered circumstances of the times. We must be prepared to modify our schedules . . . in the various years of the academic and collegiate courses, when necessary, in order to conform to the government [*sic*] requirements. Where no such requirements exist, it may still be advisable to make such modifications, in order to place ourselves in such a position with regard to non-Catholic institutions of learning, that our work may be readily compared and measured with theirs. . . .
>
> Another duty incumbent upon us in view of the changing conditions of the educational world undoubtedly is to keep ourselves fully informed as to movements in that world outside the Society. The meetings and discussions of public and private educators, which are so

frequent at the present day, lead to the modification of programs and requirements, and with these we must be familiar, if we would preserve the place in the educational world belonging of right to the Society.

Finally we must be taught by our present experience that a firm and intelligent adherence to the methods of our own *Ratio Studiorum* will bring us success and triumph, however we may be compelled to change or modify the matter to which those methods are, according to the varying circumstances of time and place, to be applied.

Need of Adaptation to American Needs Realized

At the meeting of the provincial, rectors, and prefects of studies of the Maryland-New York Province, held at Woodstock shortly after,

> . . . one of the first points taken up was Entrance Requirements, and the adaptation of our course to the demands of the country. . . . A committee was appointed to investigate the entrance requirements of non-Catholic colleges throughout the United States, and the subjects, authors, and the amount of matter taught in the various high schools. . . . A committee of five was appointed by Father Provincial to be a standing committee on studies. . . . This committee will meet four times a year.[35]

In the West, the Missouri Province had, as early as 1887, a central committee of studies for the whole province, and a local committee for each college, in an effort to formulate a uniform curriculum adapted to the needs of this section of the country.[36]

The period from 1895 to 1905 was a time of storm and stress for the Jesuit colleges of the country. Their college registration actually decreased during this decade.[37] The high-school enrollment had begun to fall off somewhat earlier about 1890, but in the early nineteen hundreds it was on the rise.[38] This decrease cannot be attributed entirely to economic reasons. A contributing factor in the decreased registration in the Jesuit high schools was, of course, the dropping of preparatory classes. It is probable, however, that the principal reason for the falling off in attendance during these years was that the opposition of the more conservative element in the Order prevented a complete realization of the adaptation needed to meet the momentous changes taking place in American education.

The *Report of the Committee of Ten,* in 1893, is an important document in American educational history. A searching investigation was made into educational values that had been long held sacrosanct. An effort was made to establish standards for appreciating the worth of the various subjects in the secondary-school program.[39] About this time, too, the standardizing agencies became increasingly active, particularly in the Middle West. This restatement of educational values and the pressure brought to bear by standardizing agencies were not immediately felt in the Order. Indeed, there were some who thought that they should be ignored.

> It used to be supposed by some . . . that we could and should adopt the policy of calmly ignoring circumstances and conditions in the outside world; says the author of *Report on Educational Policy,*[40] an apologia for the rather definite program of adaptation to the times, formally undertaken by the Missouri Province. We were to set up and follow out definitely our own standards of education, not considering whether they fitted in or not with accepted standards in secular schools. Father Burrowes [Provincial of the Missouri Province from 1913 to 1919] and others have all along vigorously opposed this suicidal policy. Were Catholics in this country many times more influential than they are, they might succeed in enforcing educational standards different from those actually in vogue. In all that pertains to the fixing of educational standards whether by legal enactment or public opinion, the determining voice is that of the non-Catholic elements of the country. It is the part of wisdom to recognize the fact and be guided accordingly. As Father Burrowes phrases it, "if we cannot set the standard, we shall have to follow it."

By 1910, it may be maintained that the Jesuits generally throughout the United States came to see the need of regarding the high school and college as altogether distinct units in the general educational scheme. The idea of high school and college being conducted in the same building and under the same administration, an almost universal practice in the American Jesuit colleges up to this date, was seen not only to be utterly at variance with the general educational practice of the country, but it no longer commended itself to Jesuits generally as a desirable arrangement. Of course, the separation was not introduced immediately everywhere, nor was it introduced without protest by those who wished to retain the gymnasium type of school. At a somewhat later period, the custom was introduced of granting diplomas to high-school graduates and the holding out to students such diplomas as something "worth working for and working for hard."[41]

Relations with Standardizing Agencies

The final stage in the evolution of the American Jesuit high school was really brought about largely through standardizing agencies, such as the North Central Association of Colleges and Secondary Schools. Before 1917, some high schools here and there had applied for recognition to these associations; but no general policy was accepted by all. Some thought it meant the abandonment of Jesuit pedagogical principles. However, in 1917, at a meeting of the rectors of the Missouri Province, all high schools of that province were directed to apply for a place on the accredited list of the North Central Association and for membership in that association.[42]

A fairly conservative point of view with regard to this change is represented in the following extract from an article appearing in *The Teacher's Review*, a Jesuit publication, in 1910:[43]

> . . . We are simply recording a fact, one indeed that has had its influence on our province and American Jesuits in general in spite of an extremely conservative policy. This influence is seen in the way we yielded to some of the requirements of the times. We have given to our Grammatica Suprema, Media, and Infima, an end and unit of their own, we have, in a measure, shaped our high-school studies so as to form of them a complete, independent whole. We have given to our high schools, as far as circumstances have allowed, an existence separate and distinct from the colleges to which they are attached. We issue for them their own prospectuses, we draw up for them their own course of studies, we assign to them their own faculties, we have adopted for our classes the names of those in use about us, we bestow on those who have successfully completed the four years of high-school study a diploma which has the same value as the Regents'

certificate or the diploma of the secular high schools. We have put ourselves under the Regents of the State of New York and we hold ourselves ready at any moment to submit to their inspection . . . both as to the manner and matter of our instruction.

Of course, this departure from traditional methods has not failed to awaken criticism. Those steps which have been taken to bring our high schools into conformity with the other high schools of the country were at the time regarded at least by some, with disfavor, and are still regarded with regret. . . . Still those [who have favored the movement] are to be congratulated for having made possible its practical fulfillment and for having made the new world run so smoothly, for they have given to our high schools an efficiency that has not only passed muster when submitted to the expert official inspection of the State's Board of Regents, but has won their public commendation.

Summary

Various factors were at work during the nineteenth century shaping the Jesuit educational policy in the United States. There was the clearly discernible Jesuit tradition, handed on from one generation to another, conservative for the most part, making for a common pattern in America and in Europe; there was the directive force that came from the General of the Order, that made, too, for conservatism and uniformity. On the other hand, there were factors at work on the American scene itself; namely, the spirit of democracy and the spirit of practicality that did not view the classical tradition with too kindly an eye. Most of all, there was the ever-growing force that came from the current of modern educational thought, manifested for the most part in voluntary associations that had almost the power of governmental bureaus, a manifestation of the American passion for standardization. By 1910 — or soon after — throughout the United States, the Jesuit high school emerged as a distinct entity, separate from the college in administration, and instructional staff for the most part, differing very little in curriculum from the classical course of the public high school, and yet retaining the characteristic Jesuit spirit in its objective and in its method.

Footnotes

[1]Pachtler, *op. cit.*, IV, 355; Duhr, *op. cit.*, pp. 21 ff.; *Liber Saecularis Historiae Societatis Jesu*, pp. 322–3.

[2]Pachtler, *op. cit.*, IV, 357 ff.; Duhr, *loc. cit.; Liber Saecularis*, pp. 327.

[3]Pachtler, *op. cit.*

[4]The comment of Godinot, the Swiss vice-provincial, is typical. "Gentilium nostrorum, tum Helveticorum et Germanorum, tum Belgarum ingenium postulat: 1o, ut in Inferioribus [scholis] juventus non solum latinis et graecis litteris pari fere passu, sed speciatim vernacula litteratura, eloquentia et arte declamatoria informetur. 2o, Ut sedulo exerceatur in Mathesi, praecipue prout haec commercio et communis vitae negotiis et publicis utilitatibus et usibus subservit. 3o, Ut accedat historiae tum sacrae tum profanae, tum universalis et particularis, patriae praesertim, una cum Geographia ac Chronologia, per omnes classes distributae traditio" Pachtler, *op. cit.*, IV, 259–60.

[5]"Reliquum nunc est RR. PP., ut quae hic parata vobis offerimus, studiose ac diligenter in opus deducantur. Licet enim quaedam in his nunc quidem nonnisi temporaria sint, donec ipso usu atque experientia duce quid fortasse immutandum, quid adjugendum, quid tollendum sit, appareat; si tamen, quod nondum definita penitus ac stabilita sint, ideo segnius in actum deducerentur, nunquam posset de successu certum ferri judicium." *Ratio atque Institutio Studiorum Societatis Jesu*, p. xi.

[6]*Liber Saecularis*, p. 348.

[7]Editorial note in the *Classical Bulletin* (Missouri Province), II, No. 5, 37 (Feb., 1926): "The *Ratio* which held undisputed sway as an educational instrument during the centuries preceding the suppression, lost its commanding position in the revived Society; new ideals were set up in Europe and elsewhere under the influence of the 'scientific spirit' of the times."

[8]See Pachtler, *op. cit.*, IV, 507 ff. Various emendations proposed by the German Provinces to the 1832 *Ratio.*

[9]"Observationes quibus innititur accommodatio Rationis Studiorum," Pachtler, *op. cit.*, IV, 471. See also *Ratio Studiorum*, "Reg. prof. inf. class. gram.," 2; "Reg. prof. med. cl. gram.," 2, etc.

[10]Casagrande, *De claris sodalibus Provinciae Taurinensis S.J. commentaria.* Augustae Taurinorum, 1906, p. 285.

[11]*Ibid.; Liber Saecularis*, pp. 330 ff.

[12]*Liber Saecularis*, p. 331.

[13]See Vasco, *op. cit.*, *passim.* But particularly "Quadro Sinottico," in Vol. IV, facing p. 312.

[14]Casagrande, *op. cit.*, p. 287. "Quam maxime commendaret eique faveret."

[15]*Ibid.*, p. 296. "Qui tantum munus ultro amplexus esset, ultro deseruit."

[16]*Histoire Religieuse, Politique et Littéraire de la Compagnie de Jésus*, VI, 433 ff.

[17]*Beleuchtung der Schrift des Herrn Dr. Johann Kelle "Die Jesuiten Gymnasien in Oesterreich,"* pp. 679–80.

[18]Gruggen and Keating, *Stonyhurst College*, p. 123.

[19]Gruggen and Keating, *op. cit.*, p. 129.

[20]January, 1924, p. 34.

[21]*Woodstock Letters*, XXII, 106. "Nam in materia hodie non sumus liberi, illa praescribitur nobis. . . . Sed si vellemus retinere materiam sicut antea, possemus claudere collegia nostra. Tamen adhuc liberi sumus in forma et methodo docendi. . . ."

[22]*Decreta Vigesimae Quintae Congregationis Generalis*, pp. 23 ff. "Quod nonnullae Provinciae postularunt ut nova Rationis Studiorum fieret redactio, id hac nostra aetate, in tanta legum scholasticarum et disciplinarum varietate atque inconstantia, Congregatio Generalis censet tentandum non esse. . . . Enixe commendatur studium sanae illius paedagogiae cuius principia a S. Patre nostro in Const. P. IV sobrie exponuntur, in Ratione Studiorum evolvuntur, et a scriptoribus societatis haud paucis luculenter explicantur.

"Cum tamen fatendum sit, ne novam quidem Rationem Studiorum Patris Roothaan hodiedum satis observari posse et cum aliae in aliis provinciis difficultates atque necessitates existant, Praepositi Provinciales, auditis Consultoribus et Magistris probatissimis, pro sua quisque Provincia, atque adeo pro singulis regionibus quarum una ferme sit conditio, ordinationem de studiis inferioribus conficiant, eamque Patri nostro approbandam subjiciant."

In the discussion at this same General Congregation of 1908, Father Moeller, the Missouri Provincial, heard an almost unanimous opinion expressed that the *Ratio* was a *method of teaching and grading* [and administration?] rather than a program of studies and that Jesuit Colleges could not hope to succeed if their courses differed greatly from those common to the country in which they were situated. The revision of the *Ratio* was considered inopportune, but the Provincials were told they could arrange their own programs of studies, suitable to the needs of their own country, and submit it to the General for approval. See *Province News-Letter,* III, 25. See also, *Constitutiones,* Pars IV, 12, 2; IV, 13, 5; and *Cong. Gen. XXIII,* dec. 16; *XXIV,* dec. 24.

[23]"The high school may be described as the legal successor to the Latin grammar school and the natural offspring of the academy." Grizzell, *Origin and Development of the High School,* etc., p. 359.

[24]Garraghan, in *The Dauphin,* II (1925), 143. See also Brown, *The Making of our Middle Schools;* Lull, *Inherited Tendencies in Secondary Education.*

[25]II, 106 ff.

[26]The development of the Jesuit College, and still more of the Jesuit university in the United States, is a fertile field for the investigator. Here even more radical deviations from the *Ratio* were made; again, this is truer of the western colleges than of the colleges along the Atlantic seaboard.

[27]See Burns, *The Growth and Development of the Catholic School System in the U. S.*

[28]VII, 48 ff.

[29]"The Princeton College Convention and the Society," *Woodstock Letters,* XX (Feb., 1891), 6 ff.

[30]The entire correspondence is in the *Georgetown Archives,* Vol. 214, fol. 8; see also *Woodstock Letters,* XXV (Feb., 1896), 124 ff.

[31]Richards to Parsons, Director of Examining Dept. Regents' Office. In *Georgetown Archives.*

[32]*Georgetown Archives.*

[33]*Ibid.*

[34]*Woodstock Letters,* XXV (Feb., 1926), 133–4.

[35]*Woodstock Letters,* XXV (Oct., 1896), 541.

[36]Letter of Rev. Rudolph Meyer, Provincial of the Missouri Province, in *Missouri Province Archives,* under "Courses of Studies."

[37]See Table II, p. 122.

[38]Table II, p. 122.

[39]See Lull, *Inherited Tendencies in Secondary Education,* pp. 227 ff.; and Rooney, *The History of the Modern Subjects in the Secondary Curriculum,* pp. 54 ff.

[40]MS. in the *Missouri Province Archives* (circa, 1922).

[41]"Report of the Meeting of the Presidents of Jesuit Colleges of the Missouri Province, April 2, 1917," *Missouri Province Archives.*

[42]*Ibid.*

[43]J. Havens Richards in *The Teacher's Review,* I (July, 1920), 45 ff.

CHAPTER IX

OBJECTIVES OF JESUIT TEACHING

BEFORE examining the curricular development in Jesuit high schools and the methods of teaching there employed, it is essential to visualize clearly the objectives the Jesuit Order had in mind in undertaking educational work. The phenomenon of a body of men giving their whole lives without stint and without remuneration to the work of education naturally suggests the question: Why does the Society of Jesus engage in the work of teaching youth? Underlying this question is a more fundamental query: Why does this Order exist at all? The contention that its main purpose is political aggrandizement or the undermining of governments, a contention advanced by the Eugene Sue school of romancers, hardly merits serious consideration nowadays. But another school, numbering among its adherents Catholics and Protestants alike, regards the Order as primarily founded to combat heresy. They form this judgment, no doubt, because of the association of St. Peter Canisius with the Catholic Counter-Reformation in southern Germany. Yet, as Duhr shows,[1] the combating of heresy was never mentioned in the Constitutions nor in the Papal Bulls approving the Society.

Still, inasmuch as the combating of heresy is one of the objectives of the Catholic Church, it may be said that the defense of the faith against unbelievers and, more explicitly, the defense of the faithful from the contagion of heresy does fall within the compass of Jesuit aims; for in a very real sense, the purpose of the Society is the same as that of the Catholic Church.

The end of the Society is not only to care for the salvation and perfecting of their own souls with divine grace, but, with the same, seriously to devote themselves to the salvation and perfection of their neighbors. . . . For it was especially instituted for the defense and propagation of the faith and the progress of souls in Christian life and doctrine.[2]

Although organizing a system of academic education was not intended as a primary work of the Order, still this was not excluded. As has been seen,[3] circumstances led the Society first to draw up a scheme of education for its own scholastics, and later to establish schools for extern youth. Once this work of education was accepted, however reluctantly at first, it became very shortly and has since remained one of the distinguishing marks of the Jesuit Order. From the beginning, there has been a distinctive philosophy underlying their educational work. Nor is this surprising. For as Bode well says:[4]

A theory of education is at bottom a theory regarding the nature of man and his place in the universe. The question of aims in education is inextricably bound up with questions such as evolution, democracy, and the nature of ideals and of duty; while the problem of method is determined largely by our conception of the nature of interest and intelligence. It is not surprising, therefore, that our theory of education should be just an expression of our philosophy of life. Our view of man's nature will inevitably direct our choice of the methods that are suitable for his training and our selection of the ends that are most worth while.

William James,[5] too, insists on the importance of knowing a man's philosophy:

In the preface to that admirable collection of essays of his called *Heretics,* Mr. Chesterton writes these words: "There are some people — and I am one of them — who think that the most practical and important thing about a man is still his view of the universe. We think that for a landlady considering a lodger it is important to know his income, but still more important to know his philosophy. We think that for a general about to fight an enemy it is important to know the enemy's numbers but still more important to know the enemy's philosophy. We think the question is not whether the theory of the cosmos affects matters, but whether in the long run anything else affects them."

I think with Mr. Chesterton in this matter. I know that you, ladies and gentlemen, have a philosophy, each and all of you, and that the most interesting and important thing about you is the way in which it determines the perspective in your several worlds. . . . The philos-

ophy which is so important in each of us is not a technical matter; it is our more or less dumb sense of what life honestly and deeply means. It is only partly got from books; it is our individual way of just seeing and feeling the total push and pressure of the cosmos.

The Jesuit Philosophy of Education

There is no lack of definiteness regarding the Jesuit educational philosophy. From the first days that the Society undertook the conduct of a school in sixteenth-century Italy, down to the present day, there has been one clear-cut objective, one entirely independent of time and place. What, then, is the Jesuit philosophy of education? It differs no whit from the Catholic philosophy of education which is inextricably bound up with scholastic philosophy and with the dogmatic teaching of the Church. The Jesuit—and Catholic—concept of man regards him as not merely a citizen of this or that commonwealth; he is more than that, he is a citizen of the larger commonwealth of the Kingdom of God. Therefore, while the Jesuit would agree with the theory that education should be a preparation for life, the two concepts of life might be diametrically opposed. The Jesuit would hold that education must prepare him, not merely for life in this world, but for life hereafter. The Jesuit school prepares not merely for citizenship, but for Christian citizenship. Moreover, the Jesuit teacher must insist on training in belief and conduct. Purely intellectual training, it may safely be asserted, occupies a subordinate position in the Jesuit philosophy of education. Not that this means that the intellectual training imparted should be a matter of minor importance; but intellectualism is not enough. Nor does it mean that formal instruction in religion should occupy a dominant place in the curriculum; in the American Jesuit high schools two periods a week is the maximum time-allotment for religious instruction. But religion must permeate the whole atmosphere of the Catholic school. For the Jesuit, "religion's all or nothing." The whole intellectual training must be surrounded and colored by Catholic principles and practices.

Père Chossat in his book on the Jesuits of Avignon[6] cites an interesting document, dated 1732, a discourse given by the spiritual father to the young Jesuit scholastics at Avignon, preparing to teach in the colleges.

> The purpose which the Founder of the Company of Jesus had in mind in establishing colleges was to attract Christian youth for the purpose of training them in piety by instructing them in liberal arts. . . . Let your students clearly understand that so many religious, devoting their lives to their instruction, have not given up the pleasures of the world simply to teach them Latin and *belles-lettres*. Their principal aim has been to sanctify them by teaching them the liberal arts. This point is of considerable importance and it is exceedingly necessary to convince your pupils of this in order to give them the viewpoint of those who are desirous of imparting to them a Christian education.
>
> Speak of God, in class, every chance that you get; there will be no lack of opportunities if only you seize hold of them.

Père de Rochemonteix[7] presses home the same point:

> This, then, is the supreme purpose which the Jesuits have in their educational work; namely, to aid their neighbor to know and serve God. Placing the Faith and holiness of life in the foremost place, they must naturally pay attention above everything else to the religion and the virtue of their students.

In another place in the same book, he says:[8]

> The Jesuits deserve great praise for inaugurating a system of pedagogy, having for its foundation religion, without which no solid virtue can exist. On this foundation, they built up their entire literary education in such a fashion that in their plan of studies, *instruction is a means, and education the end*. . . . If the state is concerned to have well-informed subjects, it is indispensable that it have upright subjects. The moral phase of education requires beyond all doubt the principal attention. . . . St. Ignatius rightly judged that instruction is not the whole of education, nor is it even the principal part. . . . He places religion at the top of his educational program, and in that program Catechism occupies a primary place. . . . The study of religion and the duties derived therefrom are fundamental; the Catechism is then in our Institute the groundwork of all instruction; it is the first subject to be taught and the most important. And it is not enough to teach the boy what he should believe and practice; he must be formed. The moral and religious formation of the boy is the principal work

of the Jesuit, the main objective of all his efforts. His single ambition will be to keep him [the boy] from evil and lead him to good, to prepare his young heart for the love and the service of God. [See *Ratio,* Common Rules of the professors of the lower schools, 5, 6, 7, 8, 9, 10.] . . .

The master must be an apostle. He cannot become an apostle in a few days: accordingly, before teaching, he makes two years of novitiate and three years of philosophy, and during this time of retreat and labor, he practices solid virtues. To the apostolate of example, he will add that of the word; let him take occasion in class to prepare the still plastic souls of his pupils to serve God, to love Him, to practice those virtues which make us pleasing in His eyes; he should exercise the apostolate also out of class time, in private interviews during which he must never fail to throw in some thought which may help to foster Christian piety. [*Ratio,* Common Rules, 1 and 6.] Finally, the Jesuit master should pray often for his pupils. (Common Rules, 4, 5, 7, 9, 10.)

An English Jesuit writer expresses similar views:[9]

One thing at least would seem to be essential. We must bring it home every day more and more, to those we have to teach that religious education, Catholic education, as distinct from any other, non-Catholic or nonreligious, really does mean something. Somehow or other, they must be made to feel that they are better men for being Catholics, and for having been educated at a Catholic school. Their Catholic training as such must give them something which more than compensates for all they have lost by the surrender of a public-school or other education. It will not be enough that they should learn Christian doctrine, whether positive or dogmatic; that by itself is neither Catholic education, nor is it a thing which will of itself make much difference in the future. It is not always those who are best grounded in the teaching of the Church that ultimately prove its most loyal champions, or who even best appreciate the boon of the faith. It will not suffice that they should be trained in pious practices; pious practices alone will never produce strong men, a fact which our late Father General [Louis Martin], in a memorable address emphasized in no measured terms. What then will suffice? It is difficult, perhaps it is impossible to speak with precision; but in general, one may say that our boys must be impressed with a sense of the tremendous reality of religion. They will learn from us, if we teach according to our traditions, that religion is something which enters into all their lives, which colors all their thoughts, which modifies their aspects of life and the things of life, and which makes them better, sounder men, just because of this sounder judgment which it gives them. If it can be made to do that, then religion becomes a reality, not only in itself, but as a factor in education. It was on these accounts that Laynez and his fellow workers put religion in the first place. For the sake of religion they had adopted education. . . . From the motive of religion they strove to draw out of their boys the best that was in them. The promotion of religion they set before them as the noblest end in life. And finally by means of religion, more than by any other means, they developed that refinement of mind and character which is the best fruit of any education. In this way they fought their battle. Religion had been tabooed by the intellectuals of the day; the Jesuit schoolmasters introduced it into every nook and corner of their schools. It had been declared bankrupt as a power over reasoning men; they taught their boys to pay it homage as the chief promoter of right reason.

Education not an End in Itself

In the same article,[10] Dr. Goodier maintains that Jesuit education is mainly intended to counteract the evil tendencies of the day. The spirit of the Society's educational work should be the same at every time, in every country, and under every condition. This work is not education as such, as an end in itself; the Jesuits try to give the best education possible, not because of any value that they believe to be in the thing itself, but simply that it might serve the better to secure some further end in view.

So long as our aims are higher, he continues, so long as our nobler ideals are kept well in view, so long as our teaching of grammar, and mathematics, and history does not stop at an examination but reaches forward to the years beyond, inspires a spirit that will last a lifetime, above all, instills that faith, which more than anything else it is our profession to instill, so long we shall be conscious to ourselves that we possess a power which to others is wanting. With this power behind us we can face any criticism. What is more, with this power to support us, there can be no doubt — as our rivals have more than once acknowledged — that we can hold the field and win battles for the Church as St. Ignatius and his companions won them of old.

Just as clearly Ebner[11] outlines the ultimate objectives of Jesuit teaching:

Instruction in the sciences and the Christian education of youth are, according to the *Institute* and the *Ratio Studiorum,* in the schools of the Society intimately bound together. . . . In the *Ratio,* Christian education is emphasized in the first place and is regarded as the main task of the school. . . .

The *Institute* and the *Ratio* look upon the youth who enters the schools of the Society as that which he really is, namely the creature and property of God, a child of God, redeemed by the blood of the God-man, whose last end and purpose, appointed by God Himself, is nothing else than to know God and to honor Him, to practice conscientiously all the duties that arise from this knowledge of God and so to reach his last destiny, union with God in everlasting bliss. This is the unchanging viewpoint, and guiding principle from which the *Institute* and the *Ratio* start out, to which the Society has clung tenaciously. And who can say that it is not the only right one, the only salutary one?

Education in Faith, Piety, and Character

The Twenty-fifth General Congregation of the Society, held at Rome in 1906, under the General, Father Louis Martin, in a pronouncement regarding the adaptation of the course of studies for different countries, added:[12]

Due attention should be paid, as is right, to the special purpose which the Society has in conducting colleges, namely, not only that all the faculties of our students should be developed by a proper methodology, but especially that they be educated in faith, piety, and character, that they become accustomed to discipline, and learn to live virtuously. But above all, care must be taken that they be taught Christian doctrine. . . .

Identical Objective of American Jesuit Educators

That the American Jesuits are in entire accord with their brethren in other lands in accepting this theory of education, could be proved by almost any page of their pedagogical writings. For the purpose of this chapter, it will be sufficient to cite a few American Jesuits. Thus, the Reverend Charles Coppens, in an article on "The Spirit of Jesuit Education," in *The Teacher's Review*,[13] says:

> St. Ignatius was not himself a great scholar, a purist in Latin and Greek, an enthusiastic admirer of the classics, choosing for his followers the work of education that he might thus promote the study of literature and spread taste and refinement throughout the world. . . . The only motive that made him assume for his followers the work of education was the opportunity it afforded to train young hearts for God and mold them after the image of Christ. He had no mission . . . to elevate the standard of scholarship, but he had a mission to elevate the standard of virtue in many lands. . . . To establish the kingdom of Christ in the hearts of men is the mission of his society, its *raison d'être,* and it is the mission of every one of us, it is what we are Jesuits for. . . . Therefore, we labor in our colleges first and last to sanctify our students, and by gaining them for God to gain also through them many other souls for God. Whatever effort does not in any way contribute to this end is so much labor lost. . . .
>
> Of course, we must teach literature and science and mathematics and all the branches of the course and teach them well. Why? That we may get more boys to educate and boys who will hereafter be capable of exercising a wider influence, able to do greater things *A. M. D. G.*,[14] that we may gain their confidence, their love, gain their minds and hearts and fill them with God and zeal for the things of God. . . . Thus understood, our education is something of extreme value in the Church and in the State; it is the copious source of sound thought in literature, of sound morals in ethics and politics, in public and private life.

In a sermon delivered at the Golden Jubilee of St. Francis Xavier College, New York, June 21, 1897, Father Pardow maintained that "there is one thing that the Jesuit system insists on more than anything else, namely the absolute need of divine faith in education. It will not do to teach simply broad morality; for, unless the moral teaching rests on clear, positive, definite, unmistakable religious dogmas, it will not be able to resist the onslaught of passion and self-interest."[15]

Jesuit Theory of Education is the Catholic Theory

This theory of education to which the Jesuits subscribe is the only one authoritatively approved by the Catholic Church.

But in the past few years in the United States, a theory of Catholic education, called by a Jesuit writer "a false and most dangerous theory,"[16] has found some acceptance, notably by some of the promoters of Catholic foundations at secular universities. Although this theory deals largely with higher education, yet if pushed to its logical conclusion, it would also hold for secondary and even for parochial schools.

> Catholic education according to this theory, says the writer already quoted, consists essentially in the teaching of the Catholic religion. Remove that from the curriculum of the Catholic college and you would have but secular education. Instill that into the secular curriculum and you preserve the essential features of Catholic education. . . . This is *not* a Catholic education.

In the same paper, this writer explains what precisely is a Catholic education, citing Canon Law and pronouncements of ecclesiastical authorities. From these official utterances, he draws the following conclusions:[17]

1. There is an approved system of education and a system of education, so called, which is condemned.
2. The approved system is that only which is joined to "the Catholic Faith and power of the Church."
3. To expel the authority of the Church from education is contrary to the natural and divine law.
4. It is the office of the Church, received from Christ, to teach Catholic youth.
5. Catholic education is that system which tends to elevate and direct men chiefly to a future life and everlasting beatitude.
6. In a Catholic education, religious and moral training must take the chief place.
7. All branches of knowledge must expand in the closest alliance with religion, and all types of study be enlightened by Catholic truth.
8. Catholic educators must have nothing more at heart than to ground the student in religion and morality, and to educate him in letters and sciences according to the mind of the Church.
9. *The soul of the entire academic education is our divine religion.*

In a later article in *America*,[18] the same writer places in succinct outline the Jesuit — and Catholic — philosophy of education:

A. *Organization*

1. A system of education joined to the "Catholic Faith and power of the Church" is maintained in every department. Its principles . . . are exclusively those approved by the Catholic Church. This system does not concern itself solely or even primarily with the knowledge of natural things or with the ends of social life. On the contrary, it assigns the chief place to religious and moral training. (Cf. *Syllabus of Pius IX, Prop. 48; Canon 1372 of the Code of Canon Law.*)

2. To expel from education the authority of the Church exposes youth to loss of Faith. (*Pius IX to the Archbishop of Freiburg, July 14, 1864.*)

3. "Our divine religion must be the soul of the entire academic education." (*Pius IX to the Bishops of Ireland, March 20, 1854.*)

B. *Purpose*

1. The purpose of the Catholic college is to "educate the young zealously in letters and science, according to the mind of the Catholic Church, the pillar and guarantee of truth." (*Ibid.*)

2. Let all branches of learning expand in the closest alliance with religion. (*Ibid.*)

3. Let "all types of study be enlightened by the bright rays of Catholic truth." (*Ibid.*)

C. *Faculty*

1. Professors must be chosen who are "models of well-doing in their teaching and in their integrity of life." (*Ibid.*)

2. Professors "should have nothing more at heart than to fashion with all care the minds of young men to the practice of religion, to uprightness of conduct, and all virtuous dealing." (*Ibid.*)

Jesuit Objective Extrapedagogic?

It is this insistence at all times and in all places on this one central aim that led a keen and fairly discerning critic[19] of the Jesuit system to characterize the purpose of Jesuit education as "extrapedagogic." By this he means a purpose that embraces something more than the mere education of the child, reserving the term "genuinely pedagogic purpose" to that education whose objective is the individual efficiency of the child, the educator having no ulterior aim in view.[20]

Jesuit education, says Dubois, is only a means to form the individual for the Church, not for himself. . . . The objective, envisioned by Jesuit pedagogy, is the triumph of the Catholic Church; hence, its first characteristic. It is an *ecclesiastical* pedagogy rather than religious; indeed, what it attempts to stir up and foster is not so much a religious spirit in general as full and entire submission to the authority of the Roman Church, the acceptance of the dogmatic truths she teaches, the fulfillment of the practices she has instituted. . . . From the intellectual, religious, and moral viewpoint, the youth is to become a subject of this Church, the guardian and font of truth. Jesuit educators in general do not aim at proselytism, at recruiting subjects for the Society of Jesus; what they desire is to establish their influence in particular over the higher classes of society for the triumph of the Church.[21]

This characterization of Jesuit educational objectives as extrapedagogic is hardly just; under the same condemnation would fall all modern educational systems that include in their aims the civic education of the child. Indeed, educationists generally would quarrel with Dubois' preference for individual efficiency over group solidarity as a desirable educational objective. Jesuit education does not stop with civic education; it aims at turning out not merely good citizens, but loyal Catholics as well. Their position is well summarized in the following statement of a Jesuit writer:[22]

But we train the body and the soul, we educate for earth and for heaven, for time and for eternity; for we aim at turning out men and women who will be perfect citizens physically, mentally, and morally, and live as other Christs — Catholic in life, Christian at death, and Christlike with God in heaven.

To say that this is "ecclesiastical pedagogy rather than religious" is to miss the point. True, the religious spirit that Jesuit schools impart is not an abstract religious spirit — it may be questioned if there be any such spirit — but a definite Catholic religious spirit. For this, conduct is not enough; conduct must go hand in hand with belief. The Jesuit believes that "the only education worth while must be vitalized by faith. God bestowed upon us His likeness, His image, and intelligence and a will, a heart and a conscience, so that we became intelligent and moral beings. The education, then, that we aim for must rest foursquare — body, mind, heart, and will — upon the solid basis of religion."[23] The late Archbishop Ireland authoritatively enunciated the fundamental principle of Catholic education, when he said:[24]

> The contention of the Catholic school is the principle that religion should permeate and vivify the education of childhood and youth. On this principle the Catholic Church rests her case before public opinion. Differ from us who may; combat against us who may, provided the principle we uphold is understood and honorably admitted.

With regard to Dubois' assertion that the Jesuits attempt to "establish their influence in particular over the higher classes of society for the triumph of the Church," it may be said that when the Society was established, secondary education was practically restricted to the "higher classes," as, indeed, has been the case in Europe until very recently. The Society aimed at educating an élite, true; but its gratuitous instruction made this education available to poor youths. In America, Jesuit schools have very definitely reflected the democratic spirit, partly due, no doubt, to the fact that Catholics were not found to any appreciable extent among the "higher classes." Jesuit students came from the same walks of life as students in the public high schools.

Jesuit Education and Faculty Psychology

The Jesuit philosophy of life, then, determines the Jesuit philosophy of education. God and religion play a definite part in that philosophy; they are warp and woof of their educational aims. Man has duties to his fellows, duties to the State; but over and above are his duties to his God. Education must prepare him for a proper appreciation of these duties, for an adequate accomplishment of them. Just as his philosophy of life determines his educational objectives, so too the Jesuit's theory of man's nature and of man's mental machinery, colors his pedagogic procedure. There are no different schools of psychology in the Jesuit Order; all are definitely scholastic.

All Jesuit masters, before they take up the work of teaching, must follow a course in scholastic psychology. That psychology postulates for man a soul as well as a body; and by soul, the scholastic means "the subject of our mental life, the ultimate principle by which we feel, think, and will."[25]

Scholastic psychology supposes that the mind, or soul, is capable of undergoing a particular kind of activity; and this capability it calls a *faculty*.

> Thus, our sensations of color are due to the faculty of vision, our judgments to the faculty of intellect, and our volitions to the faculty of will. Such a method of classification, continues this Jesuit writer, is justified by the conspicuous differences found both in the quality of the several kinds of mental life, and in the manner in which the latter put the mind in relation with the object.[26]

It is, of course, a misrepresentation of scholasticism to suppose that a mental faculty or power is a particular part of the soul or mind, or a member distinct from it as a limb is distinct from the rest of the body.[27] Scholastic psychologists do not regard the faculty as an independent reality, a separate agent, which originated conscious states out of itself apart from the mind. The faculty is a special mode through which the mind itself acts. The mind is regarded as a permanent indivisible energy, and the faculty as "the proximate ground of some special form of activity of which the mind is capable."[28]

The scholastic school of psychology maintains that to see and to hear, to know and to will are essentially different kinds of consciousness, though all come from the same source. The proposition "our soul possesses different faculties," they declare, means nothing else than "our soul is a substance which as active principle is capable of exerting different species of energies."[29]

It must be admitted, however, that some of the older scholastic writers have at times used crude phraseology in regard to the faculties and their functions which, if taken literally, would be irreconcilable with the essential unity of the mind — a fundamental tenet of scholastic psychology.

This explanation of the scholastics' concept of faculties is necessary for the proper appreciation of much Jesuit pedagogical writing about mind-training and will-training. Thus, the Reverend R. J. Meyer, writes:[30]

In the first place, education which is worthy of the name, must expand all the human faculties with all their activities and properties. Even the ordinary branches of learning must be directed toward that end. They must be such as will improve the memory, discipline the understanding, refine the feelings, cultivate the taste, form the manners. It was this that the ancients meant to express by the word *humanities* which was their equivalent for liberal education or culture; because they conceived education to consist in the full and harmonious development of all that is distinctively human in man. . . . In the second place, since "character comprises the whole sphere of the educated will and stands for the sum of the ethical traits which give each one his moral individuality," it is plain that education must aim especially to cultivate the will and to develop the moral and religious side of human nature. With this object in view, it must never weary of inculcating correct principles of morality, until they have penetrated so deeply into the pupil's mind that they have, so to speak, become a part of it.

The same ideal that Jesuit education is striving for is expressed in Father Tierney's book, *Teacher and Teaching*:[31]

Real education is a process of guiding a human being from a state of imperfection to a state of perfection. It is the development of man according to the highest attainable standards, the discipline of soul and body into the best that can be had. Such a process concerns itself . . . with the body and the senses, with the soul and all its powers . . . all must be developed harmoniously. If the intellect is trained at the cost of the will, the outcome is a rascal. If the imagination be fostered to the neglect of the other faculties, the product is a mild lunatic. If memory alone be strengthened, we have a machine. If the will receive all attention, behold a fanatic or a pious dolt. . . .

No one should doubt the importance of this faculty [of the memory]. It is a real handmaid, on whose action most of the higher powers of the soul depend in a marked degree. . . . Hardly less important than the memory is the imagination. By it man can live with angels and saints or wallow with the animal. . . . All the efforts of a school in mind-training should be exerted to give pupils a love of learning, a desire to be learned, and a knowledge of how to become so.

The will . . . remains for discussion. To our mind there is no objective reason for any difference of opinion about the training of this faculty. It needs education and should get it.

The Jesuits and the Theory of Formal Discipline

One more citation may be added to show that the Jesuits are committed to the doctrine of formal discipline. The writer, the late Father A. J. Burrowes, at one time Provincial of the Missouri Province, was for long prominent in Jesuit educational circles. He says:[32]

The old idea of education held that the mental faculties were mere instruments for acquiring knowledge and that the best way to acquire knowledge quickly and accurately was first to develop the faculties of the soul by a course of mental gymnastics, similar to those by which the muscles of the body are developed, and subsequently to put before the mind any particular branch of study that it chooses to master. Education, in the old way of thinking, was intended to give a general training to all the mental faculties. The aim was not so much to store a number of facts in the mind, as to prepare the faculties, by proper exercise, to acquire knowledge subsequently. . . . Bishop Spalding, commenting on Plato's idea of education, says: "The ideal presented is that of a complete, harmonious culture, the aim of which is not to make an artisan, a physician, a merchant, a lawyer, but a man alive in all his faculties; touching the world at many points; for whom all knowledge is desirable; all beauty lovable, and for whom fine bearing and noble acting are indispensable."

. . . The task before the educator is to discover by what means he may be able to draw out all the faculties, give each one its suitable exercise so that the combined action of all may produce the best results. The human mind is a complicated bit of mechanism, requiring the highest skill of the educator to adjust its parts.

Undoubtedly the Jesuits would subscribe whole-heartedly to Dr. Henry S. Pritchett's remarks in the *Fifth Annual Report of the Carnegie Foundation for the Advancement of Education.*[33]

√ We have to some extent lost our ideal of what education means. To learn a little about many subjects, to dip superficially into the study of English and Latin and chemistry and psychology and home economics, and a dozen things, is not education. Only that human being has gained the fundamentals of an education who has acquired soundly a few elementary branches of human knowledge and who, in acquiring these, has so disciplined his mind that it is an efficient instrument ready to be turned to whatsoever task is set before it. The high-school student is led to believe that education is attained by learning a little of each of many things; he gains, therefore, a superficial knowledge of many subjects and learns none with thoroughness. He lacks the hard fiber of intellectual discipline. Such a youth has not been educated. That only is education which sets a boy on the way to use his own mind for his pleasure and his profit; which enables him to attack a problem, whether it be in school or in business, and to think out the right answer. Education, rightly understood, is a power-producing process; and the serious indictment against the secondary-school system today is that its graduates do not acquire either discipline or power. The real struggle in the American high school is between that influence which makes toward thoroughness and that which makes toward superficiality; and if the high school is to become the true training place of the people, the ideal of thoroughness must supplant the ideal of superficiality.

The boy who desires to enter college and the boy who desires to enter business alike need to be well grounded in fundamental studies and to gain a real mastery of a few things. It appears equally clear that the educational ideal which makes for a single and thorough curriculum for the individual serves equally well the boy who looks toward college and the boy who goes directly from the high school into a vocation.

Briefly, then, the Jesuits believe that the mind can be trained; they would maintain that certain subjects are better suited to give this training than others. Their whole history shows their preference for linguistic studies over the other branches in the curriculum.

Reasons for Emphasis on Latin

Nevertheless, it is not so evident that this is the reason why the Jesuits have always upheld the classical tradition in their schools. As has already been seen, Jesuit educators of the first generation were frankly utilitarian. They taught Latin because it was the language of the educated in that day and age.

The purpose of the *Ratio,* then, in teaching Latin was . . . *culture.* The *Ratio* wishes Latin taught because without it one could not pretend to that fine appreciation and that delight in beautiful things and that feeling of being normal and at home among them that is the mark of the cultured mind. The *Ratio* wishes the pupil to learn Latin, that is, to become a master of it in expression and in appreciation; to find his reading in Latin books; to express his thoughts in Latin; to talk, to plan, to argue, to dream, to pray, to *live* in Latin. Mind training was a "by-product" of Latin teaching.[34]

It was only in recent years, with the disappearance of the utilitarian objective, that the Jesuits have had recourse to the theory of formal discipline. In this way they were but following the lead of the upholders of the classical tradition everywhere against the assault of the utilitarian school. The fact that Latin was the language of the Church had little or nothing to do with the matter; the primary purpose of their schools has never been the training of youth for the ecclesiastical state; rather it has been the formation of Catholic laymen for active participation in the world about them. The conservative tendency in a world-wide religious organization such as the Society is the principal factor in the retention of the classics in so prominent a place in the curriculum. If they were convinced that a better instrument was at hand than the classics for their purpose, they would undoubtedly jettison Latin and replace it by the modern subjects. Indeed, the whole history of Jesuit education in the United States has been a slow but steady encroachment of the modern branches upon the classics.

Apropos of this very point, the Reverend H. S. Spalding wrote in *The Teacher's Review* in 1914:

> If I have read the *Ratio* right, its object is now what it was three hundred years ago — to form Christian youths and Christian men. The times now call for modern languages, science, history and sociology, political economy . . . as well as for the ancient classics. Latin and Greek hold, and will continue to hold, an honorable place in the curriculum. . . . Even so, many will not study Greek, some will not study Latin. Why should we force these students to leave our colleges and to enter schools where faith is endangered? . . . The authors of the *Ratio* aimed at attracting students in the sixteenth century; let us attract those of the twentieth century.[35]

The Conscious Jesuit Influence

Above all and through all, the Jesuits look upon the individual as of paramount importance; their effort is mainly directed to him, not to the class, not even to the college. St. Ignatius wished the educational process of his Society to reach down to the very soul and fiber of the man; he emphasized the development of Christian manhood, rather than the formation of scientists and scholars. Jesuit education is intended to leave a definite impress on the youth; to give him a definite philosophy of life, to prepare him as far as possible to be a forceful leader of Catholic thought and action.

I am endeavoring, says Goodier,[36] to mark out that feature or those features of a Jesuit education which, as men working among men and for men, should, if we are only faithful to our tradition, be manifest. That Jesuit education has a character of its own is evident; whether we like it or not, the goods we produce and put into the market have a trade-mark stamped upon them by which they may be known. Implicitly, then, we accept a conclusion which is by no means accepted by the educational world at large. There are those who claim that it is of the essence of good education to eliminate personal influence. . . . They talk of the sacred liberty of the child and its right to its own free development; and even we ourselves, in our moments especially of failure and of depression may be inclined to side with the principle, renouncing all other responsibility in regard to those who come under us beyond that of merely meting out knowledge, of getting them through their schools and examinations. Nevertheless, the fact is plain that the whole principle implied in that position is the direct opposite of that laid down by St. Ignatius; and in proportion as our schools, and the masters who are in them, lose their own strong character, and become identical in spirit, in practice, and in fruit with schools of any other type, in such proportion, whatever other success we may achieve, one may say that the peculiar spirit of St. Ignatius is wanting. . . .

The stamp of the master must be left upon the boy, and the impression must be a lasting thing; so that, not merely during a single school year, but throughout the rest of his life, the effect of the man shall be upon the boy a permanent and a beneficial reality. . . . Whether or not he has learned from us anything of value in the matter of book knowledge, he has at least received into himself a spirit which he never had before, an insight which enables him to distinguish truth from fiction, a realization of what is of importance as opposed to what is nonessential, an energy to stand up and be a man no matter what may be his circumstances; so that whatever may be said as to the course he has followed, or the restrictive method under which he has been trained, he would not have missed the year or years he had under us for anything else in all the world.

Summary

The Society of Jesus, then, from the very beginning has had a distinctive theory of education, a theory that mirrors its philosophy of life. That theory, that philosophy, consists essentially in this: education is not an end in itself, nor is it merely a preparation for participation in civic life; Jesuit education rather envisages something beyond this — a preparation for participation in the kingdom of God. Hence, their primary objective, for which the American Jesuits as well as their brethren in the Old World have striven consciously and unfailingly, an objective that gives to their system a startling and powerful unity, namely, the formation of Christian men, loyal to Church and loyal to State. This objective applies to all their teaching. But in a special manner, the Jesuit teacher strives to attain this objective in the high school. Here is youth plastic, and ready to be shaped according to this ideal. To this purpose, Jesuit educators in the secondary field devote themselves with enthusiasm.

Their emphasis on classical studies, their adherence to a theory of education quite at variance with modern theories, the theory of formal discipline, are quite accidental to the primary objective. God and man's duties to God have an important place in the curriculum of the Jesuit school. And the Jesuit system of education does not rest content with knowledge; conduct also must be considered. Their theory of education has always been that mind-training is not its exclusive function. To knowledge it adds will-training. Beyond this, the Jesuit strives to inculcate in the boys under his charge a sense of the tremendous importance of religion; he endeavors to impregnate every shred and fiber of education with Catholic principles and practice. This objective must be kept in mind in the discussion in the succeeding chapters concerning curriculum, methodology, and administration as they were applied in the American Jesuit High School.

Footnotes

[1]Duhr, *Jesuiten-Fabeln*, pp. 1–11. Hyma, *The Christian Renaissance*, pp. 275, has a rather novel theory. "Those writers," he says, "who cling to the old belief that Loyola's new brotherhood was founded primarily to counteract the rising wave of Protestantism are greatly mistaken; for both the Reformation on its religious side and the Counter-Reformation owed their origins in part to the same religious movement — the New Devotion."

[2]*Institutum Societatis Jesu*, "Examen," cap; i, n. 2, p. 1.

[3]See *supra*, Chap. I, "Jesuits and Education."

[4]*Fundamentals of Education*, p. 163. Quoted by permission of the Macmillan Co., Publishers.

[5]*Pragmatism*, pp. 3 ff.

[6]*Les Jésuites et Leurs Oeuvres à Avignon*, p. 365. "Le but que le fondateur de la Compagnie de Jésus se propose dans l'établissement des collèges fut d'y attirer la jeunesse chrétienne pour la former plus aisement à la piété en lui enseignant les lettres humaines. . . . Faites bien comprendre aux écoliers que tant de religieux, qui se consacrent à leur instruction, ne se sont pas privés des douceurs du siècle pour leur apprendre précisément la langue latine et les belles-lettres; mais que leur but principal a été de les sanctifier en leur enseignant les lettres humaines. Ce point est d'une très grande importance, et on ne saurait croire combien il est nécessaire d'en convaincre les enfants pour les faire entrer dans les vues de ceux qui songent à leur donner une éducation chrétienne.

"Parlez de Dieu dans la classe, toutes les fois que vous aurez l'occasion: les occasions ne vous manqueront point pour peu que vous vouliez en profiter."

[7]*Un Collège de Jésuites aux xvii et xviii Siècles: Le Collège Henri IV de la Flèche*, II, 121.

[8]*Ibid.*, pp. 104 ff.

[9]Goodier, "The Society of Jesus and Education," *The Month*, CIX, 22 ff.

[10]*Op. cit.*, CX, 284 ff.

[11]Ebner, R., *Beleuchtung der Schrift des Herrn Dr. Kelle, "Die Jesuiten-Gymnasien in Oesterreich,"* pp. 673 ff.

[12]*Decreta Vigesimae Quintae Congregationis Generalis*, dec. 12, No. 3, p. 24: " . . . ratio habeatur, ut par est, ejus imprimis finis, quem sibi in suis Collegiis Societas proponit, ut nempe non tantum discipulorum nostrorum facultates omnes apta methodo evolvantur, verum praesertim ut ipsi educentur ad fidem et pietatem ac bonos mores, assuescant disciplinae, discant ex virtute agere. Proinde ante omnia curandum, ut doctrinae christianae docendae. . . ."

[13]VI, No. 2 (April, 1915), 25–26.

[14]*Ad majorem Dei gloriam:* "To the greater glory of God," — the motto of the Society of Jesus.

[15]*Woodstock Letters*. XXVI (Nov., 1897), 434 ff.

[16]Blakely, Paul, "What is a Catholic Education?" a paper read at the 1926 meeting of the "Catholic Educational Association," *The Catholic Educational Association Bulletin*, XXIII, No. 1 (Nov., 1926), 70–81.

[17]Blakely, *op. cit.*, pp. 72–73.

[18]Blakely, Paul, "The Catholic College and the College for Catholics," *America*, XXXVI No. 17 (Feb. 5, 1926), p. 407. Although there is question in this article only of the *college*, yet all that is said applies *a fortiori* to the high schools. This article is but one of a series, appearing for the most part in *America*, and written mainly by Jesuits, championing the orthodox Catholic view of education against those Catholics who held that it was an adequate and even a better plan for the state or a secular institution to impart the secular training, the Church authorities merely giving instruction in religion and morality, through "religious foundations," chaplaincies, and the like. It is doubtful if the advocates of this latter view would have favored the extension of such a practice to the secondary schools. For the controversy, see articles by Claude Heithaus, S.J., in *America* for Aug. 22, 1925, Aug. 29, Sept. 3, Sept. 19, Sept. 26, Oct. 3, Oct. 10.

Also the articles by Wilfrid Parsons, S.J., editor of *America,* reprinted by the America Press, New York, under the title, "Chaplaincy, Newman Club or Catholic College?"

[19]Dubois, *Le Problème Pédagogique,* pp. 60–65.

[20]"Nous appelons *but* réellement *pédagogique* d'une éducation un but desinteressé quant à l'éducateur, une formation de l'enfant pour lui-même, et nous entendons par *but extra-pédagogique* celui qui est en somme autre que la seule éducation de l'enfant." Dubois, *op. cit.,* p. 61, note.

[21]*Ibid.,* pp. 61–62.

[22]Ford, John J., "Education and Character," *The Catholic Mind,* XV, No. 2 (Jan. 22, 1917), 42.

[23]Dunney, Joseph A., *The Parish School,* p. 17. Quoted by permission of the Macmillan Co., publishers.

[24]"Catholic Schools for Catholic Youth," *The Catholic Mind,* XIII, No. 14 (July 22, 1915), 382.

[25]Maher, M., *Psychology* (9th Edit., London: Longmans, Green & Co., 1925), p. 461.

[26]*Ibid.,* p. 29.

[27]Boyd Barrett, *The New Psychology,* pp. 253–4, protests against the misinterpretation of scholastic psychology by many modern writers. They say that "in our psychology we partition the mind into little compartments, placing memory in one, imagination in another, intellect in a third, will in a fourth. From out these little boxes we make the will or intellect hop. Then they do little 'stunts,' and return to their kennels. Such is the psychology that is attributed to us. And we are accused of dishonesty when we deny that any scholastic psychologist ever taught such rubbish."

[28]Maher, *op. cit.,* p. 39.

[29]*Ibid.,* p. 36 and Note. Further on (p. 40), Maher remarks that "every scientific psychology that seeks to give a rational analytic account of our complex mental life is invariably led back to some scheme of 'faculties,' however it may name or even conceive them."

[30]*Science of the Saints,* pp. 266 ff.

[31]Pp. 15 ff.

[32]*Why Study Latin and Greek?* (Milwaukee, 1901), pp. 5–6.

[33]Quoted in Burns, J. A., *Catholic Education in the United States,* pp. 102–3.

[34]Morrison, R. B., "Objectives of Latin Teaching," *The Classical Bulletin,* II, 39. Schimberg contends that the Jesuits' insistence on Latin was due to their desire to promote an international scientific language which was at the same time the language of the Church. (*L'éducation morale dans les collèges de la Compagnie de Jésus,* p. 167.) However, in the sixteenth century, Latin *was* the international scientific language. The Jesuits merely accepted the existing fact and adapted their school programs accordingly.

[35]V, No. 3 (July, 1914), 35. At this time Greek was still obligatory in all Jesuit schools in America.

[36]"The Society of Jesus and Education," *The Month,* CVIII, 596–7.

CHAPTER X

THE HIGH-SCHOOL CURRICULUM — EXTRA-CURRICULAR ACTIVITIES

THE Jesuit educational system has a well-defined fundamental objective, an objective that differs in no way from the primary purpose of the Order. The environment in which the Jesuits started their educational work in Europe in the sixteenth century committed them to a rather rigid classical type of education. In this, they achieved conspicuous success to such an extent, in fact, that many writers seem convinced that the classical curriculum is inseparably connected with the Jesuit school. True, their schools are and always have been strongholds of the classical tradition. But, from the very beginning, the Jesuit Order has, in the main, regarded the curriculum as accidental, to be determined by the exigencies of time and place. If their fundamental objective, the formation of Catholic youth according to the mind of the Church, could be better attained by a type of school entirely different from what they have conducted, there is nothing in their Constitutions to prevent them from adapting their schools to that pattern. This partially explains the willingness on the part of some Jesuit schools in the United States to conform to the curricular standards of other schools. The factual evidence at hand shows that there has been some measure of elasticity in the curriculum of the Jesuit secondary school in America and that the same factors that were transforming the non-Jesuit academy and high school in the United States were not without effect on American Jesuit education.

In tracing the curricular development of the American Jesuit high school, two difficulties confront us. First, there is the lack of documents. This is more marked in the case of Georgetown, which was for long the most important Jesuit college in America. Its first catalogue did not appear until 1851; before that date only prospectuses were issued. The second obstacle is this: The lack of demarcation between college and college-preparatory instruction makes it difficult to determine which classes are of secondary grade and which beyond. However, for practical purposes, it may be assumed that the first four years of the Jesuit colleges, no matter what the nomenclature, represent roughly the secondary curriculum. On the other hand, the continual striving for uniformity makes the task less difficult insofar that the curriculum of one Jesuit school in America corresponds, in the main, to the curricula in all other American Jesuit schools for the same period. This does not imply that all the schools attained to the same degree of efficiency. A school like Georgetown, for example, situated in the East, where students came with some background of culture, was undoubtedly superior to a school placed on the Western frontier.

Jesuit Curriculum Similar to Curricula in Other American Schools

In the first decades of the nineteenth century, the Jesuit secondary curriculum probably differed but slightly from that of other college-preparatory schools in the United States, if the prospectuses issued in those days mirror faithfully the practice. Thus, the curriculum of Phillips Exeter Academy for 1818,[1] or the Boston Publick Latin School for 1820,[2] was very like that of Georgetown. In the earliest extant prospectus for Georgetown, which bears the date of January 1, 1798, great insistence is placed on the classics as is to be expected.

> The study of the dead languages, that foundation of universal knowledge, which in every academy calculated for the purpose of extensive utility, ought to engage a large proportion of the attention of the professors, must have been indeed cultivated in *this* with uncommon application, of which the extraordinary proficiency of many of its pupils, in so short a period, is unequivocal proof. . . .
>
> The English and French languages come next, and are encouraged both in theory and daily practice, no pains being spared in training up the foreigners to a correct and familiar use of the former, and the

natives to that of the latter . . . in which the mixture of American and French pupils afford a considerable assistance. Writing, arithmetic in all its branches, mathematics, geography, the use of the globes, and the art of an elegant elocution close the courses of instruction hitherto embraced in the College.[3]

Grassi, who became president in 1812,[4] left his impress on the curriculum. In the *Georgetown Archives*,[5] there is a transcript of an old prospectus for 1814, signed by John Grassi, President, in which it is stated:

The students are taught English, French, Latin, Greek and all the other branches of classical education, Sacred and Profane History, Geography, Use of the Globes, Arithmetic, Book Keeping, Algebra, Geometry, Trigonometry, Mensuration, Navigation, Surveying, Astronomy, Fluxions, and the other parts of Mathematics, in general comprising a complete and regular course.

It is hardly probable that all these branches were taught at Georgetown at this period, although undoubtedly there were men on the staff qualified to impart instruction in these subjects; Grassi himself had received a thorough training in mathematics and science at European universities.[6]

Grassi was far-sighted enough to realize that some adaptation was needed to fit the Jesuit school into the American environment. The civilization developing in the new republic was quite different from the civilization in Europe. A preparation in practical subjects was needed for commercial life. Undoubtedly, too, he was acquainted with the system of education in vogue in the American academies and drew up Georgetown's curriculum accordingly.

In the Georgetown prospectus for 1820—printed in French and English—the subjects taught in the respective classes are indicated:[7]

In the lowest school or class of Rudiments, the scholars study the English and French grammars, Arithmetic, etc., and at the conclusion of this year . . . they are supposed to be able to read and write English correctly. During the next [third class of grammar] the scholars continue to study the English and French grammars. . . . Arithmetic is continued, and toward the end of the year, the students commence the Latin grammar. In the second class of Grammar, they continue

English and French composition . . . and Arithmetic; they begin Latin exercises and read several books of the easy Latin and French authors, as Cæsar, Bossuet's Universal History, etc. During this year a course of Geography is studied. In the first class of Grammar they read portions of Cornelius Nepos, Sallust, Livy, Cicero's minor works, and some of Ovid's Elegies, Telemachus, Bossuet, etc., and commence History. In this class the students begin Greek and read portions of the Greek Scriptures, Lucian's Dialogues, and Xenophon. Algebra is also commenced.[8]

This was practically the course of studies for the secondary department at Georgetown until 1830. In the prospectus of 1835, some rather definite changes are made. In the class of rudiments they study the elements of Latin and English grammar and read in Latin the select letter of Cicero.[9] This change was undoubtedly due to the arrival in the United States of Roothaan's revised *Ratio* of 1832.

The St. Louis Curriculum in 1832

The Jesuits in the Middle West introduced similar curricula at the school they founded. Indeed, as has been seen,[10] Georgetown's method and curricula played a large part in the development of other Jesuit schools in America, just as later, St. Louis served as an exemplar for the western colleges. However, a classical education made no strong appeal to the hardheaded people of the Middle West. Consequently, from the very beginning, the Jesuit schools in this region offered in addition to the conventional classical course, a "mercantile education" as well. Thus, the St. Louis catalogue of 1832–3 states:[11]

The course of studies embraces both a Mercantile and Classical education, but so conducted that the student may apply himself to either or both of these according to his destination or the desire of his parents. The Mercantile Department embraces Reading, Writing, the English and French Languages, Poetry, Rhetoric, History, Geography, Mythology, Bookkeeping, Arithmetic, Algebra, Geometry, the Use of the Globes, Trigonometry, Mensuration and Surveying.

The Classical Department, besides the above-specified subjects, comprises the Latin and Greek Languages, Logic, Metaphysics, Moral and Natural Philosophy, and the Higher Branches of the Mathematics. The

Spanish, if required, is taught to the students of both departments without any additional charge. The English is the ordinary language of communication in all the classes, the French and Spanish excepted; but the students speak French and English indiscriminately during the hours of recreation.

Probably very few of the subjects enumerated were taught in this year, 1832–3. According to Jesuit custom, premiums were awarded in practically every branch. No premium list is given in the catalogue for this year, but that of the following year, 1833–4, gives a complete list. According to this, there were four classes in Latin, none in Greek, two classes of Spanish, one class of algebra and geometry combined, five classes of arithmetic, six classes of French, five grammar [English?] classes, and a class of rhetoric. Premiums for Greek were first announced in the catalogue for 1835–6, although according to De Theux's letter cited above,[12] elementary Greek had been taught as early as 1832.

The Cincinnati School in 1842

After the appearance of Roothaan's *Ratio* in 1832, the curriculum in American Jesuit schools was for many decades practically uniform, with slight changes in terminology, as a study of the catalogues will show. The catalogue of St. Xavier College, Cincinnati, Ohio, for 1842–3, represents the typical course of studies for that period.[13]

DISTRIBUTION OF TIME AND ORDER OF THE CLASSES

A.M.

5½ o'clock	Prayer — Studies
5½ o'clock	Recess[14]

A.M. *Classical Course*		*A.M.* *Mercantile Course*	
8	Penmanship or Studies	8	Bookkeeping, Penmanship
8½	Latin	8½	Studies, Penmanship
9½	Greek	9	English, Penmanship

Classical and Mercantile Course

A.M.

10¼ English

11 History and Geography for the Junior Classes
11¼ History, Mythology, Geography, use of the Globes, and Elocution for 3rd Senior Class
11¼ Chemistry, Physics, Philosophy, and Elocution for the 1st and 2nd Senior Classes
12 Recess
P.M.
1½ Studies
2½ French
3½ Arithmetic, Mathematics
4½ Recess
5 Studies
6½ Studies continued — German Class
7¼ Moral Lecture
7½ Recess

N.B. The day scholars are not only permitted, but are required, as far as practicable, to attend the morning and evening studies.

Course of Studies

Sixth Class [equivalently first-year high]

Latin: Adam's Grammar, Epitome Historiae Sacrae, Phaedri Fabulae.

English: Murray's Abridged Grammar, Grimshaw's United States.

French: Porney's Syllabaire, Bolmar's Colloquial Phrases.

Accessory Branches: Smith's Arithmetic, Mitchell's Abridged Geography, Loriquez' Sacred History.

Fifth Class [equivalently second-year high]

Latin: Adam's Latin Grammar, Mair's Syntax, Phaedri Fabulae, Cornelius Nepos.

Greek: Goodrich's Grammar and Exercises, Grimshaw's Rome.

French: Letellier's Grammar, Perrin's Fables.

Accessory Branches: Smith's Arithmetic, Mitchell's Geography and Atlas, German Grammar and Reader.

Fourth Class [equivalently third-year high]

Latin: Adam's Grammar, Mair's Syntax, Cæsar, Sallust, Cicero's minor works.

Greek: Graeca Minora, Grammar and Exercises.

English: Murray's Grammar, and Exercises, Grimshaw's Greece, Irving's Mythology.

French: Letellier's Grammar and Exercises, Telemaque.

Accessory Branches: Smith's Arithmetic, Mitchell's Geography and Atlas, and Geographical Reader, Bookkeeping.

Third Class [equivalently fourth-year high]

Latin: Alvarez' Prosody, Ovid, Vergil, Horace.

Greek: Grammar and Exercises, Xenophon.

English: Blair's Lectures abridged, Parker's Exercises, Modern History.

French: Telemaque, Art Poetique de Boileau, Grammaire de Chapsal.

Accessory Branches: Bourdon's Algebra, Playfair's Euclid, Keith on the Globes.

The Curriculum in the 50's

From time to time there were minor changes, for the most part either in textbook or nomenclature of classes. The two following courses of studies, for 1852–3, one for St. Joseph's College, Bardstown, Kentucky, the other for Georgetown College, Washington, are typical of the Jesuit curriculum in the 50's.

The Bardstown Course of Studies, in 1852[15]

In Mathematics

Third Class [fourth-year high]: Algebra; Davies' Bourdon; Linear and Plane Geometry; Davies' Legendre.

In Arithmetic

[Presumably in third, second, and first years]: Davies' Arithmetic (University Edition).

In the Greek Department

Third Class: Homer, Xenophon's Anabasis, Grammar, Syntax, Exercises.

Fourth Class: Lucian's Dialogues; Xenophon's Anabasis; Grammar, Syntax, Exercises.

Fifth Class: Graeca Minora, Grammar; Exercises.

Sixth Class: Grammar, Exercises.

In the Latin Department

Third Class: Sallust, Vergil's Eclogues and Georgics, Syntax, Prosody, Exercises.

Fourth Class: Cæsar's Commentaries; Cicero de Amicitia and Senectute. Ovid's Metamorphoses; Grammar, Syntax, Exercises.

Fifth Class: Cornelius Nepos; Cicero's Letters; Grammar, Exercises.

Sixth Class: Epitome Historiae Sacrae; Viri Romae; Grammar. Exercises.

In the English Department

Third Class: Murray's Grammar; Parker's Exercises; Epistolary Composition; Fredet's Modern History; Mylius' England; Mitchell's Geography and Atlas.

Fourth Class: Murray's Grammar and Exercises; Hale's History of the United States; Sacred History (abridged); Mitchell's Geography and Atlas.

Fifth Class: Murray's Grammar (abridged); Kearney's History of the United States; Mitchell's Geography (abridged).

Sixth Class: Spelling, Reading, Mitchell's Geography (abridged).

NOTE: Worcester's Dictionary has been adopted as the standard of Orthography and Pronunciation.

The Georgetown Curriculum in 1852[16]

First Class [equivalently first-year high]

Latin Grammar, Viri Romae, or Cicero's Select Letters, Geography, English Grammar, History of the Bible, Latin and English Exercises, Arithmetic, Writing.

Second Class

Nepos' Lives, Cicero's Letters, Fables of Phaedrus, Greek Grammar, Latin Grammar, English Grammar, Æsop's Fables in Greek, Geography of North America, History of the United States, Latin and Greek Exercises, Arithmetic, Writing, and Bookkeeping.

Third Class

First Term: Curtius, Ovid's Metamorphoses, Graeca Minora, Ancient History of the Republics of Athens and Sparta, Greek Grammar, Latin Grammar, English Grammar, Latin, Greek and English Exercises, Geography of South America and Europe, Mythology.

Second Term: Cæsar, Ovid's Tristium, etc.

Both Terms: Algebra.

Humanities[17]

First Term

Sallust, Vergil (Eclogues and Georgics), Lucian's Dialogues, Geography of Asia and Africa, History of Greece, Doctrine of Particles

(Tursellini), Alvarez' Prosody, Scanning and construction of Latin verse, Latin Grammar, Greek Grammar. Rules for the Formation of style, Exercises in Latin, Greek, and English.

Second Term

Cicero's Minor Works, Vergil's Æneid, Xenophon's Cyropædia, Theocritus.

Both Terms

Plane and Solid Geometry (Davies' Legendre), and Algebra continued.

Both of these institutions had a four-year French course, but it is not clear from the catalogues whether these classes were open to the preparatory students. As many of the students at both schools during this period were of French ancestry, and spoke that language at home, it is probable that some of the younger students were admitted to the higher French classes. The *Georgetown Catalogue* states:

> The study of the French language is an essential part of the collegiate course. There are four Professors of French, among whom the students are divided according to their proficiency and instructed four hours every week. The Italian, German, and Spanish languages will be taught, if required; but together with Music, Drawing, Dancing, Fencing and other similar accomplishments, they will form additional charges.

Curriculum Remains Static

It is obvious, of course, that the Jesuit curriculum for these and succeeding decades remained conventionally static. Latin, Greek, and English were the principal branches; geography and history were bound up with the English class; some instruction was given in arithmetic, algebra, and geometry. In the main, their courses did not differ greatly from the courses offered in the college-preparatory institutions of that period throughout the country.[18] The curriculum of the classical course at St. Louis University for 1857–58 remained practically unchanged for several decades; it is sufficiently typical of the Jesuit curriculum during the Civil War and succeeding period to warrant its inclusion here.

Curriculum of the St. Louis School, 1857–58[19]

First Year

Third Grammar Class

First Term:	English — Grammar, Exercises, History and Geography of the United States, Elocution.
	Greek — Grammar, Exercises, Æsop's Fables, Hierocles
	Latin — Grammar, Exercises, Epitome Historiae Sacrae
Second Term:	English.
	Greek — (The same authors continued).
	Latin.
Both Terms:	Arithmetic, Penmanship.

Second Year

Second Grammar Class

First Term:	English — Syntax, Exercises, History of England, Geography of Europe, Elocution.
	Greek — Syntax, Exercises, Palaephatus; Old and New Testaments.
	Latin — Syntax, Exercises, Nepos.
Second Term:	English — (The same authors continued).
	Greek — Syntax, Exercises, Plutarch, Lucian's Dialogues.
	Latin — Syntax, Exercises, Cæsar, Phaedrus.
Both Terms:	Arithmetic, Penmanship.

Third Year

First Grammar Class

First Term:	English — Comparative Grammar of the English, Greek and Latin Languages. General Principles of Style, Epistolary Composition, Descriptions, Essays; Modern History, Geography of Asia and Africa.
	Greek — Applications of Grammar to Composition; Lucian's Dialogues; Anacreon.
	Latin — Application of Grammar to Composition; Ovid; Cicero de Senectute et Amicitia.
	Arithmetic continued.
Second Term:	English — General outlines of English Literature; Composition.
	Greek — General outlines of Greek Literature, Composition, Xenophon's Cyropaedia.
	Latin — General Outlines of Latin Literature, Composition, Algebra.

Fourth Year

Second Rhetoric Class

First Term:	English — Prosody, Aids to Composition, Ancient History and Geography; weekly Debates and Essays.
	Greek — Prosody, Dialects, Homer, Composition.
	Latin — Prosody, Livy, Vergil, Composition.
	Algebra continued. Olmsted's Application of the Principles of Mechanics; Hydrostatics; Hydraulics; Heat; Chemical Combinations; Non-Metallic Elements.
Second Term:	English — (The same authors continued).
	Greek — Demosthenes; Composition in Verse and Prose.
	Latin — Vergil, Horace; Composition in Verse and Prose; History of the Poets and Poetry of the English, Greek and Latin Languages.
	Geometry, Pneumatics, Meteorology, Acoustics.
	Chemistry — Metallic Elements; Salts and Mineralogy.

The "Mercantile" Course

Besides this classical course, there was also a four-year mercantile or commercial course. The course in English was the same, but bookkeeping was added; and more time was given to mathematics, chemistry, and physics. Very probably the mercantile students were obliged to take one of the modern languages. This same catalogue announces; "The study of the French, German, Spanish and Italian languages is optional in either course."

In the succeeding years only minor changes were made; and the usage of St. Louis is typical of Jesuit schools the country over. Names of classes varied in different cities, but the curriculum was practically uniform. Occasionally an author was substituted, or a new textbook introduced. Here and there slight changes crept in for a time, due very possibly to educational practice in local non-Jesuit schools; thus, modern languages, generally French, were obligatory at Georgetown in 1861 and took up four hours in the weekly schedule.[20] A more generous allotment was given to mathematics — five hours a week.[21] Elementary astronomy was taught at St. Francis Xavier, New York, in fourth-year classes in 1870.[22]

The "distribution of classes" at the St. Louis school appears for the first time in the catalogue for 1877–8.

Distribution of Classes[23]

A.M.		
8	German, French, Study	
	Classical Course	*Commercial Course*
8¾	Greek	Mathematics or Arithmetic
9½	Recess	
9¾	Latin, English, Bookkeeping	
10¾	Chemistry or Natural Philosophy; or Study and Penmanship for both courses	
11¾	Recess	
P.M.		
1½	Study	
2	Mathematics or Arithmetic; twice a week Religion for both courses	
3	English, History, and Geography	
4	Recess	

Ratio Not Introduced in Its Entirety

Two observations are pertinent here with regard to the above schedules and curricula. First, in the main, the courses in Jesuit colleges differed but little from those in American schools of the college-preparatory type of this period. The same textbooks are used. Yenni's Latin Grammar, a Jesuit textbook, was not introduced until 1870; Yenni's Greek Grammar in 1877. The one exception was the history text; Fredet's History, a book by a Catholic, was commonly used in Jesuit schools. But the same Latin and Greek authors were read for the most part; in Greek, Xenophon and Homer; in Latin, Cæsar, Cicero, and Vergil.[24] The second observation is this: although the Jesuit curriculum differs only in accidentals from that of the American academies up to approximately 1880, it does differ radically from the revised *Ratio* of Roothaan. This supposed that "of the five hours of teaching on ordinary days, two in the morning are to be given to the study of Latin, and two in the afternoon to that of Latin and Greek. The remaining half hour at the end of each class is to be employed in teaching *ex professo* the vernacular tongue and the accessories."[25] It is obvious, from the typical curricula submitted, that this quantum of time was never given to the classics in American Jesuit schools.

The purpose of each of the first four years of the course is stated in the St. Louis catalogue for 1878–9.

First Year — Third Humanities. This class is meant to impart chiefly an elementary knowledge of Latin and Greek. Besides furthering the pupil in Arithmetic, English, American History and Geography, it introduces him to the Classical Course and begins to fit him for professional life. While the Commercial branches are carefully attended to, the talent for classic culture is closely observed and the pupil directed accordingly.

Second Year — Second Humanities. The object of this class is to develop more perfectly the knowledge of Greek and Latin in the idiom. The Commercial Branches — English Grammar and Composition, History, Geography, and Arithmetic — are continued and much attention is paid to them, though the class is appreciated chiefly in proportion as it may promise graduation in the Classical Courses.

Third Year — First Humanities. This class cultivates talent for style in Epistolary, Narrative and Descriptive Composition. While the Classics are well cared for, and History and Geography, Arithmetic and Algebra are of daily recitation, Bookkeeping and other branches suitable to commercial life are not forgotten, even though the student is supposed to aim chiefly at success in a profession.

Fourth Year — Poetry. In this class the student begins to study the nature of poetry and to familiarize himself with the various kinds of poetical composition. Original poems and essays form a daily exercise in class work, and the Greek and Latin authors are given as models for imitation.

Absence of Electivism

Up to 1880 — and indeed, for the next two or more decades — there was practically no electivism in American Jesuit schools. Most of the western schools and a few of the eastern offered a commercial course as an alternative to the classical course, but there was no choice offered within these courses, with the exception of French and German, an "accessory" in most places. Despite the uniformity in the Jesuit curriculum, divergent practice had developed in some schools with regard to branches like English, mathematics, history, and science. To secure efficiency, it was thought desirable that each of the Jesuit provinces should draw up a curriculum, binding on all the schools, clearly defining the branches to be taught and the amount of matter to be seen in each branch.

A letter of the Provincial of the Missouri Province, Father R. J. Meyer, to his province, calls attention to this need in a letter dated October 1, 1886.[26] He orders each rector to appoint a local committee on studies in his college; and he himself appoints a central committee for the province to collate and codify the findings of the local committees. Various suggestions are offered by the Provincial in this letter "for the purpose of facilitating the work of the Committees, but without any intention of dictating their course of action." He insists that the *Ratio Studiorum* should be adhered to as closely as possible in the classical course both with regard to grading and method as well as to textbooks and exercises. The method of the *Ratio,* according to this letter, consists "in making the Precepts [rules of Rhetoric, Composition, Grammar, etc.], Models [authors read and translated], and Practice correspond to one another." Other questions were proposed for discussion by the committees, notably the need of uniformity in the teaching of mathematics and the desirability of assigning one teacher exclusively to this branch.

Attempts at Uniformity

In 1887, Father Meyer submitted the final report of these committees to his province.[27] The rectors are told to print in their catalogues the course of studies agreed upon. No changes are to be introduced without the Provincial's permission. "Other methods may have their merit, but not all of them can be engrafted on the method of the *Ratio Studiorum* . . . which though capable of being accommodated to the exigencies of the times, cannot be set aside or ignored by us without the risk of abandoning all method."

This "Report of the Central Committee," dated May 17, 1887,[28] is the first of a series of similar documents, prescribing a course of studies for a group of schools, and specifying with some detail the matter to be seen in each class. This report. with its subjoined course of studies, was mandatory only for the schools of the Missouri Province. This document is well worth examining.

The report opens with some general remarks about education; it calls attention to the fact that the work of education is "a primary object of our Institute. Though the Society is not adverse to special schools, where they are needed, it is not her object in establishing colleges to turn out specialists, but to develop all the mental and moral faculties of the students by means of a liberal education of which thorough instruction in the principles of religion forms an essential part." The committee says that the *Ratio* has been their guide in their work. Attention is called to the need of a fixed standard; without it "we shall go on promoting from class to class and graduating them before they are able to write correctly in any language." The direction of the *Ratio* in regard to the *Prelectio* should be carried out. Students ought not to be left unaided to contend with the intricacies of the text and the difficulties of dictionary work. "It should be the aim of the professor to make all class-work, especially the study of the classics, as agreeable and instructive as possible."

Mention is made of the number of branches introduced into the ordinary course of a liberal education since the *Ratio* of 1832. "So much more attention is given to mathematics, sciences, history, geography, that time formerly given to the classics is now divided between these extra branches and a more thorough study of the vernacular." The committee urged the abandonment of scientific and commercial courses, that is, courses without Latin and Greek. The study of chemistry and physics should be relegated to the college, but it is recommended that in the lower classes some instruction should be given in elementary geology, botany, etc. The committee did not think that formal classes with textbooks were needed for this; it would be sufficient for the professor to prepare a talk on these topics from time to time. It may well be doubted whether this indefinite recommendation was ever put into effect.

There is no mention of a formal course in history for the lower (i.e., high-school) classes. French and German were optional branches, that is, the more capable students might take these languages in addition to the regular studies; it was not permissible to substitute them for Latin or Greek. The teachers of English are urged not to be content with merely reading selections; models for reading and study should be in the hands of the students.

Missouri Province Course for 1887

The course prescribed for the high-school classes of the Missouri Province schools in 1887 was as follows:[29]

Third Academic [First Year]: Latin: Yenni's Grammar; Historia Sacra. Daily themes and drill. English: Choice selections pointed out or dictated. Reading and Spelling, Arithmetic, History of the United States, Geography, Elocution, Penmanship.

Second Academic [Second Year]: Latin: Yenni's Grammar. Models: Phaedrus, 150 lines. Prose fables and dialogues. Second Term: Viri Romae. Greek: begun Second Term. Grammar and drill. Easy themes. English: Murray's Grammar, Choice selections pointed out or dictated. Easier Compositions. Arithmetic. Accessory Branches: Fredet's Modern History. Geography, Elocution. Penmanship daily.

First Academic [Third Year]: Latin: Nepos, 500 lines. Second Term: Cæsar, 300 lines; Cicero, Letters. Greek: Yenni's Greek Grammar. Greek Anthology, 100 lines. Second term: 200 lines. English: Coppen's Rhetoric. Models: Irving's *Rip Van Winkle, Legend of Sleepy Hollow,* Goldsmith's *Deserted Village;* Selections from Longfellow. Mathematics: Algebra. Accessory Branches: Fredet's Modern History. Geography. Elocution. Penmanship daily.

Class of Humanities [Fourth Year]: Latin: Cæsar, 300 lines; Ovid, 300 lines. Second Term: Four Eclogues of Vergil. Cicero, Extracts. Selections from Christian Poets. Themes and Verse-making. Greek: Greek Anthology, 300 lines; 150 lines into Latin. Second Term: Anabasis, 500 lines, 200 into Latin. English: Coppens' Rhetoric. Models: Longfellow, Scott, *Lady of the Lake,* Irving, Selections from Standard Novelists. Selections from Knight's *Half Hours with the Best Authors,* etc. Mathematics: Wentworth's Geometry. Accessory Branches: Ancient History. Elocution, Bookkeeping. Catechism.

It will be noted that arithmetic, grammar, and geography were taught in the first three years of the Jesuit high schools even at this date. This was due to the fact that boys were admitted to the Jesuit school upon the completion of the sixth grade. Another point of interest is that Greek was obligatory for all those that took the classical course. The distribution of time for the various branches at this period was as follows:[30]

Distribution of Hours per Week in Missouri Province Schools

Classics	9	hours per week
Mathematics	4	hours per week
English and Accessories	12	hours per week
Science	0	hours per week

Distribution of Hours per Week in Maryland-New York Province Schools

Classics	13½	hours per week
Mathematics	5½	hours per week
English and Accessories	8	hours per week
Science	0	hours per week

The 1887 course outlined above was given a fair trial in the Missouri Province schools for five years and seems to have met with general satisfaction according to the letter of Reverend J. P. Frieden, the Provincial, addressed to all rectors of the province.[31] "Owing to local and temporary causes," he says, "it has been found hard at times to carry out all the provisions in this or that particular class or college; but the higher standard which now prevails in our schools, especially where the course has been strictly followed, proves the advantages connected with its observance."

The Course of 1907

A new general committee drew up a new course in 1893,[32] but this differed only verbally from the 1887 program. It can safely be said that this course of studies (1887) remained in force with minor changes for twenty years in the Jesuit schools of the Middle West. In February, 1907, the Provincial, Reverend Henry Moeller, submitted a revised course of studies. The changing conditions of the modern educational world urgently demanded a complete reorganization of the Jesuit high-school curriculum. The 1907 course of studies marks an important date for the American Jesuit high school. This course prescribed for the first time the completion of the eighth grade before entrance, although in many places this had been the rule for several years. Moreover, the course was increased to eight years, making four years' high school and four years' college; but as yet there was no differentiation in administration. Three courses were recommended. Besides the classical course and the commercial course, a new course was introduced, the Latin-English which differed from the classical only by the substitution of a modern language for Greek. But this was the first time in America that a Jesuit school made Greek an elective. However, a new provincial and a new committee in the following year[33] vetoed the non-Greek course.

The schedule of class periods a week in this 1907 schedule was formidable: first year, 26; second, 24; third, 28; fourth, 25. Two periods a week were assigned to science in each year, besides one entire semester of four periods to physics. The schedule of 1908 reduced the class periods somewhat: first year, 24; second, third, and fourth, 25. On the other hand, 10 hours a week were assigned to Latin in the first year, and 7 hours in the second, third, and fourth years. This generous allotment to Latin was probably due to the Maryland-New York Province schedule of 1905,[34] which likewise prescribed 25 hours of class in each year of the high school distributed as follows:

	Lt.	*Gk.*	*Math.*	*Hist.*	*Eng.*	*Sci.*	*Mod. Lang.*	*Miscell.*
1st Year, 1st Term...	10	0	5	2	6	1	0	1
1st Year, 2nd Term..	7	5	5	2	4	1	0	1
2nd, 3rd, 4th Year...	7	5	4	2	3	0	3	1

A rather interesting comment in this same Maryland-New York schedule is the following: "The sciences have been omitted in the high-school course as they are not considered of any great educational value during this period of a boy's education."

Coöperation Among the American Provinces

From this date there were annual reports of the committee on studies in both these provinces as well as in the California and New Orleans Provinces. A notable tendency toward uniformity in all American Jesuit schools is observable. Thus, in the 1911 course of studies for the Missouri Province,[35] the foreword states that this course had been "elaborated by experienced educators well acquainted with the *Ratio Studiorum* and the requirements of modern times, who had availed themselves of the work of other committees and of the findings of a similar committee in another American Province." This course, approved by the General of the Society, was decidedly conservative. No more electives were allowed than in the earlier schedules; Greek was demanded of all who wished to secure a high-school diploma. The opponents of Greek in the Missouri Province continued their agitation. A "memorial" was sent to the General from the Missouri Province in 1916,[36] showing the impossibility of continuing obligatory Greek in the schools of the province. The reasons alleged for the dropping of Greek were the prejudices of parents and students against the language and the fact that the majority of pupils do not go beyond the high school and therefore do not obtain sufficient knowledge and appreciation of Greek literature which alone justify giving Greek a place in the curriculum. Moreover, many boys cannot study the language with profit. The Maryland-New York schools, however, were not in favor of making Greek an elective, and a heated controversy was carried on in the pages of *The Teacher's Review* and *The Province News-Letter,* both Jesuit publications, by representatives of the two provinces. Not until 1919 were the American Jesuits allowed to give a classical diploma in the high school without Greek.

Conservatism of Jesuit Curricula

While all Jesuit high schools have conservative leanings, it may be safely said that this is particularly marked in the case of the schools east of the Alleghanies. They have shown themselves distinctly unfriendly to any encroachment on the time-honored curriculum. The other Jesuit schools of the country, under the leadership of the Missouri Province, while clinging loyally to the Jesuit method, have shown a readiness to conform in curricular requirements to the high-school standards in the localities where they are placed. Possibly this is due to the pressure brought to bear by standardizing agencies, much more potent in the West and South than along the Atlantic coast; or it may be due to the presence of better traditions of classical culture and a truer appreciation of a strictly classical education in the eastern states than in the West.

Adaptation of Curriculum in the West

This readiness to submit to change was clearly indicated by the Missouri Committee in the "Supplement to the Course of Studies of 1911,"[37] where it is stated that "the Committee recognizes that the present course, though prepared with much care, is capable of being perfected from year to year; and for this reason, they invite further comments and suggestions, which they promise to give the most careful consideration." In 1914, Father A. J. Burrowes, the Missouri Provincial, projected a revision of the high-school schedule then in operation with a view to bringing it more in harmony with the accepted standardized schedules followed more or less uniformly in the public secondary schools of the country.[38] In August, 1915, the General Report of the Committee of Studies for the Missouri Province appeared.[39] One reason for reorganizing the curriculum was the fact that

> . . . state governments are ever more and more taking in hand the work of regulating and supervising educational matters. The sooner we forestall this by bringing our schools up to required standards and putting our work into such shape as is intelligible to those outside of the Society, the easier will it be for our schools to receive due recognition. . . . The . . . interchange of students between our . . . high schools and the state high schools makes it expedient to have a common ground of uniformity, as far as possible.

Further on in the same document is a passage not without interest:

It need not be said that we do not regard with unqualified approval all the methods and practices of other schools, but there are good elements, too, in modern educational effort; and it would not be a wise policy to shut our eyes to these even though they are of recent discovery or introduction. On the contrary, we ought to take advantage of them. Our early Fathers, who put together the *Ratio Studiorum,* availed themselves of all that was best in the educational methods of their time. We should pursue the same policy . . . with reference to the educational methods of our time. . . . It is well for us to know the practice of other schools and to consider whether and to what extent it is advisable for us to conform to them. We cannot remain isolated and shut our eyes as though we were the only laborers in the field. This might do very well, if we educated boys exclusively for the seminary; but our work is not exclusively, it is not even mainly, directed toward educating candidates for the priesthood. We are instructing young men in secular branches of learning and in doing this we set ourselves up, whether we will it or no, as rivals of other institutions engaged in the same work — institutions that have the wisdom and wealth of the world at their backs and are not slow to utilize these means for the purpose of challenging comparison and drawing even Catholic boys into their own halls. We cannot and need not rival such schools in worldly prosperity, but we must not be behind them in the quality and standard of education they profess to impart. For this reason, if for no other, we must know of their work and their standards. But there is another reason that is becoming more and more urgent. It is a fact that secular institutions of learning through their various organizations are beginning to set the standard of what shall be required of a school in order to receive due recognition as a secondary school. This standardizing tendency is the natural result of organization in the field of education and is bound to have its way. . . . If they know nothing of our colleges, or knowing them, find that they do not measure up to the standards set by themselves, we are simply left out of account. . . . We have a perfect right to stand apart and follow our own line, regardless of the practices of other colleges; but then we need not be surprised to find that our students suffer from it in various ways.

Place of Classics in Jesuit High Schools

The high-school schedules drawn up by the Missouri Province in 1915 represent a further stage in the development of the secondary curriculum in Jesuit schools. It was a definite recognition that there must be conformity to local standards if the Jesuit high school was to continue. Accordingly, while the classics still hold their dominant place in the curriculum, other courses are offered without Greek, and even a scientific course without Latin.

But it should not be forgotten that the Jesuit high schools are still strongholds of the classics; this is particularly true of the Maryland-New York high schools. Although the schools of this province are free to make Greek an elective, yet four[40] of the twelve still require all to follow the rigid Latin-Greek curriculum. In the *Revised Program of Studies for the High Schools of the Maryland-New York Province for 1923*,[41] there is the significant recommendation:

> Both teachers and prefects are expected to foster the Greek course in preference to the science course by their advice and encouragement and by their whole declared attitude in favor of Greek. They should create the understanding in the school that the non-Greek course is intended for less-talented students and for such as have no aptitude for going on to college.

That this recommendation has been effective is evident from the fact that of the 6,989 high-school students in this group of schools in 1924–25, only 889, or less than 13 per cent, were non-Greek students.

The percentage of Greek students in the other Jesuit high schools of the country is considerably lower; yet Greek is taught in all but three of the schools. And Latin is everywhere in honor. In the Maryland-New York Province all must take Latin; in the rest of the country, approximately 80 per cent of the students take Latin, no matter in what course they are enrolled. It will be noted in the typical curricula, representative of present practice in the various Jesuit provinces in this country, that the eastern schools allot more time to Latin than do the other schools; moreover, no science is obligatory, and is not even offered as an elective in some schools of this group. The curricula in the other Jesuit high schools of the country differ but little from the classical and scientific curricula in public high schools of the more conservative type.

Typical Courses of Studies: Maryland-New York Province[42]

SCHEDULE OF PERIODS PER WEEK

First Semester

First Year		*Second Year*		*Third Year*		*Fourth Year*	
Algebra	5	Algebra	5	English	4	English	5
Religion	2	Religion	2	Religion	2	Religion	2
English	5	English	3	Greek	5	Greek	5
Anc. History	4	Greek	5	Latin	6	Latin	6
Latin	9	Am. History	4	Mod. Lang.	4	Mod. Lang.	4
Phys. Train.	2	Latin	6	Pl. Geometry	4	Phys. Train.	2
		Phys. Train.	2	Phys. Train.	2	Trigonometry	4

Second Semester

First Year		*Second Year*		*Third Year*		*Fourth Year*	
Algebra	5	Algebra	5	Religion	2	Religion	2
Religion	2	Religion	2	English	4	English	5
English	5	Civics	4	Greek	5	Greek	5
Anc. History	4	English	3	Latin	6	Latin	8
Latin	9	Greek	5	Mod. Lang.	4	Mod. Lang.	4
Phys. Train.	2	Latin	6	Pl. Geometry	4	Phys. Train.	2
		Phys. Train.	2	Phys. Train.	2		

On page 24 of the same document, the subjects to be offered in place of Greek, where that is an elective, are enumerated: "In second year, biology; in third year, physics; in fourth year, chemistry; each to be taken for the same number of semester hours as the Greek course . . . either for three lecture periods and two double periods of laboratory, or for four lecture periods and one double period of laboratory."

Missouri Province[43]

I. CLASSICAL COURSE

First Semester

First Year		*Second Year*		*Third Year*		*Fourth Year*	
English I	5	English II	5	English III	5	English IV	5
Latin I	5	Latin II	5	Latin III	5	Latin IV	5
Algebra I	5	Geometry I	5	History I	5	Greek II	5
History I	5	History II	5	or Algebra II	5	Physics	6
				or Biology	5		
				Greek I	5		

Second Semester

First Year		*Second Year*		*Third Year*		*Fourth Year*	
English I	5	English II	5	English III	5	English IV	5
Latin I	5	Latin II	5	Latin III	5	Latin IV	5
Algebra I	5	Geometry I	5	Greek I	5	Greek II	5
History I	5	History II	5	History III	5	Physics	6
				or Sol. Geom.	5		
				or Biology	5		

II. SCIENTIFIC COURSE

First Semester

First Year	*Second Year*	*Third Year*	*Fourth Year*
English I....... 5	English II...... 5	English III..... 5	English IV..... 5
Latin I 5	Latin II........ 5	Latin III....... 5	Latin IV....... 5
		or Mod. Lang. 5	or Mod. Lang. 5
Algebra I....... 5	Geometry I..... 5	Algebra II...... 5	Amer. History... 5
History I....... 5	History II...... 5	Chemistry 6	Physics 6
or Gen. Sci... 5	or Drawing... 5	or Biology.... 6	Trigonometry .. 5

Second Semester

First Year	*Second Year*	*Third Year*	*Fourth Year*
English I....... 5	English II...... 5	English III..... 5	English IV..... 5
Latin I......... 5	Latin II........ 5	Latin III....... 5	Latin IV....... 5
Algebra I....... 5	Geometry I..... 5	or Mod. Lang. 5	or Mod. Lang. 5
History I....... 5	History II...... 5	Geometry II.... 5	Civics 5
or Gen. Sci... 5	or Drawing... 5	Chemistry 6	Physics 6
		or Biology.... 6	Adv. Algebra.... 5

III. LATIN-ENGLISH COURSE

First Semester

First Year	*Second Year*	*Third Year*	*Fourth Year*
English I....... 5	English II...... 5	English III..... 5	English IV...... 5
Latin I......... 5	Latin II........ 5	Latin III....... 5	Latin IV....... 5
Algebra I....... 5	Geometry I..... 5	Mod. Lang...... 5	Mod. Lang...... 5
History I....... 5	History II...... 5	History III..... 5	Physics 6
	or Biology.... 5	or Algebra II.. 5	

Second Semester

First Year	*Second Year*	*Third Year*	*Fourth Year*
English I....... 5	English II...... 5	English III..... 5	English IV..... 5
Latin I......... 5	Latin II........ 5	Latin III....... 5	Latin IV....... 5
Algebra I....... 5	Geometry I..... 5	Mod. Lang...... 5	Mod. Lang...... 5
History I....... 5	History II...... 5	History III..... 5	Physics 6
	or Biology.... 5	or Geom. III.. 5	

New Orleans Province[44]

COURSE I. THE HONORS-CLASSICAL COURSE

First Year	*Second Year*	*Third Year*	*Fourth Year*
Latin I........ 5	Latin II........ 5	Latin III....... 5	Latin IV....... 5
English I....... 5	English II...... 5	English III..... 5	English IV..... 5
Algebra I....... 5	Plane Geom..... 5	Alg. II (1 sem.) 5	Sol. Geom. (1 sem.) 5
Med. History ... 5	French I........ 5	Am. Hist. (2 sem.) 5	Civics (2 sem.).. 5
Elocution 1	or Spanish I.. 5	French II...... 5	Physics 6
Superv. Study... 4	Elocution 1	or Spanish II.. 5	or Chemistry.. 6
	Supervised Study 4	Greek I........ 5	Greek II....... 5

COURSE II. THE CLASSICAL COURSE

First Year	*Second Year*	*Third Year*	*Fourth Year*
Latin I........ 5	Latin II........ 5	Latin III....... 5	Latin IV....... 5
English I....... 5	English II...... 5	English III..... 5	English IV...... 5
Algebra I....... 5	Geometry I..... 5	Alg. II (1 sem.) 5	Sol. Geom. (1 sem.) 5
Med. History... 5	French I....... 5	Am. Hist. (2 sem.) 5	Civics (2 sem.).. 5
Elocution 1	or Spanish I.. 5	French II...... 5	Physics 6
Superv. Study... 4	Elocution 1	or Spanish II.. 5	or Chemistry.. 6
	Superv. Study... 4	Elocution 1	Elocution 1
		Superv. Study... 4	Supervised Study 4

California Province[45]

ACADEMIC SCHEDULE

First Semester

First Year		*Second Year*		*Third Year*		*Fourth Year*	
Religion	2	Religion	2	Religion	2	Religion	2
Latin	5	Latin	5	Latin	5	Latin	5
English	5	English	5	English	4	English	5
Algebra	5	Geometry	5	Physics	5	Chemistry	5
European Hist...	5	Med. Hist......	5	Amer. Hist......	5	Civics	5

Second Semester

First Year		*Second Year*		*Third Year*		*Fourth Year*	
Religion	2	Religion	2	Religion	2	Religion	2
Latin	5	Latin	5	Latin	5	Latin	5
English	5	English	5	English	5	English	5
Algebra	5	Geometry	5	Physics	6	Chemistry	5
European Hist...	5	Mod. Hist......	5	Amer. Hist......	5	Mod. Europ. H..	5

Electives

First Year		*Second Year*		*Third Year*		*Fourth Year*	
				French	5	Biology	5
		Greek	5	Spanish	5	Stenography ...	5
				Greek	5	French	5
				Mech. Draw.....	5	Spanish	5
				Alg. Theory.....	5	Mech. Draw.....	5
				Trigon.	5	Trigon.	4
						Alg. Theory	5

Factors That Have Fashioned the American Jesuit High-School Curriculum

The curriculum in the American Jesuit high school has undergone a number of changes. There was in the beginning an attempt at a college not unlike its European prototype. The example, however, of the American academy, and very probably the same forces that fashioned it, influenced the curriculum of the Jesuit school. Economic and social factors were also at work; the desire of the pioneer communities for material advancement, especially in the West, brought about the introduction of "mercantile" courses into the Jesuit institutions, not without protest from the Order. The external force that kept the Jesuit school from going the way of the secular academy and high school was Roothaan's *Ratio,* and repeated insistence on the classical course from the central governing head of the Order. Yet, it is not without interest that nowhere in the United States was the *Ratio* ever introduced in its entirety, as far as curricular recommendations are concerned.

With the growth of the high-school movement in the United States, and the realization that its purpose was not primarily to prepare for college, the Jesuit college, hitherto a single entity, began to disintegrate into two distinct institutions, high school and college. Again, the same forces that were at work transforming the public high school helped to broaden the Jesuit high-school curriculum. Dissatisfaction with the strict classical course, demands for more practical preparation for life brought about a gradual, but perceptible change in the Jesuit schools. These factors were directly at work through the environment in which the Jesuit schools were placed; but undoubtedly a greater force was brought to bear indirectly. First, they could not afford to remain entirely outside the channel of current American educational practice, and secondly, they were obliged to adapt their curriculum to meet the requirements of the various standardizing agencies. Despite all this, the Jesuit school has remained distinctly conservative, still dominated by the classical tradition. The conservative and classical tendency is much more marked in the schools along the Atlantic seaboard than it is in the West.

Extracurricular Activities

From the very beginning the Jesuits encouraged extracurricular activities in their schools. The "academies," for example, received ample attention and encouragement in the *Ratio Studiorum.*[46] They were designed as an outlet for the more gifted students. The drama, too, was always held in high esteem in Jesuit schools; many pretentious tragedies and comedies were staged by Jesuit colleges in the heyday of their prosperity in Europe.[47] This tradition has always been preserved by the American Jesuits. The Puritan prejudice against the theater never took hold of the Jesuit schools. Thus, the Kentucky Jesuits presented a play shortly after their arrival from France.[48] At Santa Clara in California, the earliest records show that classical productions were an annual event even in the fifties. At the Chicago World's Fair in 1893, St. Francis Xavier College of New York presented a Latin play, the "Duo Captivi" of Plautus. As soon as a school was well established, an annual dramatic performance was undertaken — a practice still in vogue in Jesuit high schools.

Literary and debating societies flourished from the beginning, some with queer-sounding names. At Georgetown in the early days there were the Philodemic, the Phileleutherian, the Philonomosian, the Philhistoric, and the Philophrastic Societies.[49] These were matched at Cincinnati in the 50's by the Philopedean, the Philhermenian, the Cosmopeon, the Himirolectic, the Phileoglossian, and Euterpean Societies[50] — all intended to foster a taste for literature and eloquence. Indeed, during their entire history, the American Jesuit schools have been active in promoting what used to be known as "forensics." There were annual elocution, oratorical, and debating contests. And their modern successors have ably upheld this tradition.

At Santa Clara in California, debating received an early impetus with the arrival of Father Edmund Young, who had been in his youth a page in the United States Senate. He conceived the idea of a literary congress modeled on the Congress of the United States. He organized the two branches of the House and the Senate in the 70's. Yale and Harvard established each a similar congress in imitation of a Jesuit college in California where it has been in use for over thirty years. (*Yale-Alumni Weekly.*)[51]

Games and athletics, intramural and interscholastic contests have received due encouragement. High-school papers, too, are common to the Jesuit schools. But besides their literary and athletic organizations, common to all American schools, public and private, the Jesuits have one organization that is distinctively Catholic, and in its origin distinctively Jesuit — "the Sodality." This organization is found in all Jesuit schools the world over. Founded at the Roman College in the sixteenth century, it admitted to membership only those distinguished in talent and virtue.[52] In the American schools of the Order, it has become an organization for the cultivation of practical piety among the students. Sections are organized for the promotion of various activities; frequent Communion, charity to the poor, aid for the foreign missions, reading of good books. All the Sodalities are under the patronage of the Blessed Virgin Mary, and "the members of the Sodality strive in imitation of her to render themselves more and more worthy of her intercession and the protection of her Divine Son, and more Christlike by the promotion of all the spiritual and corporal works of mercy. These latter especially, fostered as they are throughout the school year, cannot but result in a spirit of active charity."[53] Another religious organization found in all Jesuit schools is the "Apostleship of Prayer"; its object is "to put in practice the law of universal charity by mutual prayer for the intentions of all members."[54]

Footnotes

[1]Davis, *Public Secondary Education*, pp. 58–9; see also Grizzell, *Origin and Development of the High School in New England before 1865*, p. 290.

[2]Grizzell, *loc. cit.*

[3]*Georgetown Archives*, LXII, 11.

[4]*Supra*, Chap. V.

[5]Vol. VII, 8.

[6]*Supra*, Chap. V.

[7]*Georgetown Archives*, LXII, 11.

[8]Branches are also assigned for two higher classes, humanities and rhetoric, but they are clearly intended to be beyond the secondary level.

[9]*Georgetown Archives.*

[10]*Supra*, Chap. VI.

[11]*Catalogue of St. Louis University for the year 1832–3.*

[12]See Chap. VI, "The Middle West."

[13]*Catalogue of St. Xavier College for the year 1842–3.* St. Xavier's was at this time a boarding school.

[14]This is probably a typographical error for 7½ o'clock. The order does not appear in succeeding catalogues.

[15]*Annual Commencement of St. Joseph's College, Bardstown, Kentucky, 1852–3* (Bardstown, 1853).

[16]*Catalogue of the Officers and Students of Georgetown College, District of Columbia, for the Academic Year 1852–1853.*

[17]The class of "Humanities" at Georgetown at this period is at the same time the fourth-year high (equivalently) and the first year of college. As has been noted before, little distinction was made between collegiate classes and preparatory classes.

[18]See Brown, *Making of Our Middle Schools*, Chap. XI; also classical department of Worcester High School and Hartford High School in Grizzell, *op. cit.*, pp. 303, 306.

[19]*Catalogue of St. Louis University for 1857–58.*

[20]*Catalogue of Georgetown College 1861–2.*

[21]*Ibid.*

[22]*Catalogue of St. Francis Xavier College, New York, 1870–1.*

[23]*Catalogue of St. Louis University, 1877–8.*

[24]See Monroe, *Cyclopedia of Education*, V, 100 ff.

[25]Archambault, *Notes on the Ratio Studiorum*, p. 47. Woodstock, 1889. See also *Ratio Studiorum*, "Reg. comm. prof. class, inf." 14.

[26]Letter in *Missouri Province Archives.*

[27]Letter of R. J. Meyer, June 2, 1887. *Missouri Province Archives.*

[28]*Missouri Province Archives.*

[29]"Report of Central Committees, 1887." *Missouri Province Archives.*

[30]Hughes, *Loyola and the Educational System of the Jesuits*, p. 282. The date treated

of in Hughes is 1891, a few years later than the Missouri schedule mentioned above. But this schedule was still in force at this date.

[31]Letter of J. P. Frieden to the Rectors of the Province, March 3, 1893. *Missouri Province Archives.*

[32]"Course of Studies for the College of the Missouri Province" (July 31, 1893). *Missouri Province Archives.*

[33]"Report of Committee of Studies" (1908). *Missouri Province Archives.*

[34]"Revised Schedule for High School," (August, 1905). *Maryland-New York Province Archives.*

[35]"Course of Studies for the Colleges of the Missouri Province" (1911). *Missouri Province Archives.*

[36]"Memorial to Very Reverend Father General on the Question of Compulsory Greek" (1916). *Missouri Province Archives.*

[37]*Missouri Province Archives.*

[38]"Our Educational Policy," MS. in the *Missouri Province Archives.*

[39]*Missouri Province Archives.*

[40]Boston College High School; Loyola School, New York; Regis High School, New York; Gonzaga High School, Washington, D. C.

[41]P. 24.

[42]*Revised Program of Studies for the High Schools of the Maryland-New York Province, 1923*, pp. 22–23. Equally typical of the recently created New England Province.

[43]Typical of all the schools in this and the new Chicago Province. Taken from the *Catalogue of Campion Preparatory School, Prairie du Chien, Wis., 1925–6.*

[44]From the *Catalogue of the Jesuit High School, New Orleans, 1925–26.* Typical of all the schools of this province.

[45]From the *Catalogue of the St. Ignatius High School, San Francisco, Cal., 1925–26.* Typical of all schools of this province.

[46]See *Appendix*, "Rules for the Academies."

[47]*Province News-Letter*, V, 52 ff.; Duhr, *Studienordnung*, pp. 137 ff.; Duhr, *Geschichte*, II, 1, 665; Chossat, *Les Jésuites à Avignon*, pp. 115 ff.; Schimberg, *L'Éducation Morale*, pp. 372–6.

[48]See *supra*, Chap. VI, "The Jesuits in Kentucky."

[49]Shea, *History of Georgetown College*, pp. 11 and 127.

[50]*Catalogue of St. Xavier College*, 1858–9.

[51]*America*, XXXIV, No. 24 (March 27, 1926), 566.

[52]Rochemonteix, *op. cit.*, p. 122. "Dans l'origine elle ne s'adressait qu' à l'élite de la jeunesse des écoles." See also Duhr, *op.cit.*, pp. 32 ff.

[53]*Regis High School Bulletin*, Denver, 1926.

[54]*St. Ignatius High School Catalogue*, Cleveland, 1926.

CHAPTER XI

JESUIT METHOD OF TEACHING

AS HAS been seen, the curriculum in American high schools has undergone considerable change. Even the 1832 *Ratio* regarded Latin as the principal study in the high-school course. While the vernacular and sciences are mentioned in this document, no one could possibly maintain that they are emphasized or that any directions are given for teaching these branches. Even in Latin, the amount of matter read has increased so radically that one must admit the modern American Jesuit high school has set up an aim for teaching the classics different from that visualized in the *Ratio*. The explanation of this change is, of course, that they regard curriculum as accidental; the branches taught in Jesuit schools may change so long as the main objective is attained.

In the same way, Jesuit methodology in the United States has been sensibly affected by the changed curriculum. The minute, painstaking method of teaching Latin, suitable for the seventeenth-century Jesuit school, where Latin was almost the sole subject in the curriculum, has been gradually eliminated in the American high schools. Some vestiges of their time-honored method still remain. But, despite the regret of many Jesuits, new teaching methods have come into their schools. This change has been allowed to take place because methodology, too, is regarded as accidental. New methods in no way interfered with their primary purpose, the imparting of a Christian education to Catholic youth.

Latin Methods

If there is a distinctive methodology in Jesuit schools, it should be apparent in the teaching of Latin. There is no question that the Jesuit method of teaching Latin was once quite definitely different from the method employed in the American public high school of today. The Jesuits of the seventeenth century, and their American successors in the early decades of the nineteenth century, were not bothered with determining objectives immediate and ultimate; they probably would not have understood what was meant by classifying "development of an historical and cultural background" or "development of right attitudes toward social situations"[1] as some of the purposes of Latin teaching.

The objective of Latin teaching, implicitly contained in the early *Ratio,* was, as has been seen, *eloquentia* — that is, the ability to talk and write Latin.[2] That objective was reëmphasized in Roothaan's *Ratio,* but unquestionably this became obscured in the course of curricular development in America with the addition of modern subjects and the lessening of the time allotted to Latin. The means adopted to foster *eloquentia* was the direct method of Latin teaching. The direct method is no longer in use in American Jesuit schools, and its gradual disappearance was regarded as a great loss. Thus Father Peter Beckx, the General of the Society from 1853 to 1883, deplores the passing of this method of teaching in Jesuit schools.

> Due to its neglect, he says,[3] nowadays there are very few, even after the completion of the gymnasium course, who have any facility not merely in expressing their thoughts in Latin speech or writing, but even in understanding Latin authors.

In the *Woodstock Letters* for 1893, an eloquent plea was made for the perpetuation of the direct method:[4]

> There can be no doubt of the possibility of having American boys speak Latin; it is a thing that has been done before, and is now being done in certain of our colleges, at least in some classes. A few, not many, of our professors object that Latin is, indeed, a good training for the mind, but need not be spoken. It does not require much acquaintance with teaching to know that our course of instruction is impossible in the higher classes, quite impossible, if Latin has not been taught the boys earlier as a living language.[5] It will be remembered, that do what we will about it, our course is a Latin one throughout, that the models of literary excellence we propose for study and imitation are in Latin; can it then fail to be clear that a literary estimate of an oration of Cicero, or a description from Vergil, or an ode of

Horace, is utterly out of the question unless the boys know Latin thoroughly, even to appreciating the niceties of its rhythm and taking delight in elegance of Latin diction? Is there any way of effecting these ends without insisting on Latin talk? The innovation of teaching Latin through the vernacular was introduced by the Port Royalists.

In fact, the direct-method tradition died very slowly in the American schools. Even as late as 1910, the Schedule of the Maryland-New York Province Committee of Studies strongly recommended that Latin conversation should be "more carefully attended to in the lower classes, as a tendency has been noted to neglect more and more the traditional practice of the Society."[6] Of course, it must not be imagined that in the American Jesuit schools of the nineteenth century at any time this objective of talking and writing Latin was attained with the same thoroughness as it was in their schools of the seventeenth century when Latin was the main subject in the curriculum Yet so inextricably was this objective bound up with the *Ratio*, that the Jesuits felt, unconsciously perhaps, that the newer objectives — formal discipline, for example — could be best attained by this painstaking, laborious process.

The Prelection

In their Latin teaching, too, they clung persistently to the method of *prelection*, which may be defined as the explanation beforehand of the lesson which the pupil has to study. The word occurs a great deal in the *Ratio*[7] and in Jesuit pedagogical writings. An American Jesuit writing on the prelection in the *Woodstock Letters*, 1893, says:[8]

The three rules (Rules 27, 28, 29 of the Common Rules for the Masters of the Lower Classes) on prelection are unquestionably the most essential for method of the entire *Ratio Studiorum*. They are distinctive of our method, "the typical form" as Father Hughes says (*Loyola*, p. 232) "of Jesuit instruction," and cut us off sharply from those teachers who are content with assigning so many lines of an author, or so many pages of precepts, and bidding the pupils to get them up by themselves. The Society's plan is entirely at war with this. We are bidden on every page of the *Ratio* to give no lesson without first explaining it, and explaining it thoroughly, bringing it down to the pupil's mind, smoothing its difficulties, making the road plain for him, so that when he comes to study his lesson at home he will find it attractive from being made easy, and interesting from his being made to see what it contains. With this start, a mighty help on his way, he can set to work on his imitation theme with a zest heightened by the consciousness of having within his grasp the aids he requires to do it well. He can discard dictionary and grammar; they contain with regard to this theme nothing that he has not already fully mastered. Later on in the "Academies," or in Humanities and Rhetoric, he writes his own occasional prelections on the model given by his Professor and studies for himself in the passages assigned for them the precepts exemplified and the beauties of style and the literary worth of all. Then again in his private reading of extra authors his eye is continually under the light shed on the authors of class by the Professor.[9] The Professor's correct views mold his mind to a true shape and enable him finally to judge for himself with accuracy and taste. Such is the end aimed at by the *Ratio;* it attains it by insisting on the Professor daily explaining and explaining, until the pupil drinks in the very essence of good taste, if from nothing else, at least from constantly witnessing the employment of the æsthetic faculty by the Professor. Oral teaching is the Society's great motto and is certainly a fundamental principle of the *Ratio.*

Hughes' *Loyola and the Educational System of the Jesuits,* published in 1892, mirrors the method of teaching in vogue in American Jesuit schools at that period. In speaking of the prelection in the high-school classes, he says:[10]

In the classes of Grammar, then, let the Master follow this method of explaining Cicero, or any other author. First, he will sketch, in the briefest way, the meaning of the author, and the connection between what has gone before and what is now to be explained. Then he will give a version of the period literally, preserving to the utmost the collocation of words, as they stand in the author; and also the figures employed. As to the collocation or arrangement of the words, this is of such consequence that sometimes, if a single word is put out of its place, the whole thought seems to lose its force and fall flat. Herein, too, is perceived that rhythmic flow of the style, which, of itself, even if other ornaments are wanting, pleases the ear wonderfully and gratifies the mind. Thirdly, the whole period is to be resolved analytically into its structural elements, so that the boys understand distinctly what every word governs; and their attention should be directed to some useful points of good Latinity. As to this structural analysis, I may be allowed the passing remark, which is familiar to every judge of a classical education, that the disciplinary value of literary studies reaches here its highest degree of mental exercise; and that the two classical tongues, Latin and Greek, are altogether eminent as supplying materials for this exercise in their own native structure. . . .

After this, each word is to be examined, as to what it signifies, and to what uses it may be applied; the boy is to understand, as far as may be, the original and proper idea and force of every word, not merely its general significance, as in a shadowy outline; he should know, too, the phrases in his native tongue, which correspond with precision and propriety to the Latin. The metaphors and the figurative use of words, especially as found in Cicero, are to be explained to the boys in an extremely plain manner, and by examples drawn from the plainest objects. Unless this use of words is understood, the true and genuine knowledge of the tongue is seriously obstructed. Then, picking out the more elegant turns of style, the Master will dictate them to the scholars, and afterwards require the use and imitation of these phrases in their themes. Lastly, he will go back and translate the words of the author over again, as he did at the beginning; and, if need be, do so a third and a fourth time. . . .

Repetition is now in order. . . . As soon, therefore, as the prelection is over, the Professor is to require at once an account of all that he has said, and he is to see that the whole line of his explanation is followed in the repetition. . . . Not all of what has been explained should be repeated by one only, but as many as possible should be practiced every day.

This method of the prelection supposes only a small amount of Latin to be seen daily; the final *Ratio* notes that the daily lesson should not exceed four lines in the lowest class of grammar, and seven in middle grammar.[11] After the arrangement of the Jesuit curriculum in the 1900's in conformity with the public-high-school curriculum and its very decided increase in the amount of Latin to be read, it was felt that this lengthy prelection was out of the question. Yet as late as 1914, Father Francis P. Donnelly of the Maryland-New York Province, one of the ablest American interpreters of the *Ratio,* maintained[12] that "the prelection should be the central point of the class. It is intended to develop the art of expression. It aims at training faculties, not simply at imparting facts. Artistic in its scope, it is directed to imitation or reproduction." He quotes with approval from Pachtler,[13] *"Imitatio est anima praelectionis."*

Father Donnelly pleads for a short prelection; that is, for a few lines of Latin taken thoroughly. This seems to be an echo of a controversy then being waged in Jesuit circles relative to the increase of the content in the high-school Latin course.

My vote, he concludes, is for a short prelection with drill and practice, rather than for long prelections which do not seem to develop any faculty except that of memory. And as our time for Latin is shorter than formerly, there is less reason for increasing the amount read.

Recognition of Changed Objectives

More and more the American Jesuits began to question the old objective of Latin teaching. And if the objective had changed, possibly there was need of changing or at least adapting the traditional Jesuit method. Thus, a writer in *The Teacher's Review,*[14] comments on a question proposed in an earlier issue of the same publication, as to the primary end of Latin teaching:

So fundamental a question might at first sight seem to allow little room for discussion where all are committed to so highly systematized a scheme of instruction as the *Ratio Studiorum.* Not the least merit of the *Ratio* is the precise defining of the scope of each class in this very branch and the careful specification of means to the end.

As matters stood in earlier days a reply to the query was comparatively easy. In the grammar classes, a thorough mastery of Latin Grammar as an *"ars utens"* was the immediate primary end of the three or four years' [high-school] course. This meant ability not merely to read but to write and speak Latin fluently, correctly, and even idiomatically. The aim corresponded more or less closely to that which our present-day grammar school sets before itself in regard to the vernacular. . . .

To what extent do present conditions interfere with the carrying out of this admirable plan? That conditions have changed and new difficulties have arisen is undeniable. The utility of Latin as a preparation for life work is not what it was except in the case of the clergy. Pupils generally come to us at an age quite in advance of that for which many of the rules and methods were framed. . . . The limited time at our disposal [for Latin], owing to the crowding in of other studies, makes the attainment of those high standards almost chimerical

Classical culture does not appeal in the same way to men of our generation. These are a few of the changed conditions which make this query a very pertinent one. How far, if at all, have they affected or modified the traditional immediate end of our teaching of Latin?

Another writer in the same *Review* for July, 1919, speaks in similar vein:[15]

Despite the ever-increasing opposition to the study of Latin and Greek, we are holding tenaciously to our traditional curriculum. Because of our steadfast championship of the classics, we are in open disagreement with most of the educational leaders. . . . It is imperative that we clearly understand in what way our teaching is distinctive and what are our special needs. . . . We may quote the aims and ideals of the *Ratio*, and point out that the purpose of each class and the methods to be employed are clearly stated. We must, however, remember that the classics in our present curriculum have changed their status. Latin and Greek may no longer be pursued in that leisurely and exhaustive way that produces splendid scholarship. We have had to sacrifice them, in some part, to the trend of modern education, and wisely or not, have found it advisable to conform to the requirements of the Regents and the College Entrance Examinations.[16]

As a result, our system has been merging more and more into the system followed by the public high schools. At the present time the authors studied in Jesuit and secular high schools, and the amount required to be read is practically the same; the graduates of one system are not inferior to those of the other. The difference between the two systems then is that of method rather than of matter. In former days they were unlike in both regards, and the precise points of dissimilarity were evident.

Present-Day Latin Methods and Ratio Methods Contrasted

In a very illuminating article in another Jesuit publication, *The Classical Bulletin,* Father Corcoran, lecturer on education at the National University of Ireland, draws an interesting contrast between present-day methods of teaching Latin and the method of the *Ratio*.[17]

Dr. Corcoran maintains that a great transformation of aims and methods has taken place as compared with what prevailed when the Society taught Latin as the main subject of earlier education. His contention is that less aid is given the student now and greater demands made on him with the result that Latin teaching has suffered. He instances:

1. A class was always taught a passage thoroughly before it was required to study that passage. The reverse is usually the case both in Jesuit and non-Jesuit schools.

2. The *prelectio* was made use of — the substantive teaching process. It was elaborate, detailed, slow. Lesson-hearing or recitation was an incidental, though necessary, sequel to teaching. The reverse is often the case today even in schools of the Society.

3. The teacher explained precisely beforehand the exact meaning of every phrase in the text dealt with in the prelection. Learners took down that meaning if they wished. The texts were often printed with wide spaces between the lines to enable meanings to be written in over the relevant phrases. There is no evidence that dictionaries were in general use or that they were regarded as necessary instruments for the learner. They were always spoken of as teacher's instruments. The real source of vocabulary was the living text of the Latin language, copiously explained and clarified by the teacher. A contrary practice is in use now.

4. Idiomatic vocabulary in phrases was the aim of the learner studying a text. On the contrary, at the present day, a vocabulary of single words is often the substituted aim. Single words never make a language. The essence of language — above all, of Latin and Greek — is in words combined on an idiomatic structural principle into a phrase. Mere erudition is still far too much the aim of the teacher of Latin. What the pupil is required to know in the modern classroom is the accidental accessory element in Latin — the mere dust of its chaff.

5. Down to the eighteenth century, the learner of Latin had to learn and use Latin. The study of the vernacular by way of accurate and idiomatic translation was not imposed. Such a process was almost unknown in Jesuit schools before the suppression of the Society. It was at most tolerated at times. It can be said to be a great hindrance to the full command of Latin.

A great increase of effort is required in the modern Latin class, often far beyond the ability of the average learner. He has to deal with Latin in about one third of the weekly time allowance which he formerly had for it. He must prepare alone for the most part what formerly the teacher provided him with in the prelection. The teacher now tends to exact knowledge which he has not really taught. Much valuable time is wasted in the profitless hunt for meanings of single words in vocabularies and dictionaries; this was entirely avoided in the past. Reading of Latin has been transformed during the past century into a much severer study than it ever was in the schools of the old Society.

In a succeeding article in the same journal,[18] Dr. Corcoran discusses the changes that have taken place in methods of teaching Latin composition.

Latin values include and markedly depend on teaching methods. The Society guarantees that Latin is a superb instrument of culture. It does so, if, and so far as, it is handled as directed in the *Ratio Studiorum*. No other aims and teaching processes are contemplated.

The test applied by the Society to Latin was this: power over it as an instrument of personal expression. All prizes went to the written word in "free" composition. The main test was writing. Its freedom did not exclude a fixed subject or a fixed plan. Reading existed not for itself but for use. The living phrase set in the text was the source of idiomatic vocabulary; not dictionary, not phrasebooks, of which pupils knew but little. Composition subjects were to be the personal choice of teacher and class. Closely analogous to the matter read, the composition allowed ample transfer of phrase, sentence form, and lines of treatment. The teacher's function was to teach, with liberal suggestion and ample aid, how to handle both the matter and the manner of writing on the subject proposed. A composition was a sequence of related sections; it usually took a month to do a composition. It was coherent throughout in phrase, aim, and general content. Each day's work was very short, not more than four sentences at the most. It was meant to be a very personal achievement of the pupil, the teacher, and the class.

Latin composition is very different in schools today, and the difference is to the disadvantage of the modern learner of Latin, especially if he be of merely average ability. Hence, the widespread belief today that the classics are only for the intellectually élite. In the old days the Society never held that view; Latin rationally taught, it was believed, could be taught fruitfully to all pupils whatever, once they could read and write.

Formerly there was not in the Jesuit method an elaborate approach through vernacular accidence — syntax, idiom, style, etc. — to Latin writing. To transfer a vernacular idiom into a Latin idiom is an exacting comparative process — and quite unnecessary in making a Latinist. Grammar meant one thing — Latin, and this Latin Grammar was for personal writing. It was extremely brief both in accidence and syntax. There was no place for exceptional usages and structures. Such a book as Gildersleeve's Latin Grammar was never taught in a Renaissance classroom. It might be shown to the clever pupil at the top of the school.

In conclusion Dr. Corcoran proposes that the aim of the Society's schools today should be to restore the old method of giving more aid to the student. He does not help his class adequately. He gives a quarter and wants a dollar; and, of course, he never gets anything like his dollar. That Latin yields very insignificant results, in very many cases, is due to the widespread failure of the teacher to teach.

Has the *Ratio's* idea of prelection, "the most typical form of Jesuit instruction,"[19] been whittled down in the modern Jesuit high school until only the name remains? Certainly the American Jesuit teacher of today makes use of it in a vastly different fashion from that of his predecessors. Another writer in *The Teacher's Review* for 1914 says:[20]

> We all admit that it [the prelection in the *Ratio*] is a good method, that it is the best method. And yet who can say that he follows it out strictly? . . . The teacher finds himself confronted with the fact that he has to do in ten minutes work for which the *Ratio* demands thirty minutes. . . . I fear that with many of us the prelection consists of translation and nothing else. Now, to my mind, it is a mistake under ordinary circumstances to translate the lesson for the class. In the first place, translation occupies a minor place in the *Ratio* prelection. . . . The items put first in the *Ratio,* and which for this reason may be considered more necessary and important, are the *argumentum,* a statement of the substance of the passage studied, and the interpretation, or explanation of the meaning, structure, and connection of sentences, etc. . . . Man is educated not by having things done for him, but by doing them himself under proper guidance. For this reason . . . I would rigidly exclude from the prelection a translation of the lesson. As boys are at present, a translation of the passage by the teacher, before they themselves have spent serious effort on the same, puts a dead check in the way of progress.

A conservative presentation of what the prelection should be today is found in the 1924 high-school syllabus of the Maryland-New York Province for the "Ancient Classical Languages." The directions are for the second year of Latin, but *mutatis mutandis,* they hold for all the high-school classes.[21]

> The method of the prelection is approximately as follows:

a) Deliberate and painstaking reading of the next day's assignment.

b) A very brief synopsis of its meaning or content. This should be dictated, and may be enlarged on orally (but by no means literally) in order to arouse interest in the story.

c) Explanation of puzzling collections of words that would be apt to baffle the class at this stage . . . ; of idiomatic turn of phrase . . . ; of the analysis of long and intricate sentences, and the like. At times it will be necessary to translate both freely and literally some obscure part of the assignment. . . . Unusual constructions that are not within the scope of the class should be passed over lightly, lest more harm than good be done by going into explanations.

d) Any Latin idioms that may seem useful may next be dictated.

e) Whatever time remains may be spent in a general discussion of the Gallic War so far unfolded.

This prelection must never be a random performance. . . . Much of this matter will be provided for the pupil in the printed notes accompanying the text so that the teacher can dispatch his share in the prelection in a few minutes.

So much space has been given to the Jesuit method of teaching Latin, and to the distinctively Jesuit contribution to Latin methodology, the *prelection*, because it is believed that, if there is a Jesuit method of teaching, that method will be apparent in their teaching of Latin, and, though to a less extent, of Greek. For the Jesuit schools have ever been loyal to the classical tradition; the various *Ratios* deal almost exclusively with Latin teaching; it is only fair to assume that if they have any traditional methodology, it will be found in their conduct of Latin classes.

Latin Composition Emphasized

Can it be maintained, then, in the face of the foregoing citations from Jesuit sources, that there is a Jesuit method of teaching Latin essentially different from that pursued in the public high schools? Certainly more emphasis is placed on Latin composition in Jesuit schools than in the average American high school. In this they approach nearer to the English public-school method. Thus, in the *Ancient Classical Languages Syllabus*[22] of the Maryland-New York Province, already referred to, the purpose of the Latin high-school course is stated as follows:

> The immediate object which the teacher should put before his eyes in the teaching of high-school Latin is that the pupil acquire, first, the art of translating understandingly (that is, with an accurate comprehension of the meaning of Latin words, and of the relation of words and phrases, and with a certain ability to render the same in their natural English equivalents), and, *also, together with this, and as an aid to it, the art of turning English sentences into the Latin idiom.* [Italics added.]

The similarity of the unitalicized portion of the foregoing statement to the immediate objective of the Latin course as formulated in the *Classical Investigation*[23] will be apparent. The last phrase, however, "the art of turning English sentences into the Latin idiom" finds no place in the objectives of the American Classical League, although elsewhere, it is true, the writing of Latin is recommended,[24] presumably as a test of grammar and syntax. It may then be safely maintained that the line of cleavage between Jesuit Latin classes and others is to be found in their striving to impart to their students the art of writing Latin, unquestionably a survival of the earlier objective of all Latin teaching, *eloquentia Latina.* But in reading Latin texts, it must be admitted that there is but slight difference. The prelection is usually retained but it functions merely as a rapid explanation of the advance lesson, not as the essential Jesuit method of Latin teaching, "the typical form of Jesuit instruction," that it formerly was. The textbooks used[25] in the Latin and Greek classes, the authors read, and the amount seen, correspond *pari passu* with the public-school Latin curriculum.

Methods in Other Branches

The Jesuit method of teaching science, history, and mathematics differs only slightly, if at all, from that in other American schools. Again, the texts[26] in these subjects, edited for the public high schools, are also used in the Jesuit schools. In teaching English, however, they have retained something from the *Ratio's* method of teaching Latin, largely manifest in the emphasis on composition work. The *Woodstock Letters*[27] for 1897 published *in extenso* the correspondence between the New York Board of Regents and the authorities of the College of St. Francis Xavier of New York City. Mr. Richard Jones of the Regents had written a letter, under date of December 16, 1896, asking coöperation and criticism of the proposed plan for uniform entrance examinations in English. The Rev. James P. Fagan, S.J., answered this letter, January 28, 1897. He thought the proposed scheme particularly vulnerable, and he takes the occasion to outline the Society's aims and objectives in teaching English in the high school.

> In the first place we look for development in the candidate for Freshman, rather than scrappy and ill-digested information. . . . What we ask is that the candidate demonstrate to us first and foremost his possession of awakened faculties to such a degree as will warrant us in assuming that he will be able to follow the college course with profit and pleasure.
>
> In English, in particular, we exact (1) a thorough knowledge of grammar and the general principles of Composition and Rhetoric; (2) a degree of familiarity with the more usual forms of prose composition, narrations, descriptions, and simple essays, such a familiarity as an average boy of sixteen or seventeen may be expected to derive from exercises in analysis, imitation, etc. . . .; (3) a fairly wide acquaintance with what is best in our literature, obtained by systematic reading under the direction of the masters.
>
> To obtain these results in each class of the Academic Department [high school] (1) the principles of composition are explained and the work of each year is carefully graded; (2) specimens of literature in prose and verse are read and commented on in class as far as they exemplify the precepts studied; (3) every week a piece of written work is submitted by each student and the work is corrected; oftentimes read and criticized by the master in class and not infrequently rewritten by the pupil after this criticism; (4) every student is obliged finally to use his library privileges. The books in this library are carefully selected, especially in the department of literature, fiction, history, and biography. The masters are required to direct the reading of their pupils and to this end they are expected to study each one's peculiar tastes and capabilities.
>
> We do not pretend that this work is exhaustive or final; it is in a sense elementary and wholly preparatory. . . . It results in this much,

at least, that on their entrance into Freshman, our average student has a very fair knowledge of English works — knowledge which is to a great extent ill-defined and ill-digested. . . . Besides this, our average freshman has a notion, at least, of style and the first rude beginnings of a style of his own. Finally, he is able to think and to give expression to his thoughts. These we feel are reasonably satisfactory qualifications for college.

That English composition is still stressed in the Jesuit high school, and that a somewhat distinctive method of teaching English composition is followed, is manifest from the widespread use of the Reverend Francis P. Donnelly's *Model English,* Book I and Book II.[28] These books are almost a perfect adaptation to English composition of the *Ratio's* method of teaching Latin composition. Imitation is the device employed.

Model English, says the author,[29] as its name implies, teaches composition in the way every art must be taught, by the following of master-models. Definitions are given in the form of directions, and technical terms are kept subordinate. Definitions and terms have their legitimate use, but to commit them to memory does not make writers or speakers. The speaker or writer is made by speaking and writing, and though each one should furnish his own thoughts, he need not, and for the most part, cannot, devise new words or new forms of sentences and paragraphs. For these he must go to the best authors.

In the "Directions for Teachers,"[30] he says:

The method of models is the chief kind of composition work insisted upon in this book. To keep the idea of the model while changing the expression is an exercise in paraphrasing, useful and at times necessary, but it is not imitation. In imitating, the student should furnish his own ideas and express them with that particular excellence which he aims at in the model. He may follow closely the sentence structure or he may follow only one single point, say the use of the right words. In no case, should he permit the model to force him to say what he cannot sincerely and truthfully say of his own subject.

Models are used in the mechanical arts as well as in fine arts; models must be used in the art of composition. "That, like it or not," says Stevenson, "is the way to learn to write." Science is systematized knowledge and may be gained, in part at least, by the understanding and memorizing of facts and principles. Art, however, is the power of doing something, and though rules may keep from error and point out the way to right performance, the actual work must be done by watching someone doing it and doing it after him. One learns to run a machine, to play a musical instrument, to paint a picture, not by memorizing rules but by following the master who does the work first.[31]

Whether this method effectively secures its objective — the art of writing — whether this is the only, or even the best, method, of attaining this objective, is open to question. Certainly, the continuous use of sentence and paragraph models all during the high-school course would seem to be deadening to all interest and initiative. However, that is beside the point. Father Donnelly's method is interesting as an application of *Ratio* principles to English writing. In the teaching of English literature, the Jesuit method probably differs little from that of the public high school. The same conventional classics are read in both courses.

It is manifest, then, from what has been said, that the Jesuit method, insofar as there is a method, is a method solely of teaching languages; it is distinctive in its emphasis on expression, both oral and written. Indeed, if the American Jesuit teacher of today can be said to have retained anything from the traditional Jesuit method of the past, it is this: insistence on frequent exercise in writing and speaking. One of the latest pronouncements of an American Province[32] crystallizes this principle in an official statement:

Oral and written expression we hold to be the chief of all the results to be derived from a high-school education for every walk of life.

Rivalry and Emulation in Jesuit Schools

To one perusing the *Ratio Studiorum* it is obvious that in the Jesuit system, rivalry and emulation were held in high esteem; in fact, one of the stereotyped objections brought against Jesuit education by its opponents of a generation ago was that the emulation they recommended merely stimulated baser feelings. Their fostering of ambition was regarded as one other instance of corrupt Jesuitical morality. Even so impartial an observer as Kemp[33] remarks that emulation "was carried to such extremes that, apparently, it must have obscured the true ends of study and cultivated improper feelings among the students."

Here again the Jesuits did not invent emulation, but they did popularize and systematize the practice in their schools. Each class was divided into two sides or camps, "Romans" and "Carthaginians." At their head were the class leaders, the officers, the generals, or consuls with their aids. Each student had his opponent or *aemulus,* of approximately equal ability. Each watched the other's written and oral work, his recitations, his answers to questions. If the *aemulus* slipped, the other pounced upon him, and for his alertness was given a mark of distinction. In addition, there was the class contest, the *concertatio,* a formal competition on class matter between two classes of the same grade, or, more frequently, a contest between the rival sides or "camps." Besides this ordinary feature of the school life, there were competitions in Latin composition, in elocution, interclass debates, and the like. And for these, prizes were awarded.[34]

How much of this was introduced into the American Jesuit schools it is difficult to say. Very probably the almost continuous contest of opponent with opponent, demanded by the *Ratio,* became a burden and defeated its own end; or more probably, American youth were a bit too sophisticated for this teaching technique. Yet for occasions out of the ordinary, they did resort to the stimulus of emulation. Thus, even now there are occasionally contests between parallel sections of the same class. It still is a universal custom to award a medal for the highest average of the year in each class. In many schools, it is still common to give prizes to those who achieve distinction, first or second place, in individual branches, such as Latin, English, mathematics.

The use of emulation, perhaps, has less need of defense nowadays than it did a generation ago; other schools resort to the "unmoral practice" of having scholastic contests and of awarding prizes to the victors. The Jesuit system would seem to be rooted in human nature. Boys are more aware apparently of the motives influencing their conduct than their elders and organize their sports on a competitive basis; nor do they withhold admiration from those who succeed therein. In later life, they must meet competition in whatever vocation they follow. Surely, if education is to mirror life or prepare for life, there is no harm in capitalizing this, and within proper limits adapting it to the school.[35]

Footnotes

[1]*The Classical Investigation,* Part I, pp. 79–80.

[2]Astrain, *Historia de la Compañía,* etc., IV, 16 f., has a pertinent remark on the difference between the old objective in Latin teaching and the modern: "El maestro moderno de lenguas y literatura . . . enseña *la ciencia del lenguaje y no su ejercicio.* El maestro antiguo, por el contrario, enseñaba las lenguas *artísticamente.* . . . De aquí provenía el diverso resultado. . . . El antiguo discípulo salía de las aulas escribiendo correctamente en la lengua del Lacio, lo mismo en prosa que en verso; el moderno discípulo sale de los colegios con un caudal mayor o menor de noticias y datos lingüísticos e históricos, con los cuales podrá expresarse científicamente en su lengua, pero nunca sabrá usar cómodamente la lengua que ha aprendido. El procedimiento moderno es en esto, como en casi todo, científico; el procedimiento antiguo era principalmente artístico."

[3]"Hac methodo neglecta, factum est ut exiguus nunc temporis sit numerus eorum qui absolutis gymnasii studiis, non dicam cogitata sua scripto vel voce latine exprimendi, sed etiam latinos auctores intelligendi aliqua facilitate polleant." Quoted by Passard, *La Pratique du Ratio,* p. 29.

[4]XXIII, 322.

[5]An allusion to the practice, then prevalent, in Jesuit colleges, of using a Latin textbook for the course of scholastic philosophy (a college subject) and even in some schools of giving the lectures in that language.

[6]*Maryland-New York Province Archives;* see also, *Teacher's Review,* IV, No. 4 (Oct., 1913), 61.

[7]"Regulae Comm. Prof. Class. Inf." 27, 28, 29; "Reg. Prof. Cl. Rhet." 6; "Reg. Prof. Human.," 5 et passim.

[8]XXIV, 222 ff.

[9]Till the end of the 90's, "Professor" was the common term applied to all the teachers in Jesuit schools, the result of a literal rendering of the Latin. Father Hughes in his book calls the high-school teacher "Master," an English usage, never in vogue in American Jesuit schools.

[10]Pp. 238.

[11]Hughes, *op. cit.,* p. 241.

[12]*Teacher's Review,* V (1914), 53 ff.

[13]IV, 194.

[14]I, No. 3 (July, 1910), 35 ff.

[15]*The Teacher's Review,* X, 47.

[16]The writer is a member of the Maryland-New York Province; hence, he does not mention the North Central Association and other standardizing agencies that were influential factors in the change of curriculum that took place in the western schools.

[17]"Rational Aids for Readers of Latin," *The Classical Bulletin,* II, No. 5 (February, 1926), 37 ff.

[18]"Rational Aids for Writers of Latin," *The Classical Bulletin,* II, No. 6 (March, 1926), 49 ff.

[19]Hughes, *op. cit.,* p. 232.

[20]Germing, M., "A Note on the Prelection," V, No. 1 (Jan., 1914), 4 ff.

[21]"Notes on the Second-Year Program," *The Ancient Classical Languages Syllabus for High Schools.* Maryland-New York Province, 1924, pp. 17, 18.

[22]*Op. cit.,* p. 1.

[23]*The Classical Investigation,* Part One, General Report, p. 79.

[24]*Ibid.,* p. 124.

[25]The American Jesuits have published Latin and Greek textbooks that are widely used in their schools. In Latin: Yenni, *Latin Grammar* (the revised edition published by Allyn and Bacon is still used); Cotter, *Latin Composition Exercises;* Bunse, *Latin Grammar;* Dowd, *Loyola Latin Elements;* Rockcliff, *Latin Exercises,* etc. In Greek: Yenni, *Greek Grammar;* Connell, *Short Grammar of Attic Greek;* Connell, *First Greek Reader;* Kaegi-Kleist, *Greek Grammar;* Kleist, *First Lessons in Greek,* etc. Besides, they have published a number of college textbooks.

[26]An exception should be made for the history texts. Betten, *Ancient World;* Betten-Kaufmann, *Modern World;* and Guggenberger, *General History of the Christian Era,* all by Jesuit authors, are generally used in their schools.

[27]"College Entrance Requirements in English," *Woodstock Letters,* XXVI (1897), 140 ff.

[28]Published by Allyn and Bacon.

[29]*Model English,* Book II, Preface, p. iii.

[30]*Ibid.,* p. 291.

[31]*Ibid.,* p. 289.

[32]*Ancient Classical Languages, High School Syllabus,* 1924, p. 2.

[33]*History of Education,* p. 191.

[34]*Ratio Stud.,* "Reg. Praef. Class. Inf." 3, 13, 32, 36. "Reg. Comm. Prof. Cl. Inf." 31, 34, 35. "Leges praemiorum," etc.

[35]See Lowell, A. Lawrence, "The Art of Examination," *Atlantic Monthly,* CXXXVII, No. 1 (January, 1926), 59.

CHAPTER XII

ADMINISTRATION — DISCIPLINE — FINANCE

WHATEVER change the Jesuit system of education has undergone relative to curriculum and methodology, the administration of its schools remains essentially what it was in the sixteenth century. There are two characteristics of Jesuit government: first, it is highly centralized; secondly, it is international. This does not mean, of course, that a Jesuit school in America does not differ from a Jesuit school in Spain and Italy. It does differ, radically; almost as much as the American public high school differs from the Italian *ginnasio*. Nevertheless, it is true that the system of government of these different types of Jesuit schools is, within certain limits, very similar. This again must be explained by the identity of objective, toward which Jesuit schools the world over are aiming. Every Jesuit school is, in a sense, independent; nevertheless, the local superiors are very definitely subordinate to the central authority of the Order, the General.

The Society of Jesus, as has been seen,[1] was not originally planned as a teaching order; yet almost from the beginning it definitely assumed education as one of its primary works; and a teaching order it has always been in popular esteem. This has been particularly the case in the United States. Of the 3,052 Jesuit priests and scholastics in the United States in 1926, 1,018 were engaged in educational work and 915 more were definitely preparing for that work as undergraduate or graduate students. Besides this, there were 473 divinity students of whom 60 per cent or 283, a very conservative estimate, will engage in educational work after the completion of their theological studies.[2] Thus, 2,216, or 70 per cent of the total personnel, are actually engaged in the work of education or are being prepared for it. Of this number, 466 are in the field of secondary education. Of those in their studies, under-

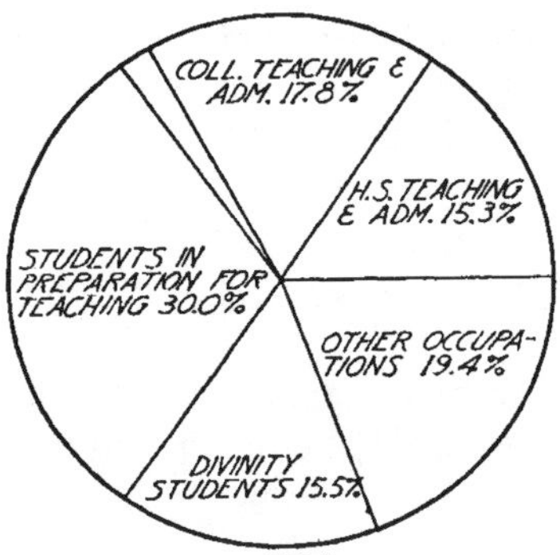

FIG.1

Distribution of Jesuit Personnel in the Four American Provinces, 1926

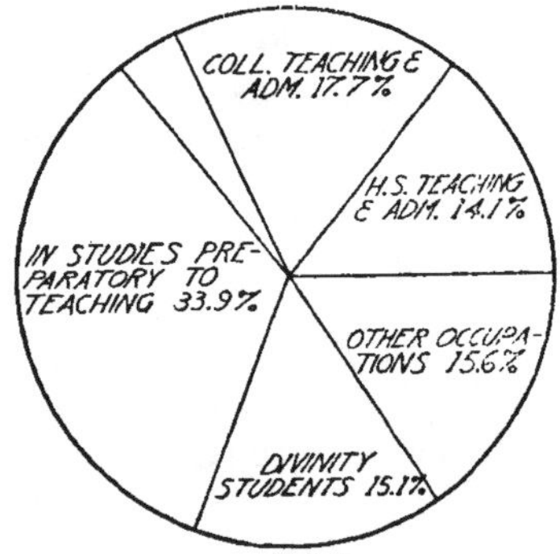

FIG.2

Personnel of Maryland-New York Province, 1926

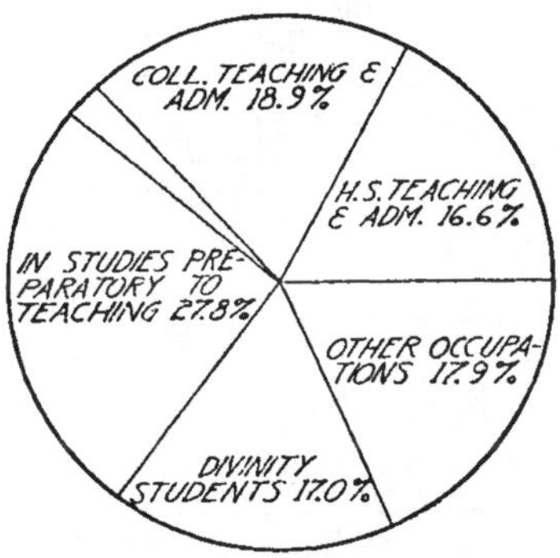

FIG.3

Personnel of Missouri Province, 1926

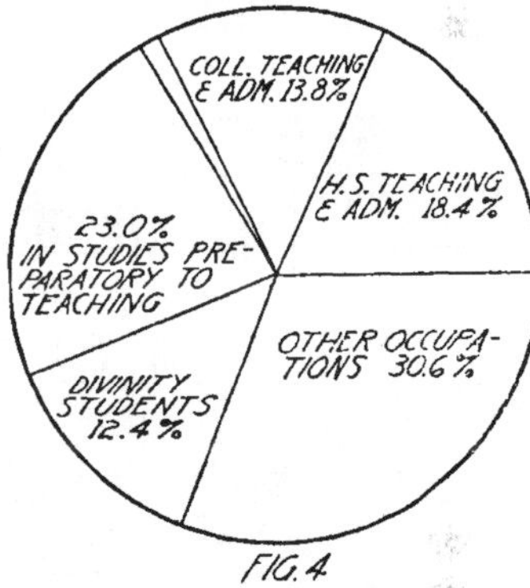

FIG.4

Personnel of New Orleans Province, 1926

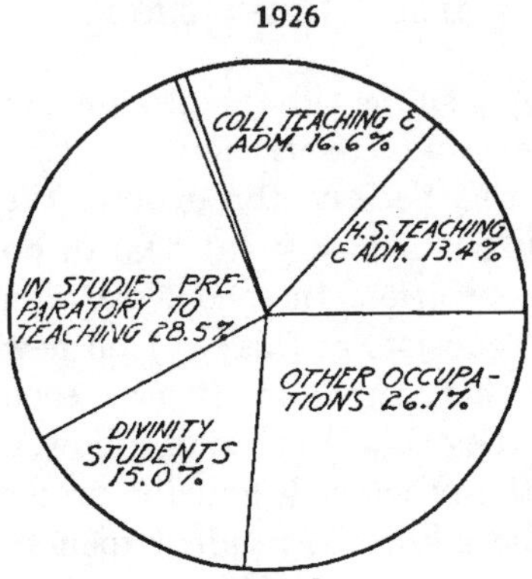

FIG.5

Data taken from the province catalogues for the year 1926.

The small segment unmarked represents the percentage engaged in general administration.

Personnel of California Province, 1926

graduate, graduate, and divinity, it is difficult to estimate with any degree of accuracy the number that will engage in *high-school* work; 50 per cent or 694 would be a very conservative estimate.

The General of the Society[3]

This personnel is subject directly to the rector or superior of the house or college in which they reside; he in turn, as well

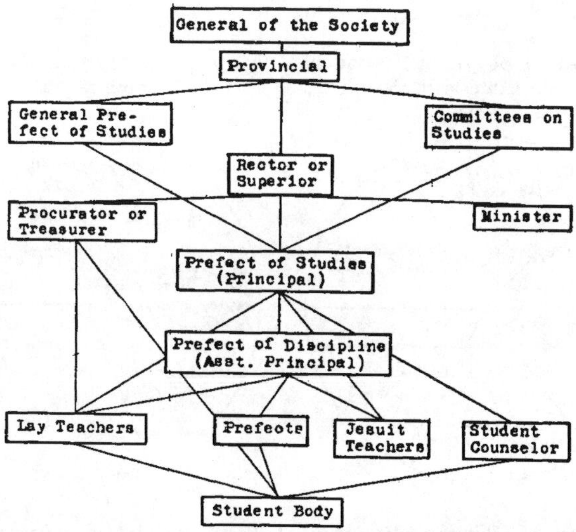

FIG. 6. ADMINISTRATION OF A JESUIT HIGH SCHOOL

as the members of his community, is subject to the provincial; and over all the provinces is the general of the Society. In 1930, there were 21,678 members of the Society throughout the world. Naturally, the general will not have a great deal to do directly with this world-wide organization. In school matters, the actual function of the general consists in this: (1) no new school may be opened without his permission;[4] (2) each province submits for his approval the course of studies followed in its schools;[5] (3) he appoints the provincial, and the rector or local superior, after taking the advice of prudent men in the province.[6] In practice, he may make recommendations to the provinces; thus, he recommended to the American provinces two periods of religious instruction a week and permitted them to make Greek an elective.[7] But the particular details of school administration are left to the provincial, the regional superior, to whom the rectors are directly responsible.

TABLE VIII. DISTRIBUTION OF JESUIT PERSONNEL IN THE FOUR AMERICAN PROVINCES 1925–1926 (*a*)

Occupation	*Number of Jesuits in Each Province According to Occupation*				
	Md.-N. Y.	*Missouri*	*New Orleans*	*California*	*Total*
H. S. Teachers	130	144	50	51	363
H. S. Administr.	45	31	14	13	103
Total in H. S.	175	175	52	64	466
Coll. and U. Teachers	176	151	31	57	415
Coll. and U. Administr.	442	49	8	22	121
Total in Coll. and U.	218	200	39	79	536
Gen'l. Administr.	4	5	5	2	16
Total in Education in U. S.	397	380	96	145	1,018
Undergraduates	314	223	55	99	691
Graduate Students	106	71	10	37	224
Divinity Students	187	179	35	72	473
Teachers Outside the U. S.	41	14			55
Foreign Missions	20	27		20	67
Writers, Editors	15	14	2	4	35
Parish Work	108	102	70	80	360
Lectures, Retreats	21	19	8	4	52
Miscellaneous	28	27	6	16	77
Total	1,237(*b*)	1,056(*c*)	282	477(*d*)	3,052(*e*)

(*a*) Data taken from *Catalogi* of the four provinces for the year 1926.
(*b*) Twenty-seven of this total are members of other provinces, stationed in the Maryland-New York Province.
(*c*) Twenty are members of other provinces, stationed in the Missouri Province.
(*d*) Thirty-nine are members of other provinces, stationed in the California Province
(*e*) This total does not include lay brothers.

TABLE IX. PERCENTAGE DISTRIBUTION OF JESUIT PERSONNEL IN THE FOUR AMERICAN PROVINCES 1925–1926

Occupation	*Percentage of Jesuits in Each Province According to Occupation*				
	Md.-N. Y.	*Missouri*	*New Orleans*	*California*	*Total*
High-School Work	14.1	16.6	18.4	13.4	15.3
College and University	17.7	18.9	13.8	16.6	17.8
Total in Educational Work (*a*)	35.4	37.3	34.	30.4	35.1
In Studies Preparatory to Teaching	33.9	27.8	23.	28.5	30.0
Divinity Students (*b*)	15.1	17.	12.4	15.	15.5
Other occupations (*c*)	15.6	17.9	30.6	26.1	19.4

(*a*) Including American Jesuits engaged in educational work in the foreign missions.
(*b*) Probably the majority of the divinity students will engage in educational work after the completion of their studies.
(*c*) Parochial work, foreign missionaries, etc. This does not include the lay brothers

The Provincial

The provincial has under his jurisdiction all the houses and educational institutions of the province. He does not appoint the rectors or local superiors; he submits to the general a list of candidates, ordinarily three; from this list the general names one to the rectorship.[8] The provincial sends to each school a certain number of teachers, but leaves to the rectors the assigning of their respective duties. Usually this latter office is subdelegated by the rector to the "prefect of studies" or, as he is now designated in the American Jesuit high schools, the principal. The provincial also appoints all the local principals. Each of the American provinces has a general prefect of studies, appointed by the provincial, to assist him in his work of administration. Each year he visits all the high schools of his province, observes the teaching in the various classes, and confers with the teachers. It is his duty to see that the provincial course of studies is faithfully observed. In two of the American provinces, Maryland-New York and Missouri, the general prefect of studies, with his assistants, draws up the semiannual examinations for all the high schools. Neither the *Ratio* nor the *Constitutions* make any provision for this office. Indeed, until very recent years, the supervisory work of the general prefect of studies was assumed, even in the American schools, by the provincial or his assistant, on the occasion of the annual visitation. The provincial is also assisted in his work of administration by various committees on studies, appointed by himself — history committees, mathematics committees, classics committees, and the like. Their function is to draw up programs of studies, approve textbooks, and by means of printed bulletins see that the teachers of the province are kept in touch with the best educational theory and practice.

The Rector

The head of a Jesuit school is usually called the rector, sometimes simply superior; to him all the members of the community owe obedience.[9] Upon him lies the responsibility of seeing that the Society's educational and moral standards are maintained in the school.[10] He is expected to visit the classes from time to time,[11] and he should see that there are faculty meetings once a month, or at least every other month.[12] Ordinarily to the rector alone belongs the right to dismiss a student.[13] But all the details of school administration are intrusted to the prefect of studies, or principal, "to whom he shall give all the power which he shall judge necessary for the fitting administration of his office."[14]

The Prefect of Studies

The office of principal or prefect of studies is the pivotal point in Jesuit school administration. The first rule in the *Ratio* for the prefect of studies in the lower (high) schools is:

> He should understand that he has been chosen for the purpose of aiding the rector in the direction and government of our schools in every possible way to the end that our students may advance in uprightness of life as well as in the liberal arts.[15]

The *Ratio* enters into great detail concerning this office; fifty rules are listed under the *Regulae Praefecti Studiorum Inferiorum*. Of these, however, Rule 2 and Rules 38 to 50 pertain to discipline. According to the 21st rule of the rector, all disciplinary matters belong to the principal's assistant, if one is assigned.[16] In many of the American schools, there is such an official, usually called the prefect of discipline.

The prefect of studies should see that the teachers observe the rules;[17] he is to be the guardian and interpreter of the *Ratio*;[18] his is the directive hand in the Jesuit system of education; he is charged with maintaining unity in that system.

> He must zealously see to it that new masters retain the system of teaching and other methods of their predecessors, provided, of course, that they are in accord with our system. Thus there will be less cause for complaint at our frequent change of masters.[19]

Accordingly, he is obliged to observe the teachers in every

class once a fortnight to see whether they are giving sufficient time to Christian doctrine, whether they are making adequate preparation for class, and finally, "whether they conduct themselves with their students in all things in a proper and praiseworthy fashion."[20] The principal is to attend to all details of admission of new students, examine them as to their fitness, and assign them to their proper classes.[21] He sees that examinations are held at stated times, that records are kept of the grades given by the examiners,[22] and he also presides at the distribution of prizes.[23] It is his duty to care for extracurricular activities, such as the "academies" or literary societies, public specimens, exhibitions, declamations, and public-speaking contests.[24]

The Principal in American Jesuit Schools

This outlines in brief the duties as they are found in the *Ratio Studiorum.* The principal in the American Jesuit high school retains all these functions. He is the responsible leader of the school; he has charge of the organization of all activities. Yet, his powers differ essentially from that of a principal in a public high school. First of all, he has little or no voice in selecting his Jesuit teachers. He must make use of the personnel supplied by the provincial. He has, however, the power to employ lay teachers to assist the Jesuit masters; and the increasing use of lay teachers in Jesuit high schools is more and more characteristic of the Jesuit educational system in the United States. Secondly, the Jesuit principal has very little to say about the curriculum in his school. He must follow the province schedule of studies, formulated by the provincial committee on studies. For any deviation from this course, permission must be obtained from the general prefect of studies. Nor has he, as a general rule, power to expel a student; that belongs to the rector, but naturally the recommendation of the principal will be acted upon. In an organization like the Society of Jesus there can be no clash of authority; the principal is very definitely subordinate to the rector or superior who, by rule, delegates to his prefect of studies all the power needed for the right administration of this office.

The Prefect of Discipline

The assistant principal, called "praefectus atrii"[25] in the *Ratio,* and, in American schools until very recent times, the prefect of discipline, has control of the discipline of the school.[26] He keeps a check on absences and tardiness[27] and reports to the rector incorrigible students.[28] This sometimes disagreeable office must be performed "in a spirit of gentleness, safeguarding in every way peace and charity."[29] The 43rd rule gives a startling picture of what the prefect of discipline had to contend with in former times:

> Neither in the school yard nor in the classes, not even the higher classes, should anyone be permitted to carry weapons. Loafing, rushing about, and noisy disturbances should likewise be prohibited. The prefect should permit no swearing, insulting or injurious behavior, in short, unbecoming or improper conduct. Should anything of this sort occur, he should immediately suppress the disorder and then report the disturbance to the rector.

The "Prefects"

In the disciplinary control of the school, the assistant principal is aided by "prefects," sometimes called in Jesuit pedagogical literature, *sub-praefecti,* or *praefecti cubiculorum.* As a general rule, they are scholastics, not priests. In a day school, in addition to their regular teaching schedule, they supervise games, or supervise the pupils during recreation periods. In a boarding school, however, the prefects play a much larger part in the school life; usually their teaching load is lightened, as they have the heavy task of caring for almost the entire extracurricular life of the boy at boarding school.

The assistant principal, or prefect of discipline, aided by the scholastic prefects, attends to all disciplinary matters in the American Jesuit school of today. Yet prefects and "prefecting" in this restricted sense are not even mentioned in the *Ratio;* indeed, the *Ratio,* by its assignment of the duty of reporting and punishing delinquents to non-Jesuit "censors" and "correctors," would seem to discountenance all surveillance on the part of the Jesuits. Even Roothaan's *Ratio* recommends this:[30]

He [the prefect of studies] should appoint in each class, in accord with local usage, a public censor, or if the term censor is not acceptable, a chief decurion or pretor. That he may be honored by his schoolmates, he should be granted certain privileges. He should have the right with the master's approval of begging off his classmates from lighter punishments. It will be his duty to note anyone who wanders about the school yard before the signal is given, or who enters a classroom not his own, or leaves his own class or his appointed place. He should report daily to the prefect those who have been delinquent in class, anyone not a student who has entered the classroom, finally any fault committed in class whether in the presence of the master or not.

It is practically certain that these two offices of corrector and censor never existed in the American Jesuit school; certainly there is no reference to them in any American documents; the spirit of the country was too strongly set against such a system of student inspectors. Instead, there grew up in this country (and the same holds true of the modern Jesuit school everywhere), the prefect system, the prefects being Jesuit scholastics, members of the faculty. The establishment of boarding schools made prefects necessary, and it is in the boarding schools that the Jesuit system of "prefecting" is seen in fullest vigor even today.

Boarding School not a Typical Jesuit School

The boarding school[31] is not, of course, the typical Jesuit school; it is only mentioned incidentally in the *Ratio*.[32] In that part of the *Ratio* that treats of the lower schools, there is no mention whatever of *convictores*, or boarders. The reason is not far to seek; when the 1599 *Ratio* was written — and as is obvious, Roothaan's *Ratio* follows this almost verbatim — the lower schools of the Jesuits were for the most part only for day students. The boarding schools were merely tolerated, hardly encouraged.[33] Thus, the Fourth General Congregation of the Society, held in 1581, decreed:[34]

While it is highly desirable that the Society be freed from the care of boarding schools as far as possible, yet it is left to the prudence of the General to determine . . . what is most expedient in this matter for God's greater services and the common good of the Society.

It is certain that at no time in the Society's history was there a predominance of boarding schools. In France, for example, in 1762, when the Jesuits gave up their colleges in that country, of nearly 100 institutions under their charge,[35] 92 were day schools. In the United States in 1930, there were only 6 high schools with resident students out of a total of 37 high schools. Of these, the Maryland-New York Province has 1, Missouri 3, California 1, and New Orleans 1. A considerable number that were at one time boarding schools have been transformed into day schools, as has been noted before.[36]

Of the prefecting in Jesuit day schools, very little need be said. There is more supervision than in the average public high school, but the time spent on the school premises outside of classes is so limited that prefecting becomes more or less a nominal function. However, in a Jesuit boarding school this is quite another matter. The Jesuit system of *surveillance* — the French word has a hateful sound in American ears — has given rise to many bitter attacks. Compayré[37] and others[38] have singled it out as specially worthy of execration.

Surveillance

Before evaluating this system, it must be noted, first, that the *surveillance* they attack is characteristic of relatively few Jesuit schools, since they are describing the prefecting in a boarding school; secondly, a practice that may seem altogether inadmissible in modern America may possibly have been not without merit in seventeenth-century France, or even nineteenth-century Italy. No observer can fail to be impressed, even at the present day, by the difference between an American high school and a Continental *lycée* or *gymnasium*. The régime of a modern French *collège*, for example, with its rigid *horaire* and strict supervision, would be quite intolerable for an American youth. The same is true, almost to the same extent, in Jesuit schools in America and Europe; the subjoined daily schedule for Jesuit schools in various countries at the present day is ample evidence of this.[39]

TABLE X. DISTRIBUTION OF TIME IN JESUIT BOARDING SCHOOLS ON ORDINARY CLASS DAYS

Country	*Hours of Class*	*Hours of Study*	*Recreation and Meals*	*Hours of Sleep*	*Miscellaneous**
United States	3 3/4	3 3/4	5 5/6	9 1/2	1 1/6
France	4 1/3	6 7/12	3 7/12	8	1 1/2
Belgium	4 2/3	3 11/12	4 2/3	9 1/2	1 1/4
England	4 3/4	4	5	8 1/2	1 3/4
Austria	4 1/12	4 1/6	5 2/3	8	2 1/12
Jugo-Slavia	4 5/12	6 5/12	4 1/12	8	1 1/12
Malta	5	5	4	8 1/4	1 3/4
Colombia (S. A.)	5	3 11/12	5 5/12	8 1/4	1 5/12
Italy	5	4 1/3	4 1/2	8 3/4	1 5/12

*This includes approximately three quarters of an hour for prayer and religious exercises.

But this is certain, that the Jesuits in founding their American schools brought with them from Europe their traditional ideas of *surveillants* or *Hofmeisters* and introduced them into the American boarding schools, as prefects. What the function of the Jesuit prefect was in continental schools is perfectly obvious from any documents. They were to exercise a strict and unfailing supervision over the pupils, to establish and maintain order, prevent evil, and repress abuses.[40] What it was in practice in the French *Collège de la Flèche* in France in the eighteenth century can be seen from the following document, an *Ordre du Jour pour le Collège des Pensionnaires de la Flèche*:[41]

> The prefects will often visit their pupils [in their rooms or study halls] to be sure that they are studying, that they are not reading forbidden books or those not pertaining to class matter, that they are not looking out of the windows or over the partitions. If, in case of necessity, they permit a student to leave, they will see to it that he is accompanied by a servant, particularly in the lower classes; they will never permit them to go out in pairs. They will never allow a pupil to enter another's room or study under the pretext of asking for paper, pens, books, or anything else.

It would seem that the practice of prefecting was carried to extremes in the French schools. Quicherat, in his history of the Collège Ste. Barbe, says:[42]

> In the colleges of the Jesuits, the youths are never left to themselves; they are the object of unflagging surveillance; and this surveillance has for its object not merely the prevention of faults of conduct; it is also a study of their characters and habits in order to discover the method of guidance best suited to each boy.

In a little book,[43] published by one of the French provinces in 1842, there is a section devoted to *Observations Relatives à la bonne tenue d'un pensionnat*. The second chapter contains "*Observations Particulières pour les Préfets*."[44]

Their function is to supervise the students in the study halls as in other places where they are officially in charge, to see to the observance of the daily order, and to take part in their recreations. They must always keep their eye on what is going on, correct what seems wrong, either by warning the offenders, or correcting them, or even punishing them, according to need; but they should take no extraordinary measures without the approval of the prefect of studies. . . .

They should devote themselves courageously to this laborious work, and master the task of prefecting . . . mingling with the students in order to become acquainted with them, to cheer them up or to repress them, making use of whatever gifts of mind, of talent, of skill God has given them, to lead the pupils to the end proposed, that is to transform them into intelligent and Christian youths. . . .

Each prefect has charge of the dormitory where he sleeps and makes his morning meditation. . . . They should see to it that the students rise and retire promptly. . . .

During walks they assign bands of three, never permitting two mischievous youths together, but always a model youth with two others less exemplary in conduct. . . .

During recreations they mix with the students when there are no games, they join in their conversation, always avoiding being placed in a position where they cannot see what is going on elsewhere. They should take special care to see that new arrivals are not left to their own devices, and that they do not fall into the hands of those who would tease them or hurt them. They should be all things to all, boys with boys, but at the same time not losing that dignity which breeds respect, nor stooping to that imprudent familiarity which brings contempt in its train. . . .

They should endeavor to stir up enthusiasm for games, with the assurance that there is less to fear when the students engage actively in sports than when they merely dawdle about or spend the time in walking up and down. The prefects will also pay special attention to those who often gather together in little cliques as well as those who walk about in pairs. . . .

They should never lose sight of the students and never permit them to get too far away or to hide from view, no matter where they may be, but especially on walks.

This passion for meticulous observance is insisted on in another French book of a much later date, styled the *Practical Manual of the Prefect*.[45] The mere titles of the chapters are sufficient evidence of this.[46] Other continental schools placed almost equal emphasis on pupil supervision. Indeed, even today in many Jesuit boarding schools on the continent, as well as in boarding schools not under Jesuit direction, a system of surveillance is enforced that appears very odious to the American observer.[47]

Surveillance Unsuited to American Schools

Whatever the value of surveillance of this nature may have been in Jesuit schools in the past or in modern continental schools, it was early found quite unsuited to American youth. Undoubtedly in the early days in the United States, European disciplinary methods were employed, as is evident from Bishop Carroll's complaint that Georgetown was "governed on the principles and in the system of a convent."[48] The more liberal concept of discipline, as formulated in Jesuit schools in England, grew in favor in this country. What that concept is may be seen in the writings of the Reverend Ernest Hull,[49] an English Jesuit, who has done much to popularize this more modern theory of discipline in American Jesuit schools.

In his *Collapses in Adult Life*,[50] he says:

> Discipline is often conceived as merely a system of restraint on liberty; that is to say, making the boys do by rule everything they ought to do. But this is to overlook the other half of discipline, which is to provide the pupils with a legitimate field of liberty, within which they may learn the practice of self-discipline.
>
> It is true that a rigid code of restraints exercises the pupils in self-control. It makes them do things whether they like it or not, thus forcing them to restrain their inclinations and submit to the law. It gets them into the habit of conforming to any regulations which happen to be imposed on them, which is quite a good thing in itself. But on the other hand, this is only one part of true discipline; and it is the least important part just because it is enforced by penalties, and is therefore a kind of moral coercion. Of far greater importance for the development of character is the free field for choice, in which a boy

is confronted with the principles of law and duty and is left to decide for himself whether to obey the law or disregard it; to follow the law of right and wrong or the instinct of like and dislike.

A rigorous system of routine, which leaves practically no scope for choice, but determines by rule everything which the pupils must do and everything they must not do, is simply suicidal when viewed in relation to character. It turns the boys into machines, and effectually cuts off from them every chance of developing character. . . . It is only in a fairly free field that character can be developed. In a totally restricted field, character cannot be developed at all; and even allowing that some routine-discipline is necessary for order and system and for the production of mechanical habits, still it must be remembered that routine is never a good in itself, but always a means to an end. As a means it is valuable so far as it promotes that end, and is worthless or even pernicious so far as it defeats that end.

Now the great end of education is certainly the formation of volitional habits, which are the very quintessence of character. A volitional habit . . . is never a mechanical thing. . . .

The aim of discipline should be on the one hand to give the boys as much scope for liberty as is good for their healthy self-development, and at the same time to impose on them as much restraint as is necessary for instilling habits of regularity and submission to external rule and to provide safeguards against moral evil. . . . But the necessary degree of restraint should involve as little routine as possible, and rely on elastic personal supervision rather than a wooden code of rules.

Boxing up pupils, and warding off all possibilities of their choosing wrong may be pious, but it is extremely unpractical. It creates an unreal situation not conformed to life in general, which leaves the will untried and weak, and deprives it of all opportunities of gaining strength by the practice of virtue under opposition. . . . We must not forget that innocence which springs from ignorance and from hermetically sealed surroundings is to a great extent a negative thing; not so much virtue, as weakness fostered and cherished by protective methods; whereas virtue is strength developed by the exercise of the will confronted with opposition. . . . If habits of good action are merely the result of a coercive routine of rules and exhaustive supervision, they are likely to be nothing but mechanical habits. But these, in the ethical and moral and character-making sense are not habits but mere customs, which will drop out as soon as the pressure of routine and supervision are removed. . . .

Not only must the routine system be restricted so as to leave pupils scope for the exercise of free choice and the development of the habit of self-control based on interior motives, but the supervision exercised over the pupils must also be restricted even in the way of seeing to their observing of the code. There must be no sustained lynxlike watching under which a child cannot move a finger unobserved. . . . This does not mean, of course, giving the pupils *carte blanche* and reducing rule and supervision to practically nothing. . . . The aim must be to reach the golden mean. . . .

In the final stages of training . . . the school régime should approximate to the conditions of after-life, by affording to the pupils increased opportunities for developing volitional habits of the kind which will be needed in the future struggle. Experiments have been made in the way of relaxing supervision, and removing routine discipline, and throwing the boys of the upper classes on their own corporate spirit of honor and duty by adopting the "monitorial system" of the English public schools, and so on. But the experiments we have heard of have usually proved a failure. . . . We Catholics cannot in conscience adopt such methods in their entirety. We do hold ourselves responsible for the morality of the boys under our charge down to the moment they leave our hands, and cannot run such risks. At the same time it is well for us to realize the disadvantages incidental to our otherwise excellent system, namely, that by emphasizing the restraint and safeguard aspect of our discipline we diminish the opportunities of development of character, and thus leave our pupils comparatively weak and unprepared for the shock of the world.

There is a danger of imagining that if our pupils have been models of good behavior throughout their school course, and have gone through it with an unspotted record, all is well with them. We have done for them all that could have been done, and think our system is perfect. In other words, we are apt to mistake mechanical habit, evolved by a perfect routine, for volitional habit evolved from internal principles and self-determining choice.

That American Jesuit teachers concur in this view of discipline can be seen from the following citation from an American Jesuit's book on education:[51]

The pedagogue who is an officious spy does scant courtesy to his own character and to his profession. Whatever his verbal profession may be, his conduct is measured and directed by the gratuitous and perverse doctrine of total depravity. . . . Of course, there should be supervision. But supervision and espionage are worlds apart. There is nothing offensive or inordinate about the former. It is reasonable and necessary. Its method is directive rather than coercive . . . its purpose is not so much the observance of a rule as the acquisition of that for which the rule was instituted.

The Student Counselor

Another official in the American Jesuit school of today is the student counselor, or as he is sometimes called, the spiritual father. His function is to keep the morale of the school at a high level according to Catholic ideals, to give personal and vocational guidance to the students. The office is thus described in the bulletins of the Maryland-New York schools:[52]

> One of the Fathers of the Faculty is appointed as counselor or adviser of the students. His principal duty is to direct the spiritual activities of the school and the various religious societies and sodalities, in regard to which he exercises much the same supervision as the prefect of discipline exercises in his department.
>
> He provides opportunities for the students to receive the Sacraments in addition to the times assigned for the general student body.
>
> He is in a special sense the friend and adviser of the students not only in matters directly spiritual, but also material and temporal, in their studies, their social duties, and in other intimate and personal matters as each one may wish.
>
> One of the questions of highest importance to every high-school graduate is the wise choice of a profession or vocation according to one's character, talents, and attractions, both natural and supernatural. No student with a serious outlook on life will fail to determine, well in advance of his graduation, the career which under God's providence will best assure his temporal success and his eternal happiness. In this matter the assistance of the student counselor will be invaluable. His hours will be arranged to afford ample opportunity of conferring with him.

The student counselor ordinarily has a very light teaching load or none at all in the larger schools. In the smaller schools, however, with a small personnel, one of the teachers has this duty of direction in addition to his regular classwork. In fact, the assignment of one man for the specific work of personal and vocational guidance is a very recent growth in American Jesuit schools. No mention is made of the office of spiritual father of the students either in school or province catalogues, earlier than the 90's;[53] and it did not become a regular feature of Jesuit administration in the United States until the last decade. Indeed, one searches in vain in both the *Monumenta Paedagogica* and the various *Ratios* for any trace of this office. Dr. Goodier describes the genesis of this office:[54]

> No doubt its beginning is obvious. When our boys began to live under the same roof with their masters, it was natural that they should be permitted to share in many of their spiritual privileges. Among these would be the care of the spiritual father; indeed, it is possible that many a scholastic might deem his boys more in need of this protection than himself.[55] The growth of sodalities would foster the movement. These in the first instances were in the hands of the [scholastic] masters and even today a master is usually their nominal director; but for obvious reasons the further assistance of a priest was indispensable. Thirdly, there would be the everpresent necessity in intern colleges of a fixed confessor for the boys. These and other cognate duties, not least that of exponent of Christian doctrine, would naturally gather around one and the same individual; and the growth of the modern curriculum, demanding as it does the master's whole energies has, no doubt, helped to further the change.

The Jesuit Teachers

Both theory and practice in the Society in this matter seem to have been until very recent years to leave to the teachers the major portion of direction and guidance. At the same time, confessors were assigned to whom the students could have recourse for more intimate direction in their personal lives. Thus, Père Jouvancy's *Ratio discendi et docendi,* the classic Jesuit work on pedagogy, assigns two sections of the *Ratio docendi* to means the Jesuit master is to use to instill piety in his pupils: *Articulus II, De Piis sermonibus qui haberi cum discipulis possunt* and *Articulus III, De variis artibus fovendae adolescentum pietatis.*[56] A method of stirring up intellectual interest is treated in a later chapter; *Articulus VI, De duplici studiorum stimulo* and *Articulus II, De privatis discipulorum studiis*.[57]

Class Teachers versus Branch Teachers

This function of the teacher accounts for the Jesuit practice, universal in American schools until the last decade and still in vogue in some places, of having class teachers rather than branch teachers. The reason for this was stated in *The Teacher's Review* in 1912.[58]

> The main teaching for one class should be done [in the high school] as far as possible by one teacher. And if it be objected that occasionally some branches may be slighted owing to a less perfect knowledge in the teacher, the general gain in efficiency, in character training, and moral development will far more than compensate such inconvenience.

So tenacious were some of the American Jesuits of this practice, so convinced of its value, that even when the general of the Society, Father F. X. Wernz, recommended to the American provinces the adoption of the branch system even in the high schools,[59] it by no means received unanimous acceptation. In the Missouri Province, the general's letter helped to crystallize the growing sentiment in favor of branch teachers, and ultimately was adopted generally by the western schools. But when one of the Missouri men ventured to write enthusiastically of the branch system as "absolutely necessary for the future success of our schools and the standing of the Society in the educational world,"[60] he was vigorously attacked in the same review by Father Francis P. Donnelly, of the Maryland-New York Province, who maintained that the departmental system utterly destroyed the unity and thoroughness of Jesuit teaching. He spoke bitterly of those in favor of it as being guilty of "obsequious truckling to half-baked theorists . . . who have no solid pedagogical principles."[61] The rather sharp controversy on this subject lasted for two years.[62] There was apparently no yielding on either side. The western schools have generally conformed to modern usage, while the Maryland-New York schools still remain faithful to the traditional Jesuit practice of class teachers.[63]

Whether the branch teacher or the class teacher is favored, whether one individual is assigned to the special duty of student counselor or not, all Jesuits would agree that the function of a teacher in a Jesuit school is not merely one of teaching. He is to use his influence in class and out of class to secure the advancement of his students not merely "in letters but in Christian character."[64] Undoubtedly the most distinctive characteristic of the American Jesuit school, a characteristic that marks it off, not only from public high schools, but even from other Catholic schools, is the spirit of camaraderie that exists between master and boys.

Lay Teachers

An interesting phenomenon, however, that has accompanied the growth in enrollment in American Jesuit schools is the presence of lay masters who are not members of the Society. A study of the catalogue of the American schools reveals the fact that the high-school faculty was for many decades predominantly Jesuit; here and there a layman taught the commercial branches in the "mercantile course." But in the past decade, all that has changed; in the American schools of the present day, lay teachers are factors to be reckoned with in administration. In some places they constitute more than 50 per cent of the total personnel.[65] They are graduates, generally of Jesuit colleges or universities, and possess the usual academic and professional qualifications demanded of public-high-school teachers, receiving usually a lower salary than do teachers in secular institutions. They are a genuine problem. First of all, in the Jesuit system they can never rise beyond the rank of teachers, all administrative offices being reserved, in the main, for members of the Order. As a consequence, their length of tenure is short. Moreover, they occupy a somewhat anomalous position in the school organization and rarely, if ever, have an equal voice with the Jesuit staff in determining policy, curricula, and the like.

TABLE XI. NUMBER OF JESUITS AND LAYMEN ON THE STAFF OF AMERICAN JESUIT HIGH SCHOOLS*

School	*Total Faculty*	*Jesuits on Faculty*	*Laymen on Faculty*	*Percentage of Jesuits*
Boston College	48	23	25	48
Brooklyn Academy	37	18	19	48
Campion Preparatory	26	19	6	73
Canisius H. S.	28	13	15	48
Creighton H. S.	26	11	16	42
Georgetown Preparatory	16	8	8	50
Gonzaga H. S., Spokane	15	12	3	80
Gonzaga H. S., Washington	19	13	6	68
Immaculate Conception H. S.	21	18	3	86
Loyola H. S., Baltimore	24	18	6	76
Loyola Academy, Chicago	20	12	8	60
Loyola H. S., Los Angeles	17	10	7	59
Loyola H. S., Missoula	5	3	3	60
Loyola School, New York	10	6	4	60
Marquette U. H. S., Milwaukee	21	10	11	48
Marquette H. S., Yakima	4	2	2	50
Regis H. S., Denver	15	12	3	80
Regis H. S., New York	26	12	14	46
Rockhurst H. S.	15	10	5	67
Sacred Heart H. S., Tampa	10	9	1	90
St. Ignatius H. S., Chicago	29	20	9	69
St. Ignatius, Cleveland	19	11	8	58
St. Ignatius, San Francisco	27	15	12	56
St. John's, Fordham	28	14	14	50
St. John's H. S., Toledo	18	14	4	78
St. John's, Shreveport	10	9	1	90
St. Joseph's, Philadelphia	32	14	18	43
St. Leo's, Tacoma	7	3	4	43
St. Louis U. H. S.	35	18	18	51
St. Mary's, St. Mary's, Kansas	27	15	12	55
St. Peter's, Jersey City	37	17	20	46
St. Xavier's, Cincinnati	30	13	18	43
Santa Clara U. H. S.	14	9	5	64
Seattle College H. S.	14	10	4	71
Xavier H. S., New York	49	19	30	39
University of Detroit H. S.	22	10	12	45

*Data compiled from province catalogues and school catalogues for 1926.

Finances

The finances of Jesuit high schools show an interesting development. According to the intention of Ignatius and the express law of the Society, instruction was gratuitous.[66] In fact, the Society was not to take charge of a college unless it was sufficiently endowed to make such fees unnecessary.[67] This was rigorously observed in the early history of the Society, when princes and prelates generously endowed Jesuit colleges in Catholic Europe.[68] But the American Jesuits were early confronted with the problem of how to live without accepting a tuition fee from their students. Thus the Washington Seminary which charged tuition was closed by the General, Father Fortis, in 1827 for violating the rule.[69] The same problem confronted the Missouri Jesuits; at St. Louis in the early days, a small tuition fee of $5 a year was charged. The rector, Peter Verhaegen, pointed out in a letter to the general, the need of some charge to meet absolute living expenses. Moreover, he maintained that parents of the better class did not wish to send their children to what was in effect a free school. But the general insisted on the strict and literal interpretation of the rule in this matter. Fearing for the existence of the St. Louis school, Bishop Rosati of St. Louis petitioned the Congregation of Propaganda late in 1832 for a modification of the Jesuit rule. In January, 1833, Pope Gregory XVI granted the dispensation. Accordingly, Father Roothaan, the general, drew up an ordination, carefully limiting the conditions under which Jesuit schools could avail themselves of this privilege of accepting tuition fees: (1) Tuition fees are to be similar to those prevailing in other reputable schools of the country; (2) Poor boys are not to be turned away nor in any way neglected through inability to pay; (3) Lawsuits are never to be instituted to recover tuition money; (4) The income from tuition fees is to be spent on the support of the Jesuit teachers and on school equipment.[70] The endowed school continues to be the Jesuit ideal[71] but, in America, tuition is charged in all Jesuit high schools, with two exceptions: namely, Regis High School, New York City, and St. John's College High School, Shreveport, Louisiana.

The tuition varies in the day schools from $500, in the exclusive Loyola School, New York City, to $50 in Creighton University High School, Omaha. In the boarding schools the range is from $1,200 for board and tuition, at the Georgetown Preparatory, Garrett Park, Maryland, to $500 at Campion Preparatory. No figures are available as to the cost of instruction per pupil. Undoubtedly it varies greatly in different localities. Where the Jesuit personnel is large, the cost is proportionately low, as the members of the Order receive no salary. Each school is financially independent of all the others, and of the province as well; each school, too, provides for the living expenses of its own Jesuit staff. While the rector has the final word in financial as in other matters, the finances are cared for by the *procurator*. The superintendence of grounds and buildings, the hiring of workmen, the supervision of the "common table" for the Jesuit community are handled by the *minister*. Both these officials are Jesuit priests.

Footnotes

[1]See *supra*, Chap. I, "The Jesuits and Education."

[2]See Tables VIII and IX, p. 219; also Figs. 1 to 5, p. 217.

[3]See Fig. 6, p. 218.

[4]*Epitome Instituti Societatis Jesu*, No. 377, p. 162; *Constitutiones*, Pars. IV, c. 7, n. 1, A.

[5]*Epitome*, No. 396, p. 169.

[6]See *Supra*, Nos. 733, 734, pp. 306, 307.

[7]*Ibid.*, Chap. XI.

[8]*Epitome Instituti Societatis Jesu*, No. 734, 1, p. 307.

[9]*Epitome*, 466, No. 1, p. 201; *Constitutiones*, Pars. VI, c. 1, No. 1.

[10]*Ratio Studiorum*, "Regulae Rectoris," 1 et 3.

[11]*Ibid.*, Reg. 3.

[12]*Ibid.*, Reg. 4; Epitome, 334, and 402.

[13]*Epitome*, 390, No. 4, p. 167; *Rat. Stud.*, "Reg. Praef. Stud. Inf.," 40.

[14]*Ratio Studiorum*, "Regulae Rectoris," 2.

[15]*Ibid.*, "Reg. Praef. Stud. Inf.," 1.

[16]*Ibid.*, "Regulae Rectoris," 21.

[17]*Ibid.*, "Reg. Praef. Stud. Inf.," 4.

[18]Passard, *La Pratique du Ratio*, p. 15.

[19]*Rat. Stud.*, "Reg. Praef. Stud. Inf.," 5.

[20]*Ibid.*, 6.

[21]*Ibid.*, 9, 10, 11, 12.

[22]*Ibid.*, 15–26. See also "Scribendi ad examen leges."

[23]*Rat. Stud.*, "Reg. Praef. Stud. Inf.," 35. See also "Leges praemiorum."

[24]*Ibid.*, "Reg. Praef. Stud. Inf.," 3, 32, 33, 34.

[25]"Reg. Rectoris," 21; *Woodstock Academy for the Study of the Ratio*, p. 23.

[26]"Reg. Praef. Stud. Inf.," pp. 38 et sqq.

[27]*Ibid.*, 39.

[28]*Ibid.*, 43.

[29]*Ibid.*, 41.

[30]"Reg. Praef. Stud. Inf.," 37 et 38. See also *Monumenta Paedagogica*, No. 96, "Regulae Correctoris," p. 712; No. 99, p. 743; No. 29, p. 301; No. 70, p. 643.

[31]Usually called "convictus" in Jesuit official documents.

[32]"Regulae Provincialis," 2; "Regulae Rectoris," 12; "Regulae Praef. Studiorum," i.e., the prefect of studies in the higher faculty or university, 21 and 22.

[33]Rochemonteix, *Un Collège de Jésuites*, etc., I, 6.

[34]Decretum xiii, in *Institutum Societatis Jesus*, I, 231. Rome, 1869.

[35]Rochemonteix, *op. cit.*, I, 57.

[36]See chapters on Jesuit educational activity in the United States.

[37]*Histoire critique*, p. 177.

[38]Schimberg, *L'Éducation Morale*, p. 484, pp. 342 ff.; Kesseler, *Das Lebenswerk der grossen Pädagogen*, p. 26.

[39]See Table X, p. 226.

[40]Passard, *La Pratique du Ratio*, p. 77.

[41]Rochemonteix, *op. cit.*, IV, 188, "Pièces Justificatives": "Les Préfets visiteront alors souvent leurs écoliers pour voir s'ils étudient, s'ils ne lisent pas des livres defendus ou

étrangers à la classe, s'ils ne regardent pas par les fenêtres ou par dessus les cloissons. S'ils permittent en cas de nécessité à un élève de sortir, ils le feront accompagner par le valet de chambre, surtout dans les basses classes; jamais ils n'en laisseront sortir deux à la fois. Ils ne permittront à aucun élève d'entrer dans la chambre ou dans la cellule d'un autre sous pretexte de demander du papier, des plumes, des livres, ou autre chose."

[42]Quicherat, *Histoire de Sainte-Barbe: Collège, communauté*, II, 60.

[43]*Manuel des Jeunes Professeurs* (Paris, 1842). This book was held in high esteem by Jesuits everywhere. Besides the *Observations*, it contains Sacchini's *Paraenesis ad Magistros Scholarum Inferiorum Societatis Jesu*, first printed in 1625; the same authors, *Protrepticon ad Magistros Scholarum Inferiorum;* Père Le Gaudier's *De Recto Modo Agendi Nostrorum cum iis Qui Ipsorum Subsunt, praesertim Convictoribus;* Père Judde, *Instruction pour les Jeunes Professeurs qui enseignent les Humanités; Instructio pro Magistris Societatis Jesu; Ratio Studiorum pro Scholis Inferioribus Societatis Jesu* — that part of the *Ratio* which pertains to the "lower" schools.

[44]*Ibid.*, pp. 9 ff.

[45]Barbier, Père, *La discipline dans quelques écoles libres. Manuel pratique du surveillant* (Amiens, 1884).

[46]Table des Matiéres.

I. Organisation du Collège sous le rapport de la discipline.
II. Nature et esprit des fonctions du Surveillant.
III. Rapports avec les Supérieurs.
IV. Rapports avec les Collègues.
V. Rapports avec les Élèves.
VI. Le Règlement.
VII. Les Exercises de piété.
VIII. Les Récréations.
IX. Les Jeux.
X. La Classe.
XI. L'Étude.
XII. Les Promenades.
XIII. Les Repas.
XIV. Le Dortoir.
XV. Le Parloir. Les Sorties.
XVI. L'Infirmerie.
XVII. Principaux Moyens d'émulation et de répressions.

[47]See, for example, "Regeln für Hofmeister" in the German translation of F. X. Kropf's *Ratio et Via Recte atque Ordine Procedendi in Literis Humanioribus Aetati Tenerae Tradendis* (1736). German translation in *Gymnasial-Pädagogik*, Vol. X of Herder's *Bibliothek*, pp. 464 ff.

[48]Hughes, *op. cit.*, "Documents," I, Part II, 799.

[49]*The Formation of Character; Collapses in Adult Life; Man's Great Concern — the Management of Life; A Practical Philosophy of Life.* All published by Herder (London and St. Louis).

[50]Pp. 42 ff.

[51]Tierney, Richard H., *Teacher and Teaching*, pp. 91–92.

[52]*Boston College High School Catalogue for 1926*, p. 52A. See also *Georgetown Preparatory School Bulletin, 1926–7*, p. 11.

[53]The first regular appearance of a *praefectus spiritualis alumnorum* in the Missouri Province catalogue is in 1889. *Catalogus Provinciae Missourianae ineunte anno 1889*, p. 18.

[54]Goodier, "The Society of Jesus and Education," *The Month*, CIX, 143 ff.

[55]In every Jesuit community there is a *praefectus spiritualis* to give individual spiritual guidance to the members.

[56]Juvencius, *Ratio discendi et docendi*, Pars II, Caput I, Art. II et III in *Thesaurus Spiritualis Magistrorum Scholarum Inferiorum Societatis Jesu*, pp. 66–71.

[57]*Ibid.*, pp. 72–79.

[58]III, 44.

[59]"Eadem praxis [i.e., of the subject teacher] saepe utilis esse potest in omnibus classibus, etiam in Schola Alta." From letter of F. X. Wernz to the Maryland-New York Province, May 10, 1910. Quoted in *The Province News-Letter*, III, 26. Transcript of letter in *Missouri Province Archives*.

[60]H. S. Spalding, in *The Teacher's Review*, VI, No. 4 (October, 1915), 49 ff.

[61]*Ibid.*, VII, No. 1 (January, 1916), 4 ff.

[62]See *The Teacher's Review*, VII, 18 ff.; VII, 50; VIII (January, 1917), 2.

[63]For example, in the *Boston College High School Catalogue for 1927*, pp. 6 ff., the faculty is listed under "Instructors in Fourth Year," "Instructors in Third Year," etc., instead of in the more conventional fashion.

[64]*Ratio Studiorum*, "Reg. Com. Prof. Class. Inf.," 1–10.

[65]See Table XI, p. 235.

[66]*Constitutiones* Pars. VI, c. II, 7. See also Paulsen, *Geschichte des gelehrten Unterrichts* I, 383; Schwickerath, *op. cit.*, pp. 246 ff.

[67]*Epitome Instituti Soc. Jesu*, 516, No. 2, 224.

[68]Schwickerath, *op. cit.*, p. 256; Rochemonteix, *op. cit.*, II, 58.

[69]See *supra*, Chap. V, "The Maryland-New York Province."

[70]Garraghan, *The Jesuits in the Middle United States*, I, Chap. 5.

[71]*Epitome Instituti Societatis Jesu*, Pars. VI, Chap. II, Art. IV, No. 516, p. 224.

CHAPTER XIII

THE TRAINING OF JESUIT TEACHERS

THE first Jesuits were determined, once the work of education had been accepted, that neither pains nor expense should be spared in the formation of the Jesuit master. As a consequence, rarely have they been reproached with inefficiency or inadequacy in the training imparted their own men. In fact, educators whose ideal is almost the contradictory of theirs, have acclaimed them as "the most efficient corporation of schoolmasters then at work."[1] These sixteenth-century Jesuits did much to elevate the status of the schoolmaster. Their theory and practice of pedagogical training were in advance of their day, as almost any page of contemporary educational writing will show. The masters of that period were obliged to resort to humiliating stratagems in order to eke out a meager subsistence and keep the specter of debt from the threshold. Vives[2] speaks bitterly of the ease with which academic honors came to those who were generous in their payment, no matter how tenuous their knowledge, tender their age, or despicable their character. This, he maintains, is one of the causes of the decadence of letters. Leibnitz,[3] too, at a later date, declared that the miserable recompense kept men of talent out of the teaching profession.

To rehabilitate teaching in the eyes of the members of the Order, to make it respectable, two things were done. First, practically all, no matter how distinguished their talents, were obliged to teach before the priesthood. Secondly, all anxiety and worry about the necessities of life were removed. The vow of poverty prevented members of the Order from owning anything as their own, but all their needs were taken care of. They received no salary, but all their debts were paid, their room, their table, their books were provided by the community. In this manner self-respect and personal dignity were safeguarded.

It is curious and somewhat anomalous that enough time was granted members of the Order during their years of training to make them great savants; and yet at the end of their training a large percentage of them were assigned to the tedious task of teaching small boys. If there be inefficiency in the formation of the Jesuit teacher, obviously the error is not in a niggardly time allotment for his religious, literary, and philosophical formation.[4]

Choice of Candidates

First of all, unlike some other religious orders in the Catholic Church, the Jesuits do not provide secondary schools as seminaries for candidates to the Order. Whether from principle or merely from expediency, none is admitted who has not finished his gymnasial course, or at least the major portion of it.[5] In America, the minimum academic requirement demanded of all candidates is the completion of the high school. Very probably all Jesuits consider it desirable that members of the Order should have some contact with the world before admission, should pursue their secondary studies in a school with other youths, not destined for the ecclesiastical profession. Of course, it is but natural that in founding secondary schools, the Jesuits looked on them not merely as institutions of learning for secular youth, but also as recruiting posts for the Order.[6] But this is a subordinate function of their schools. In fact, they are forbidden by rule to induce youths to enter the Society. One of the questions asked of the candidate for the Society is whether he has been influenced by a Jesuit "to choose this manner of life."[7] If so, this constitutes an impediment to his entry. Nevertheless, it is undoubtedly true that the attraction of Jesuit life, with its opportunities for intellectual advancement, serves as a powerful inducement to promising youths in their colleges.

Requisites for Admission to the Society

What qualities does the Society expect of its recruits? The *Constitutiones*[8] provide that only those be admitted who give hope "by their character and talents of becoming upright and learned men, fit to labor in the vineyard of Christ, our Lord." It is not precisely that geniuses are looked for. Francis Piccolomini,[9] the general of the Society (1649–1651), in a letter dated October 28, 1650, insists that gifts of mind (*excellentiam ingenii*) can be compensated for by strength of character and purity of heart. Nevertheless, certain minimum scholastic requirements should be demanded. At a later date, Father Brzozowski, the first general of the restored Society (1814–1820), in a letter to Père Leblanc, the Jesuit superior in Belgium, protests against the interpretation of Jesuit regulations regarding candidates which would exclude from the Society all but towering geniuses. "Mediocrity" he maintains, "also has its value. . . . Not infrequently subjects of mediocre talents do splendid work, better even than others of exceptional talents."[10]

Of course, everyone that applies for admission is not to be accepted. Father Peter Beckx, the general (1853–1883), urged examiners to be severe in their judgments as to the fitness of candidates, and to approve only those youths whose character and talents are suited to the spirit of the Society.[11] The minimum academic requirements of candidates varied slightly at different times. In Europe, where the gymnasium is regarded as the end of secondary studies, it is usual to demand the completion of the gymnasial course, or as the 27th General Congregation[12] puts it, "the completion of rhetoric class," which is roughly the equivalent of sophomore year in an American college. In the United States, however, where the secondary studies end with high school, the question arose as to whether it was wise to demand two years of college from candidates for admission. At a meeting of delegates from the two major American provinces, Maryland-New York and Missouri, held in 1905,[13] the question was debated. The eastern province thought that the completion of high school was sufficient; and they instanced the danger of loss of vocation if young men were obliged to wait longer; many, too, discontinued their studies after high school or entered on direct preparation for a professional career. In defense of their position, they urged that while the American high-school graduate probably had not that academic training which the 20th General Congregation desired, namely, the completion of a gymnasial course, yet graduates of American high schools were for the most part eighteen years of age, and of sufficient intellectual and moral maturity. The Missouri delegates, however, wished to continue their existing custom of demanding the completion of "humanities," that is, freshman college. Eventually, in the *Ordinatio Studiorum*[14] for the English Assistancy, issued in 1912—to which Assistancy[15] the American provinces at that time belonged—it was definitely determined that the completion of fourth year in a classical high school or its equivalent should be the minimum requirement for admission to the novitiate, although the completion of "rhetoric class" is still recommended in the latest legislation of the Society, the *Epitome Instituti*, published in 1924. Present American usage regarding the admission of candidates is reflected in the following excerpt from *The Province News-Letter* (Missouri Province):[16]

Requirements of Candidates for the Society

1. *Latin.* A 4-year course or its equivalent in Latin. An exception may be made in favor of mature candidates of extraordinary ability.
2. *Greek.* While we must direct all students who are preparing for the Society to study Greek, candidates otherwise fit, who have had no Greek may be admitted.
3. *Ability.* Students having only the minimum requirements in studies (completion of the fourth year of high school) should not be recommended for admission unless they surpass mediocrity.

The Novitiate

A novitiate in Catholic religious orders is a time of probation, a period of testing, and of mutual trial for both candidate and order. In the Society of Jesus this lasts two years. A novice is perfectly free to depart at any time during this period if the life or work is found to be uncongenial; on the other hand, the Society may for just reasons dismiss a novice whom it deems unsuited to its work.[17] During the novitiate, the rules, the manner of life are explained and practiced, the theory and practice of asceticism, the prime requisite for religious life, are imparted; study is made of the life of Christ and its application to Christian living.

In the first year of the novitiate, all the novices make the thirty-day retreat, the most influential single factor in the formation of the Jesuit. This consists of an entire month of silence and absolute retirement devoted to the *Exercitia Spiritualia*,[18] St. Ignatius Loyola's great contribution to Christian asceticism, consisting of basic meditations on the relations between God and man, enforced and vivified by the study of the life of Christ as presented in the Gospels. These thirty days of spiritual exercises might well be styled academically a *Practicum in the Philosophy of Christian Living*. It aims to develop in the novice certain attitudes, certain desires, certain habits. He must strive to "reproduce in himself the life of Christ. The long retreat and the whole period of novitiate for that matter train the youthful recruit to habits of self-examination, self-mastery, and self-realization. The novitiate has been aptly termed a perfectly equipped laboratory for experiments in habit formation."[19]

During these two years some time is allotted every day for private study in the classics. Except during the month of the long retreat, classes are held twice a day. Besides this, some training is given in public speaking, and in English writing, and the novices are free to explore the whole field of patristic Latin and Greek. But the major portion of this time is devoted, not to academic training, but to making them *religious*, to what modern terminology would call "character education." This training of the will is Ignatius's contribution to the formation of the masters; his motto *ad majorem Dei gloriam* is held before the novices, not as a mere verbalism, but as a vibrant living reality, to be realized in the novices' own lives, first of all by putting God's interest before all human interests, and secondly, by serving as a practical working ideal for their first field of action, the classroom.

The by-products of these two years of novitiate are invaluable to the future Jesuit master.

Mental concentration is aided by the rule of silence, and the will receives its quota of development from the short periods which are assigned for the various exercises. These brief periods school the novice to use time carefully, to drop engaging work at a moment's notice and to throw himself enthusiastically into an uncongenial task — accomplishments whose difficulty is hardly apparent to one who has never tried them.[20]

The Juniorate

After the two years of noviceship, the novice — his average age in America is about 20 — is free to pronounce his vows of poverty, chastity, and obedience. It is hardly necessary to remark that these voluntary promises are made not to the Jesuit superior but to God. Henceforth he is a Jesuit scholastic. His vows bind him to a life of celibacy, to obedience to his superiors, and to the renunciation of all ownership and of all rights to remuneration for services rendered. He will receive no salary, although all his legitimate wants will be supplied; food, clothing, books, are his for the asking. His superiors may put him to teach this subject or that, although it would be absurd to imagine that the Society deliberately places its men in positions to which they are altogether unsuited.

The juniorate in the United States ordinarily lasts two years; for special reasons in some provinces, a third year is occasionally added. These two years are given over exclusively to literary study; in the old Society its purpose was the perfection of *eloquentia;* in the modern American juniorate its object is

> . . . to complete and perfect the scholastic's literary training and to furnish him with the pedagogic instruction required for his future work in the classroom. . . . The juniorate is the normal school of the province. The studies in the juniorate are principally thorough courses in Latin, Greek, English, and history. . . . Latin will be for him all during his studies a most necessary instrument and every effort is made to give him a complete mastery of the language. . . . Greek is not to be of so extensive or practical a character; but he must get such a hold of it as to benefit by its culture and to be able to teach it in the ordinary high-school classes. . . . The English course . . . makes a serious demand upon the junior's attention and time. . . . The insistence on public speaking is a most important phase. . . .
>
> During the whole course in both novitiate and juniorate, the peda-

gogic course is not for an instant lost sight of. The young man is to be a teacher . . . and in addition to the study of his Order's famous method, the *Ratio Studiorum,* and practical exercises in teaching, there is a constant stream of help flowing to the student from association. . . . The professors transmit the centuries-old pedagogic lore of the Society and indicate during the lecture period points of theory and practice, bits of advice drawn from their personal experience.[21]

The 25th General Congregation, held in 1906, decreed that "the junior . . . should be thoroughly instructed in grammar, humanities, rhetoric, and especially in sacred eloquence, Latin, Greek, and vernacular literature. . . . Special care is to be taken that our juniors understand and highly esteem the *Ratio Studiorum* of the Society and in general that they complete a regular liberal-arts course which serves as an excellent preparation for the course in philosophy and is rightly expected of every priest of culture in our day."[22]

Thorough Training in the Classics

Great care is taken in selecting the professors for the juniorate. The ablest classicists in the province, with a record of successful experience in the classroom, are chosen for this office. Vitelleschi, the general from 1615 to 1645, in a circular letter to the provincials,[23] called attention to the importance of securing excellent professors for the juniors; on their training depended the success of Jesuit schools. "Care should be taken," he said, "to have excellent and experienced masters . . . who will devote all their efforts to the promotion not merely of learning, but of character as well." And Visconti, general from 1751 to 1755, wrote in similar vein: "Our juniors should have the most capable professors. Not only should they be distinguished rhetoricians but they must be able to explain and communicate this art to others. . . . For their task is to fashion not merely good students, but also good masters."[24] And Father Beckx, general from 1853 to 1883, insisted on the same point. "A provincial's first care should be to see that those intrusted with the education of our juniors are picked and proven men."[25]

Since the juniors are later to be masters in classical schools, there is naturally great insistence on the classics. Father Beckx, in a letter to the whole Society, dated June 16, 1881,[26] cited the commendation of classical studies by the 14th General Congregation,[27] and repeated their plea that "there may never be a falling off in the study of the humanities which up to the present the Society has cultivated with such honor." Father Beckx then urges provincials to see to it that the juniors receive thorough instruction in "their national literature as well as in Latin and Greek . . . and if the province is not supplied with competent professors, they should be borrowed from another province."

It would be a mistake, however, to suppose that the course in the juniorate is the same for all. The Society early resorted to homogeneous grouping of its men on the basis of natural aptitude. Thus, in theology, there is the "long course" with its *examen rigorosum* at the end, and the "short course" with less rigid requirements. In the course of philosophy there is a similar line of demarcation. In the juniorate, too, there are classes for the more advanced, conducted on the plan of a seminar, while the average group follows more conventional courses.[28]

The Course in Philosophy

After the completion of his literary studies in the juniorate, the scholastic passes on to the school of philosophy for a term, ordinarily, of three years. This is a very thorough course in neo-scholastic philosophy. Other systems of philosophy, of course, are treated formally in the lectures on the history of philosophy and come up for investigation when contrasting the theories of these systems with scholastic theories in the courses in logic, epistemology, cosmology, theodicy, and ethics. These courses, as well as the courses in rational and experimental psychology, are obligatory for all the scholastics.[29] Besides these, the scholastics may take courses in science or mathematics or continue their literary studies on the graduate level. Courses in education are now required of all during this triennium in the American Provinces.[30]

The lectures in philosophy are for the most part in Latin.

A great deal is made of the weekly disputations when one scholastic must defend a thesis against all comers. Three or four times a year public disputations are held in the presence of the faculty and the entire body of scholastics.[31] The purpose of the course in philosophy for the Jesuit is to furnish a necessary complement to the ascetic formation of the novice and the literary training imparted to the junior, to supply him with a rational philosophy of life.[32] It is not the aim to turn out specialists precisely — although specialization has its place in the Jesuit training, at a later period — not merely to turn out efficient secondary teachers, although the theory and practice of education is not neglected during these years; but the main purpose of these seven years that precede the Jesuit's classroom experience is to turn out a well-rounded man, well informed, possessed of principles that will serve as a definite philosophy of life. The Jesuit is meant to be a man of the world, not merely a teacher, not even a college professor. For those who contemn academic training in the preparation of secondary teachers, there will seem to be exaggerated emphasis on this phase of the Jesuit's training. Complaint will be made, not that the time devoted to preparation is insufficient, but rather that there is a lack of specific direction in the training of the Jesuit teacher, a waste of time that might better be spent in turning out expert educationists. To many it will seem like clinging to an impossible medieval ideal, a desire for knowledge, *"de omni scibili."*

However that may be, one thing seems certain: of no other group of American secondary teachers has there ever been so rigid a requirement in regard to their years of preparation. There are five years after high school entirely devoted to intellectual work; and it must be remembered that this is the irreducible minimum. A large percentage of the candidates in America enter with one or more years of college work to their credit. Besides this, there are the two years of novitiate, which, with its emphasis on character training and habit formation, should not be passed by in reckoning up the years devoted to teacher-training. Undoubtedly in the early history of the Society in this country, these years of preparation were shortened for some, due to stress of circumstances, but this was always regarded as an exceptional practice, and the ideal of seven years' preparation was always considered the usual procedure.[33]

Professional Preparation of Jesuit Teachers

All during these seven years, informal training in educational practice is imparted. During the novitiate, the novice is obliged to give, from time to time, a practice class in the teaching of religion. In the juniorate, practice classes in the classics, in English literature, or history are conducted.[34] In addition, "academies"[35] are recommended to the juniors and philosophical students, a combination of pedagogical seminar and education club. Thus, there is the "Ratio Academy" at Woodstock College, started in 1893;[36] a similar academy was started at St. Louis University some years later.

Yet it is a curious fact that though the *Ratio* contains much about school administration and curriculum, there is very little about teacher training. Another interesting point is that while the literary output of the Society has been immense,[37] nevertheless "it has produced little or nothing that can be classed as pedagogic literature."[38] Laurie's comment[39] is not without significance: "The school organization of the Jesuits became a tradition; the *Ratio Studiorum* and the *Ratio Docendi* were handed down. They have not written much on pedagogy, but their system embodies a pedagogy."

Practical Training in Teaching

However, even from the days of the first *Ratio* some attempts were made to impart the practical art of teaching to the Jesuit master before he entered the classroom.[40] Thus Ledesma prepared some *annotationes*,[41] suggestions suitable both for the prefect of studies in his supervision and for the master in his conduct of the class. Magius, the official visitor of the college at Paris in 1587, prescribed practice classes (*exercitatio magistrorum*) for those in the last year of the course of philosophy, who would be sent as masters to the colleges the following year.[42] Similarly, in another document, evidently for a Spanish college, it is recommended that judgment be used in selecting teachers and that they give proof of their ability beforehand by teaching, in the presence of a teacher of experience, a class similar to the one to which they are to be assigned.[43]

However, it was early learned from bitter experience that there was need of more definite pedagogical training. Complaints came to Rome in the early days before the drawing up of the definitive *Ratio* of 1599 that some of the teachers were incompetent, without sufficient religious, intellectual, and pedagogic formation.[44] One reason seems to have been that during this first stage in the Society's history too many colleges were accepted. Polanco, writing of the situation in 1554, maintained that it was harmful not only to individuals but to the good repute of the Society.[45] Consequently, the *Ratio* of 1599 ordered the rectors to have a special care of the intellectual and pedagogic formation of the future masters. Rule 9 of the rector ordered the establishment of a pedagogical seminar or "academy" in the scholasticates. A thoroughly experienced teacher was selected to supervise the future masters. Toward the end of their philosophical course they were to meet with him three hours a week and receive instruction and practice in the art of teaching.[46] Moreover, all during their course in philosophy, and theology as well, the prefect of studies was to take care that the scholastics under his charge did not lose contact with the classics which they were to teach later on.[47]

In the American provinces, it is probable that from the beginning there was this minimum pedagogical preparation of equivalently three hours a week in the last year of philosophy, prescribed by the *Ratio* and the General Congregations. Since 1890 at least, there has been, in addition, in the juniorate a regular course of instruction on the *Ratio Studiorum*.[48] But in later years this was felt to be insufficient. No doubt, the influence of standardizing agencies and their requirements brought about a larger allotment for pedagogy in the Jesuit curriculum. In 1910, it was proposed at a meeting of provincial delegates to give an entire year after the juniorate to educational subjects.[49] This, however, was never put into practice.

At a meeting of the rectors of the Missouri Province colleges in April, 1917, it was recommended that the normal work already in force at Florissant (the juniorate of this province) be arranged so as to conform to established practice throughout the country in departments of education. Moreover, teachers' courses should be added to the courses in Latin, Greek, English, and other juniorate branches. Finally, in view of the "branch system which is coming more and more into vogue especially in certain subjects, greater encouragement should be given to those who give promise of attaining a marked degree of proficiency in any branch or branches somewhat along the lines of majoring in other schools."[50]

The present practice in the American provinces is to give courses in high-school methods and history of education, together with a course on the *Ratio Studiorum,* in the juniorate. During the philosophical triennium, besides the obligatory course in experimental psychology, courses are offered in administration, educational psychology, educational sociology, tests and measurements, statistics, and the like.[51]

Examinations

All through the Jesuit course, rigorous examinations are demanded. If a scholastic fails in the juniorate, he may be made to repeat the course; if his case seems hopeless or if he fails a second time, the matter is left to the decision of the general who may offer him the choice of leaving the Society or becoming a lay brother.[52] The case is not of frequent occurrence, as great care is taken in admitting only candidates who give promise of sufficient intellectual ability to succeed in the Jesuit course of studies. Besides the usual annual examinations, an examination in the whole field of philosophy is held before a board of examiners at the end of the philosophical triennium. Those that attain only mediocrity in this examination will be placed in the "short course" in theology.[53] If he fails absolutely, the case is again referred to the general's decision. Those that surpass mediocrity in this final examination in philosophy will be admitted to the "long course" in theology. But each year of their divinity studies, they must appear before the board of examiners for an oral examination; if they fail, they are transferred to the "short course." At the end of the fourth year of theology, those who have been successful throughout their course are given four months of private study to prepare for the severe examination in the whole field of philosophy and theology.[54] If they succeed in this final examination *"ad gradum,"* an examination equivalent to the examination for the doctorate in theology in Catholic universities, they are admitted after a year more of probation to the rank of the "professed." All other Jesuit priests are classed as "spiritual coadjutors." In actual practice, there is but little distinction between the two grades, although certain offices are open only to the professed.[55]

Degrees

Formerly Jesuits were forbidden by rule to make use of the degrees they received.[56] Those who made all their studies in the Society were not given degrees. But because of the urgent need of teachers in American schools being equipped with academic degrees, the present general, Father Ledochowski, approved the permission, granted by his predecessor, Father Wernz, to the American Jesuits to accept degrees and to make use of them. He further approved the laying down of certain requirements relative to examinations and theses for these degrees in addition to the usual examination demanded in the Jesuit course of study. The bachelor's degree, he writes, could be conferred on the scholastics who had successfully finished their two years' juniorate and two years of philosophy. The master's degree could be given after the successful completion of the third year of philosophy. The Jesuit university where the scholastics study will, of course, demand additional requirements, usual in other American universities. The degree of doctor of philosophy should only be given to those who had devoted several years to research after the completion of their course in philosophy. He further forbade the use of these academic degrees, for example, after an author's name in books or periodicals or in school and college catalogues, except on a twofold condition: (1) their use is only sanctioned insofar as they are required by the laws of the State; (2) after the name and degree, the initials *S.J.* must always be added.[57]

Some of the American Jesuits felt — and still feel, no doubt — that the master's degree, held by most of them, did not adequately represent the amount of education they had received. They desired a reorganization of the seven years' course after high school in such a way that would not sacrifice any of the essential thoroughness of the old training. At a meeting of the presidents of the colleges of the Missouri Province, held in 1917,

> . . . suggestions were asked for toward such organization of the studies of the scholastics, as without interfering with the required program of juniorate or scholasticate study, will enable individuals to qualify promptly for such degrees as they are competent to attain in virtue of natural ability or academic attainments, realized before their entrance into the Society. . . . Those who enter with a bachelor's degree might with proper direction and organization of their studies on the part of superiors, qualify for the Ph.D. as early as the end of their philosophy or within a year of that time. Such policy, however, as will be readily understood, should work no prejudice to the essential features of our educational course in the Society. . . . The requirements we set for the Ph.D. degree ought not to be in excess of those normally demanded from candidates for this degree in secular universities, neither ought they to fall below that level.[58]

At a meeting of the rectors and prefects of studies of the Missouri Province, the question came up of securing adequate recognition by outside institutions for the long course of studies, pursued in the Order.[59]

> It was pointed out that the American academic degrees indicate a time value rather than a content value; that an A.B. means four years of study beyond the high school and that an additional year of study can secure the master's degree. To outsiders, therefore, the master's degree which is the highest degree thus far conferred on most of our teachers, does not adequately represent the amount of education they have received. It was accordingly suggested that the Faculty List, as printed in our catalogues, include some account of the academic record and teaching courses of each teacher. Such a statement . . . would enlighten secular educators and college officials and would go far to-

ward counteracting the lack of higher degrees commensurable with our years of study.

Specialization

The *Ordinatio Studiorum*[60] provides for specialization after the philosophical triennium. It is recommended that one, two, or three years be given to some of the scholastics to specialize in the classics, in mathematics, science, or in other branches.[61] In recent years, now that the American provinces are emerging from the pioneer stage, more and more men are being given opportunities at other universities to work for the doctorate. For philosophy, they ordinarily go to continental universities, for the classics and history to Oxford and Cambridge, for science and education to American universities.

Training of Teachers in Service: Summer Schools

Because of the peculiar organization of the Jesuit Order, with its community life, Jesuit teachers have a unique opportunity to develop professionally. Their vacations, for example, are spent together. The *Constitutiones* provide a vacation of two months for all the scholastics, both students and teachers. Two weeks of this time, the *feriae majores,* are a complete rest from studies. The rest of the time, the *feriae minores,* "is to be spent usefully in study under the direction of superiors."[62] In the American Provinces, the philosophy students have their vacations in one house, a "villa"; the divinity students in another; and the scholastic teachers from all the schools of a province in a third. For many years, the six weeks of the *feriae minores* were devoted to something like a "teachers' institute." Lectures were given by experienced teachers, practice classes conducted, discussions of ways and means of improving instruction, and the like. In addition, for the students of philosophy especially, regular classes were given in modern languages. For a long period, no thought was given to assigning credits for this work. But with the growth of the summer-school movement in America, the Jesuits began to see possibilities in their own "summer school." The first record of a regularly conducted summer school for Jesuits, seems to be a course in qualitative chemical analysis, conducted by a Mr. Tarr, not a Jesuit, at Georgetown University, in the summer of 1882, for a class of Jesuit scholastics.[63] In 1907, three weeks' courses in education were offered the Maryland-New York scholastic teachers at their villa, Keyser Island, New York. The next summer, there were courses on the teaching of English, teaching of history, teaching of high-school mathematics. Two professors from Columbia University gave courses in methods of teaching German and French.[64] At about the same time, summer courses in science were given to the scholastics in the same province; in 1907, at Boston College; in 1908–10, at Holy Cross; in 1911, at Georgetown.[65] Similar courses were inaugurated in the Missouri Province; in addition, some of the scholastics attended summer courses at secular universities. But the Missouri Province organized a summer school in a more definite way in 1920. Campion College, Prairie du Chien, Wisconsin, was selected as the "villa" for the scholastic teachers of the province. A corps of Jesuit professors was secured, courses of six weeks duration in a variety of subjects, mainly education, were offered.[66]

Jesuit Educational Association

Out of this summer school grew the Jesuit Educational Association, an organization to promote better teaching in all the schools of the province. At the first annual convention, the provincial, Father F. X. McMenamy, voiced the hope that these meetings "would improve the fine *esprit de corps* that we have already in our schools, by inspiring even greater and more self-sacrificing coöperation of the teachers with rectors and prefects of studies, and of teachers among themselves. Our strength is in our unity."[67] This Association began in 1921 with the organization of the Missouri Province Science Association, "modeled on existing outside scientific societies."[68] This was a rather significant departure in the history of Jesuit education. A paper read at the Third Annual Convention of the Jesuit Educational Association explains its genesis:[69]

Five years ago, the thought of a science association for the Missouri Province was first broached; at that time, the weak spot seemed to lie in a certain lack of professional attitude, due chiefly to lack of contact with outside colleges. If teaching were to become merely a task imposed by authority, no enthusiasm behind it, no curiosity, no interest in current happenings, no news of recent books or researches, or scientific meetings, how could a professional mood, or frame of mind flourish? We felt that the remedy lay not so much in the hands of superiors, as in our own; we had to stay in the general current of scientific activity; and to accomplish this, an organization . . . seemed to be essential. The annual meetings, the papers read, the formalities of applying for membership and of electing officers, and especially the *purely optional and voluntary* character of the association — all these, we hoped, would create an atmosphere in which enthusiasm and scholarship could develop.

The attitude of superiors was friendly — unusually so, considering that it was the first time in the history of the Society of Jesus that such an experiment had been tried. . . . We organized, elected officers, drew up constitutions and by-laws; and after the second annual meeting, published our proceedings. . . . This was the turning point of the experiment.

The same writer goes on to explain how other teachers in the province, interested in subjects other than science, began to think of organizing along similar lines. In 1922, besides the science teachers, there were present at the convention, representatives of "The Classical Association of the Missouri Province," "The Missouri English Association," "American Jesuit Historical Association, Middle-West Division" — all of these organizations newly formed after the model of "The American Association of Jesuit Scientists, Central States Section." This latter organization was divided into various sections, biology, chemistry, mathematics, physics. The proceedings of this first convention were published privately under the title, *Missouri Province Teachers' Association: Proceedings of the First Annual Convention.*[70] Thereafter there have been annual conventions, and each year the proceedings have been printed. The name of the general organization has been changed to "Jesuit Educational Association — Central States Division."

The place of meeting was changed from Campion College to Loyola University, Chicago, to allow for a larger attendance.[71] At the Fifth Annual Convention of the Jesuit Educational Association, held in Chicago from August 16–23, 1926, seven Jesuit teachers' associations comprising nearly the entire teaching personnel of the Missouri Province were present.[72] It is hoped that great good will come of these meetings by developing professional consciousness, and by coöperative effort toward reorganizing curricula and defining objectives of Jesuit education.

Jesuit Educational Periodicals

At an early date (1908), a member of the Maryland-New York Province proposed the publication of an educational periodical exclusively for Jesuit teachers in the United States. He urged the advisability of starting such a magazine "as it would help very much to foster an *esprit de corps* among us."[73] This suggestion bore fruit in *The Teacher's Review,* first issued in January, 1910, and for long the only periodical of the kind in the country. In the foreword, Father Joseph F. Hanselmann, at that time provincial of the Maryland-New York Province, said:[74]

> Meant for private circulation among Ours only, it is hoped that it will serve as a sort of clearing house, a distributing center for views and practical suggestions on our studies and teaching. . . . In this way its work will be subsidiary to the *Ratio Studiorum* whose methods and principles it will illuminate, make more familiar and popular and applicable to the needs of our day. There are many mooted questions . . . that challenge reflective and scientific study of our *Ratio,* of its history and traditions, and call upon the practical experience of successful teachers for proper solution.

In the past few years, the Missouri Province, due to the encouragement of the Jesuit Educational Association previously mentioned, has been issuing several educational journals. *The English Bulletin, The Classical Bulletin, The History Teachers' Bulletin,* and *The Modern Schoolman* are published at St. Louis. In addition, there are privately printed monthly bulletins for the teachers of biology, of mathematics, of chemistry, and of physics. All circulate among Jesuit teachers in the four provinces of the United States.

Summary[75]

As is obvious, the training of the Jesuit teacher is distinctly *sui generis*. The candidate for the Society must have completed a four-year high-school course before gaining admission to the Order. Between his entry and his first year of teaching, there are seven years of preparation — two years of novitiate, two years of juniorate, and three years of philosophy. His years of teaching as a scholastic over — usually three or four years — there are for all, four years of theology. Some are given a biennium or a triennium for special studies. All in all, a complete course designed for the formation of the Jesuit. In giving these long years of preparation to this task, the Society has a triple aim in view; the Jesuit is expected to be an efficient educator of youth, an able priest, and at the same time, a cultivated man of the world.

One cannot but be struck by the emphasis in this training on philosophy and the classics. As to the latter, even utilitarians will admit that if the Jesuit is to be a master in a classical school, he should have a thorough knowledge and wide acquaintance with classical literature. More will find fault with the number of years devoted to scholastic philosophy; this is probably due to preconceived notions of scholasticism as a relic of medievalism. But there seems to be a growing tendency in the intellectual world to evaluate scholasticism anew, and if a renascence of this system ever takes place in America, as it has in Belgium and France, the Jesuit Order, whose members are all trained in this philosophy, will be ready to participate in its revival.

TERTIANSHIP* 1 Year Average age at close: 33	SPECIAL STUDIES
THEOLOGY 4 Years Average age at close: 32	
TEACHING 3–4 Years Average age at close: 28	
PHILOSOPHY 3 Years (Including courses in education, science, mathematics, psychology, etc.) Average age at close: 25	SPECIAL STUDIES
JUNIORATE 2 Years (Includes classics, English, history, etc., undergraduate courses in education.) Average age at close: 22	
NOVITIATE 2 Years Average age at close: 20	
Studies preparatory to admission to the Order. Minimum in America: completion of 4th-Year High. Average age at entry: 18	

Fig. 7. THE TRAINING OF THE JESUIT IN AMERICA

*"Tertianship," the final year in the Jesuit's formation, has for its aim the renewal and deepening of the spiritual life. It is called the third year of probation. The life is not unlike the novitiate. One month is again devoted to the "long retreat."

But over and above all this, it is brought home to the Jesuit teacher in training that his work is not merely the teaching of youth. He is to form their characters, not simply train their minds. Latin, Greek, mathematics, science, history, literature — all these are accidental, though the Society gives its members ample opportunities to attain proficiency in the subjects they are to teach. But the branches in the curriculum are only means to an end; the end is the formation of Catholic leaders, enthusiastic for Catholic principles, who will stand out in their community as examples of Catholic manhood.

Footnotes

[1]Adamson, *Pioneers of Modern Education*, p. 13.

[2]*De dignitate et augmento scientiarum*, I. Cited by Herman, *op. cit.*, p. 177.

[3]Leibnitii, *Opera Omnia*. Genevae, 1768, V, 382–383. Cited by Herman, *op. cit.*

[4]Generous tributes to the efficiency of the Jesuit Order in teacher training are given by Fleischmann in Rein, *Handbuch der Pädagogik*, p. 668; Kesseler, *Das Lebenswerk der grossen Pädagogen*, p. 27; and Schimberg, *L'Éducation morale dans les collèges de la Compagnie de Jésus en France sous l'ancien régime*, pp. 41 ff.

[5]*Congregatio Gen. XX*, d. 12, in *Institutum, S.J.*, p. 438.

[6]Graves in his *History of Education During the Middle Ages*, supposes all students in Jesuit colleges are destined for the novitiate. This is, of course, absurd. The primary purpose of the Jesuit colleges was — and is — the fitting of Catholic youths to take their place in the world, not in the cloister.

[7]*Constitutiones*, "Examen Generale," c. iii, n. 14 in *Institutum S.J.*, p. 6.

[8]*Constitutiones*, Pars IV, Prooemium, A, in *Institutum, S.J.*, p. 48, "admittendi nimirum juvenes qui bonorum morum et ingeniorum indole spem facerent, quod in probos simul ac doctos viros ad colendam Christi Domini nostri vineam essent evasuri."

[9]*Epistolae Praepositorum Generalium ad Patres et Fratres Societatis Jesu*, II, No. 5.

[10]"Je désire sans doute qu'il y ait dans la Compagnie un très grand nombre de sujets excellents, mais je ne sais où vous avez pris qu'elle ne doit avoir que des sujets excellents. Si vous l'entendez sous le rapport de la piété, vous avez raison, et il ne faut recevoir que ceux, qui ont le désir, et la volonté d'y exceller; mais pour ce qui est de talents, la médiocrité a aussi son prix et elle n'a jamais été un titre d'exclusion. Il arrive aussi souvent que des sujets de talents médiocres rendent de très grands services, et de plus grands que bien d'autres qui ont des talents distingués." Quoted in *Ordinatio Studiorum in Assistentia Angliae* (May 16, 1912), a document in *Missouri Province Archives*.

[11]In *Epistulae Praepos. Generalium ad Patres et Fratres Soc. Jesu*, III, 272: "Moneant examinatores ut severe potius quam remisse officio suo fungantur, nec candidatos probent, nisi inspecta intime eorum indole, ingenio, ceterisque animi et corporis dotibus, quae ad hauriendum genuinum Societatis spiritum et ad ministeria cum fructu et laude exercenda necessariae et aptissimae sint. . . ."

[12]"Collectio decretorum Cong. Gen. XXVII" in *Acta Romana* for 1923, p. 37: "Optandum est ut qui admittuntur in Novitios scholasticos rhetoricam vel studia quae cum ea aequantur absolverint." Cf., also *Cong. X*, decr. 12, No. 1; *Epitome Inst. S.J.*, Pars. I, Tit. III, 44, p. 29.

[13]*Relatio Patrum Deputatorum Provinciae Marylandiae-Neoeboracensis et Missourianae. Pro studiis scholasticorum ordinandis*. Dated 1907. MS. in *Missouri Province Archives*.

[14]*Ordinatio Studiorum in Assistentia Angliae*. MS. in *Missouri Province Archives*. Dated May 16, 1912.

[15]"Assistancy," a term in Jesuit usage to designate an administrative unit of several provinces, usually of the same country, or language. Thus, the German Assistancy, the French Assistancy, etc.

[16]I (1919), 40.

[17]*Epitome Instituti, S.J.*, Pars. II, Tit. II, nn. 85, 86, p. 49.

[18]Longridge, W. H., *The Spiritual Exercises of St. Ignatius of Loyola* (London: Robert Scott, 1922), xxxvi + 351; Rickaby, Joseph, S.J., *The Spiritual Exercises of St. Ignatius Loyola* (New York: Benziger Bros., 1923), xii + 234.

[19]*Jesuit Bulletin*, I, No. 1 (March, 1922), p. 1.

[20]*Ibid.*

[21]*Jesuit Bulletin*, I, No. 1, 3 ff.

[22]Decretum xii, in *Decreta Vigesimae Quintae Congregationis*, p. 28.

[23]*Epistulae selectae*, p. 217; "Epistula ad Provinciales" (Oct. 8, 1631).

[24]*Ibid.*, p. 224 (July 17, 1752).

[25]*Ibid.*, p. 137 (February 5, 1860).

[26]*Epistulae Praepositorum Generalium ad Patres et Fratres Societatis Jesu*, III, 275: "Congregatio XIV . . . enixe commendavit 'ne umquam apud nos langueret studium litterarum humaniorum quod tanta cum laude hucusque coluit Societas' . . . Curent Patres Provinciales ut juniores nostri tum in patrio sermone tum in lingua latina et graeca diligenter ac solide instituantur . . . et si provincia in promptu non habeat apprime idoneos praeceptores, quaerat aliunde ex altera Provincia."

[27]Decretum X, *Congregatio Generalis XIV*, in *Institutum Societatis Jesu*, p. 383.

[28]Ker, *Nos Doctrines Classiques Traditionelles*, p. 339: "On comprend que la préparation littéraire, scientifique, même théologique des Jésuites ne saurait être rigoureusement uniforme pour tous. Les talents sont multiples et divers."

[29]*Ordinatio Studiorum in Assistentia Angliae* (May 16, 1912).

[30]*Ibid.* The American "scholasticates" or schools of philosophy, are usually attached to a Jesuit university. In the Missouri Province, it is an integral part of St. Louis University; in the California Province, of Gonzaga University, Spokane, Washington. In the Maryland-New York Province, it is a separate institution at Woodstock, Maryland. The New Orleans Province has as yet no scholasticate but sends its students to the other provinces.

[31]*Ordinatio Studiorum.* See also *Ratio Studiorum*, "Regulae communes omnibus professoribus superiorum facultatum," nn. 17, 18.

[32]*Jesuit Bulletin*, I, No. 2, 4 ff.

[33]*Congregatio Generalis XXII*, decretum 34 (1853). In *Institutum S.J.*, p. 457.

[34]"Le P. Préfet qui est toujours un practicien de l'enseignement explique et applique les règles de chaque classe, interroge sur les difficultés, et y repond, fait ensuite monter en chaire quelqu'un de ses auditeurs pour donner une prélection ou un autre exercice classique." Ker, *op. cit.*, p. 339.

[35]*Ratio Studiorum*, "Regulae Provincialis," 30; "Regulae Rectoris," 9.

[36]See *Woodstock Letters*, XXII, No. 3 (Dec., 1893), 559 ff.

[37]See De Backer, *Bibliothèque des Écrivains de la Compagnie de Jésus* and Sommervogel, *Bibliothèque de la Compagnie de Jésus.*

[38]Goodier, "The Society of Jesus and Education," *The Month*, CIX, 137.

[39]*Educational Opinion from the Renaissance*, p. 89.

[40]See Duhr, *op. cit.*, pp. 39 ff.

[41]*Monumenta Paedagogica*, Doc. 30, p. 313 "Arbitror enim non esse satis in universum et generatim ordinem et rationem studiorum perscribere; sed particulatim oportere per singulas classes et singula earum exercitationum genera, modum et rationem optimam magistro seruandam explicare."

[42]*Ibid.*, Doc. 99, n. 44, p. 731.

[43]*Ibid.*, Doc. 6, pp. 52–53: "Los maestros se elijan con mucho juizio, cada uno accommodado para la classa que ha de regir; y antes que empieçe á leer y se embíe donde ha de leer, lea algunos días lection de aquella schuela, que ha de gouernar, en presentia de quien en ello tenga juizio."

[44]*Chronicon Societatis Jesu*, II, 508; III, 112, 131; IV, 108; IV, 532.

[45]*Ibid.*, IV, 472.

[46]*Ratio Studiorum*, "Reg. Rectoris," 9: "Ne Magistri classium inferiorum docendi rudes ad docendum accedant, collegii ex quo humaniorum litterarum et grammaticae Magistri solent educi, Rector deligat unum aliquem docendi peritissimum, ad quem sub finem studiorum ter in hebdomada per horam conveniant proxime futuri praeceptores ad novum instituendi magisterium, idque vicissim praelegendo, dictando, scribendo. emendando, aliaque munia boni praeceptoris obeundo." See also "Regulae Provincialis," 30.

[47]*Ibid.*, "Regulae praefecti studiorum" [superiorum], 30.

[48]The 25th General Congregation, Decretum 12, No. 5 (Sept. 1, 1906), insisted on an existing practice: "Curandum quoque est ut juniores nostri scholastici Rationem Studiorum Societatis bene intelligant magnique faciant." *Decreta Vigesimae Quintae Congregationis Generalis*, p. 26.

[49]*Relatio Patrum Deputatorum pro Studiis Scholasticorum Ordinandis*. Dated Feb. 21, 1910, in *Missouri Province Archives*. The minutes of the meeting of the Maryland-New York Province delegates.

[50]MS. in *Missouri Province Archives:* "Topics Discussed at the Meeting of the Presidents of the Jesuit Colleges of the Missouri Province. St. Louis University, April 2, 1917."

[51]See *Catalogue of St. Louis University for 1926.*

[52]*Ordinatio Studiorum pro Assistentia Anglia.*

[53]All Jesuit scholastics prepare for ordination to the priesthood. Consequently, all must, according to the Canon Law of the Church, complete a four-year course in theology. In the Jesuit Order, after their philosophical course, they teach for a period of from three to five years. They then return to theology, either the "cursus minor" or the "cursus major"; both last four years, but the "cursus major" or long course, is much more rigorous. After their ordination to the priesthood, and the completion of their theological studies, they spend a year in what is known as the "tertianship" or third year of probation. They then are admitted to their final vows either as professed or spiritual coadjutors. In the American provinces, the majority of Jesuit priests are engaged in educational work after their tertianship. The rest do missionary, parochial work, and the like. See Tables VIII and IX.

[54]*Ordinatio Studiorum pro Assistentia Angliae.*

[55]*Epitome Instituti Societatis Jesu*, 722, i, n. 1; 736, ii; 738, i; 803, i; 807; 810, i.

[56]*Constitutiones*, Pars. IV, c. vi, n. 17, in *Institutum, S.J.*, p. 58.

[57]Letter from the general, W. Ledochowski, to the provincial of Maryland, A. Maas, dated, Zizers, Switzerland, Nov. 1, 1915. In the *Georgetown Archives*. The new *Epitome* of the Constitutions, published in 1924, permits Jesuits to work for degrees in Universities, "not of the Society," if the provincial judges it advisable. *Epitome*, 525, i. p. 141.

[58]MS. in *Missouri Province Archives:* "Topics Discussed at the Meeting of Presidents of the Jesuit Colleges of the Missouri Province, April 2, 1917, St. Louis University."

[59]MS. in *Missouri Province Archives:* "Meeting of the Rectors and Prefects of Studies of the Missouri Province held at St. Louis University, June 9, 10, 1920."

[60]*Ordinatio Studiorum pro Assistentia Angliae* (1912).

[61]*Ibid.*, "Studium post philosophiam unus, duo, vel tres anni specialistis in linguis classicis, vel in mathesi et scientia vel in aliis disciplinis specialibus, verbi gratia, historia, concedi possunt."

[62]*Epitome Instituti Societatis Jesu*, No. 289, pp. 127–128.

[63]Shea, *History of Georgetown*, p. 287.

[64]*Woodstock Letters*, XXXVIII, No. 1 (Jan. 1909), 10.

[65]*Ibid.*, XLI, No. 1 (Jan., 1912), 13.

[66]*Province News-Letter*, II, 11.

[67]*Missouri Province Teacher's Association: Proceedings of the First Annual Convention*, Prairie du Chien, Wis., 1922, p. 3.

[68]*Jesuit Educational Association: Mid-West Division. Proceedings of the Third Annual Convention*, 1924, p. 12.

[69]*Ibid.*, A. F. Frumveller, "The Jesuit Educational Association," pp. 12–16.

[70]Campion College, Prairie du Chien, Wis., 1922.

[71]*Proceedings of the Fourth Annual Convention of the Jesuit Educational Association. Central States Division* (Chicago, 1925), pp. 281.

[72]*Program of Annual Convention Jesuit Educational Association* (*Central States Division*). Fifth Year (Chicago, 1926).

[73]*Woodstock Letters,* XXXVII, 244.

[74]*The Teacher's Review,* I, No. 1 (January, 1910), p. 1.

[75]See Fig. 7, p. 259.

CHAPTER XIV

GENERAL SUMMARY

THIS ends the story of Jesuit educational activity in the United States. It represents a system of education whose origins are to be found in the Catholic branch of the humanistic movement. The Company of Jesus, organized on a quasi-military plan by the Spanish soldier, St. Ignatius of Loyola, was first intended to be a very small body of highly trained men, in no sense destined by its founder for the work of teaching. But with the increase in membership in the new Company, education was, so to speak, forced upon the Order. Once accepted, however reluctantly, the followers of Ignatius devoted all their energies to fashioning a perfect system of education, first for their own junior members, the scholastics, and secondly for secular youth. Their schools sprang up everywhere; princes and municipalities invited them to train their youth.

The best men of the Order collaborated for fifteen years on a plan of studies that should equal, if not surpass, any plan in the Europe of that day, and at the same time impart a thorough Catholic training to the youth under their charge. These sixteenth-century Jesuits were in no sense innovators, but organizers. They borrowed from existing schools all that was best, carefully reported to the central committee at Rome the results of tentative plans of studies, then on trial in their new colleges, and adapted all to their purpose in the compilation known as the *Ratio Studiorum,* a pedagogical document that reflects the spirit of that day and its catchword, *eloquentia,* but at the same time turns the course of humanism toward the Church and makes of the classics heralds of Christ.

This *Ratio,* with its very definite aim, its striking unity, became the program of studies, the model for discipline and organization in all the far-flung line of colleges established by the Jesuits from the sixteenth to the eighteenth century in Catholic Europe, where each school was a powerhouse for energizing youth with enthusiasm and loyalty for the Catholic Church and its principles, and secondarily, a purveyor of what was conceded to be the best secular education of the time, an education where classicism reigned supreme.

The suppression of the Society in 1773 put an end to the flourishing Jesuit schools in Europe, put an end as well to the sporadic efforts of the English Jesuits in Maryland to supply the sons of the Catholic colonists with a classical education. The important place that the Order once held in educational circles it never has regained; yet its influence in Catholic education, especially in the United States, has been considerable.

After the restoration of the Order in 1814, the American Jesuits set to work with vigor to provide educational facilities for the Catholic youth of the new republic. The work was begun by the Maryland Mission at Georgetown. These Jesuits were, for the most part, American by birth, but were the proud possessors of the English Jesuit traditions they had acquired at Liège or Stonyhurst. They were joined by the Belgians who came to the Middle West and founded the Missouri Province. The French came soon after, remained for a time in Kentucky, later moving to New York where they eventually joined forces with the Maryland Jesuits to form the Maryland-New York Province. Another group of French Jesuits settled in Louisiana. To the Far West and Colorado came the Italian Jesuits. The last national group of Jesuits to reach America were the Germans who arrived in Buffalo in the 70's forming for a time an independent mission among the German-Americans; their colleges and personnel were later divided between the Maryland-New York and the Missouri Provinces.

All of these Jesuits, of diverse nationalities brought with them different educational traditions. Yet, in time, programs and methods merged into essential unity. Naturally the newcomers consulted their brethren in the established schools — Georgetown and St. Louis. Besides this, there was another force at work making for unity in the American colleges, the traditional Jesuit system of teaching.

The *Ratio* of 1599 had been revised under the generalship

of Father Roothaan in 1832; not with conspicuous success, it must be admitted. The old *Ratio* was suited to the needs of its day; the same can hardly be said of the 1832 document. True, there were attempts at further revision — notably by the Italian, Padre Vasco. But the conservatism of his countrymen prevented his really excellent plan of studies from getting a fair trial.

Enormous changes were going on in the industrial, economic, and political world. It was a time of ferment in education; and this was particularly true in America. The democratic spirit of the New World, its demand for practical subjects, prevented the American Jesuits from ever introducing the *Ratio* of 1832 in its entirety. Yet they did place great emphasis on the classics in their teaching; and for long they kept aloof from the educational currents of thought about them.

The American Jesuit college was largely of the gymnasium type, with a year or two of scholastic philosophy added on to complete the course. The line of demarcation between college and high school was not well defined. In America, educators gradually came to the conclusion that it was not the high school's sole function to prepare for college. Eventually, this had its effect in Jesuit circles, caused the severance of the strict bonds that united all the classes of the Jesuit college into one harmonious whole, and brought about the emergence of the Jesuit high school as a distinct entity, with its own corps of instructors and administrators. Gradually, too, though not without many misgivings on the part of members of the Order, the Jesuit high school conformed in curricular standards to the secondary schools about them. Particularly marked has been the tendency of the Jesuit schools west of the Alleghanies to adapt their system to existing American usage. The schools along the Atlantic seaboard have been much more faithful in adhering to the letter of the *Ratio*. Perhaps the more radical attitude of the western schools is due to the potent influence of the standardizing agencies of this region. More probably the same forces that have made the public high school of the West develop along different lines from similar schools in the East have influenced Jesuit educators also.

At all events, the Jesuit high school, at least in the West, differs but little in externals from public high schools of conservative type. Yet, despite this external conformity, the same spirit is found in the American schools that animated Jesuit education in the past. Their traditions the Jesuits regard as a precious heritage; there hangs about the tried methods of their predecessors a glory which they are loath to lose. The American Jesuit high school has been adapted to modern requirements along conservative lines; but the American Jesuits have salvaged from the past a theory of education that is largely at variance with modern standards, a theory that mental discipline is a necessary factor in the training of the boy. This, at least partly, explains their emphasis on the classics as a splendid instrument for intellectual development.

Their work in the secondary field in the United States has been extensive; no other single organization has under its immediate control so many high-school students. In curriculum and methodology, they have been ultraconservative, judged by modern standards. Their unique distinction probably lies in their insistence on adequate preparation for the work of teaching. To insure efficiency in their schools, the Society of Jesus has made tremendous sacrifices, giving to their masters long years of preparation, and this even at a period in American educational history when the standard for the high-school teacher was lamentably low.

But over and above all this stands out the primary objective of Jesuit education — an objective from which the Jesuits have never wavered by a hair's breadth from the very beginning of their history, despite change of scene and passing of time, an objective that gives to their system an extraordinary and powerful unity. That objective is the formation of the Christian citizen, obedient to the laws of God and the Church, and obedient to the laws of the State. God and man's duties to God are considered of sufficient importance to earn a prominent place in the Jesuit school. And here the Jesuit educator does not rest content with knowledge; right habits of conduct must also be acquired. The Jesuit theory of education has always been that mind training is not its exclusive function. Their schools consciously attempt to train the will. This does not mean merely pious practices. The Jesuit strives to inculcate in the boys under his charge a sense of the tremendous importance and the intense reality of religion. In a word, for the Jesuit, curriculum and methodology are accidental, to be determined according to the exigencies of time and place, although the Order has always endeavored to make its schools the equal of others in this respect. But what is important, what is essential is that every shred and fiber of the education they impart be impregnated with Catholic principle and practice.

APPENDIX

THE *RATIO STUDIORUM* FOR THE "LOWER SCHOOLS"

APPENDIX

THE *RATIO STUDIORUM* FOR THE "LOWER SCHOOLS"

NOTE: The *Ratio Studiorum* is a document outlining Jesuit educational procedure both on the secondary and on the higher levels. In the translation given here, only those parts that pertain to the "lower schools"—equivalently, the secondary school—are set down. This comprises about half of the entire document. There is no published English translation of the *Ratio,* so far as the writer has been able to ascertain. There are, however, German translations; the best is, perhaps that of Duhr[1] in the ninth volume of the *Bibliothek der Katholischen Pädagogik.* The second volume of Pachtler[2] contains the Latin text and the German version of both the 1599 and the 1832 *Ratio.*

The translation that follows is that of Roothaan's *Ratio* of 1832;[3] where it differs from the 1599 *Ratio* indication has been made in a footnote. Although the 1832 *Ratio* was never introduced into the American schools in its entirety, yet it did shape Jesuit educational thought. While many changes have been made in curriculum and methodology, yet the spirit that still animates Jesuit education and the objectives it strives for, are outlined in this document.

The complete contents of the *Ratio* are given below. Only the starred sections are included in this translation.

I. Rules of the Provincial
II. Rules of the Rector
III. Rules of the Prefect of Studies[4]
IV. Common Rules for all the Professors of the Higher Faculties[5]
V. Rules for the Professor of Holy Scripture

[1] *Die Studienordnung der Gesellschaft Jesu* (Freiburg, i. B.: 1896), pp. viii + 286.
[2] *Ratio Studiorum et Institutiones Scholasticae Societatis Jesu,* Vols. I–IV.
[3] *Ratio atque Institutio Studiorum Societatis Jesu* (Paris, 1850), pp. xii + 156.
[4] That is, for the prefect of studies in the higher faculties of philosophy and theology.
[5] Sections III–XI, inclusive, deal with the courses in philosophy and theology, taken mainly by Jesuit scholastics, although occasionally also externs follow these courses. These rules and the studies prescribed have been largely superseded by later *Ordinationes Studiorum.*

VI. Rules for the Professor of Hebrew
VII. Rules for the Professor of Theology
VIII. Rules for the Professor of Church History
IX. Rules for the Professor of Canon Law
X. Rules for the Professor of Moral Theology
XI. Rules for the Professor of Philosophy
a) Logic
b) Metaphysics
c) Ethics
d) Physics
e) Mathematics
XII. Rules for the Prefect of the Lower Studies*
XIII. Regulations for Written Examinations*
XIV. Regulations for Prizes*
XV. Common Rules for the Professors of the Lower Classes*
XVI. Rules for the Professor of Rhetoric[6]
XVII. Rules for the Professor of Humanities*
XVIII. Rules for the Professor of the Highest Grammar Class*
XIX. Rules for the Professor of the Intermediate Grammar Class*
XX. Rules for the Professor of the Lowest Grammar Class*
XXI. Rules for the Scholastics of our Society[7]
XXII. The Training of Scholastics who are devoting a Biennium to Postgraduate Study of Theology
XXIII. Rules for the Beadle or Master's Assistant[7a]
XXIV. Rules for the Extern Students of the Society[8]*
XXV. Rules for the Academies[9]
XXVI. Rules for the Moderator of the Academy
XXVII. Rules for the Theological and Philosophical Academies
XXVIII. Rules for the Academy of the Class of Rhetoric and Humanities*
XXIX. Rules for the Academy of Grammar Students*

---

[6]The class of rhetoric was beyond the secondary level, roughly equivalent to the sophomore class in the modern American college.

[7]That is, for members of the Society studying philosophy or theology or reviewing their classical studies.

[7a]An official, usually a Jesuit, in the classes of philosophy and theology.

[8]In the main, students of philosophy and theology who are not members of the Order.

[9]Sections XXV–XXVII, inclusive, are concerned for the most part with the academies or study clubs in the courses in philosophy and theology.

XII. *Rules for the Prefect of "Lower" Studies*

1. He should understand that he has been chosen for the purpose of aiding the rector in the direction and government of our schools in every possible way to the end that our students may advance in uprightness of life as well as in the liberal arts.

2. In whatever pertains to school discipline he should consult the rector. For studies he should ask the advice of the general prefect of studies.[10] He must abide by their rulings; he should neither abolish any established custom nor introduce any new one.

3. He shall submit for approval to the same general prefect of studies the declamations either public or private to be given by students of rhetoric or of the lower classes. Whatever is to be displayed[11] publicly on the greater feast days, such as poems and other written work, should be examined beforehand by two men appointed by the rector and the best are to be selected.

4. He should have at hand the rules of the masters and students of the lower classes and see to the observance of these rules as well as those of his own office. He is to aid and direct the masters; especially should he prevent their authority and the esteem in which they are held from suffering any diminution before others, especially before their pupils.

5. He must zealously see to it that new masters retain the system of teaching and other methods of their predecessors, provided, of course, that they are in accord with our system. Thus there will be less cause for complaint at our frequent change of masters.

6. Every two weeks, at least, he is to observe every master teach; he should note whether the proper time and effort is being given to Christian doctrine; whether sufficient progress is being made in the classwork, in the prelection and in the repetition; finally whether the master's relations with his students are in every way decorous and praiseworthy.

7. He is to note in due time the occurrence of feast days and vacations, both those peculiar to his own school and those common to the province, especially the weekly holiday, as well as the hour for beginning and closing classes at the different seasons of the year. He should also inform the masters of these matters. The same holds when the students are to participate in public devotions and other exercises

[10]That is, the prefect of studies in the higher faculty. The secondary school was often attached to a university; the principal of the secondary school was subordinate to the prefect of studies in the higher studies.

[11]In the *Ratio* of 1599: "Mottoes and poems which are to be," etc.

of this nature, as well as when extraordinary orders or prohibitions are to be issued.

8. He should be careful that the grades[12] of the five lower classes, namely, rhetoric, humanities, and the three grammar classes, are kept distinct. If a class is taught in two sections by order of the provincial on account of the number of pupils, each section must keep the same grade. When more than one year[13] is in the same classroom, they must correspond to the grades described in the rules of the professors.

The better and more easily to retain this distinction, all the rules of grammar[14] should be divided into three books, one for each grammar class.[15]

The master of each class should finish his book in the first semester and repeat it in the second. However, as the book for the first class is too much for explanation and repetition in one year, it should be divided into two parts. And it would be well to admit [to the school] only those pupils who have been well instructed in the first part [of the grammar] so that the second part may be explained and repeated in one year, as in the other classes. But, where this cannot be done, the lowest class should be divided into two years. During the first semester of the first year, the first part of the textbook should be covered; in the first semester of the second year, the second part. In both cases there should be a complete repetition in the second semester. Wherever this division of a class into two years takes place, one master can teach the first year, another the second.

This repetition has a double advantage. First, the oftener a thing is repeated, the more lasting is the impression. Secondly, the more gifted boys can complete the course more rapidly than the others, since they can be advanced a class every semester.[16]

---

[12]*Gradus* and *ordo* are two words in the *Ratio* of frequent occurrence. *Gradus* refers to the matter to be covered; thus the *gradus* of rhetoric, the *gradus* of lowest grammar. It frequently, though not always, is equivalent to "year" or "class." But sometimes there are two *ordines* of the same *gradus*, as *infima grammatica primi ordinis* and *infima grammatica secundi ordinis*, each ordinarily taking a year for completion. Accordingly, to avoid confusion, in this version *gradus* is translated "grade," and *ordo*, "year." The word *classis* always means "class," in the modern sense.

[13]In some of the smaller colleges two classes were occasionally taught in the same classroom by the same master. See Duhr, *op. cit.*, p. *222*, n. 2.

[14]1599: *of Emmanuel*, i.e., Alvarez, the classic Jesuit Latin grammar.

[15]In the 1599 *Ratio* three short paragraphs follow, giving directions for the division of Alvarez.

[16]A talented boy who mastered the entire matter of the year during the first semester of the first year would be excused from the repetition of the second semester. Instead, he would go into the second year, and, while the rest of this class was repeating the entire matter of second year, he would see it for the first time. This practice of seeing the entire matter of the year in one semester and repeating it in the second together with its corollary practice of advancing the more talented, no longer exists in Jesuit schools. Some American schools retained the practice, however, as late as the early 90's.

Where there are five classes, the distinction of grades provided for in the rules of the masters should be observed. And, with the exception of lowest (grammar), there should not be more than one year for a grade.[17]

Where there are four classes, either drop rhetoric[18] and then the other four classes differ in no wise from those just described; or, what is better, rhetoric should be the highest class, which should keep the grade prescribed in the rules of the professor of rhetoric. The second class will be that of humanities; it, too, must keep the grade set down in the rules of the professor [of that class]. The third class is divided into two years; the first, the highest grammar class, the second, the intermediate grammar class. Finally, the fourth is to be the lowest class of grammar and it can be divided into two years as is explained in the rules of its master. If only the second year is admitted, the third class is to have only one year, namely, highest grammar, while the fourth will have two years, called the intermediate and lowest grammar class.[19]

Where there are three classes, the two lower classes should keep the grade prescribed for the last two classes in the college of four classes. The highest class should be simply humanities or else divided into two years, the higher to be rhetoric, the lower, humanities. However, the

[17]The arrangement of classes and years in a five-class Jesuit school was as follows:

Class	*Name*	*Year*
1st	Rhetoric	6th
2nd	Humanities	5th
3rd	Highest Grammar Class	4th
4th	Intermediate Grammar Class	3rd
5th	Lowest Grammar (A)	2nd
5th	Lowest Grammar (B)	1st

(A) and (B) after the lowest grammar class represent the first and second part of Latin grammar to be covered in these two years.

[18]Rhetoric, the highest class in the Jesuit *college* — the last year of secondary training. Roughly equivalent to sophomore class in an American college.

[19]The following scheme shows the arrangement of the four-class Jesuit college. Group A represents those who had no previous training in the classics before entering the Jesuit school; Group B, those who covered the matter of the first year before entering.

Group A			*Group B*		
Class	*Name*	*Year*	*Class*	*Name*	*Year*
1st	Rhetoric	6th	1st	Rhetoric	5th
2nd	Humanities	5th	2nd	Humanities	4th
3rd	Highest Grammar	4th	3rd	Highest Grammar	3rd
3rd	Intermediate Grammar	3rd	4th	Intermediate Grammar	2nd
4th	Lowest Grammar (A)	2nd	4th	Lowest Grammar (A)	1st
4th	Lowest Grammar (B)	1st			

higher should not be introduced without the approbation of the rector and only when there is a sufficient number of students able to profit by this higher course and on condition that the master will not fail in the due care and attention for the lower group.[20]

Where there are two classes, the lower class will consist of two years, one corresponding to the second year of the lowest grammar class, the other to the intermediate grammar class. The higher class likewise should consist of two years, one corresponding to the highest grammar class, the other to humanities.[21]

In those classes which have two years in the same classroom, there will be the same repetition of the year's matter in each year as is mentioned in the foregoing. And wherever possible, each year should see the entire matter of the year in the first semester and repeat it in the second, so that the same progress may be made by students during two years in the same class as they would make in classes not doubled up. However, where this seems too difficult, more time should be given.

To secure this result in those classes that are doubled, everything but the grammatical prelection should be taken in common. First, the prelection of the authors[22] should be common to both, the higher year being asked the harder questions; the lower, the easier ones. Then only one theme[23] should be given; the higher year should do the entire theme, but the lower year only the first or the last part, which will be accommodated to the rules they have seen. Finally, the contests[24] and drill work should also be common to all. Only the grammatical prelection, then, is different; this should be given one day

[20]This supposes that the two highest years are taught by the same master. The arrangement of the school of this type follows:

Class	*Name*	*Year*
1st	Humanities *or*	5th *or*
1st	Rhetoric and Humanities	6th and 5th
2nd	Highest Grammar	4th
2nd	Intermediate Grammar	3rd
3rd	Lowest Grammar (A)	2nd
3rd	Lowest Grammar (B)	1st

[21]The arrangement in the two-class school:

Class	*Name*	*Year*	
1st	Humanities	4th	These two years doubled
1st	Highest Grammar	3rd	under one master.
2nd	Intermediate Grammar	2nd	These two years doubled
2nd	Lowest Grammar (A)	1st	under one master.

[22]1599: prelection of Cicero. Prelection is the explanation of the Latin text. See Chap. XI, "Jesuit Method of Teaching."

[23]"Theme": the translation from the vernacular into Latin.

[24]*Concertationes:* the contest between the rival camps in the class.

to one year, another to the other; or else a daily explanation and repetition for each year, dividing the time between them.

The prefect [of studies] should, with the approbation of the provincial, so arrange the program for history, geography, elementary mathematics, and the other customary subjects that each master can finish conveniently and with exactitude the matter assigned.[25]

Where there are elementary classes,[26] he should realize that they are under his charge; he should visit the masters and demand of all the observance of rules in order that the boys may be instructed both in piety and learning.

9. He should, as far as possible, admit no one to the register of students who is not brought by his parents or guardians or whom he does not know or of whom he cannot easily secure information from others. He should, however, exclude no one merely on the ground that he is of the lower classes or poor.

10. The method of examining new students should be as follows: First, he should ask them what studies they have had and for what length of time. Then, he should have them do a written exercise on some assigned theme. Likewise, he should ask some of the precepts of the subjects they have studied. Finally, let him give them some short sentences to be turned into Latin, or when necessary, have them translate into the vernacular and interpret a passage in an author.

11. Those he finds well instructed and of good moral character he should admit. The rules for our students should be shown to them that they may know how they must conduct themselves. He should write in a book their name, surname, country, age, parents, their acquaintances among our students as well as the day and year of their admittance. Finally he should assign each one to that class and master for which he is fitted; in such wise that he seems more deserving of entering a higher class rather than that he should appear unfitted for the class to which he is assigned.

12. He should not admit to the lowest class either those who are too old or those very young, unless they are exceptionally capable. Nor should he relax this rule, even when the student is sent merely for the sake of a [Christian] education.

13. There should be a general and solemn promotion once a year after the annual vacation. If any, however, clearly distinguished themselves so that it is evident they would make better progress in a higher class than the one in which they are — and the prefect will know this

---

[25]This and the following paragraph do not appear in the 1599 *Ratio.*

[26]The so-called *abcedarii.* In the first decades of the nineteenth century, the American Jesuit schools provided these classes in the elements of the vernacular. See Chap. VI, "The Middle West" under *St. Louis University.*

by examining their records and consulting their teachers — they should not be kept back but may be promoted at any time of the year after an examination as to their fitness. However, a promotion from the highest grammar class to humanities or from humanities to rhetoric[27] is hardly feasible.[28]

14. For examination, one or, if necessary, two [Latin] prose compositions should be demanded in all the classes; in the highest grammar class and in humanities, a [Latin] poem and, if it seems good, a few days later a Greek prose composition, should be written in class.

15. The prefect must see that masters announce the examinations two or three days beforehand. And the rules for written examinations, set down after these rules, should be read in class.

16. The prefect or one assigned by him should preside during the written examination. On the appointed day, he should, when the signal is given, dictate a theme, preferably a short one.

17. He must keep the examinations in his possession, arranged alphabetically. If there is no objection, he should divide them among the examiners, who will read them and mark the mistakes in the margin.

18. There should be three examiners.[29] Generally the prefect himself should be one. The other two, good classical scholars, and, if possible, not masters themselves, are appointed by the rector at the advice of the prefect. Where the number of those to be examined is very great, there is no objection to having two or more boards.

19. Students will go three at a time, or even more in the lower classes, to the [oral] examinations. And the master shall continue to send them in the same numbers either in alphabetical order or in some other more practical way.

20. While the students are coming to the examination, the examiners should read the teacher's record of each pupil and note the grades assigned to each, comparing, when necessary the present records with earlier records of the same year in order to form a judgment of the progress each student has made or is likely to make.

21. The method of the [oral] examination will be as follows: First, if the examiners wish, each one should read a part of his [Latin] composition. Then he is to be told to correct his mistakes and to give the reason for the correction by indicating the rule [of grammar] that has been violated. After this, the students in the grammar classes should be given something in the vernacular to be translated im-

---

[27]That is, outside of the regular or solemn promotions at the end of the year.

[28]The *Ratio* of 1599 gives the reason for this. In the second semester of humanities, Latin versification was studied; and in the second semester of rhetoric, rhetorical precepts in the text of Cyprian Soarez were explained.

[29]That is, for the oral examinations.

mediately into Latin. All should be quizzed on the precepts and other matters taken in class. Then, when necessary, a brief passage of some of the [Latin] authors seen in class should be given for translation and interpretation.

22. After the examination of each group of three students, while the memory of the examiners is still fresh, they should give their votes on those examined, due regard being paid to the composition, the grades assigned by the masters, and their replies to questions.

23. To reach a decision about doubtful students, the prefect should inspect their written work for different periods, consult with the examiners so that they may decide to give them another written and oral examination, if they wish. Moreover, in doubtful cases, the age of the pupil, the time spent in the same class, his talent, and his diligence should all be taken into consideration.

24. After the examination, the grade assigned is to be kept secret. Nevertheless, before the public announcement [for promotions], the students' records should be shown to the respective masters.

25. If anyone is totally unfit for promotion, no amount of pleading should help him. If a student is hardly worthy of promotion, but on account of his age, the time he has spent in the same class, or some other reason, promotion seems desirable, he may be promoted, if there is no other objection, on this one condition that, if he fails to give evidence of his diligence to his master, he will be sent back to the lower class. And his name should not be listed in the catalogue [of those promoted]. If there are any, finally, so stupid that it would be a disgrace to promote them and of whom no progress can be expected even if they remain in the same class, the prefect should take up their case with the rector in order that the parents or guardians may be advised not to keep them any longer in the school.

26. The list of those to be promoted should be read publicly either before the whole student body in the assembly hall or else before the individual classes. Those who have especially distinguished themselves should be read first; for the rest, the alphabetical order may be followed or else according to their rank in studies.

27. Before the beginning of the school year, the prefect should consult the rector in good time about the list of books to be explained that year in our classes so that he can inform the general prefect of studies and the masters. He should do the same in case books or authors are changed in the course of the year.

28. He should make timely arrangements with booksellers so that there may be no lack of books which either we or the students use daily or will need during the following year.

29. At the beginning of each year, either personally or through the masters he should assign each student his bench and his bench mate.[30] He should also see to it that the same is done for the boarding students by those who have charge of them, unless, as in some places they are seated according to their rank of studies. He should assign better seats to the nobles, where it is the custom.[31] Ours [32] and other religious, if there are any, should have benches separate from those occupied by extern students. The prefect should not permit any notable shifting of places without his knowledge.

30. It is very important that he should so arrange the time not only for Ours, but also for the boarding students, and if possible for the extern students as well, either through the masters or through the school-prefects[33] that the hours devoted to private study may be spent profitably.

31. Only for a grave reason, and with the approval of the rector should he grant exemption, especially for a long time, from the exercises of Latin verse and from the Greek course.

32. He should see to it that not only the students of rhetoric and humanities, but also the students in the other higher classes, attend the more formal[34] declamations, given publicly in the hall by the students of rhetoric. Accordingly, the masters should be told to invite their pupils. None of Ours should absent himself without the rector's permission.

33. He should arrange the time, the place and the manner of the class contests.[35] He should lay down the rules for the conduct of the contest beforehand, and by his presence during the contest, carefully see that everything is carried out profitably, peacefully and with moderation. Likewise he should be present at the customary declamations and [public] prelections of the class of rhetoric and humanities.

34. He should take great care that the public exhibitions of class-work[36] be conducted in proper fashion so as to increase the reputa-

---

[30] "Bench mates"; *consessores* in the 1832 text. Both Duhr, *op. cit.*, p. 228, and Pachtler, *op. cit.*, p. 364, misread the 1599 *Ratio*, taking the old *s*, for an *f*, thus getting the reading *confessores*, and translating it *Beichtväter*, "confessors." In the first place the Latin word for confessors is *confessarii; confessores*, means "professors of the faith"; in the second place, there is no question of confession in the text. The writer is indebted to Dr. Josef Schroeteler, S.J., of Düsseldorf for this emendation.

[31] "Where it is the custom": omitted in the 1599 *Ratio*.

[32] *Nostri:* "Ours," the usual term in Jesuit writing employed to designate a member of the Order. Compare the usage in military circles of "Brown of Ours," etc.

[33] "Prefects," i.e., those Jesuits who had charge of school discipline; quite distinct from, and subordinate to, the prefect of studies. See Chap. XII, *supra*, "Administration — Discipline — Finance."

[34] 1599 *Ratio:* "monthly."

[35] "Contests": disputations — in the higher classes, roughly equivalent to a school debate in modern parlance, always on a classical subject.

[36] *Specimina.*

tion of our schools. Accordingly, he should notify the masters in good time, and give them needed assistance, while he himself should personally examine the fitness of the contestants before they appear in public.[37]

To insure the proper conduct of these public exercises, he should draw up a list of dates, the classes that are to participate, and the names of the students; this program may be printed, if the superior approves. Outsiders may be invited to the exercises. Finally, everything should be so arranged according to the custom of the locality that the exercise be made as festive as possible. To relieve the tedium which would result from too long an exhibition of scholastic work, the program should be varied by an occasional dialogue, and the like.[38]

Moreover to give greater prominence to literary exercises, he should with the rector's approval organize academies[39] not only in the classes of rhetoric and humanities, but also in the grammar classes. In these academies, in accord with the rules set down at the end of this book, the students should meet on fixed days and take part in prelections,[40] contests, and other exercises calculated to promote scholarship among the students.

35. The prefect should give timely reminder to the rector of the date for the distribution of prizes and of any declamations or dialogues to be given on this occasion. In the distribution of prizes, the regulations set down at the end of these rules should be followed; and these regulations should be made known in each class before the written examination.

36. He should also see that, besides the regular prizes, each master has little gifts, to be provided by the rector of the college, or some symbol of victory for his students to spur them on when they perform some noteworthy feat in their daily task, such as winning a victory over their class opponent, giving an explanation of an entire book[41] seen in class, or reciting it by heart.

37. He should appoint in each class, in accord with local usage, a public censor, or if the term "censor" is not acceptable, a chief decurion or pretor.[42] That he may be honored by his schoolmates, he should be granted certain privileges. He should have the right with the master's approval of begging off his classmates from lighter punishments. It will be his duty to note anyone who wanders about the schoolyard

---

[37]1599 *Ratio:* Rule 34 begins with the third paragraph: "To give greater," etc.

[38]Omitted in 1599 *Ratio.*

[39]"Academies": virtually study clubs.

[40]That is, reading of authors not seen in class.

[41]For example, a book of the Æneid. etc.

[42]This office never existed in American Jesuit schools. (See Chap. XII, "Administration — Discipline — Finance." p. 224.)

before the signal is given, or who enters a classroom not his own, or leaves his own class or his appointed place. He should daily report to the prefect those who have been delinquent in class, anyone not a student who has entered the classroom; finally, any fault committed in class whether in the presence of the master or not.

38. Because of those who fail in diligence or in good conduct and for whom words of warning are not enough, a corrector, not a member of the Society, should be appointed. Where this is impossible, some other means of punishing this type of pupil must be devised.[43] Rarely and only for grave reasons should they be punished in class for faults committed at home.[44]

39. Those who refuse to accept punishment should be forced to do so or, if this cannot be done without loss of dignity, they should be expelled from our school, the rector's approval having first been secured. This, too, is the method of dealing with those who are frequently absent from class.[45]

40. When neither words nor the corrector's aid suffices and there is no hope of amendment, and the offender might be a real danger to others, it would be better to expel him from school than to keep him where he himself profits but little and is a source of harm to others. This decision, however, should be left to the rector in order that all may be done to the glory and service of God, as is right.

41. If any case comes up where expulsion from school will not suffice to remedy the offense committed, it should be referred to the rector and it is for him to determine what other measures should be taken. As far as possible, he should proceed without any undue harshness and in a spirit of charity and forbearance.

42. None of those expelled or who have left our schools without a valid reason should be permitted to return without first consulting the rector; and it is for him to judge what is expedient in the matter.

43. Neither in the schoolyard nor in the classes, not even in the higher classes, should anyone be permitted to carry weapons. Loafing, rushing about, and noisy disturbances should likewise be prohibited. The prefect should permit no swearing, insulting or injurious behavior, in short, no unbecoming or improper conduct. Should anything of this sort occur, he should immediately suppress the disorder and then report the disturbance to the rector.

44. The prefect should be constantly on hand either in the corridors

---

[43] 1599 *Ratio:* "either at the hands of a pupil or in some other fitting fashion."

[44] 1599 *Ratio:* "should they be whipped for faults," etc.

[45] *Ibid.*, "Those who refuse the whipping, should be forced, if it can be done safely, or in the case of larger boys, if it cannot be done without loss of dignity, they should be expelled," etc.

or in a room from which he can see the corridors not only during the entire time of class, but he should also occasionally inspect the classrooms before the signal is given to enter and he should always be at the gate when they are being dismissed.

45. He must see to it that the students enter and leave the church without any noise or commotion; and one or more of the masters should always be present when they assist at Mass. All the students are to be present at Mass every day, each in his proper place.[46]

46. The prefect should arrange to have the confessors in their places in good time on the days and at the hours appointed for the students' confessions. During the time of confessions, he should visit the church occasionally to see that the boys conduct themselves properly and piously.

47. Even the prefect should rarely call the boys from the classroom, especially during the time of prelection. If others are negligent in this matter, he should inform the rector.

48. He should never employ any student for writing or for any other task; nor should he permit others to do this.

49. The rules common to the extern students are to be posted in a place where they can be easily read by all; besides, a set of these rules should be put in every classroom. In general, they should be read at the beginning of each month in rhetoric and the lower classes.

50. Where there is no prefect of higher studies, the prefect himself should take charge of the supervision of public declamations, with the approval of the rector. It is also his office to provide our scholastics with books, again with the approval of the rector.

XIII. *Regulations for Written Examinations*

1. All should know that absentees on the day assigned for composition will receive no consideration unless they are detained for weighty reasons.

2. All should be present in the classroom in good time to receive the assignment and instructions, given either by the prefect himself or his substitute, and they must finish the assignment before the end of school. After silence has been enjoined, no one may speak to another, not even to the prefect or his substitute.

3. All should come supplied with books and necessary writing materials so there may be no need to borrow anything during the writing period.

---

[46] Attendance at the Mass was probably obligatory only for boarding students. In the day schools, the practice varied. While Mass is said for students in all American Jesuit high schools, attendance is obligatory only in the boarding schools with few exceptions.

4. The writing should be done in a style befitting the grade of each class, clearly, and in the words of the assigned theme and according to the fashion prescribed. Ambiguous expressions are to be given the less favorable meaning. Words omitted or changed carelessly for the sake of avoiding a difficulty are to be counted as errors.[47]

5. Care should be taken that no copying be done by bench mates; if two compositions are found to be exactly alike, both of them are to be suspected since it is impossible to discover which of the two did the copying.

6. To prevent dishonesty, anyone who has permission to leave the room after the writing has commenced should be obliged to leave the assignment and whatever he has written with the prefect or with the one who is presiding.

7. After the composition is finished, each one, without leaving his place, should diligently look over what he has written, correct and improve it as much as he may wish. For, as soon as the composition is given to the prefect, if anything then has to be corrected, it should by no means be returned.

8. Each one must fold his composition according to the directions of the prefect and write on the back his full name in Latin. Thus all the compositions may be more easily arranged in alphabetical order if desired.

9. When a student brings his finished composition to the prefect, he should take his books with him and depart quietly. The students that remain should not change their places but finish their work at their own desks.

10. If anyone should not finish his composition in the allotted time, he should hand in what he has written. On this account, all should clearly know how much time is granted for writing, rewriting, and revision.

11. Finally, when they go to the [oral] examinations, let them bring with them the texts explained that year which constitute the matter for examination. While one is being examined, the others present should pay strict attention; they must, however, neither prompt the one being examined nor correct him unless told to do so.

XIV. *Regulations for Prizes*

1. In rhetoric class, eight prizes are given: two for Latin prose, two for Latin verse, two for Greek prose, two for Greek verse.[48] In the class of humanities and in the highest grammar class, in the same way, six prizes are offered, the two for Greek verse being dropped, as this

[47] As is obvious, there is question only of compositions in Latin.

[48] That is, for writing Latin prose, etc. The emphasis on written work is worthy of note and quite in accord with the Jesuit objective *efformare ad eloquentiam.*

is generally not taken before rhetoric. In all the other classes, four prizes are given, the prizes for Latin verse being omitted. Moreover, in each class, one or two prizes should be given to those who have surpassed all[49] in learning Christian doctrine, as well as to those who have excelled in the study of the vernacular and in the accessory branches. Where the number of students is great or small, the number of prizes may be increased or decreased provided always that Latin prose is kept in the most important place.

2. The contests in this written work should be given on different days so that each written exercise has a special day.[50]

3. All should assemble in their respective classrooms on the days and at the time appointed for this written work.

4. Once the assignment has been given out, no one may leave his classroom before the composition has been finished and handed in; neither should anyone talk to another either in the classroom or outside. If it be necessary to leave the room and permission has been granted, the assignment and whatever has been written should be left with the one in charge.

5. The rector may grant an extension of time for polishing the work, provided this does not extend beyond sunset. It would be well not to grant more than five or six hours' extension.[51]

6. After a student has carefully copied out his work and handed it to the prefect of the school or his substitute, with some distinguishing mark upon it, not, however, his own name, he may leave the classroom. He should also hand in another sheet of paper bearing his full name and this same distinguishing mark, carefully sealed so that the name cannot be seen.

7. The prefect of the school should faithfully guard all these papers with great care; and he should not break the seal of the papers containing the names of the contestants until the decision [as to the winners] is made.

8. Three competent and mature judges should be chosen, one of whom may be an extern[52] if the custom of the place requires it; they should not, of course, know the writing of any of the contestants. After reading through all the papers and carefully considering the matter, they should announce the winners in each subject in order

---

[49]1599 *Ratio:* "in reciting Christian doctrine." The rest of the phrase "as well as . . . accessory branches," does not appear in that *Ratio.*

[50]1599 *Ratio:* "The written composition should be spread over several days so that one day is assigned for Latin prose, another for Latin verse, and likewise two days for Greek, the first for prose, the second for verse."

[51]1599 *Ratio:* "If anyone wishes more time to perfect his composition, he may remain as long as he wishes, provided he does not leave the classroom, and that the time is not extended beyond sunset."

[52]That is, not a member of the Jesuit Order.

of merit. These, as well as those next in rank, are determined by a majority vote of the judges.

9. The one whose style of writing is better should be given the decision over the others even though he has not written so much as they. If there are any in the same subject equally good in their style of writing, the one who has written most should be declared the winner. If they are equal in this point also, the prize should be given to the one who is superior in orthography. If in orthography and the other points they are equal, then the award is to be made to the one who excels in penmanship. If they are equal in every respect, let the prize be divided, or let two prizes be given, or let the winners draw lots. If anyone surpasses all other contestants in every branch, then he should be awarded all the prizes unless in some places a contrary custom exists.[53]

10. After the winning paper has been chosen, the prefect in the presence of the rector and the prefect-general should break the seals of the papers that contain the names of the contestants and their distinguishing mark. To avoid any mistakes the prefect should carefully compare the names of the winners with their distinguishing marks. When they are known he should inform no one save the masters.

11. Then on an appointed day, with as much pomp and before as large an audience as possible, the names of the winners should be publicly announced. Each winner should come forward to receive his prize in honorable fashion. If any winner is absent, unless he has permission from the prefect for good reasons approved by the rector, he loses his prize although he has clearly won it.

12. The customary formula should precede the distribution of prizes: "Prosperity and success in literary pursuits and to all the students of our college! Prizes are awarded in the following order": Then the herald will summon each winner in the following way: "The first, second, etc., prize for Latin prose composition, Greek prose composition, Latin verse, etc., has been merited by and is hereby awarded to X." Then the prize is presented to the winner amid applause and to the sound of music. Lastly, if any have distinguished themselves in these contests, the herald should read out their names, and to them also something in the way of a prize may be given.[54]

---

[53] 1599 *Ratio:* The phrase, "unless in some places . . . exists," is lacking.

[54] 1599 *Ratio:* "12. The herald shall announce each prize winner in the following fashion: 'Prosperity and success to all literary pursuits and to the students of our college! First, second, and third, etc., for Latin prose composition, Greek prose composition, Latin verse, Greek verse, etc., has been merited by and is awarded to X.' Then he presents the prize to the winner, generally adding some short suitable (Latin) verses; these may be sung by the choir, if it can be conveniently arranged. Lastly, if any have distinguished themselves," etc.

13. If anyone violates these regulations or is guilty of any dishonesty in the contest, no attention is to be paid to his composition.

XV. *Common Rules for the Professors of the Lower Classes*

1. The master shall so train the youth intrusted for their education to the Society of Jesus that they may acquire not only learning but also a character worthy of a Christian. It should be each master's special aim not only during classes as the occasion may arise, but also outside of class time to prepare the tender minds of these youths for the love and service of God, to inculcate those virtues that are pleasing to Him. In particular, all the masters should observe the following rules.

2. Someone should be appointed to say a brief prayer at the beginning of class. The master and pupils should follow this attentively, kneeling with heads uncovered. Before the beginning of the lesson, the instructor, with uncovered head, should make the sign of the cross, and then begin.

3. The master should see to it that all are present at Mass every day and at the sermon on feast days. Moreover, twice a week during Lent, he should send them to the sermon [in the church] or, if such is the local custom, accompany them thither.[55]

4. Christian doctrine should be taught in all the classes. In the three grammar classes, and even in the others if necessary, the lesson should be recited from memory on Fridays or Saturdays. Each grade should have ampler explanation and recitations, in proportion to its need.[56]

5. Likewise on Fridays or Saturdays, each master should give a half hour of pious instruction or explanation of Christian doctrine. He should especially recommend daily prayer to God, in particular, the rosary of the Blessed Virgin, or the daily recitation of the Little Office of the Blessed Virgin, the evening examination of conscience, frequent devout reception of the sacraments of penance and Holy Eucharist, and devotion to the Sacred Heart of Jesus.[57] He should urge his charges to avoid bad habits, to hate vice, and finally to cultivate the virtues worthy of Christian manhood.

6. In private conversations too, he should strive to instill piety, not,

---

[55]In American Jesuit high schools, Mass is said daily for the students, but attendance is usually not obligatory, except in the boarding schools. Once a week, however, during class time, all must attend a short service, consisting usually of devotions and a brief talk.

[56]1599 *Ratio:* "Christian doctrine should be learned and recited from memory on Fridays or Saturdays, especially in the grammar classes, and also in the other classes, if necessary. In some places and for the new pupils it may be necessary to have these lessons oftener."

[57]1599 *Ratio:* The phrase, "devotion to the Sacred Heart of Jesus" lacking. This Catholic devotion was not so widespread at that time.

however, in such a way as to seem to influence them to enter our Order. If there be any so inclined, he should send them to their confessor.

7. He should arrange for the recitation of the litanies of the Blessed Virgin every Saturday afternoon in his class; or, if such is the local custom, he should lead his class to the church for the common recitation of the litanies with the other pupils. He should diligently foster devotion to the Blessed Virgin and also to the Guardian Angels.

8. He should strongly recommend the reading of spiritual books, especially the lives of the saints. On the other hand, not only should he be most careful never to read any passage from obscene writers or anything else likely to be dangerous to their virtue, but he should also make every effort to keep his pupils from perusing works of this type, even in their outside reading.

9. The master must see to it that all the students go to confession once a month. They should be told to hand in to their confessors a card bearing their name and class, in order that afterwards the master may know who were absent by inspecting these cards.

10. He should often pray to God for his boys and give them an example of upright character by his own manner of life.

11. In all that pertains to studies and school discipline, the master should obey the prefect of lower studies. Without his permission he should admit none to his class, dismiss none, nor take any book for class matter nor give any permission to anyone to absent himself from the common school exercises.

12. Each class must keep to its subject matter. In a separate place rules for the class of rhetoric and humanities will be given. In grammar there should be three classes, each of which has certain definite matter to cover. Hence, all the grammatical precepts[58] are to be divided into three parts, and one section assigned to each class in such wise, however, that the matter seen the previous year will always be repeated at the beginning of the next year, as will be indicated below in the rules for the masters of the respective classes.

In teaching the vernacular, practically the same method is to be observed as in the study of Latin.[59]

13. The Greek grammar should be divided about as follows. The first part, assigned to the first class,[60] should begin with the regular nouns, and include the verb "to be," and the regular verbs. The second section for the intermediate grammar class should include the contract

[58] 1599 *Ratio:* "the precepts of Emmanuel."
[59] 1599 *Ratio:* "In teaching the vernacular," etc., lacking.
[60] That is, the second year of lowest grammar, when Greek was commenced.

nouns, the circumflex verbs, the verbs in *mi,* and the easier constructions. The third class[61] should take the other parts of speech and all the syntax. The fourth class should study versification and the simpler rules of dialect.[62]

14. The time schedule for rhetoric class should be at least two hours in the morning, and an equal allotment in the afternoon. For humanities and the other classes, two and a half hours both morning and afternoon should be provided. Even on the weekly holiday, two hours should be given to class. These should always be at the same hour so that it may be known at any certain hour just what classes are being conducted.

15. The order of classes may be changed with the permission of the provincial to accord with local custom, provided that the same amount of time assigned in the rules of the respective masters be preserved and, provided that once an order of classes is adopted, it be adhered to.

16. If a holiday falls on Saturday, the exercises assigned for that day may be advanced a day or omitted altogether.

17. The same division of time is to have place on a recreation day unless some special exercises are assigned for that day. The ordinary exercises, held on other days, should be curtailed or some of them omitted altogether. Some time should be left for contest in drill work.[63]

18. Special care must be taken to have the students acquire the habit of Latin conversation. Accordingly, the master should speak Latin, beginning with the highest class of grammar, and he should require the students to speak Latin especially in the explanation of the grammatical precepts, in the correction of their Latin compositions, in the class contests and also in their conversation one with another. In translating into the vernacular, however, he should take special pains to have them use purity of diction in their mother tongue and a correct pronunciation, and he should be intolerant of any mistakes in this matter.[64]

19. The students should repeat from memory the prelections to the

---

[61]That is, the highest class of grammar.

[62]1599 *Ratio:* "The Greek grammar should be . . . The third class should take the other parts of speech and whatever goes under the terms of rudiments, excepting dialects, and the more difficult exceptions. The fourth class, that of humanities, all of syntax, and the fifth class, that of rhetoric, should study versification."

[63]That is, the concertation.

[64]1599 *Ratio:* "The practice of speaking Latin must be particularly promoted, with the exception of those classes in which the students know no Latin. They should never be permitted to use the mother tongue in what pertains to class matter. Demerit marks should be assigned to those who are negligent. For this reason, the master should always speak Latin."

decurions whose duties are explained in Rule 36. If another system seems desirable in the class of rhetoric, it may be used. The decurions themselves recite their lessons to the head decurion or to the master himself. In general, the master should ask the lesson of the lazier students and from the late-comers so as to check the fidelity of the decurions and to keep all up to the mark. On Saturday, there should be a public repetition from memory of all that has been seen in the past week or even the matter of several weeks. When a book[65] is finished, some may be chosen occasionally to recite it from beginning to end. For this a prize should be awarded.

20. Written work should be handed in by all the grammar classes every day but Saturday. In the other classes a [Latin] prose composition must be handed in daily except on Saturday and the weekly holiday. Exercises in verse should be handed in twice a week; namely, on Mondays and the day following the weekly holiday. Once a week, at least, there should be a Greek theme, to be handed in on the afternoon of any day the master chooses.

21. Daily the master should correct the written work of all his students, since very great benefit is derived from this. If, however, the number in the class is too great for this, he should correct as many as possible, so that none of the students is ever left long without correction. For this reason, on the days especially when exercises in verse are handed in, he should have some of the class opponents exchange papers [for correction]. To facilitate this, each student should write not merely his own name on his exercise, but also that of his opponent. While the recitation of the memory lesson is being heard [by the decurions] the master himself can correct some of the other papers by individual conference with the pupils in a low voice; the rest of the papers, he should correct in his room, as far as possible.[66]

22. The method of correcting written work, in general, is to note any grammatical mistake, to inquire how it may be remedied, to require the class opponents publicly to correct any mistake as soon as they notice it, and to quote the grammatical rule that has been broken. Finally, praise should be given for excellent work. While this correction is being done in class, the students should read and correct their own first copy of the exercise which should always be brought

---

[65]That is, a book of a Latin author, as a book of Vergil's *Æneid*.

[66]1599 *Ratio:* "Written work is ordinarily to be corrected by individual conference with each pupil in a low voice while the others are given time to practice their (Latin) style. It will be useful, however, daily to select some of the exercises, now from the best, now from the poorest, and to read them publicly at the beginning and end of class and post them in a conspicuous place."

to class in addition to the copy handed in to the master. The master[67] should also try as often as possible to dictate a carefully corrected version to the class.

Moreover, he should see that all the exercises are written neatly and legibly and that the penmanship in general is of good type.[68]

23. He should demand[69] different sorts of exercises at different times, suited to the grade of his class. Nothing checks the ardor of youthful spirit more than monotony.

24. Besides the daily written task to be done during class, an exercise in composition should be given to occupy them during an hour of class time, once a week, at least.[70]

25. The repetition of the previous day's work as well as of the lesson for the day should be done as follows: The entire lesson may be asked of one individual, but it would be better to question several in order that all may have practice. Only the repetition of the most important and useful points should be asked. The better students should be asked first, then the others. They should be made to answer in continued discourse or else in direct answers to the master's questions, the opponent correcting any mistakes in his partner's repetition, or if he hesitates, giving the answer himself.

26. On Saturdays, there should be a repetition of all the matter seen during that week. If any of the students say they are prepared to answer all questions on this matter or even on an entire book, let some of them be chosen whom the others may ask two or three questions. A reward should be given to those who answer successfully.

27. In the prelections, only the ancient classics, never the modern writers, are to be explained. It will be very advantageous if the master speaks, not on the spur of the moment and at random, but only what he has thoughtfully written out in his room. He should read the whole speech or oration before he begins to teach it. The method of the prelection should generally follow this plan:

First, the master should read aloud the entire passage [for translation], unless it is too long.[71] Secondly, he should explain briefly the substance of the passage and when necessary the connection with what precedes. Thirdly, as he reads over each sentence, if he gives the explanation in Latin, he should clear up the obscurities, and show the relation of part with part. This should not be done by an inept

---

[67] 1599 *Ratio:* "The master . . . of good type" lacking.

[68] 1599 *Ratio:* The 23rd rule in the 1599 *Ratio* is substantially the same as the 21st rule previously given.

[69] 1599 *Ratio:* "during the time of correction," added.

[70] This rule lacking in the 1599 *Ratio.*

[71] 1599 *Ratio:* "as in the class of rhetoric and humanities."

paraphrase, substituting one Latin word for another, but he should really explain the sentence, by casting it in a clearer version, if it is obscure in the original.[72] If he is giving an explanation in the vernacular, he should keep, as far as possible, the arrangement of words [in the Latin sentence]. Thus, their ears become accustomed to the [Latin] flow of words. If the vernacular idiom does not permit this, then he should first give a literal translation, and afterward explain the sense in the vernacular.

Fourthly, beginning over again, he should give those necessary observations, that are suited to his class, unless he prefers to give his commentary as he goes along. He should dictate, either during the explanation or later, after the prelection is finished, what he wishes the students to copy out; there should not be much of this. It is usually better for the students of the grammar classes not to write at all unless they are told.

28. The prelection of an historical writer or a poet has this special feature that the former can usually be done more rapidly, while the poet is best rendered by a careful oratorical paraphrase. The students must be accustomed to distinguish between the style of a poet and an orator.

Much after the same fashion, the vernacular classics should be read.[73]

29. In the explanation of rhetorical precepts, the art of versification, Latin, vernacular,[74] and Greek grammar, and similar subjects, the substance rather than the verbal precepts should be stressed. Brief examples from the best authors should be selected and translated. Particularly in the lower classes of grammar, when some especially difficult precept comes up, they should be drilled on this one point for one or more days. This can be varied by a repetition of some of the easier rules.

30. The assignment for theme should not be dictated *ex tempore*, but should be thought out beforehand and generally written out. As far as possible, it should be written in imitation of Cicero and built up on the model of some narrative, or argumentative prose, or some expression of congratulation, counsel, or something of that sort. Both the Latin and the vernacular version should be handed in where the master has given a verbal dictation. After the dictation, he should have the assignment immediately repeated, and he should explain the

[72]1599 *Ratio:* The phrase, "if it is obscure in the original" lacking.

[73]This sentence lacking in the 1599 version.

[74]1599 *Ratio*, "vernacular" lacking.

more difficult parts. He should supply the words, the phrases, and other needed helps. With the exception of the class of rhetoric, he should always advise them during the dictation how to write and how to punctuate the theme. An unusual and longer assignment than usual may be given when several feast days come together or when the long or short vacations are announced.

31. During class contests,[75] the master does the questioning and the opponents the correcting of their partners, or else the opponents themselves question one another. These contests are to be highly esteemed and are to be made use of as often as time allows so that praiseworthy rivalry which is a great incentive to diligence may be fostered. For the contest one can be matched against another, or several from each side. It is a good plan to put officer[76] against officer. Or one student may question several opponents. Generally, a private should be matched against private, officer against officer. Occasionally, however, a private may match his skill with an officer, and if he is victorious, he should be awarded the rank of his opponent or given another prize or sign of victory according as the rank of the class and local usage permit.

32. Exercises out of the ordinary and public exhibitions[77] are very useful. It should be noted that only those should be permitted to take part in a public examination who have been diligently prepared for it. To provide mental training for the student and not merely to exercise his memory, the master should indeed carefully polish what the students are to give before the public, but he should never write the whole of it himself. The same may be said of verse that is to be displayed in public. The students should also be carefully trained in correct enunciation, gesture, and delivery.

33. In the classes of rhetoric and humanities, every other Saturday an explanation of an author may be given or a Greek or Latin speech or poem; one class may play host to the other for this exercise. In the other classes, the explanation of an author not seen previously should not be intrusted to a student; rather he should repeat a prelection he has heard in class. No visitors should be invited to this exercise and they should be held only once a month.

34. Some time during the year, on a day appointed by the prefect of the lower schools, there should be a contest for about an hour

---

[75]Or concertations.

[76]The class was divided into camps or armies, thus the "Romans" and the "Carthaginians"; and each army had its officers and privates.

[77]"Public exhibitions" lacking in the 1599 version.

between a lower class and the one immediately above it. The subject matter should include only those topics common to both classes. The masters of the respective classes should direct the proceedings. Two, three, or more of the best students of both classes should be matched in contest, either prepared beforehand according to agreement between the two classes on set questions and answers, or asking any questions that their ingenuity suggests, or refuting the objections, especially in rhetoric, that are set forth by one side.

35. The officers [of both sides] in a class should be chosen and rewarded too, if that seems wise, every month, or at least, every other month, unless in some schools this seems unnecessary for the rhetoric class. For this purpose, the students should be given one written test in Latin prose composition and in the higher classes, if it is desired, one written test in Latin verse or in Greek composition. The entire school day should be given for this, unless in the lower classes it seems better to reserve a half hour for the contest in drill. Those who do the best work, should be honored with the highest office. The next highest should also receive honorable titles. To throw an air of erudition about it, the titles should be borrowed from the political or military offices in Rome or Greece. The class should be divided into two equal sides to stimulate rivalry. Each side should have its own officers, opposed by officers of the other side; and each individual pupil should have his opponent assigned. The chief officers of each side should have the seats of honor in the class.

36. Decurions also should be appointed by the instructor to hear the memory lessons, collect the written work for the master, and to mark down in a little book those who fail in the memory work or who fail to hand in their exercises, or fail to bring two copies of their written task to class. They should note down anything else that the master may wish.

37. For the general promotion, the students should be given during the month preceding the examination a thorough repetition of all the main points of the year's work. This holds for all the classes with the possible exception of rhetoric. If anyone has excelled during the course of the year in very marked fashion, the master should refer his case to the prefect so that he may pass at once to a higher class after a private examination.

38. At the beginning of each year, the master should give the prefect an alphabetical list of his students. He should inspect this list occasionally during the year to revise it, if necessary. Before the general examination, he should do this with special care. In this list, he should classify wherever possible the students according to ability,

namely, excellent, good, average, doubtful,[78] failures. All this can be indicated by numbers, 1, 2, 3, 4, 5, 6.

39. Nothing helps discipline so much as the observance of rules. Hence, the master should take particular care to have the students observe their own rules and those that pertain to studies. This will be more easily attained by the hope of honor and reward, and the fear of disgrace than by punishment.

40. The master should not be hasty in punishing nor petty in his investigation [of wrongdoing]. He should rather pretend not to have seen, when this can be done without disadvantage to anyone. Not only must he never strike a pupil with his own hand — that is the corrector's business — but he should also refrain altogether from sarcastic remarks and discourteous actions. He should never call a student except by his right name. In place of punishment, it will sometimes be useful to add something to the pupil's daily written task. He must leave to the prefect unusual and severe punishments, especially for offenses committed outside of school. To the prefect also should be referred the cases of those students who refuse punishment, especially if they are older boys.

41. The master should demand the greatest diligence of his students. Accordingly, he should not excuse them from class for the purpose of attending public exhibitions or plays. If anyone is absent, the master should send one of his classmates or some other person to his home. Unless proper excuses are forthcoming, the absentee should be punished. If any are absent several days without excuse, they should be sent to the prefect and should not be readmitted without his consent.

42. To avoid any interference with class exercises on account of confessions, the students should be sent to confession at the beginning of class [on confession days] in groups of three or more. When the first return, one or two others should replace them, unless in some place it should be the custom to have all go to the church for confession at the same time.

43. The master's first care should be to secure silence and becoming behavior. He should see that no one wanders about the classroom, changes his place, or exchanges notes or little gifts. The students should not leave the classroom, especially not two or more together.

44. Special care must be taken that none of the pupils be called out of the room, particularly during the time set for prelection. To avoid noise and confusion during dismissal time, the master should stand guard either at his desk or at the door, and see that those

[78] 1599 *Ratio* has *"retinendos, rejeciendos,"* that is, those who must repeat the class, and those who should not be allowed to return to school.

nearest to the doors leave first. Or he can make any other arrangement, provided the students leave orderly and quietly.

45. With the rector's approval, the master may organize academies in accordance with the rules set down later on. On feast days especially, meetings should be held in order to ward off idleness and bad habits.

46. If it seems necessary occasionally to confer with parents about a pupil, the master should consult with the rector about the advisability of the prefect or some other person summoning them, or if their rank demands it, about paying them a personal visit.

47. The master should not be more friendly to one student than to another. Outside of class time, he should speak to them only briefly and about serious matters. Their conversation should be in an open place, not inside the classroom, rather at the door of the classroom or in the yard or at the college gate so that due regard may be had to edification.

48. Without the rector's advice, the master should never recommend a private tutor to anyone, and he should never permit these tutors to burden their charges with other lessons at home, but merely allow the tutors to assist with the lessons assigned in class.

49. He should never employ a student as a copyist nor for any other work which does not pertain to the regular school exercises. Nor should he permit the students to spend their money in any way for the school.

50. Finally, the master, with the help of divine grace, should be diligent and persevering in every way, bent only on the advancement of his pupils in their daily lessons and other literary exercises. He should regard no one with contempt but devote the same care to the efforts of poor students as he does to those of the rich. Let him strive for the advancement of each and every one of his charges.

XVI. *Rules for the Professor of Rhetoric*[79]

....

XVII. *Rules for the Professor of Humanities*

1. The purpose of this class is to lay the foundation for eloquence, after the pupils have finished the grammar classes. There are three means to this: a knowledge of the language, some erudition, and a

---

[79]Twenty rules are set down for the class of rhetoric, whose purpose is to "train the students perfectly in eloquence." These rules are not given here, as the class of rhetoric is beyond the secondary level. In the old American Jesuit college, rhetoric class roughly corresponded with the sophomore class of the modern college, the class of poetry corresponding in the same fashion to modern freshman. Poetry class is not in the *Ratio;* it was intermediate to humanities and rhetoric, and partook of the nature of both.

brief introduction to the rules of rhetoric. Knowledge of the language consists principally in propriety in the use of words and a copious vocabulary. For imparting this, Cicero alone of the orators is to be explained in the daily prelections.[80] Among the historians, Cæsar, Sallust, Livy, Curtius, and others like them may be taken; among the poets, Vergil, with the exception of[81] the fourth book of the Æneid, as well as Horace's selected odes, together with elegies, epigrams, and other poems of the classic poets, provided an expurgated version be made use of. In the same way,[82] the vernacular orators, historians and poets should be studied. Erudition should be given sparingly, merely for the purpose of stimulating interest and refreshing the mind, and not in such a way as to interfere with the study of the language.

The general precepts of public speaking and writing, particularly the special rules for the shorter forms of writing, such as letters, narration, description, both in prose and verse, should be taught. That part of the Greek grammar belongs to this class which treats of prosody and gives the elementary rules of dialects. An attempt should be made to have them read the writers understandingly and to give them the ability to translate into simple Greek.[83]

2. This is the time schedule. The first three quarters of the hour in the morning, the decurions should hear the recitation of the Latin precepts and the Latin authors, while the master looks over the written work collected by the decurions and the reports they have made. Then there should be some explanation of the precepts. The following half hour should be devoted to the public correction of written exercises. Then for three quarters of an hour, there should be a repetition of the last lesson from the oration, followed by an explanation of the succeeding part. The last half hour [of the morning] should be given over to the accessory branches, or else to a class contest.

The first hour in the afternoon, there should be a recitation by heart of the rhetorical precepts and the Latin author, generally one of the poets, while the master looks over the notes assigned by the decurions, or corrects the exercises written in the morning or any of the exercises written at home that remain. Finally, there is an explanation and repetition of the precepts. The second hour, there is a lesson on a Latin

---

[80] 1599 *Ratio:* "for this his ethical writings should be chosen."

[81] *Ibid:* Add: "some of the eclogues. . . ."

[82] This sentence is not in the 1599 *Ratio.*

[83] 1599 *Ratio:* "For the rhetorical precepts, a brief summary of Cyprian should be given in the second semester. During this time, some of Cicero's simpler speeches may be substituted for his philosophical writings, for example, such as *pro Lege Manilia, pro Archia, pro Marcello* and the other speeches he delivered before Cæsar. Greek syntax belongs to this class. Moreover, care must be taken that the students understand the Greek writers fairly well and are able to translate a bit into Greek."

poet; every other day, there should be an explanation and repetition of a vernacular and Greek author. Then a theme is dictated. The last half hour is given over to a class contest or to the accessory subjects.[84]

On the weekly holiday, recitation from memory of what was seen during the prelection on the last holiday. The rest of the written exercises should be corrected as usual. During the second hour, there should be explanation and repetition of some epigram, ode, or elegy, or something[85] about tropes, figures of speech, and from the very beginning of the year the students should accustom themselves to prose rhythms and oratorical cadences. Or a short essay or some other rhetorical exercise may be assigned, or finally, there may be a class contest.

Saturday morning, during the first hour there should be recitation from memory of all the prelections of the week; during the second hour, a review of this matter. During the last half hour, a declamation or prelection may be given by one of the students; if not, they may visit the class of rhetoric or else have a class contest. The first hour in the afternoon, there should be a recitation from memory of poetry and of catechism, while the master corrects any exercises of the week left uncorrected and looks through the reports of the decurions. The following half hour is equally divided between a review of the poety and the explanation and repetition of some poem. Greek is taken in the same way. An explanation of the catechism should be given the last half hour or a pious discourse, unless one was given on Friday. In that case, the time should be spent on the study displaced by catechism.

3. In correcting the written work, the master should indicate any fault in the use of words, in propriety of expression, or rhythm; like-

---

[84]1599 *Ratio:* "This is the time schedule. First hour in the morning, Cicero and the rules of prosody should be recited to the decurions, while the master corrects the written work collected by the decurions, assigning meanwhile various exercises to the class, as explained in Rule 4. Lastly some recite in public while the master looks over the reports of the decurions. Second hour in the morning, there is to be a brief review of the last prelection, then an explanation of the new prelection for a half hour or a little longer, followed immediately by a quiz on it. If there is any time left, there should be a class contest. The last half hour in the morning: in the first semester, one of the historians or prosody on alternate days. Once the rules of prosody are covered, the historical work can be read rapidly every day. In the second semester, a daily explanation of the rhetorical rules of Cyprian, followed either by a repetition or a debate on the rules seen.

"The first hour in the afternoon, the Latin poet and the Greek author are recited from memory, while the master looks over the decurions' reports and corrects either the exercises assigned in the morning or those home tasks which are left over. At the end, a theme is dedicated. The hour and a half following is divided between a review and an explanation of a Latin poem and Greek prelection and composition."

[85]1599 *Ratio,* "from the third book of Cyprian."

wise any lack of fidelity in imitation work, any mistakes in orthography, or any other fault. He should require several versions of the same passage that through this exercise an extensive vocabulary may be acquired.

4. Exercises should be given,[86] for example, in choosing phrases from the prelections and writing down various equivalents, in rearranging a broken-up period of Cicero, in writing verses, in casting a poem of one type into another form, in imitating a standard passage, in writing compositions in Greek or the vernacular,[87] and the like. These exercises should take place every other day, either in the morning in place of the public correcting of papers, or during the second hour in the afternoon, or at some other more opportune time with the approval of the prefect. At least once a week, however, there should be an hour's exercise in composition during class time.[88]

5. Whenever the explanation of the passage permits, the prelection should be interspersed by comments pertaining to general erudition. But the master should give his principal effort to remarks on the Latin or vernacular[89] language, to the force and derivation of words, which should be chosen from approved writers.[90] Likewise he should emphasize the use and variety of expression,[91] compare the genius of the Latin with the vernacular, and use the authors as models for imitations. When, however, he is explaining a speech, he should call attention to the rules of oratorical composition. Finally, if it seems advisable, the whole passage may be rendered in a good vernacular version.

6. The assignment for written work[92] should be adapted to the precepts proper to this class and should be dictated; and it will be very useful to have it so arranged that it will contain passages taken here and there from previous prelections; and thus, as far as possible,

---

[86]1599 *Ratio:* "while he is correcting exercises."

[87]*Ibid.*, "vernacular" lacking.

[88]*Ibid.* "These exercises should take . . . during class time" lacking.

[89]*Ibid.*, "vernacular" lacking.

[90]*Ibid.*, "generally from the ancients."

[91]*Ibid.*, "and use the author as models for imitation. Nor will it be amiss to cite some passage from the vernacular, if it helps the explanation or is in any way noteworthy. When however," etc.

[92]1599 *Ratio:* "The assignment for written work in the first semester should be generally dictated word for word in the vernacular in the form of a letter; and it will be very useful to have it so arranged that it will contain passages taken outright from previous prelections. About once a week, however, they should do some original work, after an explanation of some type of letter has been given, and models indicated in the letters of Cicero or Pliny. In the second semester their ingenuity should be stimulated, by giving them first, chrias, then introductions, narratives, and even more ornate work. However, a simple, yet detailed outline should be given them. The method for the Greek theme, etc., . . . more fully." Last paragraph of Rule 6 omitted in the 1599 *Ratio.*

it will be an imitation of the author. The assignment should be dictated word for word in the vernacular according to the capacity of the students; or a free version may be given them to translate and elaborate upon. The assignment for verse should be dictated and a variety of expression suggested. The method for the Greek theme will be the same as for the Latin prose, except that generally it will be taken literally from the author, and the syntax explained more fully.

The better to practice them in the use and style of their mother tongue, exercises of various sorts in the vernacular should be strictly assigned.

7. In the class contest, or exercise, the matter shall be the mistakes a student has discovered in his opponent's theme, questions on topics stressed in the drill[93] at the beginning of class or any other time, reciting from memory choice phrases or their variants given them by the master, quoting or applying rules of[94] grammar, giving the quantity of syllables, citing the while the rule or an example from a poet, explaining the exact meaning and derivation of words, and finally interpretation of a passage from a Latin, Greek, or vernacular[95] author, and the like, at the discretion of the master.

8. Prosody should be run through rapidly, dwelling only on those points which the master sees the students need most, and spending more time on practical examples than on explanation. In the same way, the precepts[96] of rhetoric are to be briefly explained with examples from the textbook and from the daily prelections, according to opportunity.

9. In the Greek prelection,[97] the grammatical precepts and author should be explained on alternative days. In precepts, prosody and the different dialects should be taught after a brief review of the matter of the preceding classes. The text for prose study should be taken

[93] 1599 *Ratio:* "In the first hour."

[94] *Ibid.*, "rules of oratorical and epistolary composition."

[95] *Ibid.*, "vernacular" lacking.

[96] *Ibid.*, "the precepts of Cyprian."

[97] 1599 *Ratio:* "In the Greek prelection, grammar and author should be explained on alternate days. After a brief review of the precepts seen in the first Greek class, syntax and accentuation should be studied. For the prose author of the first semester one of the simpler writers should be selected, such as the speeches of Isocrates, of SS. Chrysostom, and Basil, the letters of Plato and Synesius, selections from Plutarch. In the second semester, a selection from the poets may be explained, for example, Phocylides, Theognides, St. Gregory Nazianzen, Synesius, and the like. The explanation of these authors, however, should aim at a reading knowledge rather than erudition, as required by the grade of this class. However, toward the end of the year, along with the author the rules of prosody can be studied on alternate days, and occasionally Greek verse, thrown out of its metrical form, can be recast metrically."

from the easier writers, such as the speeches of Isocrates, SS. Chrysostom and Basil, the letters of Plato and Synesius, and selections from Plutarch; for the poets, however, Homer, Phocylides, Theognides, St. Gregory Nazianzen, Synesius, and the like, may be selected. The explanation of these authors, however, should aim at the acquiring of a reading knowledge rather than erudition, as required by the grade of this class.

10. About every other month, the best poems written by the students should be posted on the wall, for the purpose of celebrating some feast day, or on the occasion of the announcement of class officers or anything else of this sort. If local custom permits it, even shorter prose pieces may be posted; as, for example, inscriptions for shields, churches, tombs, gardens, statues; or descriptions of a town, a harbor, an army; or narratives, such as, an incident from a saint's life.[98] Pictures may also be added, with the rector's permission, to illustrate the sentiment or object described.

XVIII. *Rules for the Professor of the Highest Grammar Class*

1. The objective of this class is a complete knowledge of grammar; accordingly, the master reviews Latin syntax from the beginning, adding[99] all the exceptions and idioms; then he explains figures of speech and prosody. In Greek,[100] he covers syntax with the exception of dialects and the more difficult idioms. For reading matter in prose he may take the more important letters of Cicero, the *de Amicitia,* the *de Senectute,* and the like; or where it is the practice, his easier speeches; also Sallust, Quintus Curtius, and selections from Livy. For poetry, expurgated selections from the elegies and letters of Ovid, Catullus, Tibullus, Propertius, or from the eclogues of Vergil, or the simpler books of the same author, such as the fourth Georgic, the fifth and seventh book of the Æneid. In Greek, St. Chrysostom, Xenophon, and the like. Some notions of mythology may also be given, unless this has already been taken in the intermediate grammar class.

---

[98] 1599 *Ratio,* "and finally paradoxical sayings."

[99] *Ibid.,* "adding all the appendices."

[100] *Ibid.,* "In Greek, he should cover the eight parts of speech or all that is classed as rudiments, excepting only dialects and the more difficult observations. The reading matter in prose in the first semester should be taken from the more important letters of Cicero, *Ad Familiares, Ad Atticum, Ad Quintum Fratrem.* In the second semester, his *De Amicitia, De Senectute, Paradoxa,* and the like. The poetry in the first semester should be expurgated selections from the elegies and letters of Ovid; in the second semester, expurgated selections from Catullus, Tibullus, Propertius, and from the eclogues of Vergil, or even the simpler books of Vergil, such as the 4th Georgic, the 5th and 7th books of the Æneid. In Greek, Chrysostom, Æsop, Agapetus, and the like."

2. The division of time is as follows. In[101] the first forty-five minutes in the morning, there is to be recitation from memory to the decurions of the Latin and Greek lesson both in author and precepts, while the master looks over the exercises collected by the decurions and their reports on the same; then he explains some part of the grammar, proper to this class. The following half hour is spent in public correction of exercises. Then for three quarters of an hour, there is a repetition of the last prelection of the author, a new prelection is given, followed immediately by questioning on it. The last half hour should be spent on the vernacular and accessory branches.

In the first[102] hour after dinner, Latin grammar and prosody are taken on alternate days, followed by the recitation from memory of the Latin author, generally a poet, while the master looks over the reports of the decurions, or corrects the exercises assigned that morning or any homework not yet corrected. Finally there is explanation, followed by a repetition, of either grammar or prosody. During the second hour, there should be an explanation, followed by a repetition of the Latin poet, and every other day, of the Greek author; then, the theme is dictated. The last half hour should be spent either on class contests or on the vernacular and accessory branches.[103] Saturday morning, there is the recitation from memory of all the prelection of the week or of an entire book; the second hour, review; the last half hour, class contest or declamation. The same order for the afternoon, except that during the first hour, a catechism recitation is also required, unless this was given on Friday, in which case, the time should be spent on that subject displaced by catechism.

---

[101] 1599 *Ratio*, "for the first hour in the morning, recitation of grammar and Cicero from memory to the decurions, while the master corrects the exercises collected by the decurions, assigning various tasks to the students, as detailed in the fourth rule below. In the second hour in the morning, there is a brief repetition of the last prelection on Cicero, and for a half hour an explanation, followed by a repetition of a new passage; finally the dictation of a theme. During the last half hour, after the repetition of the grammar lesson, an explanation of a new lesson, followed by questions on it, giving some time to the class contest. In the first semester, the grammatical precepts seen in the preceding class are reviewed, then the matter proper to this class is explained. Every other day the general rules of prosody, omitting the exceptions, should be taken. In the second semester, there should be a review of all the matter belonging to this class for at least two months; every other day, the rules of prosody already seen should be repeated rapidly, stressing other rules when necessary. After the grammatical review is finished, prosody should be taken every day, adding the exceptions, the forms of verse, the rules for patronymics and accent."

[102] 1599 *Ratio:* "The first hour in the afternoon, recitation from memory of the Latin poet and the Greek author, while the master looks over the reports of the decurions, and corrects the morning exercises or the homework not yet corrected. The following hour and a half is divided between the review and explanation of the poet and Greek prelection and composition in such wise that a little more than a half hour is given to Greek. The last half hour, or whatever time remains, may be spent in class contests."

[103] "Or on the vernacular and accessory branches" lacking in the 1599 *Ratio.*

3. In the correction of written work, the master should indicate the mistakes in grammar, orthography, and punctuation; moreover, he should call their attention to difficulties they have avoided, to lack of elegance in diction, or to a failure to conform to the model assigned.

4. While the master is engaged in correcting the written exercises, the students should be given work to do, such as, to translate a passage from the vernacular into Latin both for the sake of imitating[104] the author and of exercising them in Latin precepts; or to turn a Latin passage into the vernacular and then retranslate the same into Latin; to cull elegant Latin expressions from the author; to match opponent against opponent and have them propose to each other difficulties for solution and expressions for translation, taken from the grammar recently seen; to put together verse, thrown out of the metrical form, or write original poems; to do some translating into Greek, and the like. Exercises[105] of this sort can be assigned every other day, in the morning in place of the public correction of exercises, or in the second hour of the afternoon, or at any other time with the prefect's approval. But at least once a week, a whole hour of class time should be given to composition.

5. The method of the prelection is as follows. First, the master should give the substance of the passage briefly, both in Latin and in the vernacular. Then he explains each sentence, first in Latin, then in the vernacular. Thirdly, he repeats the whole passage from the beginning, and selects two or three words — unless he wishes to do this during the explanation — whose meaning and derivation he explains in detail, and compares with their vernacular derivatives;[106] and illustrates by an example or two from the same author. He should explain and show the development of the figures of speech; if there are any mythological, historical, or other references pertaining to erudition, he should briefly indicate them. Two or three fine expressions should be noted down. Finally, he should give the students a perfect[107] vernacular translation of the entire passage. It is permissible to dictate very briefly the substance of the passage in Latin, the remarks, proprieties, and elegances of phrase.

6. The written exercises should be in the vernacular in the form of a letter, a narrative, or a description,[108] based on the precepts of syntax in imitation of classic models.[109] In the same manner,[110] an

[104] 1599 *Ratio,* "of imitating Cicero."

[105] "Exercises of this sort . . . given to composition," lacking in the 1599 *Ratio.*

[106] 1599 *Ratio,* "compares with their vernacular derivatives" lacking.

[107] 1599 *Ratio,* "perfect" lacking.

[108] *Ibid.,* "a narrative, or a description" lacking.

[109] *Ibid.,* "in imitation of Cicero."

[110] *Ibid.* "In the same manner . . . from some classic author" lacking.

exercise for translation into the vernacular should be dictated or assigned from some classic author. About once a month, the students should be obliged to write an original composition either at home in place of the daily task or in class for the purpose of naming class officers by competition. This should be done only after they have made some progress and after[111] the various types of letters, narratives, and descriptions have been explained, and passages indicated in Cicero and other authors where samples may be found; the master himself should dictate some examples of the same kind.

7. For verse writing, the words of a poem can be dictated, but not in metrical fashion. Later with some of the words changed; lastly, a very simple outline with a great variety of expression to be turned into verse.

8. For the written exercises in Greek, the procedure is the same as for the Latin prose composition, except that the theme should be taken almost literally from the author, and the syntax especially emphasized.

9. The same procedure is followed with the Greek prelection[112] except that when a Greek author is being read, every single word should be explained, and, when it seems advisable, the simplest rules of syntax that apply should be indicated in general.

10. In the class contest or exercise, the matter shall be the mistakes a student has discovered in his opponent's theme, questions in topics they have been drilled upon,[113] reciting from memory phrases given them by the master, asking translations of expressions in the vernacular and rendering them in various ways for the purpose of giving them practice in syntax or in imitation of the author. An attempt should be made to have the one questioned translate the expression literally, and then after a little thought give not a word-for-word, but a continuous Latin version. Other exercises for the class contest are: recitation of the rules of letter writing; questions on the quantity of syllables, when a rule is cited or an example from a poet quoted; explanation of the etymology or proper use of a word; interpretation of a passage in a Latin or Greek author; declension of nouns and conjugation of verbs in Greek; and other exercises of this sort at the discretion of the master.

---

[111] *Ibid.*, "after the various types of letters have been explained, and the reference in Cicero's letters indicated; the master himself," etc.

[112] 1599 *Ratio:* "The same procedure is followed with the Greek prelection, which should rarely last more than a quarter of an hour, except that when a Greek author is read (it may be taken on alternate days with grammar, if the prefect approves) every word," etc.

[113] *Ibid.*, "in the first hour."

XIX. *Rules for the Professor of the Intermediate Grammar Class*

1. The objective of this class is complete, though not exhaustive, knowledge of the [Latin] grammar; genders[114] of nouns and their inflections should be explained, as also the principal parts of verbs, unless indeed this matter has already been taken in the lowest grammar class, in which case a repetition is enough.

The Greek for this class should include contract nouns, the circumflex verbs, the verbs in *mi,* the simpler constructions, and a short introduction to syntax.[115]

For reading in Latin, selections from Cicero's letters should be made,[116] together with narrative and descriptive passages, and the like from the same author; also Cæsar's *Commentaries* and the simpler poems of Ovid. In Green, Æsop's Fables, the *Tabula* of Cebes, and select expurgated dialogues from Lucian.

2. The division of time is as follows:

(*Practically the same as Rule 2 for the Professor of the Highest Class of Grammar. See supra.*)

3. In correcting the written exercises, the master should indicate all errors in grammar, orthography, and punctuation; he should call their attention to difficulties they have avoided; everything should be judged by the precepts of grammar, and as occasion offers, he should recall to memory the conjugations and the rudiments.

4. Written exercises[117] should be assigned in class, such as, to translate a passage from the vernacular into Latin in imitation of the author, especially for practice in the rules of syntax; to turn a passage of Cicero or of other authors[118] into the vernacular, and retranslate into Latin; to match opponent against opponent and have them propound to each other difficulties for solution and expressions for translation, illustrative of the grammatical precepts, especially those recently learned; to translate into Greek, and other similar exercises. Exercises of this sort[119] can be assigned every other day, in the morning in place of the public correction of written work, or in the second hour of the

[114] 1599 *Ratio,* "the matter to be explained is from the beginning of the second book (of grammar) down to figurative construction, including only the easier appendices, or, according to the Roman method, from the ordinary constructions down to figures of speech, with the addition of the easier appendices."

[115] *Ibid.,* "short introduction to syntax" lacking.

[116] 1599 *Ratio:* "Cicero's letters *Ad Familiares,* the simpler poems of Ovid should be read; and in the second semester, the catechism in Greek, and the *Tabula* of Cebes, if the prefect approves."

[117] *Ibid.,* "during the correction of the written work."

[118] *Ibid.,* "or of other authors" lacking.

[119] "Exercises of this sort . . . given to composition" lacking in 1599 *Ratio.*

afternoon, or at any other opportune time with the prefect's approval. But at least once a week a whole hour of class time should be given to composition.

5. In the repetition of the prelection, the master should take occasion now and then to ask the students to decline and conjugate the more difficult words, or to explain the grammatical construction.

6. The method for the prelection of the authors is as follows:[120] First, the master reads the entire passage aloud and gives a brief summary of the substance in the vernacular. Secondly, he gives a word-for-word translation in the vernacular. Thirdly, going through the passage from the beginning, he explains the construction, and shows the relation of each part, indicating the government of the verbs and nouns, calling attention to exemplifications of the rules of grammar already explained to the class. He may make an observation here and there on Latin usage, but these should be very simple; he should explain the figures of speech by illustrations, drawn from their ordinary experience; finally, he should choose from the passage a phrase or two to be dictated to the class together with the summary of the substance.

7. The written exercise should be dictated clearly in the vernacular, word for word.[121] Its purpose is to give them practice in the rules of grammar and in imitation of the authors studied.[122] The students should also add to their themes a short translation of the author[123] or the conjugation of the tense of a Greek verb or the declension of a Greek noun.

8. The grammar prelection should include only one rule at a time, or at most one of the notes or exceptions to the rule.

9. In teaching Greek, the same proportion holds. Custom seems to indicate the necessity of adding vernacular equivalents in the declensions and conjugations; in fact, the whole explanation should be in the vernacular.

10. In the class contest or exercise, the matter shall be the mistakes a student has found in his opponent's theme, questions on topics they have drilled upon,[124] reciting from memory, phrases given them by the master, asking each other translations of expressions in the vernacular for the sake of practice in syntax or in imitation of the authors.[125] An attempt should be made to have the one questioned

---

[120] 1599 *Ratio:* "The method for the prelection of Cicero which should hardly ever be more than seven lines is as follows."

[121] 1599 *Ratio,* "but rarely more than seven lines."

[122] *Ibid.,* "in imitation of Cicero."

[123] *Ibid.,* "of Cicero."

[124] 1599 *Ratio:* "during the first hour."

[125] *Ibid.,* "in imitation of Cicero."

translate the expression literally, and then after a little thought, give, not a word-for-word, but a continuous Latin version. Other exercises may be the more difficult nouns and verbs, especially such as occur in the prelection, giving either the entire declension and conjugation or only part of it, and either with or without the modifying adjective, noun or pronoun; and similar exercises at the discretion of the master.

XX. *Rules for the Professor of the Lowest Grammar Class*

1. The object of this class[126] is a perfect knowledge of [Latin] rudiments. It begins with the ordinary declensions and conjugations, continuing to the general, common rules of syntax, to which a few of the simpler idioms may be added. The prefect should apportion the grammar between the two years of this class. The first year should learn to read and write the Greek characters; the second year should learn the common Greek nouns, the verb "to be," and the *Verbum barytonum*. For reading, some of the easier selections, if possible a printed edition, of Cicero, the *Fables* of Phaedrus, and the *Lives* of Cornelius Nepos may be used.

2. The division of time is as follows: In the morning,[127] the first three quarters of an hour should be given to the recitation from memory to the decurions of the Latin author and the Greek and Latin grammar, while the master looks over the exercises collected by the decurions and their reports; then for each year, there should be an explanation of that part of the grammar assigned to each, each year on alternate days or both daily;[128] afterwards there should be a repetition, conducted by the master or else a class contest on this matter.

On the days when no new precept is to be taken in the afternoon —

[126]1599 *Ratio:* "is a perfect knowledge of Latin rudiments and an elementary knowledge of syntax. The class begins with the declensions and goes on to the ordinary construction of verbs. Where there are two years for this class, to the first should be assigned the nouns, verbs, rudiments, the fourteen rules for construction, the genders of nouns from the first book of grammar. The second year should cover the matter on declensions, without the appendices, as well as the perfects and supines from the first book of grammar; and in the second book, the introduction to syntax, without the appendices, up to impersonal verbs. The first year should learn to read and write the Greek characters; the second year should learn the ordinary nouns, the verb 'to be' and the *Verbum barytonum*. For reading, only the simpler selections from Cicero's letters — if possible a printed edition — should be used."

[127]1599 *Ratio:* "In the morning, the first hour should be given to the recitation to the decurions from memory of Cicero and the grammar, while the master corrects the exercises collected by the decurions, assigning in the meantime to the class various tasks as is explained in the fourth rule below. The second hour in the morning, there is to be a repetition of the last prelection of Cicero, and a new one explained for a half hour, followed immediately by questioning on this new matter. Finally a theme is dictated. The last half hour there should be for each year," etc.

[128]In case both years are taught by the same master in the same classroom.

on most days only one precept is taken a day — then[129] various tasks are to be assigned, as explained in the fourth rule. The following half hour should be spent in public corrections of exercises. Then for three quarters of an hour, there should be a brief repetition of the last prelection of the Latin author, a new passage explained, followed immediately by questioning. The last half hour should be spent on the vernacular and accessory branches.

The first hour in the afternoon should be given to recitation from memory of the Latin author and grammar, while the master looks over the reports of the decurions, and corrects either the exercises still uncorrected, or the ones just assigned. The second hour is given to an explanation of the Latin author and a repetition; a little more than a quarter of an hour should be assigned to Greek, unless it seems advisable to substitute Greek for the Latin prelection twice a week; finally a theme is to be dictated. The last half hour should be given over to a class contest or else to the study of the vernacular and the accessory branches. In the first year, however, the vernacular should take the place of Greek.

On Saturdays, the first hour of the morning should be given to the public recitation from memory of all the prelections of the week. During the second hour, review of the same; the last half hour, a class contest or a declamation.[130] The same procedure in the afternoon, except that during the first hour, the catechism is recited together with the grammar. The last half hour should be given to catechetical explanation or to a talk on spiritual things, unless this was given on the preceding Friday; in that case the time should be spent on that branch displaced by catechism.

3. In correcting written work, the master should point out mistakes in grammar, orthography, and punctuation, and indicate difficulties the students have avoided, taking for his standard grammatical correctness. And he should not lose any opportunity of repeating the conjugations and declensions.

---

[129] 1599 *Ratio:* "Then this morning prelection may take the place of the afternoon one. The last half hour in the morning should be given entirely over to the class contest or exercises.

"The first hour in the afternoon, there should be recitation from memory of the precepts of Latin and Greek grammar, while the master looks over the reports of the decurions, and corrects for about a half hour, either the exercises assigned that morning, or the home tasks that remain uncorrected. Finally, there is a review of the last grammar lesson. The second hour in the afternoon should be spent by the second year in the study of syntax, and by the first on the study of rudiments and the genders of nouns; later on, the fourteen rules of construction should be explained during this time. A little more than fifteen minutes should be assigned for Greek. The last half hour, there should be a class contest or else some dictation from the rules of grammar."

[130] 1599 *Ratio,* "declamation" lacking.

4. The exercises of the students[131] shall consist, for example, in turning into Latin something dictated in the vernacular in accord with the precept of syntax; in translating a passage from the author[132] into the vernacular and then retranslating it into Latin; in matching opponent against opponent and having them propose difficulties to each other for solution from the grammatical precepts, especially those recently seen, or give examples illustrative of these rules; in arranging words in sentences, after the model of the "Concords,"[133] to copy out passages in Greek, and the like. These exercises[134] can be assigned every other day; in the morning, in place of the public correction of written work, or the second hour in the afternoon or at any other opportune time approved by the prefect. Once a week, however, a whole hour of class time should be devoted to composition.

5. In the repetition of the prelection, the master should often[135] take occasion to ask the students to decline and conjugate or to explain any grammatical rule.

6. The method for the prelection[136] of the authors, which should not be long, is as follows. First, the master reads the entire passage aloud and gives a very brief summary of the substance in the vernacular. Secondly, he gives a word-for-word translation in the vernacular. Thirdly, starting at the beginning, he should explain the construction, and running through the sentence, show what case each verb governs, thoroughly clearing up any difficulties pertaining to the rules of grammar already seen. He may make an observation here and there on Latin usage, but these should be very simple; he should clarify the figures of speech by very familiar illustrations. Nothing should be dictated except perhaps the summary of the substance of the passage. Fourthly, he should run through the passage once more in the vernacular.

7. The written exercise should be dictated clearly in the vernacular, word for word.[137] Its purpose is to give them practice in the rules of grammar. To this theme, the students should occasionally add[138] a

---

[131] 1599 *Ratio:* "During the correction of the written work by the master."

[132] *Ibid.*, "from Cicero," etc.

[133] The "Concords" in the grammar of Alvarez are: (1) Agreement of adjectives, pronouns, and participles with their substantives in gender, number, and case; (2) Agreement of an appositive noun in case; (3) Agreement of relative pronoun with its antecedent in gender and number. They are part of the fourteen rules of construction mentioned above. Rule 1, 1599 *Ratio.*

[134] 1599 *Ratio:* "These exercises . . . to composition" lacking.

[135] 1599 *Ratio,* "often" lacking.

[136] *Ibid.*, "for the prelection of Cicero, which should hardly exceed four lines is," etc.

[137] 1599 *Ratio,* "it should not be more than four lines."

[138] *Ibid.*, "add a short translation from Cicero or some," etc.

translation from the authors studied, or some phrase illustrative of the rules of syntax, or something assigned from Greek rudiments, and the like.

8. In the grammar prelection, only one rule at most should be taken in one lesson, and until this is thoroughly mastered, no new one should be attempted.

9. In the class contest or exercise, the matter shall be the mistakes a student has found in his opponent's theme, questions on topics they have drilled upon,[139] in asking each other the translation of phrases in the vernacular for the purpose of illustrating a grammatical rule. An attempt should be made to have the one questioned translate the expression literally and then, after a little thought, give not a word-for-word, but as far as possible, a continuous Latin version. Other exercises may be the more difficult declensions of nouns and conjugations of verbs, especially such as occur in the prelection, giving either the entire declension and tense or only part of it, and this either with or without the modifying adjective, noun, or pronoun; citing definitions of the rudiments with examples; translating quickly words in different cases from Latin into the vernacular and *vice versa;* casting a sentence in the active voice into the passive; pointing out perfects and supines of verbs, genders, and cases of nouns; parsing them when asked; and similar tasks at the discretion of the master.

XXI. *Rules for the Scholastics of Our Society*

(All regulations for the Jesuit Scholastics, that is, for those members of the Order who are studying; they consist largely in recommendations concerning right intention in their intellectual work, obedience to their professors, industry, external decorum.)

. . . .

XXII. *The Training of Scholastics Who Are Devoting a Biennium to Postgraduate Study in Theology*

. . . .

XXIII. *Rules for the Beadle or Professor's Assistant*

(The beadle, usually a Jesuit, assisted the professor in arranging the program of public disputations, reporting absentees from the university lectures, and the like. The office did not exist in the lower schools.)

. . . .

---

[139] *Ibid.*, "during the first hour."

XXIV. *Rules for the Extern Students of the Society*[140]

1. Those who attend the educational institutions of the Society of Jesus should realize that no less strenuous effort, with God's grace, will be devoted to instilling piety and other virtues than to imparting instruction in the liberal arts.

2. Each one should attend the class to which the prefect, after examination, assigns him.

3. Once a month they should go to confession; every day they should assist at Mass; on feast days, they should be present becomingly for the sermon.

4. All must be present at the weekly explanation of Christian doctrine and they should learn the lessons in the manual as assigned by the master.

5. None of our students should enter the school grounds with weapons, swords, daggers or anything similar, forbidden by prescriptions of time or place.

6. They should altogether refrain from swearing, abusive epithets, detractions, lies, and forbidden sports and keep from dangerous places and those forbidden by the prefect; in short, they should do nothing that is contrary to upright conduct.

7. They should know that the masters[141] will make use of severe punishments when counsel and warnings prove futile in inciting them to good conduct or industry in their studies. If any refuse the punishment, give no hope of amendment, are harming their fellow students, or giving bad example, then they should know that they will be expelled from our schools.

8. Each one should obey his master and faithfully follow in class and at home the plan of study he has prescribed.

9. They should apply themselves earnestly and perseveringly to their studies; be prompt in coming to class, in giving their attention to the lectures and reviewing them, and diligent in all the other class exercises. If anyone is making small progress, or has any difficulties, he should confer with the master.

10. In class they should not walk about, but each one should remain at his own desk and place, quietly and becomingly attending to his own affairs. No one should leave the class without previous permission from the master. No one should deface or make any mark

---

[140]These rules are intended primarily for the extern (i.e., non-Jesuit), students in the university. However, it gives a picture of the Jesuit method of discipline. Much less liberty was undoubtedly given the youth in the lower schools.

[141]1599 *Ratio*, "by means of the corrector."

on benches, desk, chairs, walls, doors, windows or anything else either by painting, scribbling, carving, or in any other fashion.

11. They should avoid bad, even questionable, companions, and should associate only with those whose example and manner of life may assist them to progress in learning and virtue.

12. They should entirely refrain from reading idle and vicious books.

13. They should not go to the theater, to comedies, to other shows, to public executions of criminals; nor should they take part in theatrical performances with outsiders, even though they be amateurs, without the previous permission of the masters or prefect of studies.

14. Most of all, they should strive for uprightness and purity of heart, aiming at the observance of God's commandments with the utmost diligence. They should frequently and from their heart commend their interests to God, to the Sacred Heart of Jesus,[142] to the Blessed Virgin Mother of God, and to the other saints. They should often beg the assistance of the angels, particularly of their Guardian Angels. They should observe modesty at all times and places, but especially in church and in school.

15. Finally in all their words and actions, they should so conduct themselves that everyone will easily see that they are striving no less for advance in virtue and uprightness of life than they are for progress in letters and sciences.

XXV. *Rules for Academies*

....

XXVI. *Rules for the Moderator of the Academy*

....

XXVII. *Rules for the Theological and Philosophical Academies*

(Sections XXV, XXVI, XXVII deal with the academies or seminars in general, with special application to those conducted in the higher faculties, viz., in philosophy and theology. The nature and conduct of the academy will be sufficiently manifested in the rules that follow for the lower schools. It should be noted that the students of rhetoric class are beyond the secondary level; consequently some of the assignments for their academy are fairly advanced.)

....

[142] 1599 *Ratio*, "to the Sacred Heart of Jesus" lacking.

XXVIII. *Rules for the Academy of the Class of Rhetoric and Humanities*

1. Once a week, or at least every fortnight, on a day and in a place designated[143] by the rector of the college, members shall assemble; the moderator[144] of the academy should always be present.

2. The program for this academy,[145] which should be varied from time to time should be about as follows: (1) Someone may read a selection from the more advanced precepts of oratory or poetry and make observations thereon as his ingenuity may suggest, illustrating it by examples from the classics. (2) A declamation of oratorical[146] or poetical passages may be given, which the audience may criticize from the viewpoint of voice, gesture, or the general delivery. (3) A prelection may be given on striking passages from the Greek, Latin, and vernacular classics. (4) Readings of original work or imitations of a classic, such as letters, descriptions, narratives, speeches, inscriptions, symbolic devices,[147] and verses. (5) General discussion of a disputed point by the members; solution of a difficulty pertaining to classwork, after giving the reasons *pro* and *contra;* or the institution of a moot court, one group acting for the defendant, the other for the plaintiff, and a judge to give the decision. (6) Reading of oratorical analysis, not, of course, dry and jejune, but written out beforehand in a finished style; or else if not written out, delivered after some preparation. (7) Exercises in oratorical invention, by way of proof or refutation of some proposition either after preparation or impromptu; or again in arranging a speech, putting the proofs and the persuasive passages in proper order; or else exercises in delivery, fitting figures of speech to the material used. (8) Writing compositions of various types in accord with the rhetorical precepts. (9) Books may be distributed among the members from which sentences should not merely be written out and read, but also illustrated and commented upon. Finally they should have practice in anything which tends to foster eloquence or its effects. The moderator may occasionally con-

---

[143]1599 *Ratio:* "On Sundays or when it is more convenient on the weekly holiday, in a place, etc., . . . shall assemble."

[144]*Ibid.*, "the moderator . . . present" lacking. The moderator was usually a Jesuit master.

[145]*Ibid.*, "the program for this academy will be about as follows: The moderator, according to his discretion, will give a reading or propose questions from some select material or from some classic; sometimes he will give some rather advanced precept from Aristotle, Cicero, or the other rhetorical writers."

[146]1599 *Ratio:* "Sometimes he runs rapidly through a passage in an author and questions the members upon it, sometimes he gives them difficulties to solve and the like."

[147]Literally, emblems (Lat., *emblemata*), symbolic devices illustrated with verses or mottoes.

tribute to the program himself, and he should always guide the proceedings.[148]

3. Three[149] or four times a year it will be worth while for the moderator of the academy to have the more important of these programs given with some external formality before an invited audience.

4. From time to time,[150] prizes may be given to those who distinguish themselves in these programs; the prizes should be secured through contributions from the members or in whatever way the rector of the college sees fit.

5. At least once a year, some feast of the Blessed Virgin or the patron saint of the college should be chosen by the rector of the college as a day of special celebration; on this day, the members of the academy give speeches or read poems, or have verses, devices, and various insignia displayed on the wall.

XXIX. *Rules for the Academy of Grammar Students*

1. Generally the moderator should run through some passage in the grammar, not yet seen in class, or read something from a well-written and interesting book, or have[151] an exercise on what has already been seen in class.

2. At the beginning of the meeting one of the members must be prepared to recount the proceedings of the last meeting. Two or more of the others can propose difficulties to him, or give him expressions in the vernacular to translate into Latin or *vice versa*.[152] In the same way, the prelection given by the moderator to the academy may be repeated.

3. Often[153] there shall be contests between the members of the academy. Sometimes there should be exercises in [Latin] style, sometimes memoriter work, casting of phrases in various forms; again, there may be exercises in translation[154] or Greek grammar and many things of the same sort, according to the discretion of the moderator.

4. Now and then, some or even all may come prepared to recite a short epigram or narrate an historical tale.

---

[148] Rule 3 in the 1599 *Ratio* differs but little in phraseology from the Rule 2 in the 1832 *Ratio*, section 2 to the end.

[149] 1599 *Ratio:* "Three or four times a year" lacking.

[150] *Ibid.*, "(5) Private prizes should sometimes be awarded to those writing the best essays or delivering the best recitation, or solving problems and puzzles." "(6) More formal prizes can be given once a year to all the members of the academy; the prizes should be secured," etc., *ut supra* Rule 4.

[151] 1599 *Ratio:* "a repetition and . . ."

[152] *Ibid.*, "*vice versa*" lacking.

[153] *Ibid.*, "Often there shall be zealous contests," etc.

[154] *Ibid.*, "exercises in versification."

5. Occasionally they may repeat the prelections given by the master in class, adding a little formal introduction and some remarks, if it seems fitting.

6. Occasionally it will be worth while to have the members of the academy, and especially the moderator, give a formal prelection with some external solemnity and before invited guests; a contest between two or three members may be added, and some prizes may be awarded, if desirable.

7. The moderator may, if he wishes, assign as punishment some literary exercise and have the names of those who have performed poorly or without due preparation read out publicly.

8. Finally, such exercises should be assigned in sufficient variety as have besides their utility the additional value of combining pleasure and interest so that the members of the academy may joyfully and whole-heartedly draw therefrom a keen interest in their studies.

BIBLIOGRAPHY

BIBLIOGRAPHY

I. Primary Sources

Acta Romana Societatis Jesu (Romae, 1906). Published privately.

An official digest of ecclesiastical legislation, decrees, etc., affecting the Society.

Acta Sanctorum Julii, Tomus VII (Venetiis, 1759), xviii + 916 pp.

Contains the Bollandists' life of Ignatius.

American Catholic Historical Researches, Vols. I–XXI (July, 1884–Oct., 1904); New series, Vols. I–VIII (Jan., 1905–July, 1912) (Pittsburgh, 1884–6; Philadelphia, 1887–1912).

ARCHAMBAULT, FR., *Notes on the Ratio Studiorum* (Woodstock, Md., 1889), 60 pp.

An explanation of the *Ratio* for the American Jesuit scholastics. Published privately.

BELGIAN PROVINCE S.J., *Essais Pédagogiques.* Lithographed (n. d., but *circa* 1880), Vols. I–V.

These contain practical suggestions for Jesuit masters in the various classes. Detailed instructions for teaching French and Flemish.

BUFFALO, N. Y. *Canisius College Archives.*

Contains material relative to the German Jesuits who came to America to found the Buffalo Mission.

CALIFORNIA PROVINCE S.J., *Catalogus Provinciae Californiae.* Published privately.

An annual register of each college and house of this province, with a list of the Jesuit personnel, their occupation, etc.

CALIFORNIA PROVINCE, Catalogues of the various high schools of the Califoria Province.

CASAGRANDE, SALVATOR, *De Claris Sodalibus Provinciae Taurinensis Societatis Jesu Commentarii* (Turin, 1906), xii + 334 pp.

Biographical sketches of some of the prominent members of the Turin Province.

Catholic Almanac. See *Catholic Directory.*

Catholic Directory.

The first directory was issued in 1817 under the title of *The Catholic Almanac.* The second in 1822 as *The Laity's Directory.* Beginning with 1833, it appeared annually, with its list of churches, schools, priests, etc. A complete collection is in the Riggs' Library, Georgetown University.

"Collectio decretorum Congregationis Generalis XXVII," *Acta Romana Societatis Jesu* (1923), pp. 37 ff.

Constitutiones Societatis Jesu Latinae et Hispanicae cum earum declarationibus (Madrid, 1892). Ed. P. de la Torre, xiv + 420 pp.

The authentic Spanish and Latin version of the Constitutions. That part of the Constitutions which deals with education can be found in Pachtler, I, 9–69, q. v.

CORCORAN T., S.J., *Renatae Litterae saeculo a Chr. XVI in scholis Societatis Jesu stabilitae* (Dublin: National University, 1927), xv + 383 pp.

An excellent source book for the study of Jesuit education. Contains the significant material pertaining to the lower schools in the three *Ratios* (1586, 1591, 1599), together with excerpts from the *Monumenta Paedagogica.*

COUPLET, P., *Mémoire contre le Projet des Modifications à Introduire dans notre Ancien Ratio Studiorum* (Amiens, 1862), lithographed, 85 pp.

A protest from a French Jesuit against any modification of the *Ratio.*

Decreta Congregationum Generalium, in Pachtler, I, 70–125.

The General Congregation is the legislative assembly of the Order. All the decrees bearing on education are in Pachtler, *loc. cit.*

Decreta Vigesimae Quintae Congregationis Generalis a Restituta Societate Sextae (Romae, 1906), 46 pp.

Pachtler's book was published before the convening of this Congregation.

Der Jesuiten Perpina, Bonifacius, und Possevin ausgewählte pädagogische Schriften. Uebersetzt von J. Stier, H. Scheid, G. Fell, S.J., in *Bibliothek der Katholischen Pädagogik,* Vol. XI (Freiburg i. Breisgau: Herder, 1901), x + 564 pp.

A German translation of the pedagogical writings of three sixteenth-century Jesuits. See *Perpinan.*

Der Jesuiten Sacchini, Juvencius und Kropf Erläuterungsschriften zur Studienordnung der Gesellschaft Jesu. Uebersetzt von J. Stier, R. Schwickerath, F. Zorell, S.J., in *Bibliothek der Katholischen Pädagogik,* Vol. X (Freiburg i. B.: Herder, 1898), xii + 470 pp.

A German translation of the pedagogical writings of Sacchini (1570–1625), Jouvancy (1643–1719), and Kropf (1694–1746), q. v.

DEVITT, E. I., S.J., *Notes on Georgetown College.*

A manuscript in the *Georgetown Archives,* Washington, D. C.,

DEVITT, E. I., S.J., *History of the Maryland-New York Province.* A manuscript in the *Georgetown Archives.*

EBNER, RUPERT, S.J., *Officielle ungedruckte Briefe von Jesuiten-Generalen und Provinzialen und Missbrauch derselben* (Innsbruck, 1883), viii + 432 pp.

Epistolae Praepositorum Generalium ad Patres et Fratres Societatis Jesu. Tom. IV, Editio altera (Rollarii, 1909).

Epistolae Selectae Praepositorum Generalium ad Superiores Societatis. (Romae: Typis Polyglottis Vaticanis, 1911), 342 pp.

Both of these collections of letters of the generals are for private circulation.

Epistolae S. P. Ignatii. See *Monumenta Historica.*

Epitome Instituti Societatis Jesu ad Usum Nostrorum Tantum. Editio minor (Romae, 1924), xx + 396 + 127 pp.

The official summary of Jesuit legislation for members of the Order.

FOLEY, HENRY, S.J., *Records of the English Province of the Society of Jesus.*

Transcripts of original documents, official reports, letters, etc., relative to the members of the English Province during the sixteenth, seventeenth, and eighteenth centuries, including all the extant documents in the English Province Archives that pertain to the *Missio Marilandica.* Twelve series in five volumes, with a supplementary sixth volume on the English College in Rome, and two further volumes, No. VII in two parts, containing general statistics, biographical notices, etc. (London, 1877–1883).

Forty Years in the United States of America, by the late Reverend Augustus J. Thebaud. Edited by C. G. Herbermann (New York, 1904), 363 pp. *U. S. Catholic Historical Monographs,* Vol. III of "Three-Quarters of a Century (1807–1882): A retrospect written from documents and memory in 1882 or the following year by the late Rev. Augustus J. Thebaud, S.J."

GEORGETOWN, WASHINGTON, D. C. *Georgetown University Archives.*

A very valuable collection of documents and transcripts.

Institutum Societatis Jesu. Volumen Primum (Romae, 1869), xiii + 607 pp.

Contains the Constitutions, decrees of General Congregations, etc. This volume contains the *Pars Quarta* of the Constitutions, which treats of the educational policy of the Order.

Institutum Societatis Jesu. Volumen Primum. Bullarium et Compendium Privilegiorum (Florentiae, 1892), xvi + 684 pp.

This volume contains all the papal pronouncements, bulletins, etc., regarding the Order.

Jesuit Relations and Allied Documents. Edited by Reuben G. Thwaites. 73 volumes (Cleveland: Burrows Bros., 1896–1901).

JOUVANCY, J., S.J., *Josephi Juvencii Ratio discendi et docendi.* (Parisiis: apud J. Barbou, 1778), 240 pp.

Probably the best-known Jesuit pedagogical document after the *Ratio.* Père Jouvancy was a prolific writer; de Backer gives him 15 columns in his *Bibliothèque,* and Sommervogel, 29. A complete German translation of this document will be found in the *Bibliothek der Katholischen Pädagogik,* Vol. X; a large part of it is found in the *Thesaurus Spiritualis Magistrorum,* q. v.

KROPF, F. X., S.J., *Ratio et Via recte atque ordine Procedendi in Literis Humanioribus aetati tenerae tradendis* (Munich, 1736).

Kropf's work under the title *Gymnasial-Pädagogik* is in the *Bibliothek der Katholischen Pädagogik,* Vol. X. It is a very detailed account of both the method and material of teaching together with a day-to-day horarium. A faithful picture of pedagogical procedure in the German Jesuit schools during the eighteenth century.

Laity's Directory. See *Catholic Directory.*

"Leaves from an Old Diary," *Canisius Monthly,* Vol. III, No. 2.

Transcript of a diary kept by one of the founders of Canisius College, Buffalo.

Liber Saecularis historiae Societatis Jesu ab anno 1814 ad annum 1914. Edited by P. Albers, S.J. (Rome, 1914), xxi + 642 pp.

A brief summary of the history of the Order during the century following its restoration. For private circulation only.

MCELROY, FR., *Diary.*

A Manuscript in the *Maryland-New York Province Archives.* Father McElroy was one of the pioneers of this province.

Manuel des Jeunes Professeurs (Paris, 1842), 588 pp.

A manual compiled for Jesuit masters and widely used, not only in France, but in America also. It contains:

a) Observations relatives à la bonne tenue d'un pensionnat.
b) P. Sacchini's (q. v.) Paraenesis ad magistros scholarum inferiorum Societatis Jesu.
c) P. Sacchini's Protrepticon ad magistros, etc.
d) P. Le Gaudier's De recto modo agendi nostrorum cum . . . convictoribus.
e) P. Judde's Instruction pour les jeunes professeurs.
f) Instructio pro magistris Societatis Jesu.
g) Ratio studiorum pro scholis inferioribus Societatis Jesu.

MARYLAND, *A Compleat Collection of the Laws of Maryland* (Annapolis, 1727).

Contains the penal laws enforced against Catholics.

MARYLAND, *Will-books* in the Office of the Register of Wills, Annapolis, Md. *Liber I.*

MARYLAND-NEW YORK PROVINCE, *Archives of the Maryland-New York Province.*

These archives are at Fordham University, New York. Transcripts of many important documents are in the *Georgetown Archives.*

MARYLAND-NEW YORK PROVINCE, *The Ancient Classical Languages.* Syllabus for high schools (Boston, 1924), 38 pp. Privately published.

MARYLAND-NEW YORK PROVINCE, *Biology Syllabus for High Schools* (Boston, 1923), 43 pp. Published privately.

MARYLAND-NEW YORK PROVINCE, *Catalogus Missionis Americae Foederatae.*

The annual catalogue with the Jesuit personnel of each college, their teaching duties, etc., 1807–1810, compiled from old records and reprinted in *Woodstock Letters,* Vol. XVI, pp. 169 ff., 308 ff; Vol. XVII, pp. 238 ff.; 312 ff. 1824–1833 are in manuscript in the *Woodstock College Archives.*

MARYLAND-NEW YORK PROVINCE, *Catalogus Provinciae Marylandiae.*

The years 1834, 1838 in manuscript at Woodstock College. 1846 lithographed. The other years printed. The Maryland schools were united with the New York schools in 1879 forming the Maryland-New York Province in 1879.

MARYLAND-NEW YORK PROVINCE, *Catalogus Provinciae Marylandiae-Neo-Eboracensis* (1880–).

MARYLAND-NEW YORK PROVINCE, Catalogues of the various schools of the Maryland-New York Province.

Georgetown, Fordham, Holy Cross are the most important. Unfortunately Georgetown issued only prospectuses until 1851.

MARYLAND-NEW YORK PROVINCE, *English Composition and Literature.* Syllabus for high schools (Boston, 1923), 43 pp. Published privately.

MARYLAND-NEW YORK PROVINCE, *History Syllabus for High Schools and Colleges* (Boston, 1926), 53 pp. Published privately.

MARYLAND-NEW YORK PROVINCE, *Physics Syllabus for High Schools* (Boston, 1925), 29 pp. Published privately.

MARYLAND-NEW YORK PROVINCE, *Proceedings of General Committee on Studies of the Maryland-New York Province* (April, 1908), Manuscript in *Georgetown Archives.*

MARYLAND-NEW YORK PROVINCE, *Relatio Patrum Deputatorum Provinciae Marylandiae Neo-Eboracensis pro Studiis Scholasticorum Ordinandis* (Feb. 21, 1910).

A document published privately, in the *Missouri Province Archives.* An official report of the delegates of Maryland-New York Province on the proposed modifications in the course of studies for the scholastics of the Society.

MARYLAND-NEW YORK PROVINCE, *Report of the Meeting of the Committee for the Revision of the Schedule of Studies of 1910 held at Georgetown University* (May 17, 1921).

Manuscript in *Georgetown Archives.*

MARYLAND-NEW YORK PROVINCE, *Revised Program of Studies for the Colleges of the Maryland-New York Province, 1923* (Boston, 1923), 26 pp. Published privately.

MARYLAND-NEW YORK PROVINCE, *Revised Schedule of Studies for the Maryland-New York Province High Schools* (1905), In the *Georgetown Archives.*

MARYLAND-NEW YORK PROVINCE, *Schedule of Studies for the Colleges of the Maryland-New York Province* (1910), 24 pp. Published privately.

MARYLAND-NEW YORK PROVINCE, *A Summary of the Proceedings of the Commission appointed by Rev. Fr. Fulton, S.J., Provincial, to help toward Improving and Unifying the Studies in the Classes below Philosophy of the Colleges of the Maryland-New York Province* (Boston, 1888).

In the *Woodstock College Archives.*

MARYLAND-NEW YORK PROVINCE, *The Teacher's Review* (Woodstock, Md.: January, 1910), Vol. I.

A pedagogical journal, published privately by the Maryland-New York Province, for the use of American Jesuit teachers.

MAUNOURY, PÈRE, *Étude sur l'Enseignement Littéraire et le Ratio Studiorum de la Compagnie de Jésus* (Lons-le-Saunier, 1876), 88 pp. Lithographed.

A French Jesuit's study on the *Ratio.*

MISSOURI PROVINCE S.J., *Missouri Province Archives.*

Preserved at St. Louis University, St. Louis, Missouri.

MISSOURI PROVINCE S.J., *Animadversiones de ordinatione studiorum* (n. d., *circa* 1910).

The report of the Missouri Province on the new course of studies for the Jesuit scholastics.

MISSOURI PROVINCE S.J., *Catalogus Vice-Provinciae Missourianae* (1835–1862).

The annual catalogue listing the Jesuit personnel, their occupations, etc. The Missouri group of Jesuits began as a Mission dependent on the Maryland Mission; in 1831, it became an independent Mission; in 1835 a Vice-Province; in 1863 a Province.

MISSOURI PROVINCE S.J., *Catalogus Provinciae Missourianae* (1863–).

MISSOURI PROVINCE S.J., Catalogues of Jesuit schools and colleges of the Missouri Province. The most valuable are those of St. Louis University; a complete file is kept in the University Archives.

MISSOURI PROVINCE S.J., *Circular letters relative to Curriculum* (1916–1918).

Letters from the Provincial in the *Missouri Province Archives.*

MISSOURI PROVINCE S.J., *Circular letters relative to Course of Studies* 1910–1913).

In the *Missouri Province Archives.*

MISSOURI PROVINCE S.J., *The Classical Bulletin.* Published monthly by the Classical Association of the Missouri Province. (Cleveland, Ohio, 1923).

A periodical devoted to the interests of the classical teachers of the Missouri Province.

MISSOURI PROVINCE S.J., *Course of Studies for the Colleges of the Missouri Province* (July 31, 1893).

In the *Missouri Province Archives.*

MISSOURI PROVINCE S.J., *Course of Studies for the Colleges of the Missouri Province* (1911).

In the *Missouri Province Archives.*

MISSOURI PROVINCE S.J., *Documenta Scholaria.*

A collection of documents, reports, etc., relating to education in the Missouri Province schools (n. d.). In the *St. Louis University Archives.*

MISSOURI PROVINCE S.J., *General Report of Committee of Studies for the Missouri Province* (August, 1915).

In the *Missouri Province Archives.*

MISSOURI PROVINCE S.J., *The Jesuit Bulletin, an Illustrated Quarterly.* Published by the Missouri Province Educational Institute (St. Louis, 1921).

A magazine for the general public, intended largely to make known the activities of the Missouri Province Jesuits.

MISSOURI PROVINCE S.J., *Jesuit Educational Association: Mid-West Division. Proceedings of the Second Annual Convention* (Chicago, 1923), 185 pp.

MISSOURI PROVINCE S.J., *Jesuit Educational Association: Mid-West Division. Proceedings of the Third Annual Convention* (Prairie du Chien, Wis., 1924), 165 pp.

MISSOURI PROVINCE S.J., *Jesuit Educational Association: Mid-West Division. Proceedings of the Fourth Annual Convention* (Chicago, 1925), 282 pp.

MISSOURI PROVINCE S.J., *Memorial to Very Reverend Father General on the Question of Compulsory Greek* (1916).

A manuscript in the *Missouri Province Archives.*

MISSOURI PROVINCE S.J., *Missouri Province Teachers Association. Proceedings of the First Annual Convention* (Prairie du Chien, Wis., 1922), 148 pp.

MISSOURI PROVINCE S.J., *Notes on Departures from the Course of Studies* (n. d., *circa* 1915).

In the *Missouri Province Archives.*

MISSOURI PROVINCE S.J., *The Province News-Letter* (St. Louis, 1920).

A monthly chronicle of events in the Missouri Province. For private circulation.

MISSOURI PROVINCE S.J., *Relatio Patrum Deputatorum Provinciae Marylandiae Neo-Eboracensis et Missourianae pro Studiis Scholasticorum Ordinandis* (*n. d., circa,* 1910).

A report of the proceedings at the meeting of the delegates of the two provinces, Maryland-New York and Missouri to discuss the new course of studies for the scholastics of the Society. This document is in the *Missouri Province Archives.*

MISSOURI PROVINCE S.J., *Report of Central Committee of the Missouri Province* (1887).

In the *Missouri Province Archives.*

MISSOURI PROVINCE S.J., *Report of Committee of Studies of the Missouri Province* (1908).

In the *Missouri Province Archives.*

MISSOURI PROVINCE S.J., *Report of Meeting of Prefects of Studies at Campion College* (Prairie du Chien, Wis., 1915).

In the *Missouri Province Archives.*

MISSOURI PROVINCE S.J., *Report of the Meeting of the Presidents of the Jesuit Colleges of the Missouri Province* (April 2, 1917).

In the *Missouri Province Archives.*

MISSOURI PROVINCE S.J., *Report of the Meeting of the Rectors and Prefects of Studies of the Missouri Province held at St. Louis University* (June, 1920).

In the *Missouri Province Archives.*

MISSOURI PROVINCE S.J., *Report on Educational Policy* (*circa,* 1921).

A manuscript in the *Missouri Province Archives,* justifying the curricular changes that had taken place in the Missouri schools.

MISSOURI PROVINCE S.J., *Reports of Committees on the Working of the Course of Studies in the Missouri Province* (1915).

In the *Missouri Province Archives.*

MISSOURI PROVINCE S.J., *Supplement to the Course of Studies of 1911* (St. Louis, 1911). Published privately.

Mittheilungen aus der Deutschen Provinz. Als Manuskript gedruckt. Nur für Unsrigen (Roermond, 1895).

A chronicle of Jesuit activity in the German Provinces and Missions, including the Buffalo Mission in the United States.

Monumenta Historica Societatis Jesu:

I. *Vita Ignatii Loyolae et rerum Societatis Jesu Historia. Auctore Joanne Alph. Polanco ejusdem Societatis sacerdote* 6 vols. (Madrid, 1894–1898). Cited as *Chronicon Soc. Jesu.*

II. *Scripta de Sancto Ignatio* (Madrid, 1904).

III. *Monumenta Paedagogica Societatis Jesu quae primam Rationem Studiorum anno 1586 editam praecessere* (Madrid, 1901).

IV. *Sancti Ignatii de Loyola Societatis Jesu Fundatoris Epistolae et Instructiones,* 11 vols. (Madrid, 1903–1911).

V. *Epistolae Mixtae ex variis Europae locis ab anno 1537 ad 1556 scriptae nunc primum a patribus Soc. Jesu in lucem editae,* 5 vols. (Madrid, 1898–1901).

VI. *Litterae quadrimestres ex universis praeter Indiam et Brasiliam locis in quibus aliqui de Soc. Jesu versabantur Romam missae 1546–1556,* 4 vols. (Madrid, 1894–1897).

NEW ORLEANS PROVINCE, *Catalogus Provinciae Neo-Aurelianensis.*

A list of Jesuit personnel and their occupations in the various colleges of this Province. Before 1881, the members were listed in the Lyons Province *catalogus* to which they then belonged.

NEW ORLEANS PROVINCE, *Report of the Committee on the Revision of Studies* (July, 1913).

A manuscript in the *New Orleans Province Archives.*

NEW YORK, *Documentary History of the State of New York,* 4 vols. Edited by E. B. O'Callagahan. Vol. II (Albany, 1850), 711 pp.

NEW YORK, *Documents Relative to the Colonial History of the State of New York.* Vol. IV. Edited by J. R. Brodhead (Albany, 1854), xix + 1192 pp.

NEW YORK, *Ecclesiastical Records of the State of New York.* Published by the state under the supervision of Hugh Hastings, State Historian. Vol. II (Albany, 1901), xxviii + 1442 pp.

Notizie Storiche e Descrittive delle Missioni della Provincia Torinese della Compagnia di Gesù nell' America del Nord (Torino: Derossi, 1898), xv + 47 + 51 pp.

An account of Jesuit activity in the Western States. The Jesuit pioneers in this region were members of the Turin (Italy) Province.

Ordinatio Studiorum in Assistentia Angliae (May 16, 1912).

Outline of studies prescribed for the Jesuit scholastics in the English Assistancy, to which the American Provinces belonged at this date. In the *Missouri Province Archives.*

ORLANDINUS, *Historiae Societatis Jesu Pars Prima sive Ignatius.* Auctore Nicolao Orlandino (Antwerp, 1620).

The first history of the Society.

PACHTLER, G. M., S.J., *Ratio Studiorum et Institutiones Scholasticae Societatis Jesu per Germaniam olim vigentes,* 4 vols. (Berlin, Hofmann, 1887–1894).

Tomus I. Ab anno 1541 ad annum 1599 (Berlin, 1887), liii × 460 pp.

Tomus II. Ratio studiorum ann. 1586, 1599, 1832 (Berlin, 1887), vii + 524 pp.

Tomus III. Ordinationes Generalium et Ordo Studiorum Generalium ab anno 1600 ad annum 1772 (Berlin, 1890), xviii + 486 pp.

Tomus IV. Complectens monumenta quae pertinent ad gymnasia, convictus (1600–1773) itemque ad rationem studiorum (anno 1832) recognitam adornavit ediditque Bernhard Duhr, S.J. (Berlin, 1894), xviii + 621 pp.

These are Vols. II, V, IX, and XVI of *Monumenta Germaniae Paedagogica,* edited by Dr. Karl Kehrbach.

PERPINAN, PEDRO JUAN, S.J., *De ratione liberorum instituendorum literis graecis et latinis.* Litt. XVI in Tomus III of *Petri Joannis Perpiniani Valentini e Soc. Jesu Opera* (Romae, 1749).

This particular document, a method of studies before the appearance of the *Ratio,* is published in full in the *Woodstock Letters,* Vol. XXII (1893), p. 257. The original appeared in 1565.

Praelectiones Scholasticae pro Suprema Grammatices Classe, faciliore atque amoeniore methodo adornatae in usum gymnasiorum Societatis Jesu ad Rhenum Inferiorem (Coloniae: apud Hilgerum Hamecher et Ludovicum Schorn, 1761) 525 pp.

An eighteenth-century Jesuit textbook, containing all the matter taught in the highest grammar class, Latin, Greek, German, arithmetic, catechism.

PONTANUS, JACOBUS, *Jacobi Pontani de Societate Jesu Progymnasmatum Latinitatis sive Dialogorum Volumen Secundum, cum Adnotationibus de Morum Perfectione. Editio decima nona castigatior.* Cum Privilegio Sacrae Caesareae Majestatis et Facultate Superiorum. (Augustae Vindelicorum: sumptibus Mathiae Wolff, 1635).

A collection of one hundred dialogues in Latin on various subjects relating to school and home life for the use of pupils in the German Jesuit schools. The Latinity is excellent; the book illustrates the emphasis placed on Latin conversation at this period. It also throws interesting sidelights on contemporary school life.

Ratio Atque Institutio Studiorum Per Sex Patres Ad id Jussu R. P. Praepositi Generalis deputatos conscripta (Romae: in Collegio Societatis Jesu, 1586).

The first *Ratio*. The entire text in Pachtler, *op. cit.*, II, 25 ff.

Ratio Atq. Institutio Studiorum (Romae: In Collegio Soc. Jesu, 1591), 332 pp.

Ratio atque Institutio Studiorum Societatis Jesu (Neapoli, 1599), 208 pp.

The final *Ratio,* the norm for Jesuit schools until the early nineteenth century. Entire text in Pachtler, *op. cit.*, II, 226 ff.

Ratio atque Institutio Studiorum Societatis Jesu (Parisiis: apud Firmin-Didot Fratres, 1850), xii + 156 pp.

Roothaan's *Ratio* of 1832. Text in Pachtler, *loc. cit.* See also Appendix to this book.

Ratio Discendi et Docendi pro Magistris Scholarum Inferiorum (Avignon: Seguin, 1825), 132 pp.

Excerpts from Père Jouvancy's book, q. v.

Records of the American Catholic Historical Society of Philadelphia (Philadelphia, 1884).

Regeln und Consuetudinarium des Pensionats Stella Matutina zu Feldkirch (Feldkirch, Austria, *circa* 1868). Lithographed. 102 pp.

Customs, etc., for the guidance of the prefects at the Feldkirch school. Probably used in the boarding schools conducted by the German Jesuits in the United States. In the *Canisius College Archives,* Buffalo.

Sacchini, F., S.J. *Paraenesis ad Magistros Scholarum Inferiorum S.J.* (Romae, 1625).

Sacchini, F., S.J., *Protrepticon ad Magistros Scholarum Inferiorum S.J.* (Romae, 1625).

These two pedagogical treatises of Sacchini (1570–1625) have always been held in high esteem by the Order. The Latin text is in the *Manuel des Jeunes Professeurs* (q. v.): and a German translation in Vol. X of the *Bibliothek der Katholischen Pädagogik.* The first treatise is translated under the title "Praktische Winke für Gymnasiallehrer aus der Gesellschaft Jesu"; the second, under the title. "Worte der Ermunterung an die Gymnasiallehrer aus der Gesellschaft Jesu."

Sadlier's Catholic Directory. See *Catholic Directory.*

San Francisco, *St. Ignatius College Archives.*

Santa Clara, California, *Santa Clara College Archives.*

Thesaurus Spiritualis Magistrorum Scholarum Inferiorum Societatis Jesu (Gandavi: e prelo C. Poelman, 1874), 370 pp.

A book, similar to the *Manuel des Jeunes Professeurs* (q. v.), for the use of Jesuit teachers. Contains a large part of Père Jouvancy's classic *Ratio discendi et docendi.*

United States Catholic Almanac or *Laity's Directory.* See *Catholic Directory.*

United States Catholic Historical Magazine (Philadelphia, 1887).

Published as a quarterly from 1887 to 1892; later in the form of periodical volumes, called *Historical Records and Studies.*

VASCO, ENRICO, S.J., *Il Ratio Studiorum adattato ai tempi presenti ossia esposizione ragionata di alcune modificazioni che salva la sostanza del Ratio Studiorum portrebbero introdursi nell' insegnamento letterario dei nostri collegi d'Italia affine di renderlo piu' efficace nell' ottenere lo scopo delle nostre constituzioni proposta all' esame e al giudizio dei superiori e dei padri della Compagnia di Gesù dal P. Enrico Vasco della medesima Compagnia* (Roma: Presso La Civiltà Cattolica, 1851), 4 vols. Vol. I, xviii + 216 pp.; Vol. II, 140 pp.; Vol. III, 338 pp.; Vol. IV, 340 pp.

An Italian Jesuit's attempt to adapt the *Ratio* of 1832 to the needs of his time. This work was printed for private circulation among members of the Order.

Woodstock Letters — A Record of Current Events and Historical Notes connected with the Colleges and Missions of the Society of Jesus (Woodstock, Md.; published privately three times a year, 1872–).

An invaluable collection of records relating to Jesuit colleges in America, transcript of official documents relating to pioneer days in the American provinces, statistics, letters, etc.

II. Other Works Cited in the Text

ADAMSON, JOHN WILLIAM, *A Short History of Education* (Cambridge: Cambridge University Press, 1919), xi + 371 pp.

ADAMSON, JOHN WILLIAM, *Pioneers of Modern Education*, 1600–1700 (Cambridge: Cambridge University Press, 1905), xxii + 285 pp.

APPEL, BENEDIKT, *Das Bildungs–und Erziehungsideal Quintilians nach der Institutio Oratoria* (Donauwörth: L. Auer, 1914), 95 pp.

ASTRAIN, A., S.J., *Historia de la Compania de Jesús en la Asistencia de España*, 7 vols. (Madrid: 1902–1920).

BACKER, AUGUSTIN DE, S.J., *Bibliothèque des Écrivains de la Compagnie de Jésus*, 3 vols. (Paris, 1869–1876).

This bibliography of Jesuit writers was continued by Sommervogel, q. v.

BAINVEL, PÈRE, S.J., *Causeries Pédagogiques* (Paris, 1898), vii + 360 pp.

Talks given to Jesuit scholastics before entering on their work of teaching.

Barbier, Père, *La discipline dans quelques écoles libres. Manuel pratique du surveillant* (Amiens, 1884), vi + 156 pp.

A French Jesuit view of discipline, especially for a boarding school.

Barrett, E. Boyd, *The New Psychology* (New York: P. J. Kenedy, 1925), x + 358 pp.

Psychology from the Neo-Scholastic viewpoint.

Biever, Albert H., S.J., *The Jesuits in New Orleans and the Mississippi Valley* (New Orleans, 1924), 173 pp.

Blakely, Paul, S.J., "The Catholic College and the College for Catholics," *America*, Vol. XXXVI, No. 17 (Feb. 5, 1927), pp. 406 ff.

Blakely, Paul, S.J., "What is a Catholic Education?" *Catholic Educational Association Bulletin*, Vol. XXIII, No. 1 (Nov., 1926), pp. 70–81.

Bode, Boyd H., *Fundamentals of Education* (New York: The Macmillan Co., 1921), xi + 245 pp.

Boehmer, H., *Les Jésuites.* Trad. de l'allemand par G. Monod. (Paris: Colin, 1910), lxxxiv + 304 pp.

An attempt at impartial history but frequently inaccurate. Monod's introduction brings up some of the traditional, often refuted, Jesuit fables.

Boehmer, H., *Studien zur Geschichte der Gesellschaft Jesu. I Band: Loyola* (Bonn: Falkenroth, 1914), vi + 344 + 104 pp.

A great improvement on his earlier work. Well documented. Impartial.

Boyle, Esmeralda, *Biographical Sketches of Distinguished Marylanders* (Baltimore, 1877), 374 pp.

Boysse, E., *Le Théâtre des Jésuites* (Paris, 1880), 370 pp.

Bray, Rev. Thomas, *Reverend Thomas Bray: His Life and Selected Works Relating to Maryland.* Edited by B. C. Steiner (Baltimore, 1901), 252 pp.

Broderick, James, S.J., *The Life and Works of Blessed Francis Bellarmine* (New York: P. J. Kenedy, 1928), 2 vols.

Brown, Elmer E., *The Making of Our Middle Schools, an Account of the Development of Secondary Education in the United States* (New York: Longmans, Green and Co., 1924), 547 pp.

Brucker, Jos., S.J., *La Compagnie de Jésus. Esquisse de son Institut et de son Histoire, 1521–1773* (Paris: Beauchesne, 1919), viii + 842 pp.

Burger, Otto, *Erasmus von Rotterdam und der Spanier Vives: Eine Pädagogische Studie* (München: Kosel, 1914), 80 pp.

Burns, James A., *Catholic Education: A Study of Conditions* (New York: Longmans, Green and Co., 1917), ix + 205 pp.

BURNS, JAMES A., "Early Jesuit Schools in Maryland," *Catholic University Bulletin,* XIII (1908), 363 ff.

BURNS, JAMES A., *Growth and Development of the Catholic School System in the United States* (New York: Benziger Bros., 1912), 421 pp.

BURROWES, A. J., S.J., *Why Study Latin and Greek?* (Milwaukee: n. d., *circa* 1905), 32 pp.

CAMPBELL, THOMAS, S.J., *The Jesuits* (New York: The Encyclopedia Press, 1921), xvi + 936 pp.

The Catholic Historical Review (Washington, 1915). Vols. I–VI, old series (April, 1915–1921); new series, Vol. I (April, 1921).

The Catholic University Bulletin, Published quarterly by the Catholic University of America (Washington, 1895–).

CHOSSAT, MARCEL, S.J., *Les Jésuites et Leurs Oeuvres à Avignon, 1553–1768* (Avignon: Seguin et Cie., 1896), xiv + 524 pp.

A thoroughly scientific piece of historical research, relative to the Jesuit College at Avignon. Out of print.

The Classical Investigation Conducted by the Advisory Committee of the American Classical League. Part One. General Report (Princeton: Princeton University Press, 1924), 305 pp.

CLINCH, BRYAN J., "The Jesuits in American California," *Records of the American Catholic Historical Society,* XVII, 64 ff.

The College of St. Francis Xavier: A Memorial and a Retrospect, 1847–1897 (New York, 1897). 273 pp.

COMPAYRÉ, GABRIEL, *Histoire de la Pédagogie* (Paris, 1901), 491 pp.

COMPAYRÉ, GABRIEL, *The History of Pedagogy.* Translated by W. H. Payne (Boston: Heath and Co., 1899), xxvi + 598 pp.

COMPAYRÉ GABRIEL, *Histoire Critique des Doctrines de l'Éducation en France depuis le XVI siècle,* 5e. edit., 2 vol. (Paris, 1885).

All of Compayré's writings betray anti-Jesuit bias.

COPPENS, CHARLES, S.J., "The Spirit of Jesuit Education," *The Teacher's Review,* Vol. VI, No. 2 (April, 1915), pp. 25 ff.

CORCORAN, T., S.J., "Rational Aids for Readers of Latin," *The Classical Bulletin,* Vol. II, No. 5 (Feb., 1926), pp. 33 ff.

CORCORAN, T., S.J., "Rational Aids for Writers of Latin," *The Classical Bulletin,* Vol. II, No. 6, (March, 1926), pp. 49 ff.

CORCORAN, T., S.J., *Studies in the History of Classical Teaching* (New York Benziger Bros., 1911). xviii + 306 pp.

CRETINEAU-JOLY, M. J., *Histoire Religieuse, Politique et Littéraire de la Compagnie de Jésus.* 6 vols. (Paris: Mellier Frères, 1846).

A highly eulogistic account of Jesuit activity.

CRIVELLI, C., "Mexico," *The Catholic Encyclopedia,* X, 259 ff.

DANIEL, CHARLES, S.J., *Les Jésuites Instituteurs de la Jeunesse Française au XVIIe et au XVIIIe siècle* (Paris: V. Palme, 1880), 306 pp.

DARIS, JOSEPH, *Histoire du Diocèse et de la Principauté de Liège Pendant le XVI siècle* (Liège, 1884), xxvi + 712 pp.

The Dauphin, published by the students of the St. Louis Academy, St. Louis, Vol. II (1923).

DAVIS, CALVIN OLIN, *Public Secondary Education* (Chicago: Rand-McNally Co., 1917). xiv + 270 pp.

DECORME, GERHARDO, "Catholic Education in Mexico," *The Catholic Historical Review,* II, 168 ff.

DE COURCY, M., *The Catholic Church in the United States.* Translated by John Gilmary Shea. (New York, 1856), 591 pp.

DENIFLE, H., *Die Universitäten des Mittelalters bis 1400* (Berlin, 1885), I Bd., xiv + 814 pp.

DEVITT, E. I., S.J., "Bohemia," *Records of the American Catholic Historical Society,* Vol. XXIII, No. 2 (June, 1915) pp. 97–139.

An account of Jesuit activity at Bohemia, Md., in colonial days.

DEXTER, EDWIN GRANT *A History of Education in the United States* (New York: Macmillan and Co., 1919), xxii + 656 pp.

Directory of Catholic Colleges and Schools for 1926 (Washington: N. C. W. C. Bureau of Education, 1926), 544 pp.

DONNELLY, FRANCIS P., S.J., *Model English,* Book I, 1919; Book II, 1920 (Boston: Allyn and Bacon Co.).

An English composition textbook, widely used in American Jesuit high schools.

DOWLING, M. P., S.J., *Creighton University: Reminiscences of the First Twenty-Five Years* (Omaha, 1903), 272 pp.

DUBOIS, JULES, *Le Problème Pédagogique. Essai sur la Position du Problème et la Rechêrche de ses Solutions* (Geneve: Kündig, 1910) viii + 538 pp.

A modern view of Jesuit education, not friendly, but relatively impartial.

DUHR, B., S.J., *Die Studienordnung der Gesellschaft Jesu mit einer Einleitung* (Freiburg i. Breisgau: Herder, 1896), ix + 286 pp. Vol. IX in *Bibliothek der katholischen Pädagogik.*

A translation of the *Ratio* with commentaries on Jesuit practice in the German schools of the Society.

DUHR, B., S.J., *Geschichte der Jesuiten in den Ländern Deutscher Zunge.* 3 vols. (München-Regensburg, 1907–1921).

The official history of the Order for the German-speaking provinces.

DUHR, B., S.J., *Jesuiten-Fabeln* (Freiburg i. Breisgau: Herder, 1892), viii + 832 pp.

Dunney, Joseph A., *The Parish School: Its Aims, Procedures and Problems* (New York: The Macmillan Co., 1921), xx + 326 pp.

Ebner, Rupert, S.J., *Beleuchtung der Schrift des Herrn Dr. Johann Kelle "Die Jesuiten-Gymnasien in Oesterreich"* (Linz, 1874), viii + 720 pp.

An answer to the strictures of Kelle on Jesuit education in Austria.

Encyklopädie des gesamten Erziehung und Unterrichtswesens. A. Lange, edit., Vol. XI (Gotha and Leipzig).

Fleischmann, I. K., "Jesuiten-Pädagogik, Jesuiten-Schulen," *Encyklopädisches Handbuch der Pädagogik,* IV Bd.

Ford, John J., "Education and Character," *Catholic Mind,* Vol. XV, No. 2 (Jan. 22, 1917), p. 42 f.

Fouqueray, H., S.J., *Histoire de la Compagnie de Jésus en France des origines à la suppresion, 1528–1762* (Paris: Picard et Fils, 1907–1910), 3 vols.

The official history for the French provinces.

Fournet, A., "Canada," *The Catholic Encyclopedia,* III, 232 ff.

Garraghan, Gilbert, S.J., *The Catholic Church in Chicago* (Chicago: Loyola University Press, 1921), x + 236 pp.

Garraghan, Gilbert, S.J., *The Jesuits in the Middle United States.*

A history of the Missouri Province. (In press.)

Golden Jubilee of Santa Clara College (Santa Clara, California, 1901), 64 pp.

Golden Jubilee of Santa Clara College and University. A History from the Founding of Santa Clara Mission to the beginning of the University (Santa Clara, 1912), 128 pp.

Gonzaga College: An Historical Sketch. From Its Foundation in 1821 to the Solemn Celebration of its First Centenary in 1921 (Washington, D. C.: published by the College, 1922), 390 pp.

Gonzaga's Silver Jubilee: A Memoir. (Spokane, Wash.: published by Gonzaga University, n. d., *circa* 1912).

Goodier, Alban, S.J., "The Society of Jesus and Education," *The Month,* CVIII (1906), 457 ff.; 585 ff.; CIX (1907), 8 ff.; 136 ff.; 391 ff.; CX (1908), 270 ff.

Gothein, Eberhard, *Ignatius von Loyola und die Gegenreformation* (Halle: Max Niemeyer, 1895), xii + 795 pp.

Frequently betrays bias; not well documented.

Graves, F. P., *History of Education During the Middle Ages* (New York: Macmillan, 1910), xv + 328 pp.

Grizzell, Emit Duncan, *Origin and Development of the High School in New England Before 1865* (New York: Macmillan Co., 1923), xv + 428 pp.

GRUGGEN, GEORGE, AND KEATING, JOSEPH, *Stonyhurst, its Past History and Life in the Present* (London: Kegan Paul, 1901), xii + 279 pp.

HERMAN, J. B., S.J., *La Pédagogie des Jésuites au XVIe siècle* (Louvain: Bureaux du Recueil, 1914), xviii + 336 pp.

The best study of the origins of Jesuit pedagogy and of its characteristics in the sixteenth century.

HILL WALTER H., S.J., "A Short Biographical Sketch of James Van de Velde," *Woodstock Letters,* VIII (1878), 65 ff.

HILL, WALTER H., S.J., *Historical Sketch of the St. Louis University* (St. Louis: Patrick Fox, 1879), x + 260 pp.

HILL, WALTER H., S.J., "Some Facts and Incidents Relating to St. Joseph's College, Bardstown, Kentucky." *Woodstock Letters,* XXVI (1896), 93 ff.

Historical Sketch of the College of the Holy Cross (Worcester, Mass., 1883), 44 pp.

HUGHES, THOMAS, S.J., *The History of the Society of Jesus in North America, Colonial and Federal* (New York: Longmans, Green and Co., 1907–1917). Text: Vol. I, 1907; Vol. II, 1917. Documents: Vol. I, Part I, 1908; Vol. I, Part II, 1910.

The author is the official historian of the Society for English North America.

HUGHES, THOMAS, S.J., *Loyola and the Educational System of the Jesuits* (New York: Scribner, 1892). The "Great Educators" series edited by Nicholas Murray Butler. ix + 302 pp.

HUGHES, THOMAS, S.J., "Properties of the Jesuits in Pennsylvania," *Records of the American Catholic Historical Society,* XI, 180 ff.

HULL, ERNEST, S.J., *Collapses in Adult Life* (St. Louis: Herder, 1920), 111 pp.

HULL, ERNEST, S.J., *Fortifying the Layman* (London: Catholic Truth Society, 1906), xi + 94 pp.

HULL, ERNEST, S.J., *Formation of Character* (St. Louis: Herder, 1910), 123 pp.

HULL, ERNEST, S.J., *God, Man, and Religion* (Bombay: Examiner Press, 1914), iv + 168 pp.

HULL, ERNEST, S.J., *Man's Great Concern: The Management of Life* (New York: Kenedy, 1920), xiii + 177 pp.

HULL, ERNEST, S.J., *Why Should I Be Moral?* (New York: Kenedy, n. d.), 2nd edition, 118 pp.

HYMA, ALBERT, *The Christian Renaissance: A History of the "Devotio Moderna"* (New York: Century Co., 1925), xviii + 501 pp.

A well-documented history of the Brethren of the Common Life and their influence. Sometimes exaggerates the influence of the Brethren, especially on the Society.

IRELAND, ARCHBISHOP JOHN, "Catholic Schools for Catholic Youth," *The Catholic Mind,* XIII, No. 14 (July 22, 1915), 382 ff.

"The Jesuits in Chicago," *The St. Ignatius Collegian,* V, No. 4 (July, 1906), 3 ff.

JAMES, WILLIAM, *Pragmatism.* (New York: Longmans, Green, 1908) xiii–309.

JONES, W. H. S., "Quintilian, Plutarch, and the Early Humanists," *The Classical Review,* XX (1907) 41 ff.

JOURDAIN, CHARLES, *Histoire de l'Université de Paris au XVII et au XVIII siècles.* 2 vols. (Paris, 1888).

KÄMMEL, H. J., *Geschichte des deutschen Schulwesens im Uebergang vom Mittelalter zur Neuzeit* (Leipzig, 1882).

KEMP, E. L., *History of Education* (Philadelphia: Lippincott, 1908). xiii + 385 pp.

KENNY, MICHAEL, S.J., *Catholic Culture in Alabama.* (New York: The America Press, 1931) 400 pp.

KER, PAUL, *Nos Doctrines Classiques Traditionelles* (Paris, 1921), ix + 389 pp.

KESSELER, K., *Das Lebenswerk der Grossen Pädagogen; Betrachtungen über die Entwicklung und Verwirklichung der Pädagogischen Ideen* (Leipzig und Berlin, 1913), vi + 137 pp.

KÖRNER, FRIEDRICH, *Geschichte der Pädagogik von den Altesten Zeiten bis zur Gegenwart* (Gera, 1886), viii + 388 pp.

LAURIE, S. S., *Studies in the History of Educational Opinion from the Renaissance* (Cambridge: University Press, 1903), vi + 260 pp.

LINGARD, J., *History of England,* Vol. X. 5th Edition. (London: Chas. Dolman, 1849) ix + 551 pp.

LOWELL, A. LAWRENCE, "The Art of Examination," *Atlantic Monthly,* CXXXVII, No. 1 (Jan., 1926), 58 ff.

LONERGAN, WM., S.J., "Another California Jubilee," *America,* XXXIV 1926), 563–5.

LONGRIDGE, W. H. *The Spiritual Exercises of St. Ignatius Loyola* (London: Robert Scott, 1922), xxxvi + 351 pp.

LUCAS, HERBERT, S.J., *At the Parting of the Ways,* 2nd Edition (London: Sands and Co., 1909), 317 pp.

LULL, HERBERT GALEN, "Inherited Tendencies of Secondary Instruction in the United States," *University of California Publications,* III, No. 3 (April, 1913), 155–281.

MACAULAY, THOMAS BABINGTON, *History of England from the Accession of James the Second,* 5th edition, 2 vols. (London, 1849).

MCGUIRE, E. J., "The Elgin Botanical Garden and the New York Literary Institute," *Historical Records and Studies,* IV, Part I and II, 332 ff.

McLaughlin, J. Fairfax, *College Days at Georgetown* (Philadelphia: Lippincott, 1899), 230 pp.

Maher, M., S.J., *Psychology,* 9th edition (London: Longmans, Green and Co., 1925), xv + 603 + xii pp.

Marquette College: A Quarter Century, 1881–1906. Stray Leaves from the College History (Milwaukee, 1906), 103 pp.

Meehan, Thomas F., "Catholic Literary New York," *The Catholic Historical Review,* IV (1918), 405 ff.

Memorial Volume of the Diamond Jubilee of St. Louis University, 1829–1904 (St. Louis, 1904), 330 pp.

Mertz, Dr. Georg, *Die Pädagogik der Jesuiten* (Heidelberg: Carl Winter, 1898), viii + 192 pp.

A doctoral dissertation, unfriendly to the Jesuits.

Meyer, F., *Der Ursprung des Jesuitischen Schulwesens* (Gräfenhainichen, 1904).

Meyer, Rudolph, S.J., *Science of the Saints,* 4th edition, 2 vols. (St. Louis: Herder, 1910).

Monroe, Paul, *Cyclopedia of Education,* 5 vols. (New York: Macmillan Co., 1911).

Mulkerins, Thomas, S.J., *History of Holy Family Parish — Church and People* (Chicago, 1923), xxiii + 980 pp.

Naumann, Dr. Viktor ("Pilatus"), *Der Jesuitismus. Eine kritische Würdigung der Grundsätze, Verfassung, und geistigen Entwicklung der Gesellschaft Jesu mit besonderer Beziehung auf die wissenschaftlichen Kämpfe und auf die Darstellung von antijesuitischer Seite* (Regensburg, 1905), x + 595 pp.

Parsons, J. Wilfrid, "The Catholic Church in America in 1819," *The Catholic Historical Review,* V (1919), 301 ff.

Parsons, Wilfrid, S.J., *Chaplaincy, Newman Club or Catholic College* (New York: America Press, 1926), 16 pp.

Passard, F. X., S.J., *La Pratique du Ratio Studiorum pour les Collèges.* Nouvelle Edition (Paris, 1896), xiv + 238 pp.

Pastor, Ludwig von, *Geschichte der Päpste.* Vol. VI (Freiburg i. B.: Herder, 1913), xl + 724 pp.

Paulsen, Dr. Friedrich, *Geschichte des gelehrten Unterrichts auf den deutschen Schulen und Universitäten vom Ausgang des Mittelalters bis zur Gegenwart.* I Bd. (Leipzig, 1896), xx + 608 pp. II Bd. (Leipzig, 1897), 726 pp. 2 Auflage.

Pollen, J. H., S.J., "The Society of Jesus," *The Catholic Encyclopedia,* XIV, 92 ff.

Quicherat, M., *Histoire de Ste. Barbe,* 2 vols. (Paris, 1886).

Ranke, Karl von, *History of the Popes.* Trans. by F. Foster. 3 vols. (London, 1896).

RAUMER, KARL VON, *Geschichte der Pädagogik vom Wiederaufblühen klassischer Studien bis auf unsere Zeit,* 3 Auflage, 5 vols. (Stuttgart, 1857).

Evidences considerable anti-Jesuit bias.

REINHARDSTÖTTNER, KARL, "Zur Geschichte des Jesuitendramas in München," *Jahrbuch für Münchener Geschichte,* III (1889), 53 ff.

RENAUDET, A., *Préréforme et Humanisme à Paris pendant les premières guerres d'Italie 1494–1517* (Paris: E. Champion, 1916), xlviii + 739 pp.

Important for the study of the intellectual life at Paris in the period preceding Loyola's arrival.

RICKABY, JOSEPH, S.J., *The Spiritual Exercises of St. Ignatius Loyola* (New York: Benziger Bros., 1923), xii + 234 pp.

RIORDAN, JOSEPH, S.J., *The First Half-Century of St. Ignatius Church and College* (San Francisco, 1905), 390 pp.

ROCHEMONTEIX, CAMILLE DE, S.J., *Un Collège de Jésuites aux XVII et XVIII siècles: Le Collège Henri IV de la Flèche.* 4 vols. (Le Mans: Leguicheux, 1889).

ROONEY, JOHN J., *The History of the Modern Subjects in the Secondary Curriculum* (Washington: Catholic University Press, 1926), 65 pp.

RYAN, JOHN J., S.J., *Historical Sketch of Loyola College, Baltimore, 1852–1902,* (Baltimore: privately printed, n. d.), 248 pp.

St. Louis Catholic Historical Review, Vol. I (St. Louis, 1919).

SANDYS, JOHN EDWIN, *A History of Classical Scholarship,* Vol. II (Cambridge: The University Press, 1908), xxviii + 497 pp.

SCHILLER, DR. HERMAN, *Lehrbuch der Geschichte der Pädagogik,* 4te Auflage (Leipzig, 1904), viii + 470 pp.

SCHIMBERG, ANDRE, *L'Éducation Morale dans les Collèges de la Compagnie de Jésus en France sous l'Ancien Régime* (Paris, 1913), xv + 592 + 8 pp.

SCHMIDT, K. A., *Geschichte der Erziehung vom Anfang bis auf Unsere Zeit,* 5 vols. (Stuttgart, 1884–1901).

SCHMIDT, CHARLES, *La Vie et Les Oeuvres de Jean Sturm* (Paris, 1855).

SCHWICKERATH, ROBERT, S.J., *Jesuit Education: Its History and Principles Viewed in the Light of Modern Educational Problems,* 2nd edition (St. Louis: Herder, 1904), xv + 687 pp.

SEDGWICK, HENRY DWIGHT, *Ignatius Loyola: An Attempt at an Impartial Biography* (New York: Macmillan Co., 1923), xiv + 400 pp.

SHEA, JOHN GILMARY, *A History of the Catholic Church Within the Limits of the United States from the First Attempted Colonization to the Present Time* (1866), 4 vols. (New York, 1886–1892).

Vol. I. *The Catholic Church in Colonial Days* (1886), xviii + 664 pp.

Vol. II. *Life and Times of the Most Rev. John Carroll* (1888), 695 pp.

Vol. III. *History of the Catholic Church from 1808–1843* (1890), xvi + 734 pp.

Vol. IV. *History of the Catholic Church from 1843 to 1866* (1892), xxxiii + 727 pp.

SHEA, JOHN GILMARY, *Memorial of the First Centenary of Georgetown College, D. C., Comprising a History of Georgetown University* (New York, 1891), xv + 480 pp.

SICARD, A., *Les Études Classiques avant la Révolution* (Paris, 1887), ix + 590 pp.

Sketch of Gonzaga College from its Foundation in 1821 till the Celebration of the Diamond Jubilee in 1896 (Washington: published by the College, 1897) 181 pp.

SOHM, WALTER *Die Schule Johann Sturms und die Kirche Strassburgs in ihren Gegenseitigen Verhältnis.* 1530–1581. Band 27 of *Historische Bibliothek* (München und Berlin: Oldenburg, 1912), xiv + 317 pp.

SOMMERVOGEL, CARLOS, S.J., *Bibliothèque de la Compagnie de Jésus.* (Paris: Picard, 1890–1900), 9 vols.

Spring Hill College, 1830–1905 (Mobile: published privately, 1908), 222 pp.

STOECKIUS, HERMANN, *Forschungen zur Lebensordnung der Gesellschaft Jesu im 16. Jahrhundert* (München: Beck, 1910, 1911). Erstes Stück, *Ordensgehörige und Externe* (1910), viii + 58 pp. Zweites Stück, *Leben im Ordenshause* (1911), x + 198 pp.

STROWSKI, F., *Pascal et son Temps,* 3 vols. (Paris, 1909–13).

TAAFFE, THOMAS GAFFNEY, *A History of St. John's College, Fordham, N. Y.* (New York, Catholic Publication Society, 1891), viii + 154 pp.

TACCHI-VENTURI, PIETRO, S.J., *Storia della Compagnia di Gesú in Italia* (Roma-Milano, Societa Editrice Dante Alighieri, 1910), xi + 720 pp.

TIERNEY, RICHARD H., S.J., *Teacher and Teaching* (New York: Longmans, Green and Co., 1914), viii + 178 pp.

TOURNIER, F., "Monseigneur Guillaume du Prat au Concile de Trent," *Études,* XCVIII (1904), 465–484.

The best analysis of the genesis of the Jesuit College.

TREACY, WILLIAM P., *Old Catholic Maryland and its Early Jesuit Missionaries* (Swedesboro, N. J.: privately published, n. d., *circa* 1889), 183 pp.

TREACY, WILLIAM P., "Some Early Catholic Grammar Schools," *U. S. Catholic Historical Magazine*, I (1887), 71 ff.

U. S. Bureau of Education Circular of Information (1894) No. 2, "History of Education in Maryland" by Bernard C. Steiner, 331 pp.

University of Santa Clara: Diamond Jubilee Volume, 1851–1926 (Santa Clara, California; published by the University, 1926), 106 pp.

VAN DYKE, PAUL, *Ignatius Loyola: The Founder of the Jesuits* (New York: Chas. Scribner, 1926), vi + 381 pp.

VAN ORTROY, P., S.J., "Manrèse et les Origines de la Compagnie de Jésus," *Analecta Bollandiana*, XXVII (1908), 405–418.

VEIL, HEINRICH, *Sturms Unterrichtsziele und Schuleinrichtungen mit Besonderer Berücksichtigung seiner Beziehungen zu dem Niederländischen Humanismus* (Strassburg, 1888).

WILLMANN, O., *Didaktik als Bildungslehre nach Ihren Beziehungen zur Socialforschung und zur Geschichte der Bildung, 2 Bande* (Braunschweig, 1903).

WILLMANN, O., *The Science of Education in its Sociological and Historical Aspects.* Translated by Felix M. Kirsch (Beatty, Pa., 1921), 2 vol.

III. Other Works Treating of Jesuit Education, Consulted, Not Cited

BADTS DU CUGNAC, ALBERT DE, *Les Jésuites et l'Education* (Lille, 1879).

BROSNAHAN, TIMOTHY, S.J., *The Courses Leading to the Baccalaureate in Harvard College and Boston College* (New York: Messenger Press n. d., *circa* 1900), 40 pp.

BROSNAHAN, TIMOTHY, S.J., *President Eliot and Jesuit Colleges* (Woodstock, Md.: Woodstock Press, 1900), 36 pp.

A spirited defense of Jesuit education in answer to President Eliot's strictures in the *Atlantic Monthly.*

BROWNING, OSCAR, *An Introduction to the History of Educational Theories*, 2nd edition, (London: 1882), xi + 196 pp.

BURNS, JAMES A., *The Catholic School System in the United States* (New York: Benziger Bros., 1908), 415 pp.

BUTEL, FERNAND, *L'Education des Jésuites autrefois et aujourd'hui: Un Collège Breton* (Paris: Firmin-Didot, 1890), 529 pp.

CAHOUR, A., "Théâtre Latin des Jésuites à la Fin du XVI Siècle et au Commencement du XVII," *Études* (Paris, 1862), I, 460 ff.

CORCORAN, T., S.J., *Renovatio Litterarum in scholas saec. A. C. XVI deducta* (Dublin: National University, 1925).

DAMAS, PÈRE DE, *Le Surveillant dans un Collège Catholique* (Paris, 1857), 383 pp.

A faithful picture of discipline in the French Jesuit schools of that period.

DANIEL, CHARLES, S.J., *Des Études Classiques dans la Société Chrétienne* (Paris: Lanier et Cie., 1853), 446 pp.

DANIEL, CHARLES, S.J., "La Géographie dans les Collèges des Jésuites aux XVII et XVIII Siècles," *Études,* XL (June, 1879), 801 ff.

DANIEL, CHARLES, S.J., "Les Distributions de prix dans les collèges" *Études,* XLI (Aug. 1879), 269 ff., and (Sept. 1879), 352 ff.

DANIEL, CHARLES, S.J., "Les Méthodes de Port Royal et les Jésuites"; *Études,* XLII (Jan. 1880), 117 ff.

DANIEL, CHARLES, S.J., "Les Jésuites Historiens aux XVII Siècle"; *Études,* XLI (Sept. 1879), 399 ff.

DELBREL, J., S.J., *Les Jésuites et la Pédagogie au XVI Siècle: Juan Bonifacio* (Paris: Picard et Fils, 1894), xi + 89 pp.

DU LAC, PÈRE, S.J., *Jésuites* (Paris: Plon-Nourrie et Cie., 1901), xxxi + 408 pp.

A defense of the Jesuits and their teaching written when the laws against the teaching congregations were being enforced in France.

DUPONT-FERRIES, GUSTAVE, *Du Collège de Clermont au Lycée Louis-le-Grand* (Paris: E. de Brocard, 1921–2), 2 vols.

EASBY-SMITH, JAMES S., *Georgetown University in the District of Columbia* 1789–1907: *Its Founders, Benefactors, Officers, Instructors and Alumni* (New York: Lewis Publishing Co., 1907), 2 vols.

ELIOT, CHARLES W., "Recent Changes in Secondary Education," *The Atlantic Monthly* LXXXIV (Oct., 1899), 433–444.

Contains a paragraph derogatory to Jesuit education, a more or less *obiter dictum,* that produced a vigorous protest from Father Brosnahan, q. v.

FUERST, CLEMENT J., S.J., "A Few Principles and Characteristics of the Ratio Studiorum," *The Classical Journal,* XXI, 3 (Dec. 1926), 204–211.

GÖTTLER, DR. JOSEPH, *Geschichte der Pädogogik* (Berlin: F. Dummler, 1923), 2e Auflage, viii + 215 pp.

HEINER, DR. FRANZ, *Der Jesuitismus in Seinem Wesen, Seiner Gefährlichkeit und Bekämpfung* (Paderborn, 1902), 140 pp.

HERMAN, J. B., S.J., *L'Explication des Auteurs d'après Les Programmes des Jésuites au XVI Siècle* (Louvain: Bulletin Bibliographique et Pédagogique du Musée Belge, 1910).

KELLE, JOHANN, *Die Jesuiten-Gymnasien in Oesterreich* (Prag, 1873), 276 pp.

A severe indictment of Jesuit education in Austria.

KLEUTGEN, JOSEPH, S.J., *De Scholarum Institutione Pristina et Recenti Disputatio* (Parisiis, 1889), 1880 pp.

An academic explanation of Jesuit practice and theory.

KLEUTGEN, JOSEPH, S.J., *Ueber die Alten und die Neuen Schulen* (Münster, 1869), 240 pp.

MAGEVNEY, EUGENE, S.J., *The Jesuits as Educators* (St. Marys, Kansas: published privately, 1906), 32 pp.

MARIQUE, PIERRE, J., *History of Christian Education* (New York: Fordham University, 1924), 2 vols.

The second volume contains a brief summary of Jesuit education, written from the Catholic viewpoint.

MAYNARD, MICHEL ULYSSE, *The Studies and Teaching of the Society of Jesus at the Time of its Suppression,* 1750–1773. Translation from the French. (Baltimore, 1885), 261 pp.

An impassioned defence of the Society.

MERTZ, DR. GEORG, *Ueber Stellung und Betrieb der Rhetorik in den Schulen der Jesuiten* (Heidelberg: Carl Winter, 1898) 60 pp.

MESCHLER, MORITZ, S.J., *Die Gesellschaft Jesu: Ihre Satzungen und Ihre Erfolge* (Freiburg i. Breisgau: Herder, 1911), x + 308 pp.

N., B., *The Jesuits: Their Foundation and History.* 2 vols. (New York: Benziger Bros., 1879).

NONELL, JAIME, S.J., *El Ratio Studiorum de la Compañia de Jesus* (Barcelona, 1878).

PORTER, NOAH, *The Educational Systems of the Puritans and Jesuits Compared* (New York, 1851), 95 pp.

QUICK, ROBERT HERBERT, *Essays on Educational Reformers* (Cincinnati: Robt. Clarke and Co., 1874), xxi + 331 pp.

Pp. 3–20 treat of Loyola and the Jesuits.

ROSENTHAL, PAUL, *Die "Erudition" in den Jesuitenschulen* (Erlangen: 1905), 126 pp.

SOUQUET, P., *Les Écrivains pédagogiques du XVIme Siècle* (Paris, 1886).

STOECKIUS, H., "Ueber die Pflege der Muttersprache in der Gesellschaft Jesus," *Monatschrift für höheren Schulen* (Jahrgang, 1911), 88–101.

INDEX

INDEX